COMPUTER, INTERNET AND ELECTRONIC COMMERCE TERMS: JUDICIAL, LEGISLATIVE AND TECHNICAL DEFINITIONS

by

BARRY B. SOOKMAN

B.A., M.E.S., LL.B.

of the Ontario Bar

Partner and Chair of the McCarthy Tétrault Internet and
Eletronic Commerce Group in Toronto
(BSookman@mccarthy.ca)

2002

THOMSON

CARSWELL

Canadian Cataloguing in Publication Date

Sookman, Barry B., 1954—
    Computer, Internet and Electronic Commerce Terms: Judicial, Legislative, and Technical Definitions/Barry B. Sookman — 2002 ed.
ISBN 0-459-27533-X

1. Computers—Law and legislation—Dictionaries. 2. Internet—Law and legislation—Dictionaries. 3. Electronic commerce—Law and legislation—Dictionaries. 4. Computers—Dictionaries. 5. Internet—Dictionaries. 6. Electronic commerce—Dictionaries. 7. Information technology—Dictionaries. I. Sookman, Barry B., 1954–   . Computer, Internet and electronic commerce law. II. Title.

K564.C6S66 2002   343.09'99'03   C2002-905751-5

THOMSON
CARSWELL

One Corporate Plaza, 2075 Kennedy Road, Toronto, Ontario M1T 3V4
Customer Relations:
Toronto 1-416-609-3800
Elsewhere in Canada/U.S. 1-800-387-5162
Fax 1-416-298-5094

Preface

Computer, Internet and Electronic Commerce Terms: Judicial, Legislative and Technical Definitions is a comprehensive collection of definitions of computer, internet and e-commerce terms. The definitions have been compiled from judicial opinions rendered throughout the world, including from judgements delivered by courts and tribunals in the United States, Canada, Australia, United Kingdom and elsewhere in Europe and the Commonwealth. Many definitions have also been taken from terms used in laws related to protecting intellectual property rights in information technologies and in regulating and facilitating use of the internet and e-commerce. Included are many terms found in legislation around the world, terms defined in model laws and uniform legislation as well as terms explained in background papers and research published internationally and used to develop policies for addressing legal issues related to information technologies, the internet and e-commerce.

The definitions found in this book are also published as part of the four-volume book also published by Carswell entitled *Sookman: Computer, Internet and Electronic Commerce Law* and written by Barry Sookman. The first edition of this glossary of terms was published in 1989 with the predecessor of that book, *Sookman Computer Law: Acquiring and Protecting Information Technology*, also written by Barry Sookman. It has been continually updated to include the terms of most interest to practitioners.

Changes in information and communications technologies, including new developments related to the internet and e-commerce, raise challenging new issues that need to be understood and addressed. Lawyers and other professionals providing assistance to clients such as in drafting contracts, litigating disputes, and in rendering opinions must understand the meaning of the terms used by their clients. They must know how courts have interpreted such terms. They must also be aware of how these terms are used in laws that relate to advice being given. The definitions collected here are intended to satisfy these objectives.

Definitions

Access

Access means to program, to execute programs on, to communicate with, store data in, retrieve data from, or otherwise make use of any resources, including data or programs, of a computer, computer system, or computer network. *State of Louisiana v. Azar*, 539 So2d 1222 (La. Sup. Ct.).

To approach or otherwise make use of any resources of a computer, directly or by electronic means. *State of Washington v. Riley*, 846 P.2d 1365 (Sup. Ct. Wash. 1993).

Access, in relation to data held in a computer, means: (a) the display of the data by the computer or any other output of the data from the computer; or (b) the copying or moving of the data to any other place in the computer or to a data storage device; or (c) in the case of a program, the executionof the program. *Property Damage and Computer Offices Act 2002 (Australia).*

Access Contract

Means a contract to obtain electronically access to, or information from, an information processing system of another person, or the equivalent of such access. *Uniform Computer Information Transactions Act*, National Conference of Commissioners on Uniform State Laws, available at http://www.law.upenn.u/bll/ulc/ucita/citim99.htm.

Access Controls

Access controls refers to the ability of computer systems to be set up so that only specified individuals of computers are permitted to have access to specific parts of the computer system. Passwords is one form of an access control. Tokens, such as a smart card . . . can also be required before a computer will permit a person to use that computer. Access controls are generally set by the administrator of the computer system, and can include both discretionary and mandatory access controls. *A Survey of Legal Issues Relating to the Security of Electronic Information*, Department of Justice, Canada.

Access Material

Means any information or material, such as a document, address, or access code, necessary to obtain authorized access to information or control or possession of a copy. *Uniform Computer Information Transactions Act*, National Conference of Commissioners on Uniform State Laws, available at http://www.law.upenn.u/bll/ulc/ucita/citim99.htm.

Access Protection

A technological protection measure that restricts unauthorised access to a copyright work, usually in the form of a software program and/or hardware as part of a computer, an audiovisual or audio device. Access protection measures include means of preventing information, films or sound recordings stored on certain optical disks from being played on certain players (such as zoning systems, for example those used to allow DVD zoning in relation to films). It can also refer to systems that use encryption or a software key to access material or information stored on a digital format. *Digital Technology and the Copyright Act 1994: A Discussion Paper, Competition and Enterprise Branch, July 2001 (New Zealand).*

Access Service

A service that enables an individual user to connect to the switching system of a local exchange carrier. The individual user could be either an individual subscriber or an interexchange carrier. Submission of the Director of Investigation and Research to the CRTC Re Public Notice CRTC 1994-130.

ADAD

Automatic equipment capable of storing or producing telephone numbers to be called, and which can be used, alone in conjunction with other equipment, to convey a prerecorded or synthesized voice message to the number called. CRTC Telecom Decision 94-10.

Add-on

Extra device, circuit, board or *peripheral* added to a computer or video games *console* to change or enhance its performance. Monopolies and Mergers Commission — Video Games: A report on the supply of video games in the UK (LONDON: HMSO Cm2781).

Address

The address is the location (particular pigeon hole) of the memory from which an instruction or datum is sought. *Apple Computer Inc. v. Mackintosh Computers Ltd.* (1986), 28 D.L.R. (4th) 178 (Fed. T.D.).

Addressability

A technology that allows cable operators to send programs or data to individual subscriber homes. Submission of the Director of Investigation and Research to the CRTC Re Public Notice CRTC 1994-130.

Address Space

The aggregation of all possible IP numerical addresses assigned to hosts on the Internet. *Domain Name System Reform and Related Internet Governance Issues: A Consultation Paper,* Industry Canada available at *www.strategis.gc.ca.*

Addressee

Addressee of a data message means a person who is intended by the originator to receive the data message, but does not include a person acting as an intermediary with respect to that data message. *UNCITRAL, Working Group IV (Electronic Commerce), Thirty-ninth session New York, 11-15 March, 2002.*

Advanced Card

A card capable of carrying information. Uses technology more advanced than magnetic stripe. Smart, Optical and Other Advanced Cards: How to Do a Privacy Assessment, Information and Privacy Commissioner/Ontario Canada, available at http://www.itc.on.ca.

Advanced Card Technologies (ACT)

Refers to any cards used for the purposes of identifying the end-user to gain access to an information system. *A Survey of Legal Issues Relating to the Security of Electronic Information*, Department of Justice, Canada.

Adventure game

Computer or video game where the player takes on a character's identity and is confronted by various tasks. The scenarios are from a fantasy world and often include goblins or magicians. Sometimes called an arcade adventure. Monopolies and Mergers Commission — Video Games: A report on the supply of video games in the UK (LONDON: HMSO Cm2781).

Agent Software

Allows users to automatically detect whether a Web site conforms to a set of standards determined by a user. It can also be used to seek out information on behalf of the user. Advancing Global Electronic Commerce: Technology Solutions to Public Policy Challenges, The Computer Systems Policy Project, July 1999, available at http://www.cspp.org/projects/july99_cto_report.pdf.

Algorithm

A finite set of well-defined rules for the solution of a problem in a finite number of steps. Computer Software Protection: Australia, Copyright Law Review Committee 1995.

An algorithm is, in general, a set of rules or processes for solving a problem in a finite number of steps. *Re Application No. 096,284* (1978), 52 C.P.R. (2d) 96 (Pat. App. Bd. & Pat. Commr.).

A procedure for solving a given type of mathematical problem. *Gottschalk v. Benson*, 409 U.S. 63 (1972).

A step-by-step procedure for solving a problem or accomplishing some end. *In Re Chatfield*, 545 F.2d 152 (C.C.P.A. 1976), cert. denied. 434 U.S. 875 (1977).

A step-by-step procedure, or defined set of instructions, designed to solve a particular problem or to produce a particular result. *E.F. Johnson Co. v. Uniden Corp. of America*, 623 F.Supp. 1485 (D.C. Minn. 1985).

Refers to methods of calculation, mathematical formulae, and mathematical procedures generally. *In Re Walter*, 618 F.2d 758 (C.C.P.A. 1980).

(1) A fixed step-by-step procedure for accomplishing a given result; usually a simplified procedure for solving a complex problem, also a full statement of a finite number of steps. (2) A defined process or set of rules that leads and assures development of a desired output from a given input. A sequence of formulae and/or algebraic/logical steps to calculate or determine a given task; processing rules. *In Re Toma*, 575 F.2d 872 (C.C.P.A. 1978). (From C. Sippl, *Computer Dictionary and Handbook*, 2nd ed. (1972).)

The fundamental processes used by a program are called algorithms (mechanical computational procedures). *Whelan Associates Inc. v. Jaslow Dental Laboratory Inc.*, 225 U.S.P.Q. 156 (E.D. Pa. 1985), affirmed 797 F.2d 1222 (3rd Cir. 1986).

The arithmetic rule and the mathematical principles governing the program. It is an instruction to the human intellect that is replaced by the machine. *Bappert und Berker v. SudWestdeutsche Inkasso*, Karlsruhe, February 9, 1983, summarized at [1984] 9 E.I.P.R. 253.

Methods of combining, in a program, instructions given to a computer. Japanese Amended Copyright Law.

An algorithm is a procedure used to solve a mathematical problem. *Autodesk Australia Pty Ltd. v. Dyason* (1989), 15 I.P.R. 1 (Aus. Fed. Ct.), reversed [1990] A.I.P.C. 36,446 (Aus. Fed. Ct.).

The procedure for solving [a] particular problem in a finite number of steps; the mathematical process or set of rules involved in the operation [of a program]. *Autodesk Australia Pty. Ltd. v. Dyason*, supra.

An algorithm is a mechanical computational procedure. *Comprehensive Technologies International, Inc. v. Software Artisans Inc.*, 3F. 3d 370 (4th Cir. 1993).

An algorithm is a set of logical rules or mathematical specification of a process which may be implemented in a computer. *National Information Infrastructure: A Preliminary Draft of the Report of the Working Group on Intellectual Property Rights, July 1994.*

An algorithm is a specific series of steps that accomplish a particular operation. *Gates Rubber Co. v. Bando American Inc.*, 28 U.S.P.Q. 2d 1503 (10th Cir. 1993).

An algorithm is a mechanical computational procedure. *Comprehensive Technologies Int., Inc. v. Software Artisans, Inc.*, F.3d 370 (4th Cir. 1993).

An algorithm is a recipe that contains instructions for completing a task. It can be expressed in any language, from natural spoken language to computer programming language. *Universal City Studios, Inc. v. Reimerdes*, 55 U.S.P.Q. 2d 1873 (S. D.N.Y. 2000).

Algorithm And Key Length

The combination of cryptographic algorithm and its key length(s) often used to establish the strength of an encryption process. *Cryptography's Role in Securing the Information Society*, United States National Research Council, 1996.

Alpha Testing

The designation given when the reliability of a computer system is verified by internal users. For example, internal Hewlett-Packard users test and verify a new computer system before external customer tests are conducted. Alpha testing of software is preliminary testing performed internally within the company to identify obvious problems with the software prior to the software reaching any customers. This testing is often done by the developers themselves as part of the development process. By identifying problems at a very early stage, they can be addressed quickly and corrected prior to any distribution outside the company. *Delrina Corp. v. Triolet Systems, Inc.* (1992), 47 C.P.R. (3d) 1 (Ont. H.C.).

Alphanumeric Domain Name

An alphanumeric domain name usually consists of two levels: a Second Level Domain and a Top Level Domain. For example, in the United States Courts' website, *"http://www.uscourts.gov,"* the Second Level Domain is "uscourts" and the generic Top Level Domain is ".gov." The http://" refers to the protocol used to transfer information, and the "www" simply refers to the World Wide Web. *Image Online Design, Inc. v. Core Association,* 2000 U.S. Dist. LEXIS 10259 (C.D.Cal. 2000).

Alphanumeric Service

Means a service consisting of letters, numbers, graphic designs or still images, or any combination thereof, that may be accompanied by
    (a) background music,
    (b) the programming service of a licensed A.M. station or licensed F.M. station, other than an educational radio programming service the operation of which is the responsibility of an educational authority,
    (c) the service of Weather Radio Canada,
    (d) the Canadian programming service of a licensed national audio network operation, or
    (e) spoken words that relate to what is represented by the letters, numbers, graphic designs or still images. Cable Television Regulations, 1986, SOR/86-831.

A.M. Station

A station that broadcasts in the A.M. frequency band of 525 to 1605 kHz, but does not include a carrier current undertaking or a transmitter that only rebroadcasts the radiocommunications of another station. Cable Television Regulations, 1986, SOR/86-831.

Analog

A term applied to any device, usually electronic, that represents values by a continuously variable physical property, such as voltage in an electronic circuit.

5

Submission of the Director of Investigation and Research to the CRTC Re Public Notice 1994-130.

Describes the way information is represented in the form of continuously varying wave forms, for example a modulated radio signal or the variation in width and depth of the groove in a vinyl music record. Copying or transcribing analogue information for storage and transmission always involves some degradation of quality since reproduction can never be perfect. *Digital Technology and the Copyright Act 1994: A Discussion Paper, Competition and Enterprise Branch, July 2001 (New Zealand).*

Analog Service

Transmission of a set of audible frequencies enabling telephony voice conversations or dial-up Internet access via a regular telephone line. Virtually all residential telephones are analog devices. Analog signals are typically converted into a digital format. *Report to the Governor in Council: Status of Competition in Canadian Telecommunications Markets, Deployment/Accessibility of Advanced Telecommunications Infrastructure and Services, September, 2001.*

Analog Signal

An analog signal is a continuously variable signal as opposed to a discretely variable signal. *Advanced Micro Devices, Inc. and Intel Corp.*, CCH Comp. Cases 60,218 (Arb. Award. 1990).

Analog Transmission

One of two major types of signal processing used in television and other areas of electronics. In analog signal processing, some property of the signal, such as its voltage, magnetic field or frequency, varies continuously such that the output is "analogous" to the input, in contrast to digital transmission. Submission of the Director of Investigation and Research to the CRTC Re Public Notice CRTC 1994-130.

Anonymizers

Remove the personal identity from a record, communication or transaction. Web sites exist that allow the user to send and receive anonymous e-mail and to surf Web pages anonymously. Advancing Global Electronic Commerce: Technology Solutions to Public Policy Challenges, The Computer Systems Policy Project, July 1999, available at http://www.cspp.org/projects /july99_cto_report.pdf.

ANSI

American National Standards Institute. "Security Requirements for Cryptographic Modules", FIPS Pub. 140-1, Federal Information Processing Standards Publication, January 11, 1994, available at http://csrc.nist.gov/fips/fips1401.htm.

Application Program Compatibility

The ability of customers to run application programs written for one party's operating system on another party's operating system. *IBM v. Fujitsu Ltd.*, Copyright L.R. (CCH) 20,517 (Am. Arbtn. Assoc. Comm. Arbtn. Trib.).

Application Programs

The application program is the program with which the ultimate user directs the computer to perform a particular task. *People v. Versaggi*, 629 N.E. 2d 1034.

A program written to perform a specific task for the user. It does not contribute to the effective functioning of the computer. Computer Software Protection: Australia, Copyright Law Review Committee 1995.

This is a set of instructions to the computer on how to do the particular tasks that it is going to be asked to perform. The instructions describe how the computer is to produce specific results in terms of output. Two identical computers may have entirely dissimilar application programs. *Continental Commercial Systems Corp. v. R.*, [1982] 5 W.W.R. 340 (B.C. C.A.).

Application programs are designed for a specific task, such as the playing of a video game, preparation of a tax return, or the writing of text. *Apple Computer Inc. v. Mackintosh Computers Ltd.* (1986), 28 D.L.R. (4th) 178 (Fed. T.D.).

An application program is designed for a specific task, ordinarily chosen by the user, such as to maintain records, perform certain calculations or display graphic charts. Application programs are normally written in high-level languages that are designed to be easily used by the unsophisticated. *Apple Computer Inc. v. MacIntosh Computers Ltd.* (1985), 3 C.I.P.R. 133 (Fed. T.D.).

This consists of material programmed to the specific requirements of the user's business and may be prepared either by the user or as part of custom programming service done by experts on the user's instructions. *Clarke Irwin & Co. v. Singer Co. of Can.*, Ont. Div. Ct., Keith J., December 3, 1979, summarized at [1979] 3 A.C.W.S. 807.

Application programs are programs that permit a user to perform some particular task such as word processing, database management, or spreadsheet calculations, or that permit a user to play video games. *Lotus Development Corp. v. Paperback Software International*, 15 U.S.P.Q.2d 1577 (D. Mass. 1990).

An "application program" is a computer program which is designed to solve a particular program; for example, to maintain personnel files or to handle a company's payroll. It is generally any computer program which is not a systems programs. *Computer Sciences Corp. v. Commissioner of Internal Revenue*, 63 T.C. 327 (U.S. Tax. Crt. 1974).

Application Programming Interfaces (APIs)

These are synapses at which the developer of an application can connect to invoke pre-fabricated blocks of code in the operating system. These blocks of code in turn perform crucial tasks, such as displaying text on the computer screen. *United States of America v. Microsoft Corporation*, 87 F.Supp. 2d 30 (D.D.C. 2000).

Application Software

An application software program directs the manipulation of data or information within a computer to produce a particular result. *Dental Office Computer Systems Inc. v. Glutting*, No. CV-86-5613DT (Mich. App. filed August 13, 1987).

Such software allows a computer to perform a specific function such as accounts payable or a general ledger analysis of financial information. *Cullinet Software Inc. v. McCormack & Dodge Corp.*, 500 N.E.2d 831 (Mass. App. Ct. 1986), reversed 511 N.E.2d 1101 (Sup. Jud. Ct. Mass. 1987).

Application software programs are to be used "on top of" the operating system, tell the computer how to perform the finished tasks that a computer desires, whether it be the recording of journal entries, the preparation of a spread-sheet, or the creation of long documents. *ISC-Bunker Ramo Corporation v. Altech, Inc.*, 765 F.Supp. 1310 (N.D. Ill. 1990).

Application System Software

Application system software includes source code, data files and utilities which are stored on the computer, as well as programme documents not stored on the computer, but which still form part of the software, e.g., specifications, file layouts, source code, report designs and manuals. *Geac J & E Systems Ltd. v. Craig Erickson Systems Inc.* (1993), 46 C.P.R. (3d) 25 (Ont. Gen. Div.).

Arcade conversion

Licensed conversion of an existing game from an amusement arcade to a home computer or *console* format. Monopolies and Mergers Commission — Video Games: A report on the supply of video games in the UK (LONDON: HMSO Cm2781).

Arcade game

Video or computer game similar to those found in coin-operated machines in an amusement arcade; see *adventure game, arcade conversion.* Monopolies and Mergers Commission — Video Games: A report on the supply of video games in the UK (LONDON: HMSO Cm2781).

Archie Server

A remote computer capable of searching directories for file names containing a particular string of characters on FTP servers permitting anonymous retrieval. *Shea v. Reno*, 1996 U.S. Dist. LEXIS 10720 (S.D.N.Y. 1996).

Architecture

Architecture is the logic processes which have lead to the layout of the computer parts, the banks of chips, memory carts, circuits, cabling and so forth which are inside the metal cases which make up the external appearance of a main frame computer. *Systems Reliability Holdings plc v. Smith*, [1990] I.R.L.R. 377 (Ch.D.).

Architecture refers to structure of the product, how its individual components are organized; how they relate together; and how someone interacts with the products. *Computer Associates International, Inc. v. Bryan*, 3 CCH Comp. Cases 46,619 (E.D. N.Y. 1992).

Arithmetic/Logical Instructions

These instructions modify data in locations according to arithmetic or logical rules; these are instructions such as, for example, "add," "subtract," "and," "or," "rotate," "clear," etc. *Apple Computer Inc. v. Mackintosh Computers Ltd.* (1986), 28 D.L.R. (4th) 178 (Fed. T.D.).

Arithmetic Processing

Applications include: general commercial accounting, inventory control, banking and point-of-sale processing, financial and econometric modeling, scientific calculations, etc. Second Computer Inquiry (Supplemental Notice), 42 Fed. Reg. 13029 (F.C.C. 1977).

Artificial Intelligence

Artificial intelligence is an expression commonly used to designate those types of computer systems that display certain capabilities associated with human intelligence, such as perception, understanding, learning, reasoning, and problem solving. Committee of Experts on a Possible Protocol to the Berne Convention for the Protection of Literary and Artistic Works.

Artwork

Artwork is a term of art which means the actual physical board on which wires, chips and other parts are placed. Special machinery is required to make the artwork. *Southern Data Systems, Inc. v. Michael Greer*, reprinted in Comp. Ind. Lit. Reptr. 9887 (D.C.E.D.N.Cal. 1989).

ASCII

An acronym for the American Standard Code for Information Interchange. This is a standard whereby a unique 8-bit binary number is assigned for each upper- and lower-case letter, numeral, punctuation symbol, and other character of the typewriter keyboard. *Apple Computer Inc. v. Mackintosh Computers Ltd.* (1986), 28 D.L.R. (4th) 178 (Fed. T.D.).

ASCII Language is an internationally understandable combination of control characters and alphanumeric characters established in the American Standard Code for Information Interchange. *E.F. Johnson Co. v. Uniden Corp. of America*, 623 F.Supp. 1485 (D.C. Minn. 1985).

Assembler

A computer program that changes assembly language into the language that the computer operates on directly, that is, the object code. *Compendium of Copyright Offices Practices*, Copyright Office, Washington D.C., 1984.

Assembler Language (Assembler Code)

A suitably trained or skilled programmer will be able to write a program in machine code for a particular model of computer. But the process is slow and tedious and the program, although intelligible to the computer, will be virtually unintelligible to anyone except an equally skilled programmer. From the comparatively early days of computers, therefore, an alternative language for writing programs was devised. This was known as "assembler language." It used a variety of abbreviations more akin to ordinary language than machine code. A computer could not itself understand such a language directly, but a program could be, and was, devised which enabled a computer to convert assembler language into the machine code which could be understood by the computer. The translation process is usually possible only in one direction. Assembler language can be translated into machine code, but not vice versa. *John Richardson Computers Ltd. v. Flanders*, [1993] F.S.R. 497 (Ch.D.).

A type of programming language used to represent programs in machine code in a convenient and readable notation. Computer Software Protection: Australia, Copyright Law Review Committee 1995.

Assembly codes may be said to be an intermediate level of language. *Apple Computer Inc. v. Mackintosh Computers Ltd.* (1986), 28 D.L.R. (4th) 178 (Fed. T.D.).

A computer program written in humanly-recognizable commands or mnemonics. An assembly language program is converted into machine-readable form by an assembler. *E.F. Johnson Co. v. Uniden Corp. of America*, 623 F.Supp. 1485 (D.C. Minn. 1985).

An "intermediate" level programming language is assembly language. Rather than in bits, assembly code is written in simple symbolic names, or alphanumeric symbols, more easily understandable by human programmers. For example, a calculation may be represented, in the assembly language of a certain computer, as follows: LOAD B; DIV C; ADD A. Because of the primitive nature of assembly language, even relatively simple computations can require long and complex programs. *Lotus Development Corp. v. Paperback Software International*, 15 U.S.P.Q.2d 1577 (D. Mass. 1990).

Association of Data Processing Service Organizations (ADAPSO)

A national trade association representing the data processing industry. *Association of Data Processing Service Organizations, Inc. v. Board of Governors of the Federal Reserve System*, Comp. Ind. Lit. Reptr. 1,1643 (Crt.App. D.C. 1984).

Assurance

Confidence that a system design meets its requirements, or that its implementation meets its specification, or that some specific property is satisfied. *Cryptography's Role in Securing the Information Society*, United States National Research Council, 1996.

Asymmetric Cryptography

Asymmetric cryptography is cryptography which uses one key to generate a digital signature and a related but different key to verify the signature. It must be computationaly infeasible to derive the key used to generate the signature from that used to verify the signature. Security and Electronic Authorization and Authentication Guideline, Communications Security Establishment, Government of Canada September 1995, CID/01/15.

Asymmetric cryptography makes it possible to divide an encryption key into two parts: one part is secret and the other part is public. For this reason, asymmetric encryption is also called private key/public key encryption. *A Survey of Legal Issues Relating to the Security of Electronic Information*, Department of Justice, Canada.

Cryptography based on algorithms that enable the use of one key (a public key) to encrypt a message and a second, different, but mathematically related, key (a private key) to decrypt a message. Asymmetric cryptography can also be used to perform digital signatures and key exchange. *Cryptography's Role in Securing the Information Society*, United States National Research Council, 1996.

Asymmetric Cryptosystem

Means a computer-based system capable of generating and using a key pair consisting of a private key for creating a digital signature and a public key to verify the digital signature. *Illinois Electronic Commerce Security Act*, 1998 5 Ill. Comp. Stat. 175.

Means an algorithm or series of algorithms which provide a secure key pair. *Utah Digital Signature Act*, available at http://www.le.state.ut.us/code/TITLE46/htm/46_03004.htm.

Asymmetrical Digital Subscriber Line (ADSL)

Telecommuications technology that allows multiple, simultaneous high-speed services to be carried over existing telephone copper-twisted pair wires, increasing the potential capacity of installed copper networks. Most of the capacity is devoted to distribution of video downstream to consumers. Submission of the Director of Investigation and Research to the CRTC Re Public Notice CRTC 1994-130.

Asynchronous Transfer Mode (ATM)

A high-speed networking technology for broadband communications. *The Challenge of the Information Highway: Final Report of the Information Highway Advisory Council* (September 1995).

A high-speed cell-switching network technology for LAN's [local area networks] that handles data and real time voice and video. It combines the high efficiency of packet switching used in data networks, with the guaranteed bandwidth of circuit switching used in voice networks. *3Com Corp.* 56 U.S.P.Q. 2d 1060 (T.T.A.B.2000).

ATM's (Automated Teller Machines)

An unattended terminal-type device that provides simple banking services such as cash withdrawals, transfer of funds between accounts and account balances. *The Challenge of the Information Highway: Final Report of the Information Highway Advisory Council* (September 1995).

ATM transactions involve the use of plastic cards which must be used in conjuction with a Personal Identification Number (PIN). After entry of the correct PIN by the customer using the card, the customer chooses the relative transaction. *Databank Systems Ltd. v. Commnr. of Inland Revenue*, [1987] N.Z.L.R. 312 (H.C. Wellington).

Automatic teller machines are terminals which dialogue with a computer to dispense cash and transfer funds between customers' accounts. The machines are located in an area separate from the remainder of the main banking facilities, usually in a lock enclosure. The enclosure that houses the machines is locked for security reasons and has door openings large enough to move machines in and out. *CIBC v. Alberta (Assessment Appeal Board)*, 75 Alta. L.R. (2d) 362, [1990] 6 W.W.R. 425, 73 D.L.R. (4th) 271, 109 A.R. 203 (Q.B.).

To use the machine, a customer inserts an encoded plastic card and enters a personal identification number on the machine's keyboard. The customer then enters the desired transaction and amount. *Independent Bankers Assn. of New York State, Inc. v. Marine Midland Bank*, Comp. Ind. Lit. Reptr. 2,390 (2nd Cir. 1985).

ATM Link

ATM Link is a system of hardware components . . . which create the (ATM) connection, or link, between different computer networks or network systems. *3Com Corp.* 56 U.S.P.Q. 2d 1060 (T.T.A.B.2000).

ATM Network

Shared ATM networks are relatively sophisticated businesses whose function is to deliver banking services at a variety of locations both during and after normal banking hours, without the need for a human teller. *Plus System, Inc. v. New England Network, Inc.*, 804 F.Supp. 111 (D. Col. 1992)

ATT

The oldest and most comprehensive numerical control language. *White Consolidated Industries Inc. v. Vega Servo-Control Inc.*, 214 U.S.P.Q. 796 (S.D. Mich. 1982), affirmed 218 U.S.P.Q. 961 (Fed. Cir. 1983).

Attract Mode (in relation to video games)

"Attract mode" refers to the audio-visual display seen and heard by a prospective customer contemplating playing the game; the video screen displays some of the essential visual characteristics of the game. "Play mode" refers to the audio-visual display seen and heard by a person playing the game. *Stern Electronics Inc. v. Kaufman*, 669 F.2d 852 (2nd Cir. 1982).

"Attract mode" refers to the audio-visual effects displayed before a coin is inserted into the game. It repeatedly shows the name of the game, the game symbols in typical motion and interaction patterns, and the initials of previous players who have achieved high scores. *Williams Electronics Inc. v. Artic International Inc.*, 685 F.2d 870 (3rd Cir. 1982).

When the game is not in play, a series of images known as the "attract mode" appear on the screen. *Avel Pty Ltd. v. Jonathan Wells* (1992), 22 I.P.R. 305 (Aust. H.C.).

Attribution Procedure

Means a procedure established by law, administrative rule, or agreement, or a procedure otherwise adopted by the parties, to verify that an electronic event is that of a specific person or to detect changes or errors in the information. The term includes a procedure that requires the use of algorithms or other codes, identifying words or numbers, encryption, callback or other acknowledgment, or any other procedures that are reasonable under the circumstances. *Uniform Computer Information Transactions Act*, National Conference of Commissioners on Uniform State Laws, available at http://www.law.upenn.u/bll/ulc/ucita/citim99.htm.

Audio Channel

A channel of an undertaking on which is distributed a frequency-modulated transmission capable of being received by subscribers by means of a conventional F.M. radio receiver. Cable Television Regulations, 1986, SOR/86-831.

Audio-Visual Works

Works that consist of a series of related images which are intrinsically intended to be shown by the use of machines or devices such as projectors, viewers, or electronic equipment, together with accompanying sounds, if any, regardless of the nature of the material objects, such as films, or tapes, in which the works are embodied. The United States Copyright Act, 17 U.S.C. s.101.

Audit Trails

Audit trails in computer systems are intended to allow management to investigate events leading up to any incident or to trace or monitor activities or transactions on the system. *A Survey of Legal Issues Relating to the Security of Electronic Information*, Department of Justice, Canada.

Auditing Technologies

Provide verifiable records of transactions that can be used to ensure integrity and resolve disputes. *Advancing Global Electronic Commerce: Technology Solutions to Public Policy Challenges*, The Computer Systems Policy Project, July 1999, available at http://www.cspp.org/projects/july99_cto_report.pdf.

Authenticate

Means:(A) to sign, or (B) otherwise to execute or adopt a symbol or sound, or to use encryption or another process with respect to a record, with intent of the authenticating person to: (i) identify that person; or (ii) adopt or accept the terms or a particular term of a record that includes or is logically associated with, or linked to, the authentication, or to which a record containing the authentication refers. *Uniform Computer Information Transactions Act*, National Conference of Commissioners on Uniform State Laws, available at http://www.law.upenn.u/bll/ulc/ucita/citim99.htm.

Authentication (See also Electronic Authentication)

Authentication means evidence (as conclusive as possible) that the person identified as the sender in the electronic message is actually the person who sent the message. *A Survey of Legal Issues Relating to the Security of Electronic Information*, Department of Justice, Canada.

"Authentication" is generally defined to mean establishing the validity of the identity of a particular entity. Electronic Commerce: Building A Legal Framework, Report of the Electronic Commerce Expert Group (Australia) to the Attorney General, 31 March, 1998.

Means a function for establishing the validity of a claimed identity of a user, device or another entity in an information or communications system. *OECD Guidelines for Cryptography Policy*, March 27, 1997, available at *www.oecd.org*.

Proof that users are who they claim to be (or that computer devices, software, etc. are what they purport to be). *Building Trust and Confidence in Electronic Commerce: A Framework for Electronic Authentication in Canada*, prepared by the Electronic Commerce Branch, Industry Canada, July 2000, available at *http://e-comm.ic.gc.ca*.

Authentication Code

A value generated from the application of a shared key to a message via a cryptographic algorithm, such that it has the properties of *message authentication* (and *integrity*) but not *signer authentication*. Equivalent to *protected checksum*, "A checksum that is computed for a data object by means that protect against active attacks that would attempt to change the checksum to make it match changes made to the data object." *XML-Signature Syntax and Processing, W3C Recommendation 12 February 2002*.

Authentication, Message

The property, given an *authentication code/protected checksum*, that tampering with both the data and checksum, so as to introduce changes while seemingly preserving *integrity*, are still detected. "A signature should identify what is signed, making it impracticable to falsify or alter either the signed matter or the signature without detection." *XML-Signature Syntax and Processing, W3C Recommendation 12 February 2002.*

Authentication, Signer

The property that the identity of the signer is as claimed. "A signature should indicate who signed a document, message or record, and should be difficult for another person to produce without authorization." *XML-Signature Syntax and Processing, W3C Recommendation 12 February 2002.*

Authentication Technologies

Verify the authenticity of data, including the identity of users using cryptographic and physical data mechanisms. Authorization technologies such as passwords ensure that only the people entitled to access a site or data actually do so. Advancing Global Electronic Commerce: Technology Solutions to Public Policy Challenges, The Computer Systems Policy Project, July 1999, available at http://www.cspp.org/projects/july99_cto_report.pdf.

Authenticity

A security service that provides a user with a means of verifying the identity of the sender of a message, a file, a computer system, a software process, or even a database or individual software component. *Cryptography's Role in Securing the Information Society*, United States National Research Council, 1996.

Authorization

Authorization means evidence (as conclusive as possible) that the person who sent a message (*e.g.* signed a contract, approved a payment, certified receipt of goods) actually had the authority to send that message. Authorization is based on the individual's financial authority, security clearance and need-to-know. *A Survey of Legal Issues Relating to the Security of Electronic Information*, Department of Justice, Canada.

Determining whether a subject (a user or system) is trusted to act for a given purpose, for example, allowed to read a particular file. *Cryptography's Role in Securing the Information Society*, United States National Research Council, 1996.

Authorized Equipment

Means terminal or other equipment that has been approved for attachment to the public telecommunications transport network in accordance with a party's conformity assessment procedures. North American Free Trade Agreement between Canada, Mexico and the United States, Article 1310.

Autocad

Autocad is a sophisticated computer program designed to assist in the process of drafting. *Autodesk Australia Pty Ltd. v. Dyason* (1989), 15 I.P.R. 1 (Aus. Fed. Ct.), reversed [1990] A.I.P.C. 36,446 (Aust. Fed. Ct.).

Automated computer system

Means a computer program or an electronic or other automated means used to initiate an action or respond to data messages or performances in whole or in part, without review or intervention by a natural person at each time an action is initiated or a response is generated by the system. *UNCITRAL, Working Group IV (Electronic Commerce), Thirty-ninth session New York, 11-15 March, 2002.*

Automated Data File

Means any set of data undergoing automatic processing. Council of Europe: Convention for the Protection of Individuals with Regard to Automatic Processing of Personal Data.

Automated Key Distribution

The distribution of cryptographic keys, usually in encrypted form, using electronic means, such as a computer network (e.g., down-line key loading, the automated key distribution protocols of ANSI X9.17). "Security Requirements for Cryptographic Modules", FIPS Pub. 140-1, Federal Information Processing Standards Publication, January 11, 1994, available at http://csrc.nist.gov/fips/fips1401.htm.

Automated Transaction

Means a transaction conducted or performed, in whole or in part, by electronic means or electronic records in which the acts or records of one or both parties are not reviewed by an individual in the ordinary course in forming a contract, performing under an existing contract, or fulfilling an obligation required by the transaction. *Uniform Computer Information Transactions Act*, National Conference of Commissioners on Uniform State Laws, available at http://www.law.upenn.u/bll/ulc/ucita/citim99.htm.

Automatic Data Processing Machines

(a) Digital machines capable of (1) storing the processing program or programs and at least the data immediately necessary for the execution of the program; (2) being freely programmed in accordance with the requirements of the user; (3) performing arithmetical computations specified by the user; and, (4) executing, without human intervention, a processing program which requires them to modify their execution, by logical decision during the processing run; (b) Analog machines capable of simulating mathematical models and comprising at least; analog elements, control elements and programming elements; or (c) Hybrid machines consisting of either a digital machine with analog elements or an analog machine with digital elements. *An Act to Implement the Free Trade Agreement between Canada and the United States of America*, S.C. 1988, c. 65.

Automatic Processing

Includes the following operations if carried out in whole or in part by automated means: storage of data, carrying out of logical and/or arithmetical operations on those data, their alteration, erasure, retrieval or dissemination. Council of Europe: Convention for the Protection of Individuals with Regard to Automatic Processing of Personal Data.

Automatic Programming Tools (APT)

APT is a universal and highly versatile part programming language developed for computer-assisted part programming for NC machines, and has the widest application and broadest capability of any parts programming language. *Re Manufacturing Data Systems Inc.*, 5 C.L.S.R. 723 (U.S. Comptr. Gen. 1974).

Availability

Means the characteristic of data, information and information systems being accessible and usable on a timely basis in the required manner. OECD Guidelines from the Security of Information Systems adopted November 26, 1992, available at http://www.oecd.org/dsti/sdi/it/secur/prod/e_secur.htm.

Means the property that data, information, and information and communications systems are accessible and usable on a timely basis in the required manner. *OECD Guidelines for Cryptography Policy*, March 27, 1997, available at *www.oecd.org*.

Back Door

An aspect of a system's mechanism that can be exploited to circumvent the system's security. *Cryptography's Role in Securing the Information Society*, United States National Research Council, 1996.

Backbone Service Provider (BSP)

Entities that operate infrastructure components of the Internet. *Public Performance of Musical Works* 1996-1998 (Tariff 22) (1999), 1 C.P.R. (4th) 417 (Copyright Board).

Backup

An alternate or redundant device that replaces a primary device in order to maintain continued operation in the event of primary device failure. Smart, Optical and Other Advanced Cards: How to Do a Privacy Assessment, Information and Privacy Commissioner/Ontario Canada, available at http://www.itc.on.ca.

Bacteria

A sub-class of viri; malicious software that does not attach itself specifically to other programs, does not use network resources, but still has a damaging effect. *A Survey of Legal Issues Relating to the Security of Electronic Information, Department of Justice, Canada.*

Bandwidth

A measure of electromagnetic frequency. It refers to a band of frequencies lying between two points on the electromagnetic spectrum. The wider the band, the more frequencies it comprises and the more information it can carry. Services requiring a lot of bandwidth are referred to as "broadband". Digital compression techniques are used to increase the amount of bandwidth on any delivery technology, e.g., fibre, coax, copper-wire. Submission of the Director of Investigation and Research to the CRTC Re Public Notice CRTC 1994-130.

The range of frequencies required for the transmission of a signal, usually given in hertz. More bandwidth is required for carrying more complex signals; for example, in the case of full-motion video as opposed to simple voice messages. *The Challenge of the Information Highway: Final Report of the Information Highway Advisory Council* (September 1995).

The carrying capacity of a network; the amount of data that can be transferred in a given amount of time. In general, the greater the bandwidth, the greater the opportunities for commerce. For example, with low bandwidth, it is not feasible to transfer the contents of a music CD over the Internet; with higher bandwidth, it is. Ministry of Revenue Advisory Committee, Report of the Committee On Electronic Commerce, April 30, 1998, Industry Canada.

The capacity of a transmission medium for transfer of information. Wide (or high) bandwidth means being able to transmit information such as a full television channel, compared with (say) a single telephone call. A digital full motion television channel requires as much bandwidth as 100 telephone conversations. *Digital Technology and the Copyright Act 1994: A Discussion Paper, Competition and Enterprise Branch, July 2001 (New Zealand).*

Banner Advertisement

Known as "banner ads", the advertisements are commonly found at the top of the screen. The adds themselves are often animated and whimsical, and designed to entice the internet user to "click here". If the user does click on the ad, she is transported to the website of the advertiser. *Playboy Enterprises, Inc. v. Netscape Communications Corp.* SA CV 99-320 A.H.S. (C.D.Cal. July 27, 1999).

A banner ad is an advertisement that stretches across the top and sometimes on the bottom of a web page which contains a link to the sponsor's website. A user clicking on the ad would be brought to the advertiser's website. *Playboy Enterprises, Inc. v. Netscape Communications Corp.*, SA CV 99-320 A.H.S. (C.D.Cal. July 27, 1999).

Banner advertisements are so named because they generally resemble flags or banners, in that they tend to be long and narrow and their width often spans a significant part of a Web page. *DoubleClick Inc. Privacy Litigation* Civ.0641 (N.R.V.) (S.D.N.Y. Mar. 28, 2001).

Barker Code

A Barker code is a pattern of 1's and 0's alternated in a pre-patterned sequence. *E.F. Johnson Co. v. Uniden Corp. of America*, 623 F.Supp. 1485 (D.C. Minn. 1985).

BASIC

Beginners All-Purpose Symbolic Instruction Code. *Apple Computer Inc. v. Computermat Inc.* (1983), 1 C.I.P.R. 1 (Ont. H.C.).

Basic Media Conversion Devices

Basic media conversion devices are two (or more) port devices which do not necessarily change the form of their input and output energy, but which serve as the interface between dissimilar media for information transfer. This category is broader than transducers, and includes transducers within it. Examples of basic media conversion devices include modulator/demodulator (MODEM) or dataset equipment which serve as the interface between analog and digital transmission media, and devices which "read" paper or magnetic tapes and which serve as the interface between a communications channel and paper or magnetic storage media, and basic communication path switching in PBX and key telephone systems. Second Computer Inquiry (Tentative Decision), 72 F.C.C.2d 358 (F.C.C. 1979).

Basic Non-Voice Service

A "basic non-voice" service is the transmission of subscriber inputted information or data where the carrier: (a) electrically converts originating messages to signals which are compatible with a transmission medium, (b) routes these signals through the network to the appropriate destination, (c) maintains signal integrity in the presence of noise and other impairments to transmission, (d) corrects transmission errors, and (e) converts the electrical signals to usable form at the destination. (In essence, the information is delivered in its original data format, code, or protocol to the addressee, and programmed actions are not taken on the basis of the content of the information transmitted in order to produce a response or control the routing of the message). Second Computer Inquiry (Tentative Decision), 72 F.C.C.2d 358 (F.C.C. 1979).

Basic Telecommunications Transport Service

Means any service, as defined and classified by measures of the regulator having jurisdiction, that is limited to the offering of transmission capacity for the movement of information. *An Act to Implement the Free Trade Agreement between Canada and the United States of America, S.C. 1988, c. 65.*

Basic Transmission Service

A basic transmission service is one that is limited to the common carrier offering of transmission capacity for the movement of information. In offering this capacity, a communications path is provided for the analog or digital transmission of voice, data, video, and other information. Different types of basic services are offered by carriers depending on (a) the bandwidth desired, (b) the analog and/or digital capabilities of the transmission medium, (c) the fidelity, distortion, or other conditioning parameters of the communications channels to achieve a specified transmission quality, and (d) the amount of transmission delay acceptable to the user. Under these criteria a subscriber is afforded the transmission capacity to suit its particular communications needs. A basic transmission service should be limited to the offering of transmission capacity between two or more points suitable for a user's transmission needs and subject only to the technical parameters of fidelity or distortion criteria, or other conditioning. Use internal to the carrier's facility of compounding techniques, bandwidth compression techniques, circuit switching, message or packet switching, error control techniques, etc. that facilitate economical, reliable movement of information does not alter the nature of the basic service. In the provision of a basic transmission service, memory or storage within the network is used only to facilitate the transmission of the information from the origin to its destination, and the carrier's basic transmission network is not used as an information storage system. Thus, in a basic service, once information is given to the communication facility, its progress towards the destination is subject to only those delays caused by congestion within the network or transmission priorities given by the originator. In offering a basic transmission service . . . a carrier essentially offers a pure transmission capability over a communications path that is virtually transparent in terms of its interaction with customer supplied information. Second Computer Inquiry (Final Decision), 77 F.C.C.2d 384 (F.C.C. 1980).

A basic transmission service is the common carrier offering of transmission capacity for the movement of information between two or more points. Various basic services are offered, depending upon the amount of bandwidth employed, the analog or digital characteristics of the transmission medium, and other line conditioning parameters that affect overall transmission quality. In providing such services a carrier offers to the public channel(s) of communications with associated network switching and routing. In this sense, a basic service is the offering of a "transmission pipeline" in contrast to the myriad services that are dependent upon, but different in kind, from the pipeline service. Second Computer Inquiry (Reconsideration of Final Decision), 84 F.C.C.2d 50 (F.C.C. 1980).

A basic service is one that is limited to the offering of transmission capacity for the movement of information. In offering this capacity, a communications path is provided for the analog or digital transmission of information of various types such as voice, data and video. Different types of basic services are offered depending on (a) the bandwidth desired, (b) the analog and/or digital capabilities of the transmission medium, (c) the fidelity, distortion or other conditioning parameters of the communications channel to achieve a specified transmission quality, and (d) the amount of transmission delay acceptable to the subscriber. Under these criteria, subscribers are afforded transmission capacity which suits their particular communications needs. A basic service should be limited to the offering of transmission capacity between two or more points, suitable for a subscriber's transmission needs, and subject only to the technical parameters of fidelity or distortion criteria, or other conditioning. Use internal to the service provider's facility of compounding techniques, bandwidth compression techniques, circuit switching, message or packet switching, error control, or other techniques that facilitate economical, reliable movement of information does not alter the nature of the basic service.

Similarly, internal speed, code and protocol conversion that is not manifested in the outputs of the service does not alter the nature of the basic service. In the provision of a basic service, memory or storage within the network is used only to facilitate the transmission of the information from the origination to its destination, and the service provider's basic transmission network is not used as an information storage system. Thus, in a basic service, once information is given to the communication facility, its progress towards the destination is subject to only those delays caused by congestion within the network of transmission priorities given by the originator. In offering a basic service, therefore, a service provider essentially offers a pure transmission capability over a communications path that is virtually transparent in terms of its interaction with subscriber supplied information. Enhanced Services, Telecom, Decision CRTC 84-18 (July 12, 1984), 9 C.R.T. 486.

Batch Mode

Until the 1970's, data processing was performed in the "batch" mode, that is, the application of a computer program was applied to data recorded (keypunched) on small cards, which were physically delivered to the computer. Batch processing requires extensive data pick-up and delivery, often involves lengthy overall turn around time, and permits only one job to be performed at a time. Technological advances now enable data to be transmitted electronically, typically over a telephone line, to and from central processing unit and the user's terminal. That capability plus other technological advances permit "timesharing": the simultaneous use of computer by many users, each of whom can interact with the computer, i.e. ask yes-no questions and receive immediate responses. *Assn. of Data Processing Service Organizations, Inc. v. Board of Governors of the Federal Reserve System*, Comp. Ind. Lit. Reptr. 1,1643 (Crt. App. D.C. 1984).

Batch Software

There is a distinction between batch software and on-line software. The nature of the distinction is not of vital importance, but in general terms, as I understand it, batch software is appropriate for a computer which prints information at one time and in one place, on-line software is appropriate for a system where a number of operators have their own terminals which display information. That information is up-to-date to the minute, whereas the information printed in the batch system may be out of date when it comes to be used. *Saphena Computing Ltd. v. Allied Collection Agencies Ltd.*, Ch. D., Recorder, July 22, 1988 (unreported); affirmed, C.A., May 3, 1989 (unreported).

Battery Backup

Battery contained in a game cartridge for storing the position, score or level attained within a game when the *console* is switched off. Monopolies and Mergers Commission — Video Games: A report on the supply of video games in the UK (LONDON: HMSO Cm2781).

Beacon

Beacon is the name given by the Stentor alliance of telephone companies to its plan for the construction of a two-way (or switched) broadband network. Competition and Culture on Canada's Information Highway: Managing the Realities of Transition, CRTC (the "Convergence Report"), May 19, 1995.

Benchmark

Benchmark is simply a demonstration of what a bidder has to offer. *Digital Methods Ltd. v. Alphatext Ltd.*, Ont. H.C., Garrett J., June 30, 1978, summarized at [1978] 2 A.C.W.S. 376.

Berne Convention

The Berne Convention for the Protection of Literary and Artistic Works.

Beta

"Beta" is the name of one of the two systems developed commercially for video cassette recording and playing equipment, the other being "VHS." *Re Application by Pioneer Kabushiki Kaisha* (1985), 5 I.P.R. 285 (Aus. Pat. Office).

Beta Test (or Beta Testing)

Beta testing is the final phase of operational testing prior to actual production release. *SAS Institute Inc. v. S. & H. Computer Systems Inc.*, 605 F.Supp. 816 (M.D. Tenn. 1985).

The designation given when the reliability of a computer system is verified in a limited customer environment. Beta testing of software is testing performed by users external to the company prior to the distribution of the software to the general public. In most cases, a pre-release version of the product (software and documentation) is made available to a few trusted users for testing prior to general release. Any problems with the software, documentation or functionality detected at this stage can still be addressed and corrected in the released version of the product. *Delrina Corp. v. Triolet Systems, Inc.* (1992), 47 C.P.R. (3d) 1 (Ont. H.C.).

Beta test means a test of a program with a real customer who pays, though rather a lesser amount than is intended once the program is established as trouble free. I suppose that an "alpha test" is one which is made by the programmer before any release. *IBCOS Computers Ltd. v. Barclay's Mercantile Highland Finance Ltd.*, [1994] F.S.R. 275 (Ch.D.).

Big Blue

IBM is the major American electronics company and apparently is known in the computer world as "Big Blue." *IBM Corp. v. Computer Imports Ltd.*, N.Z. H.C., Smellie J., March 21, 1989 (unreported).

Binary

Where only two values or states are possible for a particular condition; for example, "On" or "Off," or "One" or "Zero." *The Challenge of the Information Highway: Final Report of the Information Highway Advisory Council* (September 1995).

Binary Code

Machine language represented in numeric form by a series of 1's (the presence of a signal) and 0's (the absence of a signal). *IBM Corp. v. Ordinateurs Spirales Inc.* (1984), 2 C.I.P.R. 56 (Fed. T.D.).

The binary code version of a computer program is the program's source code translated into mechanical instructions that the computer can execute. Most software is distributed to consumers in this form. *Infosystems Technology Inc. v. Logical Software Inc.*, Vol. 6, No. 5 C.L.R. 831 (4th Cir. 1987).

Computer(s) only work in binary code, a code made up of 0's and 1's. So all data held in a computer or held on a computer storage device (such as a RAM, disc, or tape) must be so coded. *IBCOS Computers Ltd. v. Barclay's Mercantile Highland Finance Ltd.*, [1994] F.S.R. 275 (Ch.D.).

Binary Digits or Bits

A binary digit (or "bit") is a "two-way" digit in that it can have only one of two values. In digital signal processing, bits have the values "one" or "zero". Complex information is coded into bits, which processors translate into a corresponding electrical form such as "on" or "off". Submission of the Director of Investigation and Research to the CRTC Re Public Notice CRTC 1994-130.

One of the two symbols (0 and 1) that are commonly used to represent numerical entries in the binary number system. *Cryptography's Role in Securing the Information Society*, United States National Research Council, 1996.

Binary Notation

Binary notation is based on a system having a base 2. *Apple Computer Inc. v. Mackintosh Computers Ltd.* (1986), 28 D.L.R. (4th) 178 (Fed. T.D.).

Binary is number system using only two digits, 1 and 0. *Apple Computer Inc. v. Mackintosh Computers Ltd.* (1986), 28 D.L.R. (4th) 178 (Fed. T.D.).

A system of numeration consisting of only two digits, 0 and 1. *E.F. Johnson Co. v. Uniden Corp. of America*, 623 F.Supp. 1485 (D.C. Minn. 1985).

Binary notation simply consists of a series of 1's and 0's, with one digit representing the "electronically on" state and the other representing "electronically off." For convenience, binary code is sometimes expressed in hexadecimal, as a short end notation. *IBM Corp. v. Computer Imports Ltd.*, N.Z. H.C., Smellie J., March 21, 1989 (unreported).

Binary Signals

Binary signals are composed of a stream of zeros and ones, usually transmitted in groups of eight (e.g., 10101010 or 01101001). *Secure Services Technology Inc. v. Time and Space Processing Inc.*, 772 F.Supp. 1354 (E.D. Va. 1989).

Binary System

The binary system is based on the digits zero and one. Another system is known as the hexadecimal system which is based upon 16 digits: zero to 15 in decimal terminology. Computers operate on the binary system and the digits are transmitted by sending electrical signals where a low voltage or charge corresponds to the digit one and the absence of the voltage or charge corresponds to the digit zero. These transmissions operate at very great speed but always come back to the charge or no charge, the on or off, the positive or negative. Computers operate entirely in the binary language or system. Thus, instructions to a computer must be converted into the binary language when information is stored in a computer. Information is stored in binary language in the memory hardware within the computer. When information is processed within the computer it is processed in binary language and when information is transmitted from the computer to, for example, a screen or a printer, it is transmitted in binary language. Numbers can be expressed in binary language. When reduced to normal writing, the numbers are expressed in what we call 'bytes' consisting of a series of 'bits'. The bits are either one or zero and the existence and placement of these bits in a byte determine the number represented by the byte. But in the computer all this is represented by electrical signals or impulses. *Autodesk Australia Pty Ltd. v. Dyason* (1989), 15 I.P.R. 1 (Aus. Fed. Ct.), reversed [1990] A.I.P.C. 36,446 (Aus. Fed. Ct. FC).

Biographic Information

Information regarding image capture may include the date captured, the time, the operator identification, the capture device identification and location, and details of modification, if any. National Standard of Canada, Microfilm and Electronic Images as documentary evidence, Can/CGSB-72.11-93.

Biometrics

Catalogues unique physical characteristics of the user and can electronically authenticate identity. Advancing Global Electronic Commerce: Technology Solutions to Public Policy Challenges, Computer Systems Policy Project (CSPP), available at http://www.cspp.org/projects/july99_cto_report.pdf.

Is the measurement of physical characteristics such as fingerprints or retinal features using scanning technologies. Advancing Global Electronic Commerce: Technology Solutions to Public Policy Challenges, The Computer Systems Policy Project, July 1999, available at http://www.cspp.org/projects/july99_cto_report.pdf.

A biometric is a unique, measurable characteristic or trait of a human being for automatically recognizing or verifying identity. *Consumer Biometric Applications: A Discussion Paper, Internet and Privacy Commissioner/Ontario*, September, 1999.

Bios (Basic Input-Output System)

BIOS is that series of instructions which can be described as fulfilling the role of taking information into and out of the operating portion of the computer. *IBM Corp. v. Ordinateurs Spirales Inc.* (1984), 2 C.I.P.R. 56 (Fed. T.D.).

IBM Corp. v. Computer Imports Ltd., N.Z. H.C., Smellie J., March 21, 1989 (unreported).

BIT Economy

That part of the economy that earns its revenues directly from the Internet, comprises not only services such as advertising, entertainment, financial services and computer service, but also what may be defined as "digital" industries. These include newspapers, periodicals, book publishing, radio and television broadcasting, music, computer software - all those goods/services which can potentially be turned into BITS. These industries are also among core copyright industries, i.e. those industries that primarily create copyrighted works or produce copyrighted materials. Measuring Electronic Commerce: International Trade In Software, OECD dsti/iccp/ie (98) 3/Final, April 30, 1998.

Bit

A contraction of "*b*inary dig*it*"; a unit of information represented by zero or one. The speed of information transmission is measured in bits per second. The Challenge of the Information Highway Report. Report of the Committee On Electronic Commerce, April 30, 1998, Industry Canada. *The Challenge of the Information Highway: Final Report of the Information Highway Advisory Council* (September 1995).

Each digit of binary code (be it a 1 or 0) in computer terminology is called a bit. *Apple Computer Inc. v. Mackintosh Computers Ltd.* (1986), 28 D.L.R. (4th) 178 (Fed. T.D.).

The smallest unit of information used in a computer, represented as 0 or 1. *E.F. Johnson Co. v. Uniden Corp. of America*, 623 F.Supp. 1485 (D.C. Minn. 1985).

A bit is a single binary digit, i.e., a single zero or one. *Secure Services Technology Inc. v. Time and Space Processing Inc.*, 772 F.Supp. 1354 (E.D. Va. 1989).

This is generally considered to be the smallest "physical" unit of machine storage. It represents a "binary" state of TRUE or FALSE. It is the building block of all data within a computer system. It is a standard term within the industry. *Delrina Corp. v. Triolet Systems, Inc.* (1992), 47 C.P.R. (3d) 1 (Ont. H.C.).

The smallest unit of memory in a computer, a bit, is a switch with a value of 0 (off) or 1 (on). A group of eight bits is called a byte and represents a character—a letter or an integer. A kilobyte ("K") is 1024 bytes, a megabyte ("MB") 1024 kilobytes, and a gigabyte ("GB") 1024 kilobytes. *Universal City Studios, Inc. v. Reimerdes* 55 U.S.P.Q. 2d 1873 (S. D.N.Y. 2000).

Bit-map

Technique of relating screen graphics to a particular area of memory, represented by one or more bits. Monopolies and Mergers Commission — Video Games: A report on the supply of video games in the UK (LONDON: HMSO Cm2781).

Bitmap Graphics

A computer's processing unit generates, and a computer monitor displays, images by composing dots on the monitor screen called pixels which are illuminated, shaded or colored to achieve the desired effect. Bitmap graphics allow particular bits of the computer's memory function to manage each pixel, permitting programmers great flexibility in creating the visual displays actually generated. Programs written for computers having only limited amounts of such memory are forced to base their visual displays on vertically or horizontally defined lines and thus generally are confined to blinking cursors, letters, numbers and similarly limited characters. Such a visual interface is generally termed an alphanumeric or character-based interface and lacks the ability to generate the more complex shapes, forms, artistry and animation associated with a graphical user interface. A user wanting to start a word processing application, for example, in an alphanumeric or character-based interface might type the command "Exec WS" or to create a new file might type "Dup. F. Txt." *Apple Computer Inc. v. Microsoft Corp.*, 1992 U.S. Dist. LEXIS 12219 (N.D. Cal. 1992).

Bitmapped Character

A bitmapped character, whether used on a computer screen or on a dot-matrix or laser printer, is a dotted representation of an analog letter or character image where dots are so close together that when reduced to actual printed or displayed size, they form an image or character without the need to connect the dots. U.S. Library of Congress, Copyright Office, 53 F.R. 38110.

Bitmapping

"Bitmapping" refers to the technology that allows control of individual pixels on a display screen to produce graphic elements of superior resolution, permitting accurate reproduction of arcs, circles, sine waves, or other curved images. U.S. Library of Congress, Copyright Office, 53 F.R. 38110.

Bit Stream

The running stream of binary symbols representing digitized information; the term is commonly used to refer to digital communications. *Cryptography's Role in Securing the Information Society*, United States National Research Council, 1996.

Bit tax

A form of consumption tax (or tariff) levied on the transmission of digital information. Ministry of Revenue Advisory Committee, Report of the Committee On Electronic Commerce, April 30, 1998, Industry Canada.

"Blind" Signatures

Developed by David Chaum of DigiCash. . .provide the same authentication as digital signatures, but do so without revealing the originator's identity, thus rendering it "blind." The advantage of such a system is that it preserves the authenticating features of digital signatures, while protecting one's privacy at the same time. The Emerging Digital Economy, United States Department of Commerce, http://www.ecommerce.gov.

Blocking Software

Prevents the downloading of specific Web sites that are determined by the blocking software owner to be undesirable. Advancing Global Electronic Commerce: Technology Solutions to Public Policy Challenges, The Computer Systems Policy Project, July 1999, available at http://www.cspp.org/projects/july99_cto_report.pdf

Bookmark

An online function that lets you access your favourite web sites quickly. Federal Trade Commission and the National Association of Attorneys General - Cyberspeak - Learning the Language.

If you think of the Web as a book full of millions of pages, a bookmark on the Web acts much the same way as it does in a real book — it marks a site of interest for future reference. Most Web browsers keep a history of the sites you have visited and have the ability to store a list of addresses or URLs so you can retrieve them in the future. For example, with the Netscape Navigator browser, stored items are called "Bookmarks." Microsoft Internet Explorer"s equivalent is called Favorites. The Internet: A Guide For Ontario Government Organizations, Information and Privacy Commissioner/Ontario, May 1998, available at http://www.ipc.on.ca.

An online function that lets you access your favorite web sites quickly. Cyberspeak — Learning the Language, the Federal Trade Commission and the National Association of Attorneys General, available at http://www.ftc.gov/bcp/conline/pubs/online/sitesee/index.html.

A method of storing the Internet address of a Web page so that the user can go to that address without having to re-enter it manually. *Domain Name System Reform and Related Internet Governance Issues: A Consultation Paper*, Industry Canada available at *www.strategis.gc.ca.*

Boot up

To switch on and start up a computer. Monopolies and Mergers Commission — Video Games: A report on the supply of video games in the UK (LONDON: HMSO Cm2781).

Bottleneck

A bottleneck is a local telephone network service, function or facility currently subject to some degree of monopoly control, that competitors cannot economically duplicate, but require access to in order to compete. The degree to which network elements exhibit bottleneck characteristics will soon be examined in the Commission's process on local competition. Competition and Culture on Canada's Information Highway: Managing the Realities of Transition, CRTC (the "Convergence Report"), May 19, 1995. *The Challenge of the Information Highway: Final Report of the Information Highway Advisory Council* (September 1995).

Brick and Mortar

The phrase "Brick and Mortar" is often used to designate a traditional business when contrasting it with a predominantly, or entirely, on-line business. The phrase appears to refer to the historical reliance on conducting commerce within the context of a physical space made from materials such as brick and mortar, as opposed to the modern trend towards conducting commerce in a cyberspace made from computers and programs. *eBay v. Bidder's Edge Inc.,* 54 U.S.P.Q. 2d 1798 (N.D. Cal. 2000).

Broadband Network

A type of local area network on which transmissions travel as radio frequency signals over separate inbound and outbound channels. Stations on a broadband network are connected by coaxial or fibre-optic cable. The cable itself can be made to carry data, voice and video simultaneously over multiple transmission channels. Broadband networks can achieve transmission speeds of 20 megabits per second (Mbps) or greater. Cable television is an example of a broadband network. Submission of the Director of Investigation and Research to the CRTC Re Public Notice CRTC 1994-130.

Broadband Services

A range of communications services that require and use larger bandwidth than traditional voice messaging. A broadband communication system can simultaneously accommodate television, voice, data, and many other services. *The Challenge of the Information Highway: Final Report of the Information Highway Advisory Council* (September 1995).

A service enabling the two-way transmission of voice, data or multimedia communications with speed in one direction in excess of 1.544 Mbps. *Report to the Governor in Council: Status of Competition in Canadian Telecommunications Markets, Deployment/Accessibility of Advanced Telecommunications Infrastructure and Services, September, 2001.*

Broadcasting

Any transmission of programs, whether or not encrypted, by waves or other means of telecommunication for reception by the public by means of broadcasting receiving apparatus, but does not include any such transmission of programs that is made solely for performance or display in a public place. *Broadcasting Act*, S.C. 1991, c. 11.

Any radiocommunication in which the transmissions are intended for direct reception by the general public. *Radiocommunication Act*, R.S.C. 1985, c. R-2, as amended.

Means any radiocommunication in which the transmissions are intended for direct reception by the general public. *Capital Cities Communications Inc. v. CRTC*, [1978] 2 S.C.R. 141.

Broadcasting Receiving Apparatus

A device, or combination of devices, intended for or capable of being used for the reception of broadcasting. *Broadcasting Act*, S.C. 1991, c. 11.

Broadcasting Undertaking

Includes a distribution undertaking, a programming undertaking and a network. *Broadcasting Act*, S.C. 1991, c. 11.

Browse

Browse means a temporary materialization of a work on a video screen, television monitor or similar device, or the performance of the audio portion of such a work on a speaker or a similar device by a user, but does not include the making of a permanent reproduction of the work in any material form. Connection Community Content, *The Challenge of the Information Highway: Final Report of the Information Highway Advisory Council* (September 1995).

Browser

A software application that displays HTML-formatted content; used to access content on the World Wide Web and on intranets. Ministry of Revenue Advisory Committee, Report of the Committee On Electronic Commerce, April 30, 1998, Industry Canada.

Browsers are programs or software that allow you to access the World Wide Web. They are the information retrieval tools of the Web, as they allow you to view and interact with various kinds of resources available on the Web. The documents that browsers display are hypertext documents. This means that text can be linked or referenced to other texts. Browsers let you use the links in a transparent way (i.e., select a link in one document and then have the text from the referenced document presented to you on your screen). The Internet: A Guide For Ontario Government Organizations, Information and Privacy Commissioner/Ontario, May 1998, available at http://www.ipc.on.ca.

Special software that allows you to navigate several areas of the Internet and view a web site. Cyberspeak — Learning the Language, the Federal Trade Commission and the National Association of Attorneys General, available at http://www.ftc.gov/bcp/conline/pubs/online/sitesee/index.html.

A program which interprets a Web (hypertext) document allowing it to be read on a computer screen. *Digital Technology and the Copyright Act 1994: A Discussion Paper, Competition and Enterprise Branch, July 2001 (New Zealand).*

A browser is a computer program through which a user communicates on the Web. *DoubleClick Inc. Privacy Litigation* Civ.0641 (N.R.V.) (S.D.N.Y. Mar. 28, 2001).

Computer programs known as "browsers" are used on a searcher's computers to read HTML information and interact with it. The browsers read the website coding to display designs and text on the user's computer screen. *British Columbia Automobile Assn. v. OPEIU. Local 378* (2001), 10 C.P.R. (4th) 423 (B.C.S.C.).

Information is published on the Web using a formatting language known as Hypertext Markup Language or HTML. A computer user who wishes to access resources on the Web utilizes a Web "browser", such as the now generally familiar Netscape Navigator or Internet Explorer. A browser is software that can display HTML documents containing text, images, sound, and moving video. By employing a Web browser, users can access particular sites on the Web in several ways. First, they can simply type the address of a desired site directly into the address bar on their browser. That address, which is known as the Universal Resource Locator or "URL", includes, as one of its technical components, the second-level domain name. Armed with that second-level domain name, the browser software then contacts a remote computer, known as a Domain Name

Server. The Domain Name Server translates the requested second-level domain name into the assigned unique IP address associated with the name. Having acquired the appropriate numeric IP address, the browser then contacts the server located at that address, which in turn sends a copy of the text and any graphics associated with that particular Web page back to the browser for display on the user's monitor. *National A-1 Advertising, Inc. et al v. Networks Solutions, Inc.*, Civ. No. 99-033-M (D.N.Hamp. Sept. 28, 2000).

Bug

A bug is unexpected problem in a computer program which prevents the program from functioning properly. A bug fix is an adjustment that corrects the bug. *Infosystems Technology Inc. v. Logical Software Inc.*, Vol. 6, No. 5 C.L.R. 831 (4th Cir. 1987).

An error or fault. Programs undergo a 'debugging' process to eradicate errors before a game comes to market. Monopolies and Mergers Commission — Video Games: A report on the supply of video games in the UK (LONDON: HMSO Cm2781).

Bulletin Board (See also Electronic Bulletin Board)

Computer bulletin boards generally offer both private electronic mail services and newsgroups. The latter is essentially email directed to the community at large, rather than a private recipient. A bulletin board is an interactive or bidirectional service that cannot currently be offered through cable television transmissions. *MTV Networks v. Curry*, 867 F.Supp. 202 (S.D.N.Y. 1994).

A computer acting as a message board for storage and retrieval of data and programs by a number of users; accessed by telephone line and often used for pirated, pornographic or 'still in development' *software*, although many legitimate services exist. Monopolies and Mergers Commission — Video Games: A report on the supply of video games in the UK (LONDON: HMSO Cm2781).

A computing system, usually (but not necessarily) connected to the Internet, which can be accessed by diverse people to exchange messages. Electronic bulletin boards mimic many of the features of a physical notice board, with users being able to post messages for others to read. *Digital Technology and the Copyright Act 1994: A Discussion Paper, Competition and Enterprise Branch, July 2001 (New Zealand)*.

Places to leave an electronic message or share news that anyone can read and respond to. Marketers or others can get your e-mail address from bulletin boards and newsgroups. Cyberspeak — Learning the Language, the Federal Trade Commission and the National Association of Attorneys General, available at http://www.ftc.gov/bcp/conline/pubs/online/sitesee/index.html.

Bulletin Board Service (BBS)

A computer bulletin board service offers home computer owners a method for obtaining information from a central source by use of modem. Remote computers access central service through telephone lines. Files of information are stored in the central system, and subscribers may either "download" information into their home units, or "upload" information from their home units into the central files. The owner of the service controls the terms by which the remote computer owners will be able to access the system, and typically will control the conditions under which information may be downloaded or uploaded. *Playboy Enterprises, Inc. v. Hardenburgh, Inc.*, 982 F.Supp. 503 (N.D. Ohio, 1997).

Bulletin-Board System (BBS)

A computer bulletin-board system is a computer program that simulates an actual bulletin-board by allowing computer users who access a particular computer to post messages, read existing messages, and delete messages. The messages exchanged may contain a wide variety of information, including stolen credit card numbers, confidential business information, and information about local community events. *United States v. Riggs*, 2 CCH 43,316 (N.D. Ill. 1990).

As the name implies, a BBS (Bulletin-Board System) is an electronic forum for exchanging electronic mail, reading notices and features, carrying on unstructured multilogs, and copying programs stored on the host computer. Bulletin-boards are videotext systems that provide quick access to information held in databanks. They can be used to transmit information back and forth. They can be used to provide information to a closed group or an open group. Bulletin-board services are sometimes provided as a free service, but may be subject to a charge. They function as electronic notice boards and as electronic mail services. *Re Application by International Computers Ltd.* (1985), 5 I.P.R. 263 (Aus. Pat. Office).

A bulletin board system is a computer system to which subscribers have telecommunications access for many purposes, including sending and receiving electronic mail, and obtaining and delivering files (which may consist of software, text, graphic images, or anything else that may be placed in a digital format). A BBS may be (1) commercial, as in the examples of CompuServe, Prodigy, and the like, (2) institutional, as in the case of a university BBS, or (3) individually owned and operated. *National Information Infrastructure: A Preliminary Draft of the Report of the Working Group on Intellectual Property Rights, July 1994.*

A computer bulletin board system is the computerized equivalent to the bulletin board's commonly found in the workplace, schools, and the home. . . . To run a bulletin board system, three things are needed. The first item is a computer. Bulletin board systems can be run on virtually any size computer, from a small personal computer costing a few hundred dollars, to a large mainframe computer affordable only to large corporations and universities. Second, bulletin board software is needed, which can be obtained either commercially or for free. Finally, there must be a way for people (usually called 'users' in the computer jargon) to access the bulletin board. This is accomplished via a modem or connection to a computer network. *Davis v. The State of Oklahoma*, 1996 CCH Computer Law Reporter p. 47421 (Crim.App.S. Okla. 1996).

Bundling

Practice of combining separate hardware, software and services into a package offered at a single price. *The Challenge of the Information Highway: Final Report of the Information Highway Advisory Council* (September 1995).

Bundling in the computer industry is a practice by which a computer manufacturer charges a single price for hardware and software and other provided services, along with the sale of the computer system. Included in the single price is the hardware, all software that has been developed, future supportive systems, education services, and, to varying degrees, all future developments in software. This has been the practice in the computer industry since its inception, when there was little software available. *United Software Corp. v. Sperry Rand Corp.*, 5 C.L.S.R. 1492 (E.D. Pa. 1974).

Bypass

The circumvention of a telecommunications facility by means of some lower-cost alternative such as satellite, microwave or private line. Submission of the Director of Investigation and Research to the CRTC Re Public Notice CRTC 1994-130.

Byte

A string of eight digits is called a byte. *Apple Computer Inc. v. Mackintosh Computers Ltd.* (1986), 28 D.L.R. (4th) 178 (Fed. T.D.).

A grouping of eight bits. *E.F. Johnson Co. v. Uniden Corp. of America*, 623 F.Supp. 1485 (D.C. Minn. 1985).

This is generally considered to be the smallest "addressable" unit of machine storage. In most computer systems, it consists of 8 BITS of data. It is a standard term within the industry. *Delrina Corp. v. Triolet Systems, Inc.* (1992), 47 C.P.R. (3d) 1 (Ont. H.C.).

Binary digits or "bits" are the building blocks of a larger coding unit called a "byte". A byte is a string of eight bits that signify something recognizable such as letters of the alphabet, punctuation marks or numbers. Amounts of computerized information, as well as the capacity of drives and memories, are usually conveyed in multiples of bytes. Submission of the Director of Investigation and Research to the CRTC Re Public Notice CRTC 1994-130.

.ca

Canada's country code Top Level Domain (ccTLD). *Domain Name System Reform and Related Internet Governance Issues: A Consultation Paper*, Industry Canada, available at *www.strategis.gc.ca*.

Cable

The fibre optic wires, although of silicon or glass, enclosed in a protective covering and used in the transmission of signals normally transmitted by a copper cable are themselves a cable within the ordinary meaning of the term. *British Columbia Telephone Co. v. Canada*, [1991] F.C.J. No. 340 (Fed. T.D.).

Cable Internet Service

A bi-directional high-speed digital communication service, enabling Internet access through the use of cable TV coaxial network. *Report to the Governor in Council: Status of Competition in Canadian Telecommunications Markets, Deployment/Accessibility of Advanced Telecommunications Infrastructure and Services, September, 2001.*

Cable Modem

Allow a user's computer to transmit digital signals over coaxial cable infrastructure. Advancing Global Electronic Commerce: Technology Solutions to Public Policy Challenges, The Computer Systems Policy Project, July 1999, available at http://www.cspp.org/projects/july99_cto_report.pdf.

Cable Telephony

The use of a cable television distribution system to transmit and switch voice and data in a manner functionally equivalent to the public switched telephone network. Submission of the Director of Investigation and Research to the CRTC Re Public Notice CRTC 1994-130.

Cable Television

A method for distributing television signals to subscriber homes through coaxial cable links, primarily to residential customers. Submission of the Director of Investigation and Research to the CRTC Re Public Notice CRTC 1994-130.

Cache

An electronic cache is a means of temporarily storing files copied from some other source. In the context of the Web a cache is usually a section of magnetic disk storage which is used to store documents being transferred across the Internet. Such a cache is often used by an ISP or a local browser (on a user's own computer) to reduce the time and cost, and increase the reliability, of retrieval of information across the Internet. Caching is the process of storing files in a cache. *Digital Technology and the Copyright Act 1994: A Discussion Paper, Competition and Enterprise Branch, July 2001 (New Zealand).*

Cache Servers

Internet access providers, and others, may also operate "cache" servers that temporarily store material requested by end users from a host server. *Society of Composers, Authors & Music Publishers of Canada v. Canadian Assn. of Internet Providers* (2002), 19 C.P.R. (4th) 289 (Fed. C.A.).

CAD

Computer Assisted Drafting. *Autodesk Australia Pty Ltd. v. Dyason* (1989) 15 I.P.R. 1 (Aus. Fed. Ct.), reversed [1990] A.I.P.C. 36,446 (Aus. Fed. Ct.).

[CAD] allowed the individual to do the design in the computer and then, using the computer's capability, in memory and with the speed of the processor, to change that design on the screen, which afforded tremendous leverage in terms of the speed, and also the cost associated with the designs themselves. *Apple Computer, Inc. v. U.S.*, CCH Comp. L. 46,363 (Cit. 1991).

Computer Assisted Drafting. *Autodesk Australia Pty Ltd. v. Dyason* (1992), A.I.P.C. 90,855 (Aust. H.C.).

CAD Software

In general, CAD software products enable architects, engineers and other design professionals to design and alter designs of buildings, mechanical devices and electronic equipment using computers as drafting devices. They can then produce blue prints and other design drawings through their computers. *Baystate Technologies Inc. v. Bentley Systems*, 946 F. Supp. 1079 (D. Mass. 1996).

CAD-CAM System

"CAD-CAM System" stands for "computer-aided design and computer-aided manufacturing system." *Jostens Inc. v. National Computer Systems Inc.*, 318 N.W.2d 691 (Minn. Sup. Ct. 1982).

Computer assisted design and computer assisted manufacture. *Lasercomb America Inc. v. Reynolds*, 911 F.2d 970 (4th Cir. 1990).

Call

This refers to a program utilizing (calling) the services provided as part of the basic software supplied with the computer system (operating system). The program uses the "CALL" facility of the particular programming language to request the desired service. For instance, within any operating system, there are a wide variety of system supplied procedures that provide general purpose functionality such as reading data and getting the current date. These "operating system procedures" act as the building blocks for programming by providing the foundation level of basic functionality that most programs will require. *Delrina Corp. v. Triolet Systems, Inc.* (1992), 47 C.P.R. (3d) 1 (Ont. H.C.).

Call Controller

A call controller is a piece of computer hardware that enhances the utility of a telephone system by the automatic selection of a particular long distance carrier and activating optical features such as speed dialing. *MiTek Holdings Inc. v. IQTEL Inc.*, 44 U.S.P.Q. 2d 1172 (10th Cir. 1997).

CAM

Content-Addressable Memory. *Intel Corp. v. Radiation Inc.*, 184 U.S.P.Q. 54 (T.T.A.B. 1974).

Canadian Carrier

This refers to a telecommunications common carrier that is subject to the legislative authority of Parliament. *Telecommunications Act*, S.C. 1993, c. 38.

Canadian Central Facility

Is the Government of Canada Public Key Infrastructure's central Certification Authority. Public Key Infrastructure Management in the Government of Canada, Treasury Board of Canada Secretariat, May 27, 1999, available at http://www.tbs-sct.gc.ca/pubs_pol/ciopubs/PKI/pki1_e.html

Capacitive Card

A capacitively coupled memory card, where value can be stored as tokens. For example a value token can represent a bus ride, or payment for a video game. Smart, Optical and Other Advanced Cards: How to Do a Privacy Assessment, Information and Privacy Commissioner/Ontario Canada, available at http://www.itc.on.ca.

Capture

The creation of an image from a source record. National Standard of Canada, Microfilm and Electronic Images as documentary evidence, Can/CGSB-72.11-93.

Card

A rectangular paper or plastic medium used to carry information relating to its issuer and user. Smart, Optical and Other Advanced Cards: How to Do a Privacy Assessment, Information and Privacy Commissioner/Ontario Canada, available at http://www.itc.on.ca.

Cardholder

Generally the person to whom an identification card is issued. For financial transactions cards it is usually the customer associated with the primary account number recorded on the card. Smart, Optical and Other Advanced Cards: How to Do a Privacy Assessment, Information and Privacy Commissioner/Ontario Canada, available at http://www.itc.on.ca.

Card Issuer

An individual or organization that issues identification cards, to individual or corporate cardholders. Smart, Optical and Other Advanced Cards: How to Do a

Privacy Assessment, Information and Privacy Commissioner/Ontario Canada, available at http://www.itc.on.ca.

Cartridge Game

A video game installed in a cartridge that plugs into a *console* and contains one or more *ROM chips* so that the game is available for immediate access by the player. Sometimes contains *battery backup*. Monopolies and Mergers Commission — Video Games: A report on the supply of video games in the UK (LONDON: HMSO Cm2781).

Catalog

A catalog is a set of indices that contain file information and volume identifiers. *IBM v. Fujitsu Ltd.*, Copyright L.R. (CCH), 20,517 (Am. Arbtn. Assoc. Comm. Arbtn. Trib. 1988).

Cathode-Ray Tube (C.R.T.)

A cathode-ray tube is the screen on which the information requested appears. *Poly Data Inc. v. Fedsan Ltd.*, Ont. H.C., Trainor J., November 2, 1979, summarized at 1 A.C.W.S. (2d) 83.

CBC

Cipher Block Chaining. "Security Requirements for Cryptographic Modules", FIPS Pub. 140-1, Federal Information Processing Standards Publication, January 11, 1994, available at http://csrc.nist.gov/fips/fips1401.htm.

CCITT

CCITT is the standard abbreviation for the International Telephone and Telegraph Consultive Committee of the International Communications Union. *Secure Services Technology Inc. v. Time and Space Processing Inc.*, 772 F.Supp. 1354 (E.D.Va. 1989).

ccTLD - country code Top Level Domain

The Top Level domain that corresponds to each country's ISO 3166 code (e.g. .au for Australia, .ca for Canada). *Domain Name System Reform and Related Internet Governance Issues: A Consultation Paper*, Industry Canada available at *www.strategis.gc.ca*.

CD

Compact disc. CDs have a much larger capacity than cartridge or *floppy disc* formats. Monopolies and Mergers Commission — Video Games: A report on the supply of video games in the UK (LONDON: HMSO Cm2781).

CD ROM (Compact Disk — Read Only Memory)

Compact disc with read-only memory; inexpensive, high-capacity storage medium for data, text, and video. Ministry of Revenue Advisory Committee, Report of the Committee On Electronic Commerce, April 30, 1998, Industry Canada.

A CD ROM disk, or CD ROM, is identical in appearance to the compact disks used in audio players but, rather than storing music decipherable by a compact disk player, stores data which can be read by a laser into a computer via a CD ROM disk drive, just as a computer reads information off a floppy disk through a disk drive. The main advantage of CD ROM disks over floppy disks is their larger storage capacity; one CD ROM holds roughly the same amount of information as one thousand floppies. *Night Owl Computer Service v. James* (1992), Copyright Law Decisions, p. 26892 (W.D.N.Y. 1992).

A CD ROM is a five-inch wide optical disk capable of storing approximately 650 MB of data. To read the data on a CD ROM, a computer must have a CD ROM drive. *Universal City Studios, Inc. v. Reimerdes,* 55 U.S.P.Q. 2d 1873 (S. D.N.Y. 2000).

A CD ROM is a 118 mm plastic disk with information represented by holes or pits in a thin metal film and capable of storing up to 800 Megabytes. The information is read as variations in reflected light from a small laser. CD ROMs and music CDs are physically identical but the information is encoded differently. CD ROMs and music CDs are a type of, and are sometimes called, Optical Disks. Smaller size optical disks are becoming more common, such as Sony MiniDiscs. Some types of CDs are erasable or may be written to once (then the information can be read as many times as required). *Digital Technology and the Copyright Act 1994: A Discussion Paper, Competition and Enterprise Branch, July 2001 (New Zealand)..*

Cellular Telephone Service

Cellular telephone service is based upon a system of individual cellular telephone units having wireless radio transmission capabilities and which operate within a series of geographic "cells", each of which is served by a radio transmitter capable of handling as many as 666 channels. As the user moves from one cell to another, transmission of telephone calls is automatically shifted from one transmitter to the other, thus maintaining a consistent signal quality. *United States v. Brady,* 820 F.Supp. 1346 (C.D. Utah 1993).

Cellular Telephony

A mobile or "wireless" telecommunications system that allows subscribers to dial into the public switched telephone network (PSTN) while moving about freely in areas where coverage is not provided. It divides a geographic region into cells, using a low-power transmitter within each cell. Calls are transferred from cell to cell as the subscriber moves about. Submission of the Director of Investigation and Research to the CRTC Re Public Notice CRTC 1994-130.

Central Office

Facility containing telephone equipment where customers' calls are switched and transmitted. *Report to the Governor in Council: Status of Competition in Canadian Telecommunications Markets, Deployment/Accessibility of Advanced Telecommunications Infrastructure and Services, September, 2001.*

Centralized Routines

These are usually self-contained pieces of program code that provide a commonly or frequently required function within a program. They are coded once within the program and then simply "called" wherever the functionality is required within the body of the program code. In many cases, the functionality extends beyond the scope of a single program and the routine is centralized into a library for the application area much like the "operating system procedures" supplied with the operating system only on a narrower scope. Examples of this would include such tasks as the calculation of one number as a percentage of another, displaying data at a certain position on the terminal screen and printing the copyright notice at the top of all terminal screens. *Delrina Corp. v. Triolet Systems, Inc.* (1992), 47 C.P.R. (3d) 1 (Ont. H.C.).

Centrex Service

A telephone company supplied local service with associated sets of features (e.g., call display, call forwarding). *Report to the Governor in Council: Status of Competition in Canadian Telecommunications Markets, Deployment/Accessibility of Advanced Telecommunications Infrastructure and Services, September, 2001.*

Certificate

An electronic document that contains credentials bound to an entity and is signed by a certification authority which has verified these credentials. Security and Electronic Authorization and Authentication Guideline, Communications Security Establishment, Government of Canada September 1995, CID/01/15; a Cryptology Policy Framework for Electronic Commerce, Task Force on Electronic Commerce, Industry Canada, February 1998.

Means a data message or other record which is issued by an information certifier and which purports to ascertain the identity of a person or entity who holds a particular [key pair] [signature device]. Draft Uniform Rules on Electronic Signatures, UNCITRAL, 29 June 1999.

Means a record that at a minimum: (a) identifies the certification authority issuing it; (b) names or otherwise identifies its subscriber, or a device or electronic agent under the control of the subscriber; (c) contains a public key that corresponds to a private key under the control of the subscriber; (d) specifies its operational period; and (e) is digitally signed by the certification authority issuing it. *Illinois Electronic Commerce Security Act* 1998 5 Ill. Comp. Stat. 175.

A message ensured by a person, which message attests to the accuracy of facts material to the legal efficacy of the act of another person. General Usage for International Digitally Insured Commerce (Guidec), International Chamber of Commerce, 1997, available at http://www.icc.wbo.org/guidec2.htm.

Means a computer-based record created by a certification authority and issued to a subscriber for the purposes of permitting the subscriber to sign (a) electronic applications and electronic instruments under this Part, and (b) electronic returns under the *Property Transfer Tax Act. B.C. Land Title Amendment Act*, 1999 (Bill 93-1999).

Means a computer-based record which: (a) identifies the certification authority issuing it; (b) names or identifies its subscriber; (c) contains the subscriber's public key; and(d) is digitally signed by the certification authority issuing it. *Utah Digital Signature Act* 46-3, available at http://www.le.state.ut.us/code/TITLE46/htm/46_03004.htm.

An electronic document signed by the CA which: (1) identifies a Key-holder; (2) binds the Key-holder to a Key Pair by specifying the Public Key of that Key Pair; and (3) should contain the other information required by the Certificate Profile. *The Office of the Federal Privacy Commissioner (Australia), Consultation Paper, (June 2001).*

Certificate Directory

The published directory listing Certificates currently in force. *The Office of the Federal Privacy Commissioner (Australia), Consultation Paper, (June 2001).*

Certificate Policy (CP)

The document describes the PKI and the roles, functions and obligations of PKI Service Providers and End Entities (with reference to other Accredited Documents where appropriate.). *The Office of the Federal Privacy Commissioner (Australia), Consultation Paper, (June 2001).*

Certificate Profile

The specification of the fields to be included in a Certificate. *The Office of the Federal Privacy Commissioner (Australia), Consultation Paper, (June 2001).*

Certificate Revocation List (CRL)

The published list of revoked and/or suspended Certificates. The CRL may form part of the Certificate Directory or may be published separately. *The Office of the Federal Privacy Commissioner (Australia), Consultation Paper, (June 2001).*

Certificate Management

The overall process of issuing, storing, verifying, and generally accepting responsibility for the accuracy of certifications and their secure delivery to appropriate consumers. *Cryptography's Role in Securing the Information Society*, United States National Research Council, 1996.

Certificate Policy

Is a named set of rules that indicates the applicability of a public key certificate to a particular community and/or class of application with common security requirements. It indicates whether or not the public key certificate is suitable for a particular application or purpose. A Certification Authority may adopt more than one Certificate Policy. Public Key Infrastructure Management in the Government of Canada, Treasury Board of Canada Secretariat, May 27, 1999, available at http://www.tbs-sct.gc.ca/pubs_pol/ciopubs/PKI/pki1_e.html.

A named set of rules that indicates the applicability of a certificate to a particular community and/or class of applications with common security requirements. "European Electronic Signature Standardization Initiative", Final Draft of the EESSI Expert Team Report, June 18, 1999.

Certificate Revocation List

A "certificate revocation list" is a list of certificates which have been revoked and the time and date that each certificate was revoked. They may include additional information, such as the reason the certificate was revoked. Security and Electronic Authorization and Authentication Guideline, Communications Security Establishment, Government of Canada September 1995, CID/01/15.

Is a list maintained by a Certification Authority. It contains the public key certificates that it issued but revoked before their natural expiration time. Public Key Infrastructure Management in the Government of Canada, Treasury Board of Canada Secretariat, May 27, 1999, available at http://www.tbs-sct.gc.ca/pubs_pol/ciopubs/PKI/pki1_e.html.

Certification

Certificate is the testing of a magnetic disk to determine whether the media meets specific industry standards. A signal is written on the diskette and read back off. The percentage of the signal that is retained is used in the industry as a measure of the quality of the product. Greater signal retention commands a higher price in the market, although markets do exist for mircrodisks that test at lesser levels. *International Trade Commission Determination re 3.5-Inch Microdisks*, 1 CCH Comp. Cases 60,024 (ITC Inv. No. 731-Ta-389).

Certification Authority (CA)

A third party that verifies an entity's credentials, generates certificates which can be used by these entities to prove their attributes to others, and maintains adequate records to demonstrate the binding between the entity and the credentials which have been certified. Certification authorities also manage, distribute, and store certificates and certificate revocation lists. Security and Electronic Authorization and Authentication Guideline, Communications Security Establishment, Government of Canada September 1995, CID/01/15; a Cryptology Policy Framework for Electronic Commerce, Task Force on Electronic Commerce, Industry Canada, February 1998.

Means a person who authorizes and causes the issuance of a certificate. *Illinois Electronic Commerce Security Act* 1998 5 Ill. Comp. Stat. 175.

Is a person or organizational unit within a department that is responsible for: (a) the operation of an authority trusted by one or more users to issue and manage public key certificates and certificate revocation lists; or (b) the management of: (i) any arrangement under which a department contracts for the provision of services relating to the issuance and management of public key certificates and certificate revocation lists on its behalf; and (ii) policies and procedures within the department for the management of public key certificates issued on its behalf. Public Key Infrastructure Management in the Government of Canada, Treasury Board of Canada Secretariat, May 27, 1999, available at http://www.tbs-sct.gc.ca/pubs_pol/ciopubs/PKI/pki1_e.html.

A body that signs and issues digital certificates which bind subscribers to their private keys. *The Office of the Federal Privacy Commissioner (Australia), Consultation Paper, (June 2001).*

Certification Practice Statement

Is a statement published by a certification authority that specifies the policies or practices that the certification authority employs in issuing, managing, suspending, and revoking certificates and providing access to them. *Illinois Electronic Commerce Security Act* 1998 5 Ill. Comp. Stat. 175.

Means the statement approved by the director under section 168.71. *B.C. Land Title Amendment Act*, 1999 (Bill 93-1999).

A statement of the practices which a certifier employs in issuing certificates generally, or employed in issuing a particular certificate. General Usage for International Digitally Insured Commerce (Guidec), International Chamber of Commerce, 1997, available at http://www.icc.wbo.org/guidec2.htm.

Is a statement of the practices that a Certification Authority employs in issuing public key certificates. It is a comprehensive description of such details as the precise implementation of service offerings and procedures of public key certificate life-cycle management and will be more detailed than the certificate policies supported by the Certification Authority. Public Key Infrastructure Management in the Government of Canada, Treasury Board of Canada Secretariat, May 27, 1999, available at http://www.tbs-sct.gc.ca/pubs_pol/ciopubs/PKI/pki1_e.html.

Means a declaration of the practices which a certification authority employs in issuing certificates generally, or employs in issuing a material certificate. *Utah Digital Signature Act* 46-3, available at http://www.le.state.ut.us/code/TITLE46/htm/46_03004.htm.

A statement of the Certification Authority's practices with respect to a wide range of technical, business and legal issues that may be used as a basis for the Certification Authority's contract with Subscribers and relationships with Relying Parties. UNCITRAL Model Law on Electronic Signatures, A/CN. 94/483.

The document that describes the operational practices of the CA in relation to its Certification Services. *The Office of the Federal Privacy Commissioner (Australia), Consultation Paper, (June 2001).*

Certification Services

Issue of Certificates and other functions performed by the CA under the CP. *The Office of the Federal Privacy Commissioner (Australia), Consultation Paper, (June 2001).*

Certification Service Provider

Means a person who or an entity which issues certificates or provides other services related to electronic signatures to the public. Proposal for A European Parliament and Council Directive on a Common Framework for Electronic Signatures, COM (1998) 297 Final.

Certifier

A person who issues a certificate, and thereby attests to the accuracy of a fact material to the legal efficacy of the act of another person. General Usage for International Digitally Insured Commerce (Guidec), International Chamber of Commerce, 1997, available at http://www.icc.wbo.org/guidec2.htm.

Character

This is the unit of storage that is used to contain a single "readable" character within the computer system. In most computer systems, this is equivalent to a BYTE. It is a standard term within the industry. *Delrina Corp. v. Triolet Systems, Inc.* (1992), 47 C.P.R. (3d) 1 (Ont. H.C.).

Chat Room

A place for people to converse online by typing messages to each other. (Once you're in a chat room, others can contact you by e-mail. Some online services monitor their chat rooms and encourage children to report offensive chatter. Some allow parents to deny access to chat rooms altogether.) Federal Trade Commission and the National Association of Attorneys General - Cyberspeak - Learning the Language.

A chat room is a form of bulletin board that enables users to communicate with each other one on one or in a group on a real time basis. *Technical Committees' Internet Task Force Report*, International Organization of Securities Commissioners, September 13, 1998.

Provide additional online discussion forums that allow users to engage in real time dialogue with one or many other users by typing messages and reading the messages typed by others participating in the chat, analogous to a telephone party line, using a computer and keyboard rather than a telephone. There are thousands of different chat rooms available "in which collectively tens of thousands of users are engaging in conversations on a huge range of subjects". *Cyberspace Communications, Inc. et al. v. Engler*, 55 F. Supp. 2d 737 (1999).

Chat Software

Servers running "chat software", such as Internet Relay Chat ("IRC"), permit multiple users to converse by selecting one of many "discussion channels" active at any time. *Shea v. Reno*, 1996 U.S. Dist. LEXIS 10720 (S.D.N.Y. 1996).

Chatting

A way for a group of people to converse online in real-time by typing messages to each other. Cyberspeak - Learning the Language, the Federal Trade Commission and the National Association of Attorneys General, available at http://www.ftc.gov/bcp/conline/pubs/online/sitesee/index.html.

Checksum

"A value that (a) is computed by a function that is dependent on the contents of a data object and (b) is stored or transmitted together with the object, for the purpose of detecting changes in the data." *XML-Signature Syntax and Processing, W3C Recommendation 12 February 2002.*

Chip (or Microchip)

A small crystal of semi-conducting material such as silicon. Chips are usually cut from large wafers containing the imprints of integrated circuits. Integrated circuits are complete electrical circuits produced on a microscopic scale whose components are permanently wedded together. Chips containing integrated circuits are best known as the essential working components of desktop computers and other similar devices. Submission of the Director of Investigation and Research to the CRTC Re Public Notice CRTC 1994-130.

A manufactured semiconductor integrated circuit. Draft Treaty on the Protection of Intellectual Property in Respect of Integrated Circuits, WIPO Geneva, IPIC/CE/II/2, March 17, 1986.

A very thin wafer of semiconductor material such as silicon, processed to form an integrated circuit and capable of doing the work of thousands of individual electronic devices. Monopolies and Mergers Commission — Video Games: A report on the supply of video games in the UK (LONDON: HMSO Cm2781).

Silicon semiconductors. *Apple Computer Inc. v. Mackintosh Computers Ltd.* (1986), 28 D.L.R. (4th) 178 (Fed. T.D.).

Ciphertext

Data in its enciphered form. A Cryptology Policy Framework for Electronic Commerce, Task Force on Electronic Commerce, Industry Canada, February 1998.

CIRA - Canadian Internet Registration Authority

The organization proposed by the Canadian Domain Name Consultative Committee (CDNCC) to manage the .ca name space. *Domain Name System Reform and Related Internet Governance Issues: A Consultation Paper*, Industry Canada available at *www.strategis.gc.ca*.

Circuit

Means one or more facilities which, when connected in tandem, provide a single electrical transmission path between two or more points. CNCP Telecommunications: Interconnection with Bell Canada, CRTC Decision 79-11 (May 1979).

Means one or more facilities which, when connected in tandem, provide a single transmission path between two or more points. Tariff Revisions Related to Resale and Sharing, Telecom Decision CRTC 87-2 (Feb. 12, 1987).

Circuit Layout

A representation of the transistors and other components which form part of the integrated circuit memory device when fabricated. *Avel Pty Ltd. v. Jonathan Wells* (1992), 22 I.P.R. 305 (Aust. H.C.).

Circuit layout means a representation, fixed in a material form, of the 3-dimensional location of the active and passive elements and interconnections making up an integrated circuit. *Avel Pty Ltd. v. Wells* (1992), 23 I.P.R. 353 (Aust. Fed. C.A.).

Circumvention Device

Means a device (including a computer program) having only a limited commercially significant purpose or use, or no such purpose or use, other than the circumvention, or facilitating the circumvention, of an effective technological protection measure. *Copyright Amendment (Digital Agenda) Act 2000 Australia.*

Circumvention Service

Means a service, the performance of which has only a limited commercially significant purpose, or no such purpose or use, other than the circumvention, or facilitating the circumvention, of an effective technological protection measure. *Copyright Amendment (Digital Agenda) Act 2000 Australia.*

Clean Room

A "clean room" is a procedure used in the computer industry in order to prevent direct copying of a competitor's code during the development of a competing product. Programmers in clean rooms are provided only with the functional specifications for the desired programs. *Sega Enterprises Ltd. v. Accolade Inc.* (1992), 24 U.S.P.Q.2d 1561.

Clickstream Data

"Clickstream" is defined as data derived from an individual's behaviour, pathway. Canadian Marketing Association, Code of Ethics & Standards of Practice, "http://www.cdma.org/newethics.html".

Data derived from a user's navigational choices expressed during the course of visiting the world by web site or other on-line areas. Canadian Association Privacy Code.

Click Wrap Agreement

A "click wrap agreement" allows a consumer to assent to the terms of a contract by selecting an 'accept' button on the website. If the consumer does not accept the terms of the agreement the website will not complete the transaction. *American Eyewear, Inc. v. Peeper's Sunglasses and Accessories, Inc.*, 2000 U.S. Dist. LEXIS 6875 (D. Tex. May 16, 2000).

Click-wrap license

A click-wrap license presents the user with a message on his or her computer screen, requiring that the user manifest his or her assent to the terms of the license agreement by clicking on an icon. *Specht v. Netscape Communications Corp. et al*, 2001 U.S. Dis. LEXIS 907 (S.D.N.Y. 2001).

A license concerning the use of a copyright work, usually a software product, that includes pre-drafted terms and conditions of sale that consumers are required to agree to before being able to load or use the work. These terms and conditions are usually non-negotiable. A consumer is required to mouse "click" on an "agree" button before being able to load or use the program. *Digital Technology and the Copyright Act 1994: A Discussion Paper, Competition and Enterprise Branch, July 2001 (New Zealand).*

Clipper Chip

An escrowed encryption chip that implements the Skipjack algorithm to encrypt communications conducted over the public switched network (e.g., between telephones, modems, or facsimile equipment). *Cryptography's Role in Securing the Information Society*, United States National Research Council, 1996.

Clones

IBM look-a-like compatibles. *IBM Corp. v. Computer Imports Ltd.*, N.Z. H.C., Smellie J., March 21, 1989 (unreported).

Cloning

Programming a cellular telephone to have an ESN and an MIN identical to that of another cellular telephone having a valid ESN/MIN combination assigned to a customer, thereby enabling the user to obtain telephone services through having access to that customer's account. *United States v. Brady*, 820 F.Supp. 1346 (C.D. Utah 1993).

Coaxial Cable

Coaxial cable is a "broadband" transmission device, meaning that it has the ability to carry large amounts of information, like video signals. It comprises a core of solid copper wire surrounded by metallic and other sheathing all of which share a common axis (hence "coaxial"). It is unlike the wire used by telephone companies for subscriber drops, usually known as "twisted copper pair". Submission of the Director of Investigation and Research to the CRTC Re Public Notice CRTC 1994-130.

Commonly called "co-ax"; high-capacity cable used in television distribution, communications and video to carry great quantities of information. *The Challenge of the Information Highway: Final Report of the Information Highway Advisory Council* (September 1995).

CGA

Coloured graphics array. *Princeton Graphics Operating, L.P. v. Nec Home Electronics (U.S.A.), Inc.*, Comp. Ind. Lit. Reptr. 11,126 (S.D.N.Y. 1990).

CMOS

Complimentary Metal Oxide Semiconductor. *Pearl Systems Inc. v. Competition Electronics Inc.*, 8 U.S.P.Q.2d 1520 (U.S.D.C.S.D. Fl. 1988).

COBOL (Common Business-Oriented Language)

A computer language especially adapted for business applications. *Teamsters Security Fund of North Carolina Inc. v. Sperry Rand Corp.*, 6 C.L.S.R. 951 (1977).

A high-level programming language developed and used for commercial data processing. *Eurodynamic Systems Plc v. General Automation Ltd.*, Q.B.D., Steyn J., September 6, 1988 (unreported).

COBOL Compiler

The COBOL compiler's function is to translate incoming coded application programs into machine-readable electronic impulses, which the computer can process under the direction of other systems software elements; an article of software that translates coded statements into machine instructions. *Teamsters Security Fund of North Carolina Inc. v. Sperry Rand Corp.*, 6 C.L.S.R. 951 (1977).

Code

Means the binary representation of alphanumeric and control characters. Second Computer Inquiry (Final Decision), 77 F.C.C.2d 384 (F.C.C. 1980).

Any system of symbols and rules for expressing information or instructions in a form usable by a computer or other machine for processing or transmitting information. *Autodesk Australia Pty Ltd. v. Dyason* (1989), 15 I.P.R. 1 (Aus. Fed. Ct.), reversed [1990] A.I.P.C. 36,446 (Aus. Fed. Ct.).

A computer program or any part of it, in a form which can be read by the processor. Monopolies and Mergers Commission — Video Games: A report on the supply of video games in the UK (LONDON: HMSO Cm2781).

Means of representing data/information in digital form. For example, the ASCII code (American Standard Code for Information Interchange) represents letters of the alphabet and other symbols in the form of seven digital bits (single binary digits, eight of which comprise a byte). The term also refers to the representation of computer programs, as in source code (human readable form) or machine code (a form which can be interpreted by a computer), and writing a program is sometimes described as coding. Encoding is the process of converting information into a particular code. *Digital Technology and the Copyright Act 1994: A Discussion Paper, Competition and Enterprise Branch, July 2001 (New Zealand).*

Code-Breakers

Code-breakers are products that operate to defeat protective devices and to permit a possessor of a program to make copies. *Vault Corp. v. Quaid Software Ltd.*, 655 F.2d 750 (E.D. L.A. 1987), affirmed 847 F.2d 255 (5th Cir. 1988).

Coding

Once each necessary module has been identified, designed, and its relationship to the other modules has been laid out conceptually, the resulting program structure must be embodied in a written language that the computer can read. This process is called "coding", and requires two steps. First, the programmer must transpose the program's structural blueprint into a source code. This step has been described as "comparable to the novelist meshing out the broad outline of his plot by crafting from words and sentences the paragraphs that convey the ideas." *Computer Associates International Inc. v. Altai Inc.*, 23 U.S.P.Q.2d 1241 (2nd Cir. 1992).

Once each necessary module has been identified and designed, and its relationship to the other modules has been laid out conceptually, the resulting program structure must be embodied in a written language that the computer can read. This process is called "coding" and requires two steps. First, the programmer must transpose the program's structural blueprint into a source code. This step has been described as comparable to the novelist fleshing out the broad outline of the plot by crafting from words and sentences the paragraphs that convey the ideas. The source code may be written in any one of several computer languages, such as

COBAL, FORTRAN, BASIC, etc., depending upon the type of computer for which the program is intended.

Once the source code has been completed, the second step is to translate or "compile" it into object code. Object Code is the binary language comprised of zeros and ones through which the computer directly receives its instructions. The zero and one indicate an open or closed switch representing the high and low voltage signals on which the computer actually operates. The object code is usually unintelligible even to those highly skilled in programming. *Matrox Electronic Systems Ltd. v. Gaudreau*, [1993] R.J.Q. 2449 (C.S.).

.com

The generic Top Level Domain (gTLD) reserved for commercial entities. *Domain Name System Reform and Related Internet Governance Issues: A Consultation Paper*, Industry Canada available at *www.strategis.gc.ca*

Command

Command refers to an abbreviated description of a direction that a user of a software program (whether Lotus 1-2-3, Borland's Quattro Pro, or another program) may invoke to cause some operation to be performed. *Lotus Development Corporation v. Borland International Inc.*, 788 F.Supp. 78 (D.C. Mass. 1992).

Command Structure

Command structure refers to the organization of the menus and menu commands. (Other phrases used with essentially the same meaning include "menu command structure," "menu hierarchy," and "menu command hierarchy.") In Lotus 1-2-3, menu commands are organized so that less than a dozen related menu commands are displayed at any given moment. This display communicates to the user the spreadsheet operations immediately available. Each menu of less than a dozen commands is linked to preceding/succeeding menus by the operation of menu commands. All command menus are ultimately linked to a single main (root/ trunk) menu to form a "menu tree." *Lotus Development Corporation v. Borland International Inc.*, 788 F.Supp. 78 (D.C. Mass. 1992).

Command Tree

A command tree or command tree structure informs the user, in a hierarchical fashion, of the options available and also interacts with the user in requesting information from the user in order to utilize the program. *MiTek Holdings Inc. v. Arce Engineering Inc.*, 39 U.S.P.Q. 2d 1609 (11th Cir. 1996).

Comment

All computer programs contain short explanatory comments annotating the code in which they are embedded. The function of these comments is simply to inform programmers of the purpose and operation of particular sections of code. Comments have no role whatsoever in software performance. *Unix System Laboratories, Inc. v. Berkeley Software Design, Inc.*, Comp. Ind. Lit. Reptr. 16,704 (D. New Jer. 1993).

Now when a human writes he often needs to make notes to remind himself of what he has done and to indicate where the important bits are. This is true of life generally and for programmers. So it is possible to insert messages in a source code. A reader who has access to it can then understand, or understand more readily, what is going on. Such notes, which form no part of the program so far as the computer is concerned, are called "comments". They are a kind of sidenote for humans. *IBCOS Computers Ltd. v. Barclay's Mercantile Highland Finance Ltd.*, [1994] F.S.R. 275 (Ch.D.).

All programming languages permit the insertion of comments into the code. A comment is text in ordinary language written by the programmer which serves to document the program. A well-written comment explains what the code is supposed to achieve, and why, and what the programmer thinks the program is doing at that particular point. Comments give code some of its individuality, and they are also an opportunity for humour, or supposed humour, on the part of the programmer. In VAX-BASIC they are introduced by the exclamation mark "!" and continue to the end of the line. They are ignored by the compiler. *Cantor Fitzgerald International v. Tradition (UK) Ltd.*, [1999] I.N.L.R. No. 23 (Ch.D.).

Comment Lines

A comment line is one which appears as part of the source code but which appears for the limited purpose of informing or instructing the operator; a "comment" line is not converted to the object code. *CCH Australia Ltd. v. Accounting System 2000 (Developments) Pty Ltd.* (1991), 20 I.P.R. 555 (Aust. Fed. Ct.), affirmed (1993), 27 I.P.R. 133 (Aust. Fed. C.A.).

Commercial Computer Software

Means computer software which is used regularly for other than government purposes and sold, licensed, or leased in significant quantities to the general public at established market or catalog prices. U.S. D.O.D. Directive and D.O.D. F.A.R. Supplement, Federal Register Vol. 53, No. 209 43698.

Commercial Electronic Mail Message

Commercial Electronic Mail Message means that an electronic mail message sent for the purpose of promoting real property, goods or services for sale or lease. *State of Washington v. Jason Heckle doing business as Natural Instincts*, No. 69416-8 (Wash. Sup. Ct. June 7, 2001).

Common Carrier Communications Service

The fundamental characteristic of a common carrier communications service is the transmission of a subscriber's message through the telecommunications network without alteration of the content of the message in the course of transmission. *Second Computer Inquiry (Tentative Decision)*, 72 F.C.C.2d 358 (F.C.C. 1979).

Common Control Switching Arrangement (CCSA)

Is a private line system for linking the various offices of a large company through large switches on a local telephone company's premises instead of through the PBX switches on the customers' premises. *MCI Communications Corp. v. AT&T*, 4 C.L.S.R. 1119 (E.D.Pa. 1973).

Communicate

Means make available online or electronically transmit (whether over a path, or a combination of paths, provided by a material substance or otherwise) a work or other subject matter. *Copyright Amendment (Digital Agenda) Act 2000 Australia.*

Communication

The ordinary meaning of "communication" is the act of imparting or transmitting of facts or information communicated. *State of Washington v. Riley*, 846 P.2d 1365 (Sup. Ct. Wash. 1993).

Communication by Wire or Radio

Means the transmission of writing signs, signals, pictures, and sounds of all kinds . . . between the points of origin and reception of such transmission, including all instrumentalities, facilities, apparatus, and services (among other things, the receipt, forwarding, and delivery of communications) incidental to such transmission. (47 USC 153(a)(b)).

Communication to the public

The transmission to an audience or the general public of a material, audio, audiovisual content or images for immediate rather than deferred use, although recordings may be made either as a result of, or to facilitate this. The communication of works to the public encompasses a wide range of activities, including: the broadcast of a work or its inclusion in a cable programme service, and the rebroadcast of the work. Technological advances have made it possible for works to be communicated to the public in new ways, such as by webcasting. *Digital Technology and the Copyright Act 1994: A Discussion Paper, Competition and Enterprise Branch, July 2001 (New Zealand).*

Communications Common Carriage

The function or role of communications common carriage is to provide the means for transmitting subscriber initiated messages or information between two or more points, and having that information arrive at the destination intended by the subscriber without the content of the message or information being altered by the carrier in the course of transmission. Computer Inquiry (Tentative Decision), 72 F.C.C.2d 358 (F.C.C. 1979).

Communications Devices

Devices utilized to transmit input data to a computer and to service as the terminus for the processed output data transmitted from the computer. Dataspeed 40/4, 52 F.C.C.2d 21 (F.C.C. 1977).

Communications Function

The generic characteristic of the communications function is that the semantic content of information is not changed at the completion of a given process. A message entering a network is intended to arrive at its destination unchanged. Several computer operations, such as message and circuit switching, may be required to permit the message to transit the network. In this progress, individual symbols may be processed, as in code conversion and error correction. Or the message may be accompanied by addressing information, such as dial pulses or message headers, which are used by the communications network for centralized message routing. The purpose of these computer operations is, nevertheless, the transmission of an unaltered message through a network, and they do not constitute a data processing service. Second Computer Inquiry (Notice of Inquiry), 5 C.L.S.R. 1381 (F.C.C. 1976).

Compatibility

"Compatibility" has no single definition, but instead suggests a broad range of possibilities. For mainframe processors, an operating system that is truly 100 per cent compatible with another vendor's operating system — that performs all functions offered by that system in exactly the same way — might have to be virtually identical to that system. *IBM v. Fujitsu Ltd.*, Copyright L.R. (CCH) 20,517 (Am. Arbtn. Assoc. Comm. Arbtn. Trib. 1988).

Like the experts at trial, we distinguish between compatibility, or practical compatibility, and complete, absolute, or theoretical compatibility. If two products are completely compatible, they will work properly together in every possible situation, every time. Complete compatibility is almost virtually impossible to obtain. On the other hand, two products are compatible, within the standards of the computer industry, if they worked together almost every time in almost every possible situation . . . compatibility between two computer products can be testd and determined. While two computer products are not likely to be perfectly compatible, the question of whether the degree of compatibility is consistent with industry standards is a question generally for the jury, not the judge. *Step-Saver Data Systems, Inc. v. Wise Technology*, 1990 W.L. 158151 (E.D. Pa. 1990).

Compatibility becomes an issue when a firm wishes to create a single new component designed to operate with elements of a pre-existing system. For example, if manufacturer "B" would like to design a computer that can use software designed for a computer manufactured by "A," B's operating system interface must match that of manufacturer A. Without that compatibility, the software designed for A's machine will not function on B's. *Bateman v. Mnemonics Inc.,* 38 U.S.P.Q. 2d 1225 (11th Cir. 1996).

Compatible

A compatible product must meet that standard or at least perform in a manner equivalent to the standard's requirements. *Princeton Graphics Operating, L.P. v. Nec Home Electronics (U.S.A.), Inc.,* Comp. Ind. Lit. Reptr. 11,126 (S.D.N.Y. 1990).

Compatible Software

The original creation of a computer program which will perform the same overall task as an existing program. *S. & H. Computer Systems Inc. v. SAS Institute Inc.,* 568 F.Supp. 416 (M.D. Tenn. 1983).

Competitive Local Exchange Carrier (CLEC)

A facilities-based provider of local exchange service, other than an ILEC. *Report to the Governor in Council: Status of Competition in Canadian Telecommunications Markets, Deployment/Accessibility of Advanced Telecommunications Infrastructure and Services, September, 2001.*

Compilation

The process whereby a program written in a high level language is converted into equivalent instructions in machine code or object code. Computer Software Protection: Australia, Copyright Law Review Committee 1995.

Compile

To prepare a machine language program from a computer program written in another programming language by making use of the overall logical structure of the program, or generating more than one machine instruction for each symbolic statement, or both, as well as performing the function of an assembler. *Compendium of Copyright Offices Practices*, Copyright Office, Washington D.C., 1984.

Compiled Data

This is precise and particular information that the application programme works on. *Continental Commercial Systems Corp. v. R.*, [1982] 5 W.W.R. 340 (B.C. C.A.).

Compiler

A computer program that is used to change high-level programming language into machine language. It is similar to an assembler. *Compendium of Copyright Offices Practices*, Copyright Office, Washington D.C., 1984.

A "compiler" program translates the program once and for all into machine language, after which the translated program can be executed directly by the CPU without the need for any further resort to the compiler. A distinctive "interpreter" or "compiler" progam is available for each type of source code programming language and each type of CPU. *Lotus Development Corp. v. Paperback Software International*, 15 U.S.P.Q.2d 1577 (D. Mass. 1990).

A program that runs on the computer and performs the conversion from human readable instructions to the computer [source code] written in a defined format [computer language] into codes that can be readily performed by the computer system itself [object code]. Popular programming languages include COBOL, FORTRAN, "C", DBASE and SPL. *Delrina Corp. v. Triolet Systems, Inc.* (1992), 47 C.P.R. (3d) 1 (Ont. H.C.).

A program written in source code must also be used with another program, called a "compiler" or "interpreter," which translates the source code into binary instructions which the computer can understand. *Softel Inc. v. Dragon Medical and Scientific Communications, Inc.*, 1992 U.S. Dist. LEXIS 9502 (S.D.N.Y.1992).

Composite Data Service

The term "Composite Data Service" denotes an offering which combines the use of computers and terminal equipment with the use of communication services of Telephone Company to provide a single integrated data service for data processing and data message switching, or for data message switching. American Trucking Association Inc/Resale and Shared Use, 47 F.C.C.2d 644 (F.C.C. 1974).

Compression

Rearranging data for more efficient use of storage space, thus increasing the memory capacity of a particular storage medium. Monopolies and Mergers Commission — Video Games: A report on the supply of video games in the UK (LONDON: HMSO Cm2781).

Data compression is a process by which digital information can be reduced in volume so that it takes up less space on a storage device or can be transmitted over a communications link more quickly than the uncompressed information. There are many types of data compression, some of which result in the loss of some information ("lossy" compression) and thus reduced quality of reproduction. These are often used for the storage and transmission of graphical, video or audio information (MP3 is an example of a lossy compression standard for audio information.) *Digital Technology and the Copyright Act 1994: A Discussion Paper, Competition and Enterprise Branch, July 2001 (New Zealand).*

Compromise

The unauthorized disclosure, modification, substitution or use of sensitive data (including plaintext cryptographic keys and other critical security parameters). "Security Requirements for Cryptographic Modules", FIPS Pub. 140-1, Federal

Information Processing Standards Publication, January 11, 1994, available at http://csrc.nist.gov/fips/fips1401.htm.

A situation in which the secrecy of a Private Key cannot be relied on, e.g. if there has been unauthorized access to the cryptographic module in which the Private Key is stored or used, or unauthorized access to or loss or theft of media on which the Private Key is stored. *The Office of the Federal Privacy Commissioner (Australia), Consultation Paper, (June 2001).*

Computer (See also Digital Computer)

An electronic device that performs logical, arithmetic, or memory functions by the manipulation of electronic or magnetic impulses and includes all input, output, processing, storage or communication facilities that are connected or related to the device. *State of Texas v. Burleson,* CCH Comp. Cas. 60,005.

A device or group of devices which, by manipulation of electronic, magnetic, optical or electrochemical impulses, pursuant to a computer program, can automatically perform arithmetic, logical, storage or retrieval operations with or on computer data, and includes any connected or directly related device, equipment or facility which enables such computer to store, retrieve or communicate to or from a person, another computer or another device the results of computer operation, computer programs or computer data. *People of the State of New York v. Johnson,* 148 Misc.2d 103 (N.Y. Crim. Ct. 1990).

"Computer" includes an electronic, magnetic, optical, or other high-speed data processing device or system performing logical, arithmetic, and storage functions, and includes any property, data storage facility or communications facility directly related to or operating in conjunction with such device or system. *State of Louisiana v. Azar,* 539 So2d 1222 (La. Sup. Ct.).

A mechanical or electronic apparatus capable of carrying out repetitious and highly mathematical calculations at high speeds; a calculator especially designed for the solution of complex mathematical problems; specifically, a programmable electronic device that can store, retrieve, and process data; any of several devices for making rapid calculations in navigation or gunnery. Computers may be defined as systems of machines that process information in the form of letters, numbers, and other symbols, and that are self-directing within predetermined limits. *R. v. Mclaughlin,* [1981] 1 W.W.R. 298 (S.C.C.).

A computer is a complex system of interconnected, integrated electrical circuits. It consists of a circuit board (mother board) into which have been pinned or soldered a number of electronic components. The components communicate with one another by means of the traces (sometimes called buses, sometimes called wires) etched into the board. The main electronic components of the system are the input/output devices, the microprocessor (CPU) and the memory. The input/output devices connect, respectively, to whatever is being used to feed information into the computer (*e.g.*, a keyboard, magnetic tape, punch cards) and to whatever is being used to display or otherwise make use of the information which results from the computers functioning (*e.g.*, the screen of a monitor). *Apple Computer Inc. v. Mackintosh Computers Ltd.* (1986), 28 D.L.R. (4th) 178 (Fed. T.D.).

A computer is a highly complex miniaturized interconnected collection of electrical circuits. *Apple Computer Inc. v. Mackintosh Computers Ltd.* (1986), 28 D.L.R. (4th) 178 (Fed. T.D.).

A device which is programmed to carry out a specified series of steps, but generally speaking it is the hardware itself which is usually referred to as the computer, or computing apparatus. *Re Application No. 096,284* (1978), 52 C.P.R. (2d) 96 (Pat. App. Bd. & Pat. Commr.).

A computer in its pristine state is merely an automatic programmable and re-programmable, digital data processor. *Clinical Computing Ltd. v. Commnrs. of Customs and Excise*, [1983] V.A.T.T.R. 121 (London V.A.T. Trib.).

A computer is nothing more than an electronic machine. It is characterized by its ability to process data, usually by executing mathematical operations on the data at high speeds. By virtue of the speeds with which computers operate, they are capable of executing complex or otherwise time-consuming calculations in fractions of a second. Their use in technology is analogous to the use of mechanical devices, such as levers, which provide mechanical advantages in inventions of a mechanical nature; they make possible, or practicable, the solution of mathematical problems which are impracticable to solve manually due to the inordinate amount of time a manual solution would consume. *In Re Walter*, 618 F.2d 758 (C.C.P.A. 1980).

Comprehends, *inter alia:* general purpose stored program processors, general and special purpose mini-computers and micro-processors. Second Computer Inquiry (Notice of Inquiry), 5 C.L.S.R. 1381 (F.C.C. 1976).

Means a data processing device capable of accepting data, performing prescribed operations on the data, and supplying the results of these operations; for example, a device that operates on discrete data by performing arithmetic and logic processes on the data, or a device that operates on analog data by performing physical processes on the data. U.S. D.O.D. Directive and D.O.D. F.A.R. Supplement, Federal Register, Vol. 53, No. 209 43698.

Any computer has certain basic processing capabilities which include: arithmetic computation — the basic operations of count, add, subtract, multiply, and divide; logical computation — operations which include: AND, OR, NOT, compare, and branch; storage, retrieval, and transfer — of alphanumeric or graphical data. Second Computer Inquiry (Notice of Inquiry), 5 C.L.S.R. 1381 (F.C.C. 1976).

The present day computer is created by the integration of mechanical devices and electronic circuits, and may be programmed to perform a wide variety of complex functions. *GTE Service Corp. v. F.C.C.*, 3 C.L.S.R. 592 (2nd Cir. 1973).

A computer is an electrical device which operates by the reception and transmission of electrical signals. The signals are coded into what is known as binary coding or the binary system. *Autodesk Australia Pty. Ltd. v. Dyason* (1989), 15 I.P.R. 1 (Aus. Fed. Ct.), reversed [1990] A.I.P.C. 36,446 (Aus. Fed. Ct. FC).

A computer is a machine with no intelligence and has no independent stimuli. It must be instructed in minute detail as to every activity which it is requested to perform. Each computer is manufactured to accept only specified language, one of which is known as "cobol" (common business oriented language). Through the use of the binary principal, symbols made up of combinations of the figures 0 and 1 are arbitrarily assigned to denote words, numerals, phrases and processes. *Pezzillo v. General Telephone & Electronics Information Systems, Inc.*, 414 F.Supp. 1257 (D.C. M.D. Tenn. 1976), affirmed 572 F.2d 1189 (6th Cir. 1978).

Computers are machines which can do certain things based upon instructions. A computer is traditionally viewed as composed of three fundamental components: a CPU (central processing unit), some memory, and some means of getting input and displaying output. The CPU is where all the actual computing is done. Memory is used to hold the program that is being run, as well as to provide a place for the program to store the intermediate results of a calculation. *Computer Associates International Inc. v. Altai Inc.*, 775 F.Supp. 544 (E.D.N.Y. 1991), affirmed 23 U.S.P.Q.2d 1241 (2d Cir. 1992).

A computer is a machine with no intelligence and has no independent stimuli. It must be instructed in minute detail as to every activity which it is requested to perform. Each computer is manufactured to accept only specified language, one of which is known as "cobol" (common business oriented language). Throughout the use of the binary [principle], symbols made up of combinations of the figures 0 and 1 are arbitrarily assigned to denote words, numerals, phrases and processes. *Pezzillo v. General Telephone & Electronics Information Systems, Inc.*, 414 F.Supp 1257 (M.D. Tenn. 1976).

A computer is a machine that processes numerical data. Any data which are numerical, such as text, have to be translated into numerical form before a computer can do anything with it. Moreover, numerical data must be in binary form (which means that it must consist only of the numbers 0 and 1 in some combination) if a computer is to handle it. To this extent a computer operates in a very simple manner. Its advantage is that it can do simple operations very quickly; and by doing a series of simple operations extremely quickly it can achieve the effect of doing a complex operation much more speedily and accurately than could be achieved by the human mind. However a computer cannot do anything at all by itself. If it is to solve a particular problem it must be told precisely how to do it. This is the function of a computer program. *John Richardson Computers Ltd. v. Flanders*, [1993] F.S.R. 497 (Ch.D.).

Riley contends the telephone companies' long distance switch is not a "computer" — we reject this contention. The trial court explicitly found that the switch is a computer. *State of Washington v. Riley*, 846 P.2d 1365 (Sup. Ct. Wash. 1993).

Means an electronic, magnetic, optical, hydraulic or organic device or group of devices which, pursuant to a computer program, to human instruction, or to permanent instructions contained in the device or group of devices, can automatically perform computer operations with or on computer data and can communicate the results to another computer or to a person. The term "computer" includes any connected or directly related device, equipment, or facility which enables the computer to store, retrieve or communicate computer programs, computer data or the results of computer operations to or from a person, another computer or another device. Virginia Computer Crimes Act; (Va. Code Ann. § 18.2-152.2 et seq.) (amended effective July 1, 1999).

Means an electronic device that can perform substantial computations, including numerous arithmetic operations or logic operations, without human intervention during the computation or operation. *Uniform Computer Information Transactions Act*, National Conference of Commissioners on Uniform State Laws, available at http://www.law.upenn.u/bll/ulc/ucita/citim99.htm.

A computer "is a digital information processing device. . .consist[ing] of central processing components. . .and mass data storage. . . certain peripheral input/output devices. . ., and an operating system." *Universal City Studios, Inc. v. Reimerdes*, 55 U.S.P.Q. 2d 1873 (S. D.N.Y. 2000).

A programmable machine comprised of hardware, including electronic components for the storage and manipulation of digital signals and devices for storing, inputting and displaying digital information. *Digital Technology and the Copyright Act 1994: A Discussion Paper, Competition and Enterprise Branch, July 2001 (New Zealand)*.

Computers are designed to process material in the form of binary numbers, that is to say, numbers made up of 0s and 1s only. A computer receives material by means of an input device. The material is placed in the storage capacity of the computer. The material is then modified by the processor of the computer and can be transferred, in its modified form, by way of an output device. The computer keeps in its storage capacity instructions that tell the processor what to do with the material. The instructions are also in the form of binary numbers that can be received by the computer, kept in its storage capacity and, in turn, transferred by the computer. *Australian Video Retailers Association Ltd. v Warner Home Video Pty Ltd* (2001) 53 I.P.R. 242 (Aust. F.C.)

Computer Control

A computer control may be broken into five major components: (1) digital computer; (2) teletype; (3) high speed reader; (4) position control logic; and (5) machine tool control panel. *White Consolidated Industries Inc. v. Vega Servo-Control Inc.*, 214 U.S.P.Q 796 (S.D. Mich. 1982), affirmed 218 U.S.P.Q. 961 (Fed. Cir. 1983).

Computer Data

Means any representation of information, knowledge, facts, concepts, or instructions which is being prepared or has been prepared and is intended to be processed, is being processed, or has been processed in a computer or computer network. "Computer data" may be in any form, whether readable only by a computer or only by a human or by either, including, but not limited to, computer printouts, magnetic storage media, punched cards, or stored internally in the memory of the computer. Virginia Computer Crimes Act; (Va. Code Ann. § 18.2-152.2 et seq.) (amended effective July 1, 1999).

Means any representation of facts, information or concepts in a form suitable for processing in a computer system, including a program suitable to cause a computer system to perform a function. *Committee of Experts on Crime in Cyb-Space, Draft Convention on Cyber Crime (PC-CY).*

Computer Definition

A repository for information stored in such manner that it may electrically or electronically be retrieved rapidly and, if necessary, selectively. *Cdn. Real Estate Assn. v. Charco Consultants Ltd.* (1976), 33 C.P.R. (2d) 15 (Reg. T.M.).

Computer Disk Cartridge

The computer disk cartridge is comprised of two main components: a round disk platter on which data can be magnetically encoded and stored, and a plastic molding in which the disk platter is encased. *Magnetic Data, Inc. v. St. Paul Fire and Marine Insurance Co.*, 430 N.W.2d 483 (Minn. Crt. App. 1989), reversed 1 CCH Comp. Cases 46,089 (Minn. Sup. Crt. 1989).

Computer Fraud

Computer fraud is the accessing or causing to be accessed of any computer, computer system, computer network, or any part thereof with intent to (i) defraud, or (ii) obtain money, property, or services by means of false or fraudulent conduct, practices or representations, or through the alteration, deletion, or insertion of programs or data. *State of Louisiana v. Azar*, 539 So2d 1222 (La. Sup. Ct.).

Computer-Generated

"Computer-generated," in relation to a work, means that the work is generated by computer in circumstances such that there is no human author of the work. Copyright, Designs, and Patents Act 1988, 1988, c. 48.

Computer Hardware (See also Hardware)

Computer hardware is any of a large variety of devices capable of performing mathematical calculations on numbers or magnitudes. *E.D.S. Federal Corp. v. Ginsberg*, 259 S.E.2d 618 (W.Vir. Crt. App. 1979).

Consists of the machine itself, while computer software is the set of instructions, written by computer programmers, that tell the hardware to perform certain tasks. *Bateman v. Mnemonics Inc.,* 38 U.S.P.Q. 2d 1225 (11th Cir. 1996).

Computer Information

Means information in electronic form that is obtained from or through the use of a computer, or that is in digital or equivalent form capable of being processed by a computer. The term includes a copy of information in that form and any documentation or packaging associated with the copy. *Uniform Computer Information Transactions Act*, National Conference of Commissioners on Uniform State Laws, available at http://www.law.upenn.u/bll/ulc/ucita/citim99.htm.

Computer Information Transaction

Means an agreement a primary purpose of which is to require a party to create, modify, transfer, or license computer information or informational rights in computer information. *Uniform Computer Information Transactions Act*, National Conference of Commissioners on Uniform State Laws, available at http://www.law.upenn.u/bll/ulc/ucita/citim99.htm.

Computer Language

A computer language, of which there are many, is a code for writing a program. A language is said to be higher or lower depending upon the ease with which it can be read. A high-level language has symbols and rules that correspond closely enough to ordinary mathematics and English (or other common language) and it may be read and understood with relative ease. Examples are languages such as BASIC, COBOL, Pascal, and FORTRAN. A second level of language, which can be referred to as an intermediate level, consists of mnemonics which correspond more explicitly to the operations the computer must perform. This intermediate level is referred to as assembly language. A third level of language, the lowest, is sometimes referred to as machine language or object code. *Apple Computer Inc. v. Mackintosh Computers Ltd.* (1986), 28 D.L.R. (4th) 178 (Fed. T.D.).

A notation used to describe the steps required in order to complete a given task using a computer. The language is English-like and fairly easy for a programmer to understand. Common, industry standard languages include COBOL, FORTRAN C and PASCAL. SPL is proprietary language specific to the HP3000. *Delrina Corp. v. Triolet Systems, Inc.* (1992), 47 C.P.R. (3d) 1 (Ont. H.C.).

Computer language might be compared to any foreign language. *Pezzillo v. General Telephone & Electronics Information Systems, Inc.*, 414 F.Supp. 1257 (M.D. Tenn. 1976).

A computer language defines the names of each word in the language and the rules governing the use of each word (syntax). Each word in a computer language is an instruction to the computer to invoke lower level processes, the word chosen to invoke those processes is generally chosen to suggest the nature of the process that will be invoked. A computer language is comprised of a set of reserved words which are used in accordance with the rules of syntax governing their use. A computer language syntax, like the syntax of a human language, comprises the rules by which the words can be combined to form statements which are correct for the language. For each command or function there is a specific syntax which describes how arguments may be applied to the command. Arguments can be likened to a noun phrase, they describe what the command will act on. Various documents also refer to "functions" as well as commands. Functions are a type of command which perform a computation and return a result. *Powerflex Services Pty Ltd. v. Data Access Corp.* (1997), 37 I.P.R. 436 (Aust. C.A.).

Computer Memory

At the electrical level, the computer memory is an integrated circuit which is capable of holding, because of its circuitry, a pattern of high and low voltage states. *Apple Computer Inc. v. Mackintosh Computers Ltd.* (1986), 28 D.L.R. (4th) 178 (Fed. T.D.).

Computer Network

A computer network is a configuration of hardware and software products connected for information interchange through communications facilities. *IBM v. Fujitsu Ltd.*, Copyright L.R. (CCH) 20,517 (Am. Arbtn. Assoc. Comm. Arbtn. Trib. 1988).

Computer networks are systems of interconnected computers that allow the exchange of information between the connected computers. *CompuServe Inc. v. Patterson*, 39 U.S.P.Q (2d) 1502 (6 Cir. 1996).

Means a set of related, remotely connected devices and any communications facilities including more than one computer with the capability to transmit data among them through the communications facilities. Virginia Computer Crimes Act; (Va. Code Ann. § 18.2-152.2 et seq.) (amended effective July 1, 1999).

Computer Operation

Means arithmetic, logical, monitoring, storage or retrieval functions and any combination thereof, and includes, but is not limited to, communication with, storage of data to, or retrieval of data from any device or human hand manipulation of electronic or magnetic impulses. A "computer operation" for a particular computer may also be any function for which that computer was generally designed. Virginia Computer Crimes Act; (Va. Code Ann. § 18.2-152.2 et seq.) (amended effective July 1, 1999).

Computer Outline Program

A computer outliner allows a user to create, revise, expand and reorganize and outline more quickly and easily than can be done on paper. The program has two components — the computer code and the resulting displays on the computer screen. *Telemarketing Resources v. Symatec Corp.*, 12 U.S.P.Q.2d 1991 (N.D.Cal. 1988).

Computer Printout

Any statement or report which the computer may print. *Northern Office Micro Computers Ltd. v. Rosenstein*, [1982] F.S.R. 124 (S.C. S.Africa).

Computer Processing

Computer processing is the use of a computer for processing information where the output information constitutes a programmed response to input information ... "Processing" entails the use of a computer for operations upon data which include, *inter alia:* arithmetic and logical operations, storage, retrieval, and transfer. Second Computer Inquiry (Tentative Decision), 72 F.C.C.2d 358 (F.C.C. 1979).

Computer Program

A set of instructions or statements, expressed, fixed, embodied or stored in any manner, that is to be used directly or indirectly in a computer in order to bring about a specific result. [en. *An Act to amend the Copyright Act*, S.C. 1988, c. 15, s. 1].

A set of statements or instructions to be used directly or indirectly in a computer in order to bring about a certain result. United States Copyright Act, 17 U.S.C. 101.

Means data representing instructions or statements that, when executed in a computer system, causes the computer system to perform a function. *Criminal Code* (Canada), R.S.C. 1985, c. C-46, s. 342.1(2)[en. R.S.C. 1985, c. 27 (1st Supp.), s. 45].

An expression, in any language, code or notation, of a set of instructions (whether with or without related information) intended, either directly or after either or both of the following: (a) conversion to another language, code or notation; (b) reproduction in a different material form, to cause a device having digital information processing capabilities to perform a particular function. Australia, Copyright Act of 1984.

The term "program" is taken to mean a set of ordered steps or list of instructions specifying the internal changes of state of physical devices within a data processor. This set of steps or list of instructions may be recorded on a variety of media including printed or handwritten lists on paper, punched cards, or paper tapes, magnetic tapes, or electric wiring. *Re Application No. 961,392 (1971)*, 5 C.P.R. (2d) 162 (Pat. App. Bd. & Pat. Commr.).

A computer program may be thought of as that portion of computer ware which may be written or printed on paper in an alphanumeric source language, magnetically recorded on tapes, or used with punch cards in computer acceptable form. In other words, it provides the wording, directions for the computer hardware. *Re Application No. 096,284 (1978)*, 52 C.P.R. (2d) 96 (Pat. App. Bd. & Pat. Commr.).

A set of sequential instructions that direct a computer to prepare certain tasks. *Apple Computer Inc. v. MacIntosh Computers Ltd.* (1985), 3 C.I.P.R. 133 (Fed. T.D.).

Computer program is a set of sequential instructions that direct a computer to perform certain tasks. There are basically two types of computer programs: operating system programs and application programs. *Apple Computer Inc. v. Computermat Inc.* (1983), 1 C.I.P.R. 1 (Ont. H.C.).

A sequence of coded instructions for a digital computer. *Gottschalk v. Benson*, 409 U.S. 63 (1972).

A computer program is a set of statements or instructions to be used directly or indirectly in a computer in order to bring about a certain result. *Apple Computer Inc. v. Franklin Computer Corp.*, 215 U.S.P.Q. 935 (E.D.Pa. 1982), reversed 714 F.2d 1240 (3rd Cir. 1983), cert. dismissed 104 S.Ct. 690 (1984); *Healthcare Affiliated Services Inc. v. Lippany*, 701 F.Supp. 1142 (W.D. Pa. 1988).

A program is simply a set of statements, data or instructions to be used directly or indirectly in a computer in order to bring about a certain result. *Stern Electronics Inc. v. Kaufman*, 669 F.2d 852 (2nd Cir. 1982).

A program is a set of instructions for carrying out pre-arranged operations on data by use of processing equipment. *In Re Ghiron*, 442 F.2d 985 (C.C.P.A. 1971).

A set of instructions to the computer. *Whelan Associates Inc. v. Jaslow Dental Laboratory Inc.*, 225 U.S.P.Q. 156 (E.D. Pa. 1985), affirmed 797 F.2d 1222 (3rd Cir. 1986).

A set of precise instructions that tells the computer how to solve a problem. *Data Cash Systems Inc. v. J.S.& A. Group Inc.*, 480 F.Supp. 1063 (N.D. Ill. 1979), affirmed 628 F.2d 1038 (7th Cir. Ill. 1980).

A computer program is a set of detailed instructions by which the computer performs certain functions or delivers a desired result. While the program usually involves very complicated problems and procedures, these same problems and procedures could be solved with paper and pencil. The difference, of course, is the very long time it would require to perform the same functions manually that the computer, properly programmed, would perform in a matter of seconds. *Williams v. Arndt*, 626 F.Supp. 571 (D. Mass. 1985).

A computer program is a set of instructions expressed in codes, schemes, or in any other form, that is capable, when incorporated in a machine-readable medium, of causing of a computer — an electronic or similar device having information-processing capabilities — to perform or to achieve a particular task or result. Draft Model Provisions for legislation in the field of copyright proposed by World Intellectual Property Organization, CE/MPC/1/2-I, October 20, 1988.

A sequence of commands that, after being stored on a machine-readable medium, can cause a machine with data processing capability to display, execute, or achieve a certain function or task or a certain result. *Bappert und Berker v. Sud-Westdeutsche Inkasso*, Bundesgerichtshof (Federal Supreme Court), May 9, 1985, summarized at [1986] 3 E.I.P.R. 88.

A sequence of instructions expressed in any kind of language that makes it possible for a digital computer to display, execute, or achieve a pre-determined function of a task, or to arrive at a pre-determined result. *Bappert und Berker v. Sud-Westdeutsche Inkasso*, Karlsruhe, February 9, 1983, summarized at [1984] 9 E.I.P.R. 253.

The computer program is a set of instructions the purpose of which is to cause an information-processing device, a computer, to perform its functions. Green Paper on Copyright and the Challenge of Technology, The Commission of the European Communities, COM (88) 172 Final (1988).

Means a series of instructions or statements in a form acceptable to a computer, designed to cause the computer to execute an operation or operations. Computer programs include operating systems, assemblers, compilers, interpreters, data management systems, utility programs, sort-merge programs, and ADPE maintenance/diagnostic programs, as well as applications programs such as payroll, inventory control, and engineering analysis programs. Computer programs may be either machine-dependent or machine-independent, and may be general purpose in nature or be designed to satisfy the requirements of a particular user. U.S. D.O.D. Directive and D.O.D. F.A.R. Supplement, Federal Register Vol. 53, No. 209 43698.

Computer software programs consist of individual "functions", which are contained in one or more "files". Each function is first written in "source code" (readable by humans) and then translated into "object code" (readable by computers). *Forsight Resources Corp. v. Pfortmiller*, 719 F.Supp. 1006 (D.Kan. 1989).

A computer program is made up of several different components, including the source and object code, the structure, sequence and/or organization of the program, the user interface, and the function, or purpose, of the program. *Johnson Controls Inc. v. Phoenix Control Systems Inc.*, 886 F.2d 1173 (9th Cir. 1989).

Consists of a set of instructions encoded onto . . . disks. The set of instructions come from the word "information" and are sometimes referred to as "software" as contrasted with the word "hardware". Sometimes the word "software" is used to describe the disks since they are flexible but this is misleading. Software is a word in common use to describe the information constituting a computer program. *Autodesk Australia Pty. Ltd. v. Dyason* (1989), 15 I.P.R. 1 (Aus. Fed. Ct.), reversed [1990] A.I.P.C. 36,446 (Aus. Fed. Ct. FC).

A computer program, essentially, is a set of instructions to the computer to perform a function. It is based on logic and to a large extent is based on algorithms. *Autodesk Australia Pty Ltd. v. Dyason*, supra.

A computer program is a purely functional entity, the sole purpose of which is to make a piece of electronic equipment work in a particular way. *Autodesk Australia Pty Ltd. v. Dyason*, supra.

A computer program is a set of instructions designed to cause a computer to perform a particular function or to produce a particular result. A program is usually developed in a number of stages. First, the sequence of operations which the computer will be required to perform is commonly written out in ordinary language, with the help of formulae and diagrams. Next, the source program is prepared, either in source code (high level language) or in assembly code (low level language), or both. The source or assembly code cannot be used directly in the computer, so it is converted into an object code which is "machine readable". The program in object code, in the first instance, consists of a sequence of electrical impulses which are often first stored on a magnetic disk or tape and which may be stored in a ROM (Read Only Memory), a silicon chip containing many electrical circuits. *Autodesk Australia Pty Ltd. v. Dyason*, supra.

Means . . . an expression, in any language, code or notation, of a set of instructions (that is to say, orders or directions, used together, being numbers of symbols which cause a computer to perform some specified action) (whether with or without related information) intended, after either or both of: (i) conversion to another computer language, code or notation (ii) reproduction in a different material form (that is in relation to a work or an adaptation of a work, any form of storage from which the work, or adaptation, or a substantial part thereof, can be reproduced) to cause a device (that is, a contrivance) having digital (that is, of or pertaining to information represented by patterns made up from qualities existing in two states only, on and off, as pulses) information processing capabilities (that is, having the ability to manipulate data in order to abstract the required information) to perform a particular function (that is, any basic computer operation). *Autodesk Australia Pty Ltd. v. Dyason*, supra.

There are marked stages in the development of a present day computer program. It evolves through conceptual phases to a state where it is "encoded". A program . . . is written, or encoded, in a higher level language which bears an ostensible relation to the English language. The product of this stage of a program's development is called a "source code", something not directly intelligible to a computer. Through another program, or "language", that source code is translated into a series of "1's" and "0's" which tell the computer what to do. The series of 1's and 0's, so translated, is part of a "machine-readable language" and is called an "object code". *Orbitron Software Design Corp. v. M.I.C.R. Systems Ltd.* (1990), 48 B.L.R. 147 (B.C. S.C.).

A computer program is a list of instructions, one line at a time, each of which causes the computer to take a specific action. Once the program has been developed, it is preserved in the form of magnetic tapes, punch cards or some other recording medium. In the industry, computer programs are referred to as "software". *Computer Sciences Corp. v. Commissioner of Internal Revenue*, 63 T.C. 327 (U.S. Tax. Crt. 1974)

Computer programs are sequences of instructions to direct hardware to carry out specific operations. They establish in advance the operations that hardware is to go through in order to perform the desired functions. The set of instructions together solve a problem, and the creation of the coded instructions is a complex, logical task. *United Software Corp. v. Sperry Rand Corp.*, 5 C.L.S.R. 1492 (E.D. Pa. 1974).

Is a set of statements or instructions to be used directly or indirectly in a computer in order to bring about a certain result. *Autoskills Inc. v. National Educational Support Systems Incorporated*, Comp.Ind.Lit.Reptr. p. 15074 (D.C. New Mex. 1992).

Computer programs are written in specialized alphanumeric languages or "source code." In order to operate a computer, source code must be translated into computer readable form or "object code." *Sega Enterprises Ltd. v. Accolade Inc.* (1992), 24 U.S.P.Q.2d 1561.

A computer program consists of a series of instructions that cause a computer to perform certain operations. Computer programs are generally written in one of several special languages (e.g., BASIC, FORTRAN) which can be understood by a trained programmer. The "source code" is translated into a computer readable language called "object code," a series of "1's" and "0's", which is difficult for people to decipher. The object code is then imprinted into a silicon chip. *Sega Enterprises Ltd. v. Accolade Inc.*, 23 U.S.Q.D. 1440 (N.C. Cal. 1992).

Computer programs can be classified as either systems programs or applications programs. Systems programs are concerned with the operation or use of the computer. Applications programs perform a task or set of tasks for the computer user, such as payroll accouting, data base operation, or word processing. *Computer Associates International Inc. v. Altai Inc.*, 775 F.Supp. 544 (E.D.N.Y. 1991), affirmed 23 U.S.P.Q.2d 1241 (2d Cir. 1992).

Likewise computer programs — the instructions to the processor as to what to do with data — must be in binary form. *IBCOS Computers Ltd. v. Barclay's Mercantile Highland Finance Ltd.*, [1994] F.S.R. 275 (Ch.D.).

Dr Heys defined a program as a list of instructions or routines or actions set out in a logical order and designed to solve a particular problem. A series of such instructions may be combined together in order to solve a more complex problem, or a number of separate problems. Such a series might, as I understand it, equally be described as a single program. *John Richardson Computers Ltd. v. Flanders*, [1993] F.S.R. 497 (Ch.D.).

A computer program is made up of several different components, including the source and object code, the structure, sequence and/or organization of the program, the user interface, and the function, or purpose, of the program. *Prism Hospital Software Inc. v. Hospital Medical Records Institute*, B.C.S.C., Doc. Vancouver C872267, August 25, 1994.

An ordered set of data representing coded instructions or statements that when executed by a computer causes the computer to process data or perform specific functions. *State of Texas v. Burleson*, CCH Comp. Cas. 60,005.

An ordered set of data representing coded instructions or statements that, when executed by a computer, causes the computer to perform one or more computer operations. *O'Connor v. Commonwealth of Virginia*, 4 CCH Comp. Cas. 65,209 (Virg. C.A. 1993).

An ordered set of data representing coded instructions or statements that, when executed by a computer, causes the computer to process data or direct the computer to perform one or more computer operations. A computer may contain several "sets" of coded "instructions", however, and, in that sense, a computer may contain more than one "program". Indeed, computers commonly contain both "system programs" and "application programs". *People v. Versaggi*, 629 N.E. 2d 1034.

Means an ordered set of data representing coded instructions or statements that, when executed by a computer, causes the computer to perform one or more computer operations. Virginia Computer Crimes Act; (Va. Code Ann. § 18.2-152.2 et seq.) (amended effective July 1, 1999).

There are, speaking generally, three kinds of computer programs: operating system programs, application system programs and application development programs. An operating system program (such as DOS, OS/2 or Windows 95) controls the basic functions of the computer hardware such as the efficient utilisation of memory and the starting and stopping of application programs. Application programs, on the other hand are programs which permit a user to perform a particular task. Examples are word processing programs, spread sheet programs and data base programs. Application development programs exist, as has already been noted, as an aid to professional or non-professional programmers/developers to enable them to develop their own application programs. *Powerflex Services Pty Ltd. v. Data Access Corp.* (1997), 37 I.P.R. 436 (Aust. C.A.).

Computer programs are initially written in a "source code," which is a symbolic language, often using English words and common mathematical symbols, that humans can read. The source code is then translated, through a mechanical process known as compilation or assembly, into "object code," which is a concatenation of 1s and 0s readable by computer. Although a skilled programmer can read and understand small sections of object code, it is virtually impossible to develop a working understanding of a program by examining only its object code. As a result, most commercial programs are sold only in object code form, and can be run only "as is" by the ordinary user. *Bateman v. Mnemonics Inc.,* 38 U.S.P.Q. 2d 1225 (11th Cir. 1996).

Means a set of statements or instructions to be used directly or indirectly in a computer in order to bring about a certain result. *Copyright Amendment (Digital Agenda) Act 2000 Australia.*

Programs are sometimes called software to distinguish them from hardware, the physical equipment used in the operation of a computer. A distinction can also be drawn between systems programs and processing programs. Systems programs are those that control the operation of the computer. Together, they constitute the operating system for the computer. Processing programs are those whose execution is controlled by the operating system. There is a considerable variety of processing programs such as: language translators that decode source programs; service or utility programs, such as those that "dump" computer memory to external storage for safekeeping; application programs, which perform business and scientific functions, such as word processing. *Australian Video Retailers Association Ltd. v Warner Home Video Pty Ltd* (2001), 53 I.P.R. 242 (Aust. F.C.).

By itself hardware can do nothing. The really important part of the system is the software. Programs are the instructions or commands that tell the hardware what to do. The program itself is an algorithm or formula. It is of necessity contained in a physical medium. A program in machine readable format must be contained on a machine readable medium, such as paper cards, magnetic cards, magnetic tapes, discs, drums or magnetic bubbles. *St. Albans City and District Council v. International Computers Ltd.* [1996] 4 ALL E.R. 481 (C.A.).

Includes any literary work that is: (a) incorporated in, or associated with, a computer program; and (b) essential to the effective operation of a function of that computer program. *Copyright Amendment (Digital Agenda) Act 2000 Australia.*

Computer Programs Directive

Council Directive 91/250/EEC of 14 May 1991 on the legal protection of computer programs.

Computer Program Function

A program's function is to control the computer's activities. It does so by a series of instructions or statements prepared in order to achieve a certain result and input into a computer in a form acceptable to it. *People v. Versaggi*, 629 N.E. 2d 1034.

Computer Service

Any and all services provided by or through the facilities of any computer communication system allowing the input, output, examination, or transfer of computer data or computer programs from one computer to another. *People of the State of New York v. Johnson*, 148 Misc. 2d 103 (N.Y. Crim. Ct. 1990).

Includes data processing and the storage or retrieval of data. *Criminal Code (Canada)*, R.S.C. 1985, c. C-46, s. 342.1(2) [en. R.S.C. 1985, c. 27 (1st Supp.), s. 45].

Establishments primarily engaged in providing computer facilities on a rental and time-sharing basis, and such ancillary activities as programming, planning, and systems analysis etc. *Re WTH Can. Inc.*, T.M. Opp. Bd., T.M. App. No. 248, 186, J.P. D'Aoust Sr. H.O., October 6, 1986 (unreported).

Means that service, whether or not conveyed over the basic telecommunications transport network, that involves generating, acquiring, storing, transforming, processing, retrieving, utilizing or making available information in a computerized form, including but not limited to computer programming, prepackaged software, computer integrated systems design, computer processing and data preparation, information retrieval services, computer facilities management, computer leasing and rental, computer maintenance and repair, and other computer-related services, including those integral to the provision of other covered services. *An Act to Implement the Free Trade Agreement between Canada and the United States of America*, S.C. 1988, c. 65.

Includes computer time or services or, including data processing services, Internet services, electronic mail services, electronic message services, or information or data stored in connection therewith. Virginia Computer Crimes Act; (Va. Code Ann. § 18.2-152.2 et seq.) (amended effective July 1, 1999).

Computer Software

See Software.

A set of computer programs, procedures and associated documentation concerned with computer data or with the operation of a computer, computer program, or computer network. *O'Connor v. Commonwealth of Virginia*, 4 CCH Comp. Cas. 65,209 (Virg. C.A. 1993).

Means computer programs and computer data bases. U.S. D.O.D. Directive and D.O.D. F.A.R. Supplement, Federal Register, Vol. 53, No. 209 43698.

Data comprising source code listings, design details, algorithms, processes, flow charts, formulae, and related material that would enable the computer program to be produced, created, or compiled, Federal Acquisition Regulation (FAR): Rights in Technical Data (Proposed Rules), Federal Register, Vol. 55, No. 199.

Computer software consists of a logical set of instructions called programs. In its abstract form, a computer program is the intangible product of the thoughts of the programmer. Each program tells the computer how to manipulate data to achieve a desired result. These programs are embodied in a physical medium such as paper, magnetic tape, cards, or disks, to record the thoughts of the programmer and to allow him to communicate instructions to the computer. Although once embodied in some medium, the program becomes a tangible record of the programmer's thoughts, no aspect of the intellectual product is altered and it continues to exist apart from its encoded medium. *Wharton Management Group v. Sigma Consultants, Inc.*, 1990 Del. Super. Lexis 54 (Del. Sup. Ct. 1990).

Means a set of computer programs, procedures and associated documentation concerned with computer data or with the operation of a computer, computer program, or computer network. Virginia Computer Crimes Act; (Va. Code Ann. § 18.2-152.2 et seq.) (amended effective July 1, 1999).

Computer software is generally divided into two categories: operating systems and application programs. Operating systems control the internal operations of the computer and transfer the data between the components of the overall system. In essence, they function as intermediaries between computer hardware and application programs. Application programs tell the operating system to instruct the computer to perform a specific function, such as word processing. *Bateman v. Mnemonics Inc.,* 38 U.S.P.Q. 2d 1225 (11th Cir. 1996).

Computer Software Documentation

Means technical data, including computer listings and printouts, in human-readable form which (a) documents the design or details of computer software, (b) explains the capabilities of the software, or (c) provides operating instructions for using the software to obtain desired results from a computer. U.S. D.O.D. Directive and D.O.D. F.A.R. Supplement, Federal Register Vol. 53, No. 209 43698.

Computer System

Means a device that, or a group of interconnected or related devices one or more of which, (a) contains computer programs or other data, and (b) pursuant to computer programs, (i) performs logic and control, and (ii) may perform any other function. *Criminal Code* (Canada), R.S.C. 1985, c. C-46, s. 342.1(2) [en. R.S.C. 1985, c. 27 (1st Supp.), s. 45].

Means a device that, or a group of interconnected or related devices one or more of which, (a) contains computer programs or other data; and (b) pursuant to computer programs, performs logic and control, and may perform any other function. *Personal Information Protection and Electronic Documents Act,* S.C. 2000, c.5.

Means a device that, or a group of interconnected or related devices of one or more of which, (a) contains computer programs or other data, and (b) pursuant to computers, performs logical and control, and may perform any other function. *Electronic Commerce and Information, Consumer Protection Amendment and Manitoba Evidence Amendment Act,* C.C.S.M., c. E5S.

Means any device or a group of inter-connected or related devices, one or more of which, pursuant to a program, performs automatic processing of data. *Committee of Experts on Crime in Cyb-Space, Draft Convention on Cyber Crime (PC-CY).*

Computer Tampering

The crime of computer tampering involves the use of a computer or a computer service as the instrumentality of a crime . . . the defendant uses the computer to sabotage its intended operation in some way. The American Bar Association's task force on computer crime found in its survey that such tampering was the most prevalent means of computer abuse. *People v. Versaggi*, 629 N.E. 2d 1034.

Concurrent Execution

The ability of a computer system to have two or more separate and unrelated programs running at the same time. The CPU works on a program for a time, then sets it aside and works on another, etc. Eventually it returns to the first program and picks up where it left off. This is made possible by the fact that a CPU processes data much faster than its peripherals operate. Also called multiprogramming. *In Re Digital Research Inc.*, 4 U.S.P.Q.2d 1242 (T.T.A.B. 1987).

Confidentiality

Means the characteristic of data and information being disclosed only to authorised persons, entities and processes at authorised times and in the authorised manner. O.E.C.D. Guildines from the Security of Information Systems adopted November 26, 1992, available at http://www.oecd.org/dsti/sdi/it/secur/prod/e_secur.htm.

The property that sensitive information is not disclosed to unauthorized individuals, entities or processes. "Security Requirements for Cryptographic Modules", FIPS Pub. 140-1, Federal Information Processing Standards Publication, January 11, 1994, available at http://csrc.nist.gov/fips/fips1401.htm.

Is an element of data protection, but it does not equal data protection. Confidentiality is a state or quality of being confidential; treated as private and not for publication (Black's Law Dictionary). Confidential information is that which is spoken or written in confidence, entrusted with secrets (Oxford Dictionary). Ensuring Privacy and Confidentiality on the Health Iway, St.John's, Newfoundland, October 2-3, 1997, "Regulatory and Legislative Strategies in Canada", Andrea Neill, available at http://www.canarie.ca..

Means the property that data or information is not made available or disclosed to unauthorised individuals, entities, or processes. *OECD Guidelines for Cryptography Policy*, March 27, 1997, available at *www.oecd.org*.

Configuration

The word "configuration" is commonly used, not only as meaning the mode of arrangement of the physical components of a computer system, but also a collective noun for those components. *Madeley Pty Ltd. v. Touche Ross*, McGarvie, J., Aust. Fed. Ct., Dec. 21, 1989 (unreported).

Configuration Tables

The layout of the computer system, including MPE table, memory, and buffer sizes. Most computer programs are written in such a way that their specific functioning can be tailored by the user to suit a specific purpose or situation. In order to specify the characteristics to the program, a set of tables of values and/or options are often provided using a "configuration" dialog. The specific selections of options are stored in "configuration tables" for use by the program. These characteristics might include such things as the number and type of disk devices connected to the computer, the amount of main memory and the maximum number of users allowed on the system at any one point in time. *Delrina Corp. v. Triolet Systems, Inc.* (1992), 47 C.P.R. (3d) 1 (Ont. H.C.).

This term can also be applied specifically to the MPE/V operating system. The MPE/V Systems Table Manual documents the layout and contents of several hundred tables that are used to configure and manage the functioning of the computer system. These are grouped into areas of interest such as "Memory Management", "Disc Layout", "Process", "Jobs", "I/O" and "Measurement Information". Anyone who has an interest in the functioning of a particular aspect of the operating system would focus their attention on the number of table entries that had been configured as well as the contents of each of the table entries currently in use for the subset of these systems tables that relate to their particular area of interest. *Delrina Corp. v. Triolet Systems, Inc.* (1992), 47 C.P.R. (3d) 1 (Ont. H.C.).

Consequential Damages

Resulting from breach of contract include (i) any loss resulting from general or particular requirements and needs of which the other party at the time of contracting had reason to know and which could not reasonably be prevented, and (ii) injury to person or damage to other property proximately resulting from any breach of warranty. The term does not include direct or incidental damages. *Uniform Computer Information Transactions Act*, National Conference of Commissioners on Uniform State Laws, available at http://www.law.upenn.u/bll/ulc/ucita/citim99.htm.

Console

The basic unit of an electronic games machine. It may be portable ('hand-held') or connect to a domestic television, and accept games on a cartridge or *CD* format. It is not programmable. Monopolies and Mergers Commission — Video Games: A report on the supply of video games in the UK (LONDON: HMSO Cm2781).

Conspicuous

With reference to a term, means so written, displayed, or otherwise presented that a reasonable person against which it is to operate ought to have noticed it. A term in an electronic record intended to evoke a response by an electronic agent is conspicuous if it is presented in a form that would enable a reasonably configured electronic agent to take it into account or react without review of the record by an individual. Conspicuous terms include the following: (A) with respect to a person: (i) a heading in capitals in a size equal to or greater than, or in contrasting type, font, or color to, the surrounding text; (ii) language in the body of a record or display in larger or other contrasting type, font, or color or set off from the surrounding text by symbols or other marks that call attention to the language; and (iii) a term prominently referenced in an electronic record or display which is readily accessible and reviewable from the record or display; and (B) with respect to a person or an electronic agent, a term or reference to a term that is so placed in a record or display that the person or electronic agent can not proceed without taking some action with respect to the term or reference. *Uniform Computer Information Transactions Act*, National Conference of Commissioners on Uniform State Laws, available at http://www.law.upenn.u/bll/ulc/ucita/citim99.htm.

Consumer Contracts Directive

Council Directive 93/13/EEC of 5 April 1993 on unfair terms in consumer contracts.

Constants

Constants are the invariable integers that comprise part of the formulas used to perform the calculations in the programs. *Gates Rubber Co. v. Bando American Inc.*, 28 U.S.P.Q. 2d 1503 (10th Cir. 1993).

Content

Refers to any text, data, sound, program, or visual image transmitted over or made available for retrieval on an interactive computer service. *Shea v. Reno*, 930 F.Supp. 916 (S.D.N.Y. 1996).

Content Provider

Refers to any "internet speaker" that is, a user who transmits or makes available any content over the internet. *Shea v. Reno*, 1996 U.S. Dist. LEXIS 10720 (S.D.N.Y. 1996).

Persons involved in the Internet provide applications or high level services, including the World Wide Web, Internet e-mail and... Since many of these applications involve making information of any kind available to users, those who provide such information are commonly referred to as "content providers". *Public Performance of Musical Works* 1996-1998 (Tariff 22) (1999), 1 C.P.R. (4th) 417 (Copyright Board).

Content providers may be commercial corporations, or individuals with a computer at home, the appropriate software and internet access. *Society of Composers, Authors & Music Publishers of Canada v. Canadian Association of Internet Providers* (2002), 19 C.P.R. (4th) 289 (Fed.C.A.)

Content Scramble System (CSS)

CSS, or Content Scramble System, is an access control and copy prevention system for DVD's developed by the motion picture companies... It is an encryption-based system that requires the use of appropriately configured hardware such as a DVD player or a computer DVD drive to decrypt, unscramble and play back, but not copy, motion pictures on DVDs. The technology necessary to configure DVD players and drives to play CSS-protected DVDs has been licensed to hundreds of manufacturers in the United States and around the world. *Universal City Studios, Inc. v. Reimerdes,*, 55 U.S.P.Q. 2d 1873 (S. D.N.Y. 2000).

Control Flow

Control flow refers to the overall sequence of actions and events in a program. *Gates Rubber Co. v. Bando American Inc.*, 28 U.S.P.Q. 2d 1503 (10th Cir. 1993).

Control flow is the sequence in which the modules perform their respective tasks. *Gates Rubber Co. v. Bando American Inc.*, 28 U.S.P.Q. 2d 1503 (10th Cir. 1993).

Control Information

Information that is entered into a cryptographic module for the purposes of directing the operation of the module. "Security Requirements for Cryptographic Modules", FIPS Pub. 140-1, Federal Information Processing Standards Publication, January 11, 1994, available at http://csrc.nist.gov/fips/fips1401.htm.

Controller

A controller is an electronic minicomputer which consists of many small components soldered to a printed circuit board. *Eaton Corp. v. Magnavox Co.*, 581 F.Supp. 1514 (E.D. Mich. 1984).

[T]he natural or legal person, public authority, agency or any other body which alone or jointly with others determines the purposes and means of the processing of personal data. Where the purposes and means of processing are determined by national or Community laws or regulations, the controller or the specific criteria for his nomination may be designated by a national or Community law. European Union Data Protection Directive.

Controller of the File

[T]he natural or legal person, public authority, agency or any other body who is competent according to the national law to decide what should be the purpose of the automated data file, which categories of personal data should be stored and which operations should be applied to them. Council of Europe: Convention for the Protection of Individuals with Regard to Automatic Processing of Personal Data.

Convergence

This refers to the "blurring" of traditional distinctions between cable television, telecommunicaitons, satellite and wireless technologies, and multi-media businesses. Because of digitization, broadcasting is beginning to converge with computing and consumer electronics and telecommunications. Submission of the Director of Investigation and Research to the CRTC Re Public Notice CRTC 1994-130.

The "coming together" of formerly distinct technologies, industries or activities; most common usage refers to the convergence of computing, communications and broadcasting technologies. *The Challenge of the Information Highway: Final Report of the Information Highway Advisory Council* (September 1995).

Conversion Programme

A conversion programme transforms information from the format of one file layout to another file layout for the purpose of taking user data from one set of data files and transforming it into another set of data files so that a new programme can be used. *Geac J & E Systems Ltd. v. Craig Erickson Systems Inc.* (1993), 46 C.P.R. (3d) 25 (Ont. Gen. Div.).

Cookie

Cookie technology allows a Web site's server to place information about a consumer's visits to the site on the consumer's computer in a text file that only the Web site's server can read. Using cookies a Web site assigns each consumer a unique identifier (not the actual identity of the consumer), so that the consumer may be recognized in subsequent visits to the site. On each return visit, the site can call up user-specific information, which could include the consumer's preferences or interests, as indicated by documents the consumer accessed in prior visits or items the consumer clicked on while in the site. Privacy on Line: A Report to Congress, Federal Trade Commission June 1998.

When you visit a site, a notation may be fed to a file known as a "cookie" in your computer for future reference. If you revisit the site, the "cookie" file allows the web site to identify you as a "return" guest — and offer you products tailored to your interests or tastes. You can set your online preferences to limit or let you know about "cookies" that a web site places on your computer. Cyberspeak — Learning the Language, the Federal Trade Commission and the National Association of Attorneys General, available at http://www.ftc.gov/bcp/conline/pubs/online/sitesee/index.html.

A cookie is a piece of information, or unique identifier, that is placed on your computer which enables websites to remember information about the choices you make when you visit their sites. Cookies can be used to save you having to type in all your personal information and password every time you visit a site. They can also be used to build up a profile of your interests by tracking what sites and pages you visit. This can be used by advertisers to tailor their marketing to you. Some people see this as an invasion of privacy. *Consumers@Shopping: An International Comparative Study of Electronic Commerce*, Consumers International, September 1999, available at *www.consumersinternational.org*.

Cookies are computer programs commonly used by Web sites to store useful information such as usernames, passwords, and preferences, making it easier for users to access Web pages in an efficient manner. *DoubleClick Inc. Privacy Litigation,* Civ.0641 (N.R.V.) (S.D.N.Y. Mar. 28, 2001).

A cookie is an electronic file that on-line companies. . . implant upon computer users' hard drives when those users visit an internet website. *In re Inuit Privacy Litigation,* 2001 U.S. Dist. LEXIS 5828 (C.D. Cal. 2001).

Copper-Based Signal Transmission System

Copper-based systems are used as the medium of transmission copper wires arranged in cables, which may consist of a number of twisted pairs or which may be coaxial cables. Signals are conducted in the copper wire, as a flow of electrons. The technology embodied in a copper-based system is a mature technology. While the cabling materials and insulation have changed since the invention of the telephone in the late 19th century, the copper conductors and the principle of signal transmission have remained the same throughout. *British Columbia Telephone Co. v. Canada,* [1991] F.C.J. No. 340 (Fed. T.D.).

Copy

Means the medium on which information is fixed on a temporary or permanent basis and from which it can be perceived, reproduced, used, or communicated, either directly or with the aid of a machine or device. *Uniform Computer Information Transactions Act*, National Conference of Commissioners on Uniform State Laws, available at http://www.law.upenn.u/bll/ulc/ucita/citim99.htm.

Copy Protection

Includes any device or means intended to prevent or to restrict copying of a work or to impair the quality of copies made. *Copyright, Designs, and Patents Act 1988*, 1988, c. 48.

A technological protection measure that restricts unauthorised copying of a copyright work, usually in the form of a software program and/or hardware as part of a computer, an audiovisual or audio device. Copy-protection measures might prevent any copies being made or might only allow copies to be made from an original copy. *Digital Technology and the Copyright Act 1994: A Discussion Paper, Competition and Enterprise Branch, July 2001 (New Zealand).*

Copyright Directive

Directive 2001/29/EC of the European Parliament and of the Council of 22 May 2001 on the harmonization of certain aspects of copyright and related rights in the information society.

Core

The area inside a computer where instructions are stored in order to be executed and is divided into a Common Area and one or more Partition Areas. The Common Area contains sets of instructions to perform routine tasks common to almost all application programs, such as preparing data to be sent to the math storage devices. The Partition Areas contain the application programs written to accomplish a particular function such as preparing a payroll. *Clarke Irwin & Co. v. Singer Co. of Can.*, Ont. Div. Ct., Keith J., December 3, 1979, summarized at [1979] 3 A.C.W.S. 807.

Core Memory Board

The circuit board upon which the electronic components making up Core Memory are affixed. *Clarke Irwin & Co. v. Singer Co. of Can.*, Ont. Div. Ct., Keith J., December 3, 1979, summarized at [1979] 3 A.C.W.S. 807.

CPU (Central Processing Unit)

The CPU controls the operations of the computer, executes the instructions in the systems software and application programs and processes the data. *Clarke Irwin & Co. v. Singer Co. of Can.*, Ont. Div. Ct., Keith J., December 3, 1979, summarized at [1979] 3 A.C.W.S. 807.

It is the CPU which carries out the arithmetic and logic functions (*e.g.*: addition, subtraction, comparison of data presented as two fields of numbers). *Apple Computer Inc. v. Mackintosh Computers Ltd.* (1986), 28 D.L.R. (4th) 178 (Fed. T.D.).

Is the integrated circuit that executes programs. *Apple Computer Inc. v. Franklin Computer Corp.*, 215 U.S.P.Q. 935 (E.D.Pa. 1982), reversed 714 F.2d 1240 (3rd Cir. 1983), cert dismissed 104 S.Ct. 690 (1984).

This is the component within the computer that provides the "brains" of the computer. *Delrina Corp. v. Triolet Systems, Inc.* (1992), 47 C.P.R. (3d) 1 (Ont. H.C.).

CRT (Cathode Ray Tube)

A CRT is more commonly known to laymen as a television picture tube. *Motorola Inc. v. Computer Displays International Inc.*, 222 U.S.P.Q. 844 (7th Cir. 1984).

Crawler

A search engine uses specialised computer programs sometimes called "spiders" or "crawlers" to electronically visit websites, gather relevant data about those websites, and compile and index the information. *British Columbia Automobile Assn. v. OPEIU. Local 378* (2001), 10 C.P.R. (4th) 423 (B.C.S.C.).

A computer program that travels the web in search of images to be converted into thumbnails and added to the index. *Kelly v. Arriba Soft Corp.*, 53 U.S.P.Q. 2d 1361 (C.D.Cal. 1999).

Critical Security Parameters

Security-related information (e.g., cryptographic keys, authentication data such as passwords and PINs) appearing in plaintext or otherwise unprotected form and whose disclosure or modification can compromise the security of a cryptographic module or the security of the information protected by the module. "Security Requirements for Cryptographic Modules", FIPS Pub. 140-1, Federal Information Processing Standards Publication, January 11, 1994, available at http://csrc.nist.gov/fips/fips1401.htm.

Cross-Certificate

Is a certificate used to establish a trust relationship between two Certification Authorities. Public Key Infrastructure Management in the Government of Canada", Treasury Board of Canada Secretariat, May 27, 1999, available at http://www.tbs-sct.gc.ca/pubs_pol/ciopubs/PKI/pki1_e.html.

Cross-Certification

Is the process undertaken by Certification Authorities to establish a trust relationship. When two Certification Authorities are cross-certified, they agree to trust and rely upon each other's public key certificates and keys as if they had issued them themselves. The Certification Authorities exchange cross-certificates and enable users from one Certification Authority to interact electronically and securely with users from the other. Public Key Infrastructure Management in the

Government of Canada, Treasury Board of Canada Secretariat, May 27, 1999, available at http://www.tbs-sct.gc.ca/pubs_pol/ciopubs/PKI/pki1_e.html.

CRTC Interconnection Steering Committee (CISC)

A forum for parties, with CRTC assistance, to resolve local competition implementation, issues of a technological, operational or administrative nature and to resolve other telecommunications issues. *Report to the Governor in Council: Status of Competition in Canadian Telecommunications Markets, Deployment/ Accessibility of Advanced Telecommunications Infrastructure and Services, September, 2001.*

Cryptographic

Also called a cipher, this is the mathematical function used algorithm for encoding and decoding a message. *The Challenge of the Information Highway: Final Report of the Information Highway Advisory Council* (September 1995).

Cryptographic Key

A parameter used in conjunction with a cryptographic algorithm that determines: (i) the transformation of plaintext data into ciphertext data, (ii) the transformation of ciphertext data into plaintext data, (iii) a digital signature computed from data, (iv) the verification of a digital signature computed from data, or (v) a data authentication code (DAC) computed from data. "Security Requirements for Cryptographic Modules", FIPS Pub. 140-1, Federal Information Processing Standards Publication, January 11, 1994, available at http://csrc.nist.gov/fips/fips1401.htm.

Means a parameter used with a cryptographic algorithm to transform, validate, authenticate, encrypt or decrypt data. *OECD Guidelines for Cryptography Policy*, March 27, 1997, available at *www.oecd.org*.

Cryptographic Methods

Means cryptographic techniques, services, systems, products and key management systems. *OECD Guidelines for Cryptography Policy*, March 27, 1997, available at *www.oecd.org*.

Cryptographic Module

The set of hardware, software, firmware, or some combination thereof that implements cryptographic logic or processes, including cryptographic algorithms, and is contained within the cryptographic boundary of the module. "Security Requirements for Cryptographic Modules", FIPS Pub. 140-1, Federal Information Processing Standards Publication, January 11, 1994, available at http://csrc.nist.gov/fips/fips1401.htm.

Cryptography

The message is both encrypted and decrypted by common keys. The uses of cryptography are far-ranging in an electronic age, from protecting personal messages over the Internet and transactions on bank ATMs to ensuring the secrecy of military intelligence. *Bernstein v. United States Department of State*, 1996 W.L. 186106 (N.D. Cal. 1996).

Is the science of secret writing, a science that has roots stretching back hundreds, and perhaps thousands, of years? For much of its history, cryptography has been the jealously guarded province of governments and militaries. In the past twenty years, however, the science has blossomed in the civilian sphere, driven on the one hand by dramatic theoretical innovations within the field, and on the other by the needs of modern communication and information technologies. As a result, cryptography has become a dynamic academic discipline within applied mathematics. *Bernstein v. Department of State*, (9th Cir. Mar. 6th, 1999) No. 97-16686

Uses complex mathematical algorithms to convert information into formats that are virtually unreadable without having access to a specific deciphering mechanism. Cryptography not only provides a means for protecting information, it can also be used to authenticate identities and ensure the integrity of data. Advancing Global Electronic Commerce: Technology Solutions to Public Policy Challenges, The Computer Systems Policy Project, July 1999, available at http://www.cspp.org/projects/july99_cto_report.pdf.

Uses complex mathematical algorithms to convert information into formats that require deciphering with a specific mechanism before it is readable. Cryptography provides a means for protecting information and for authenticating information. Advancing Global Electronic Commerce: Technology Solutions to Public Policy Challenges, Computer Systems Policy Project (CSPP), available at http://www.cspp.org/projects/july99_cto_report.pdf.

Means the discipline which embodies principles, means, and methods for the transformation of data in order to hide its information content, establish its authenticity, prevent its undetected modification, prevent its repudiation, and/or prevent its unauthorised use. *OECD Guidelines for Cryptography Policy*, March 27, 1997, available at *www.oecd.org*.

CSS

Content Scrambling System

Custom Program

A custom program is a type of program that is specifically developed for and tailored to a particular client's business. *Management Data Systems, Inc. v. Sta-Fed Computer Tax, Inc.*, 330 N.W. 2d 247 (Ct. App. Wisc. 1982).

Customer-Premises Equipment (CPE)

Customer-premises equipment is terminal equipment located at a subscriber's premises which is connected with the termination of a carrier's communication channel(s) at the network interface at that subscriber's premises. Second Computer Inquiry (Final Decision), 77 F.C.C.2d 384 (F.C.C. 1980).

CPE is terminal equipment located at a subscriber's premises that is connected with the termination of a carrier's communication channel(s) at that subscriber's premises. Second Computer Inquiry (Tentative Decision), 72 F.C.C.2d 358 (F.C.C. 1979).

Customer-premises equipment includes all equipment provided by common carriers and located on customer premises, except over-voltage protection equipment, inside wiring, coin operated or pay telephones, and multiplexing equipment to deliver multiple channels to the customer. Second Computer Inquiry (Reconsideration of Final Decision), 84 F.C.C.2d 50 (F.C.C. 1980).

Customer Services

Means those services, whether or not conveyed over the basic telecommunications transport network, that involve generating, acquiring, storing, transforming, processing, retrieving, utilizing or making available information in a computerized form, including, but not limited to, computer programming, prepackaged software, computer integrated systems design, computer processing and data preparation, information retrieval services, computer facilities management, computer leasing and rental, computer maintenance and repair, and other computer-related services, including those integral to the provision of other covered services. *Canada-United States Free Trade Agreement Implementation Act*, S.C. 1988, c. 65.

Computer services available to the consumer, while taking many and varied forms, may be generally categorized as (1) message-switching; (2) data processing; or (3) a combination of both, i.e., a hybrid service. *GTE Service Corp. v. F.C.C.*, 3 C.L.S.R. 592 (2nd Cir. 1973).

Customized

Customized means specific changes that a client has requested where a standard is the software off the shelf without any specific changes. *Starr Data Systems Inc. v. Quasimodo Consulting Services Ltd.* (1996), [1996] O.J. No. 4030, 1996 CarswellOnt 4256 (Gen. Div.).

CWIN

Cyber Warning and Information Network

Cyber Pirate

A person who steals valuable trademarks and establishes domain names on the internet using these trademarks to sell the domains to the rightful trademark owners. *iTravel2000.com Inc. v. Fagan,* (2001), 11 C.P.R. (4th) 164 (Ont. S.J.).

[Persons] who register well-known marks as domain names in order to sell them to trademark owners. *Nutrisystem.com Inc. v. Easthaven Ltd.,* 58 U.S.P.Q. 2d 1160 (E.D. Penn. 2000).

Cyberspace

CyberSpace is a popular term for the world of electronic communications over computer networks. *Religious Technology Center v. Netcom On-Line*, 37 U.S.P.Q. 2d 1545 (N.D. Cal. 1995).

A decentralized, global medium of communications. *American Civil Liberties Union v. Reno*, 929 F.Supp. 824 (E.D. Pa. 1996).

The three-dimensional expanse of computer networks in which all audio and video electronic signals travel and users can, with the proper addresses and codes, explore and download information. *The Challenge of the Information Highway: Final Report of the Information Highway Advisory Council* (September 1995).

As commonly used today, cyberspace is the conceptual abstract 'location' of the electronic interactivity available using one's computer. Cyberspace is a place 'without physical walls or even physical dimensions' in which interaction occurs as if it happened in the real world and in real time, but constitutes only a 'virtual reality'. Cyberspace is the manifestation of the words, human relationships, data, wealth, and power . . . by people using [computer-mediated communications]. *The Hearst Corporation v. Goldberger*, 1997 WL 97097 (S.D.N.Y. 1997).

A term, coined by Canadian writer William Gibson, for the virtual three-dimensional environment created by computer networks in which textual, audio, and video electronic signals travel. Ministry of Revenue Advisory Committee, Report of the Committee On Electronic Commerce, April 30, 1998, Industry Canada.

Another name for the Internet. Cyberspeak — Learning the Language, the Federal Trade Commission and the National Association of Attorneys General, available at http://www.ftc.gov/bcp/conline/pubs/online/sitesee/index.html.

The generic term for the loosely connected network of computers that permits users of personal computers worldwide to communicate with each other. *United States v. Maxwell* 45 M.J. 406 (Ca. Armed Forces. 1996).

"Cyberspace" refers to the interaction of people and businesses over computer networks, electronic bulletin boards, and commercial online services. The largest and most visible man at the station of cyberspace is the Internet. *Blumenthal v. Drudge*, 1992 F. Supp. 44 (D.D.C. 1998).

Cybersquatters

Cyber squatting involves the registration as domain names of well-known trademarks by non-trademark holders who then try to sell the names back to the trademark owners. Since domain name registrars do not check to see whether a domain name request is related to an existing trademark, it has been simple and inexpensive for any person to register as domain names the marks of established companies. This prevents use of the domain name by the mark owners, who infrequently have been willing to pay "ransom" in order to get "their names" back. *Sporty's Farm L.L.C. v. Sportman's Market, Inc.*, 202 F. 3d 489 (2d. Cir. 2000).

In popular terms, "cybersquatting" is the term most frequently used to describe the deliberate, bad faith abusive registration of a domain name in violation of rights in trademarks and service marks. *Final Report of the WIPO Internet Domain Name Process*, April 30, 1999 available at http:\\wipo2.wipo.int

An expression that has come to mean the bad faith, abuse of registration and use of the distinctive trademarks of others as Internet domain names, with the intent to profit from the goodwill associated with those trademarks. *Shields v. Zuccarini*, Case No. 00-2236 (3rd, Cir. June 15, 2001).

Cybersquatting (or cyberpiracy) refers to the deliberate, bad faith, and abuse of the registration of the internet domain names and violation of the rights of trademark owners. *Electronics Boutique Holdings Corp. v. Zuccarini,*, 56 U.S.P.Q. 2d 1705 (E.D.P. 2000).

The internet version of a land grab. *Virtual Works Inc. v. Volkswagen of America Inc.*, 57 U.S.P.Q. 2d 1547 (4th Cir. 2001).

Cybersquatting is the practice of registering "well-known brand names as Internet domain names" in order to force the rightful owners of the marks "to pay for the right to engage in electronic commerce under their own brand name." Cybersquatting is profitable because while it is inexpensive for a cybersquatter to register the mark of an established company as a domain name, such companies are often vulnerable to being forced into paying substantial sums to get their names back. *Virtual Works Inc. v. Volkswagen of America Inc.*, 57 U.S.P.Q. 2d 1547 (4th Cir. 2001).

Individuals who...scoop up available websites that might later be in demand by large organizations. *Hasbro, Inc. v. Clue Computing, Inc.*, 45 U.S.P.Q. 2d 1170 (D. Mass. 1997).

DARPA

Defense Advanced Research Projects Agency

DASD

Direct-Access Storage Device. *IBM v. Fujitsu Ltd.*, Copyright L.R. (CCH) 20,517 (Am. Arbtn. Assoc. Comm. Arbtn. Trib. 1988).

Data

Means representations of information or of concepts that are being prepared or have been prepared in a form suitable for use in a computer system. *Criminal Code* (Canada), R.S.C. 1985, c. C-46, s. 342.1(2) [en. R.S.C. 1985, c. 27 (1st Supp.), s. 45].

"Data" is commonly used in the electronics field to refer to information provided by electronic equipment. *Smiths Industries Ltd. v. Ventek Computer Systems Ltd.* (1978), 42 C.P.R. (2d) 139 (T.M. Opp. Bd.).

"Data" in the computer field is a term used to describe information in coded form which can be fed into, stored in, and by the use of an appropriate program, worked on in a computer. *Datacall Ltd. v. The Post Office*, Ch. D., Whitford J., November 27, 1981 (unreported).

Means recorded information, regardless of form or method of the recording. U.S. D.O.D. Directive and D.O.D. F.A.R. Supplement, Federal Register, Vol. 53, No. 209 43698.

Recorded information, regardless of form, the media on which it may be recorded, or the method of recording. The term includes, but is not limited to, technical data and computer software and computer data bases. The term does not include data incidental to the administration of a contract, such as financial, administrative, cost and pricing, or management information. Federal Acquisition Regulation (FAR): Rights in Technical Data (Proposed Rules), Federal Register, Vol. 55, No. 199.

Data is a collection of information, which is used by the computer program. It is generally formatted into files, which are stored on either the hard disc of the PC or on a floppy diskette. Data can include text and pictures. *Softel Inc. v. Dragon Medical and Scientific Communications, Inc.*, 1992 U.S. Dist. LEXIS 9502 (S.D.N.Y.1992).

Data is the information of the customer to be stored and used in the computer. The customer enters its data and the programmes transfer the data into the data files as specified by the file layouts. *Geac J & E Systems Ltd. v. Craig Erickson Systems Inc.* (1993), 46 C.P.R. (3d) 25 (Ont. Gen. Div.)

A representation of information, knowledge, facts, concepts or instructions that is being prepared or has been prepared in a formalized manner and is intended to be stored or processed in a computer. Data may be embodied in any form, including but not limited to computer printouts, magnetic storage media, and punch cards, or may be stored internally in the memory of the computer. *State of Texas v. Burleson*, CCH Comp. Cas. 60,005.

Representations of information or concepts, in any form. Personal Information Protection and Electronic Documents Act, S.C. 2000 C.5.

Means a representation of facts, concepts or instructions in a formalised manner suitable for communication, interpretation or processing by human beings or by automatic means. O.E.C.D. Guildines from the Security of Information Systems adopted November 26, 1992, available at http://www.oecd.org/dsti/sdi/it/secur/prod/e_secur.htm.

Means representations, in any form, of information or concepts. *Uniform Electronic Evidence Act*, adopted by the ULCC (August 1998), available at http://www.law.ualberta.ca/alri/ulc/current/eueea.htm.

Means the representation of information in a manner suitable for communication, interpretation, storage, or processing. *OECD Guidelines for Cryptography Policy*, March 27, 1997, available at *www.oecd.org*.

Means representations of information or of concepts in any form. *Electronic Commerce and Information, Consumer Protection Amendment and Manitoba Evidence Amendment Act,* C.C.S.M.c.E5S.

The material, being binary numbers, which makes up the subject matter of the processing and the instructions for the processing is often referred to generally as "*data*". The material, being binary numbers that makes up the instructions is referred to as "*programs*". Thus, in that sense, all programs are data but not all data is programs. In many contexts, however, the term "data" is reserved for the material that is the subject of the processing in order to distinguish it from programs. In computer science, the distinction between programs and data in that sense is fundamental. Thus, Webster's New World Dictionary of Computer Terms contains the following definitions: "*Program: a list of instructions written in a programming language, that a computer can execute so that the machine acts in a predetermined way. Synonymous with software. Data: factual information (such as text, numbers, sounds and images) in a form that can be processed by a computer. ...*" Programs cause a computer to perform arithmetic and logical operations or comparisons and to take some additional action based on the comparison or to input or output data in a desired sequence. *Australian Video Retailers Association Ltd. v. Warner Home Video Pty Ltd.* (2001) 53 I.P.R. 242 (Aust. F.C.)

Data and Information

In the context of computing, there is no useful distinction to be drawn between these terms. Both describe the representation in some coded form of digital information. *Digital Technology and the Copyright Act 1994: A Discussion Paper, Competition and Enterprise Branch, July 2001 (New Zealand).*

Data Chains

"Data chains" are any combination of two or more data elements or data use identifiers. Automated Regulatory Information System, 37 Fed. Reg. 7638 (Fed. Power. Comm. 1972).

Data Code

A "data code" is a letter, a number, or a combination of alphanumeric characters, used to represent data items in facilitating machine processing. Automated Regulatory Information System, 37 Fed. Reg. 7638 (Fed. Power. Comm. 1972).

Data Compression

A term applied to various means of compacting information for more efficient tramsmission or stoarage. Submission of the Director of Investigation and Research to the CRTC Re Public Notice CRTC 1994-130.

Data Element

A "data element" is a unit of information or data class composed of a logical grouping of homogeneous pieces or subunits of information such that: 1. Each unit has a meaning in terms of "what it is" different from any other unit of information; 2. The individual subunits (data items) in such groupings are mutually exclusive; 3. In most cases, the data items of each group are exclusive to that unit of information. Automated Regulatory Information System, 37 Fed. Reg. 7638 (Fed. Power. Comm. 1972).

Data File

A data file (or file) is the portion of the software in which the customer's data is stored. The design of the data file corresponds to and is recorded in the file layout. The data file is the embodiment of the file layout. For example, the file name, order of fields in each record, field sizes, type of data, and key, are dictated by the file layout. Not all of the information in the file layout is found in the data file. A data file is created by the software programmer, owned by the developer and is part of the software. The file structure information from the file layout is incorporated into the data file. The data entered into the data file is owned by the customer. The records in the data file must conform to the file structure or design defined by the file layout and that design must be used by programmers that write programmes which access the data file. When a data file is first installed at a customer's site, there is no data in it — the files are clean — and at that stage the data file is entirely a part of the software, owned by the software owner. *Geac J & E Systems Ltd. v. Craig Erickson Systems Inc.* (1993), 46 C.P.R. (3d) 25 (Ont. Gen. Div.).

(D)ata files, to the extent of their design and structure, are part of software. Quite obviously, the customer's data in those files is not part of the software. The data belongs to the customer. *Geac J & E Systems Ltd. v. Craig Erickson Systems Inc.* (1993), 46 C.P.R. (3d) 25 (Ont. Gen. Div.).

Data Flow

Data flow is the sequence of actions taken on each piece of information, that is, how the data travels through the program. *Gates Rubber Co. v. Bando American Inc.*, 28 U.S.P.Q. 2d 1503 (10th Cir. 1993).

Data flow describes the movement of information through the program and the sequence with which it is operated by the modules. *Gates Rubber Co. v. Bando American Inc.*, 28 U.S.P.Q. 2d 1503 (10th Cir. 1993).

Data Held in a Computer

Includes—(a) data entered or copied into the computer; and (b) data held in any removable data storage device for the time being in the computer; and (c) data held in a data storage device on a computer network of which the computer forms part; "data storage device" means any thing (for example, a disk or file server) containing or designed to contain data for use by a computer. *Property Damage and Computer Offices Act 2002 (Australia).*

Data Integrity

It is important that the information stored in the databases of a computer system and the information received by one part of the system from another have integrity in the sense of being reliable. Data has integrity if it can be relied on as representing the true state of affairs. The information electronically stored in the files of the database on the hard disk may be treated as analogous to information stored in the files of a conventional filing cabinet. It would obviously be unsatisfactory if, while one user was actually engaged in writing amendments to the text of an item of stored information, so as to amend it and bring it up to date, a second user were to consult the incompletely amended text and obtain the information it contained. The second user would obtain information which was incomplete and therefore unreliable. Further, the second user's intrusion might end the first user's amendment of the text so that the item of information would remain incompletely amended and unreliable. Similarly if two users each with information which required amendment of the text to bring the information up-to-date, engaged in doing so simultaneously, it would be likely to lead to the information being corrupted by incorrect amendment and unreliable for that reason. *Madeley Pty Ltd. v. Touche Ross*, McGarvie, J., Aust. Fed. Ct., Dec. 21, 1989 (unreported).

Data Items

"Data items" are defined as "the smallest meaningful pieces or subunits of information appearing in a reporting or data system and which cannot be further subdivided and retain significant meaning". Automated Regulatory Information System, 37 Fed. Reg. 7638 (Fed. Power. Comm. 1972).

Data Key

A cryptographic key which is used to cryptographically process data (e.g., encrypt, decrypt, sign, authenticate). "Security Requirements for Cryptographic Modules", FIPS Pub. 140-1, Federal Information Processing Standards Publication, January 11, 1994, available at http://csrc.nist.gov/fips/fips1401.htm.

Data Matching

The comparison of personal data obtained from different sources, including personal information banks, for the purpose of making decisions about the individual to whom the data pertains. Generally, it applies to comparing computerized sets of data rather than comparing records from two government departments about a single individual. Thus, data matching is generally described as a "program." *A Survey of Legal Issues Relating to the Security of Electronic Information*, Department of Justice, Canada.

Data Message

Means information generated, sent, received or stored by electronic, optical or similar means including, but not limited to, electronic data interchange (EDI), electronic mail, telegram, telex or telecopy. UNCITRAL Model Law On Electronic Commerce (1996).

Means information generated, sent, received or stored by electronic, optical or similar means including, but not limited to, electronic data interchange (EDI), electronic mail, telegram, telex or telecopy. *UNCITRAL, Working Group IV (Electronic Commerce), Thirty-ninth session New York, 11-15 March, 2002.*

Data Mining

Data mining is a set of automated techniques used to extract buried or previously unknown pieces of information from large databases. Successful data mining makes it possible to unearth patterns and relationships, and then use this "new" information to make proactive knowledge-driven business decisions. Data mining then, "centres on the automated discovery of new facts and relationships in data. The raw material is the business data, and the data mining algorithm is the excavator, sifting through the vast quantities of raw data looking for the valuable nuggets of business information." Data Mining: Staking a Claim on Your Privacy, Information and Privacy Commissioner/Ontario, January 1998, available at http://www.ipc.on.ca.

Data Movement Instructions

These instructions cause the transfer of information between memory and a register or from one register to another register, etc.: for example, "load accumulator" or "store accumulator." *Apple Computer Inc. v. Mackintosh Computers Ltd.* (1986), 28 D.L.R. (4th) 178 (Fed. T.D.).

Data Object (Content/Document)

The actual binary/octet data being operated on (transformed, digested, or signed) by an application—frequently an *HTTP Entity*. Note that the proper noun Object designates a specific XML element. Occasionally we refer to a data object as a document or as a *resource's content*. The term element content is used to describe the data between XML start and end tags. The term *XML document* is used to describe data objects, which conform to the XML specification. *XML-Signature Syntax and Processing, W3C Recommendation 12 February 2002.*

Data Path

The physical or logical route over which data passes; a physical data path may be shared by multiple logical data paths. "Security Requirements for Cryptographic Modules", FIPS Pub. 140-1, Federal Information Processing Standards Publication, January 11, 1994, available at http://csrc.nist.gov/fips/fips1401.htm.

Data Processing

Means a process whereby a computer is used to manipulate information, including the functions of storing, retrieving, sorting, merging, calculating and transforming data according to programmed instructions and those activities required to support this process. The Manitoba Telephone Act, R.S.M. 1970, c. T-40, as amended.

Data processing is the computer processing of input information for the purpose of providing additional, different or restructured information. Second Computer Inquiry (Tentative Decision), 72 F.C.C.2d 358 (F.C.C. 1979).

The use of a computer for the processing of information as distinguished from circuit or message-switching. "Processing" involves the use of the computer for operations which include, *inter alia*, the functions of storing, retrieving, sorting, merging and calculating data, according to programmed instructions. Computer Inquiry (Final Decision), 28 F.C.C.2d 267 (F.C.C. 1971); Computer Inquiry (Tentative Decision), 28 F.C.C.2d 291 (F.C.C. 1970).

The use of a computer for the purpose of processing information wherein: (a) the semantic content, or meaning, of input data is in any way transformed, or (b) the output data constitute a programmed response to input data. Second Computer Inquiry (Notice of Inquiry), 5 C.L.S.R. 1381 (F.C.C. 1976).

The electronically automated processing of information wherein: (a) the information content, or meaning, of the input information is in any way transformed, or (b) the output information constitutes a programmed response to input information. The second condition, (b), brings services such as process control and proprietary information retrieval within the ambit of the definition of data processing. In the process control case, a message or other stimulus results in a change of state in the process which is being controlled. In the proprietary information retrieval case, the arrival of an input message or stimulus — the information request — is operated upon by the processing device and results in an output which is the specific information requested. Second Computer Inquiry (Supplemental Notice), 42 Fed. Reg. 13029 (F.C.C. 1977).

Data Processing Service

A "data processing service" is the offering for hire of computer processing capabilities for the purpose of: (a) transforming or altering for the subscriber of the service the information content or meaning of information provided by the subscriber; or (b) maintaining, managing, or providing a data information bank or information retrieval service whereby information may be selectively retrieved by or for a subscriber to the service; or (c) monitoring or controlling an on-going non-communications process or event. Second Computer Inquiry (Tentative Decision), 72 F.C.C.2d 358 (F.C.C. 1979).

Data processing comprehends at least three reasonably distinct subclauses, which may be commingled in specific applications: arithmetic processing-general commercial accounting, payroll, inventory control, banking and point-of-sale processing, financial and econometric modeling, scientific calculations, etc.; word processing — a rapidly developing application resulting from advances in mass memory technology and work processing software. Applications include: interactive information retrieval systems, management information systems, text editing, translation, typesetting, etc.; process control — the increased reliability and availability of computers is leading to an expansion of applications where a computer is used to monitor and control some process which is occurring continuously — such as a nuclear-powered generating station, an electric power distribution grid, an automatic machine tool, or a fire detection and control system. Second Computer Inquiry (Notice of Inquiry), 5 C.L.S.R. 1381 (F.C.C. 1976).

Data Service

Means a telecommunications service other than a voice service. CNCP Telecommunications: Interconnection with Bell Canada, CRTC Decision 79-11 (May 1979); Tariff Revisions Related to Resale and Sharing, Telecom Decision CRTC 87-2 (Feb. 12, 1987).

Non-voice services. *Report to the Governor in Council: Status of Competition in Canadian Telecommunications Markets, Deployment/Accessibility of Advanced Telecommunications Infrastructure and Services, September, 2001.*

Data Structure

The manner in which data is stored and manipulated. Soft *Computer Consultants Inc. v. Lalehzarzadeh*, [1989] Copyright L. Dec. (CCH) 26,403 (E.D.N.Y. 1988).

Data structure is a precise representation or specification of a data type that consists of (i) basic data type groupings such as integers or characters, (ii) values, (iii) variables, (iv) arrays or groupings of the same data type, (v) records of groupings of different data types, and (vi) pointers or connections between records that set aside space to hold the records values. *Gates Rubber Co. v. Bando American Inc.*, 28 U.S.P.Q. 2d 1503 (10th Cir. 1993).

Data Terminals

Are . . . miniature computers with information-processing capabilities used to generate information and to operate on and alter information received at their inputs . . . The marketing of "smart" remote-access data terminals which incorporate microprocessor technology (miniature computers) and new forms of local memory have accelerated the loss of identity between what previously was generally thought of as "communications" equipment. User versatility has been enhanced in these terminals by configuring them so that the user can determine their functions, capabilities and uses to best fit his needs by altering their programming. These highly sophisticated user terminals are being offered both by communications common carriers and by the unregulated equipment manufacturing sector. Second Computer Inquiry (Tentative Decision), 72 F.C.C.2d 358 (F.C.C. 1979).

Data Type

A data type defines the type of item that an operator acts upon such as a student record or a daily balance. *Gates Rubber Co. v. Bando American Inc.*, 28 U.S.P.Q. 2d 1503 (10th Cir. 1993).

Data Under Voice (DUV)

By this technique, a digital bitstream will be transmitted in an otherwise unused portion of the band width on 4 and 6 GHz microwave radio channels. *Re AT&T*, 41 F.C.C.2d 586 (F.C.C. 1973).

Data Use Identifier (DUI)

A "data use identifier" (DUI) is the name given to a descriptive modification of a basic data element, reflecting a specific use of or reference to it, within a data system. A DUI may be the name of a file on a card or tape or column on a report form or format. It is the name given to the date element within the system design. Automated Regulatory Information System, 37 Fed. Reg. 7638 (Fed. Power. Comm. 1972).

Database (See also Electronic Database)

A database is a collection of data elements that the user puts into the computer; the term refers also to how these elements are organized in records, and how they organized in files. *Dental Office Computer Systems Inc. v. Glutting*, No. CV-86-5613DT (Mich. App. filed August 13, 1987).

A collection of information stored and accessed by electronic means. It may be a collection of full text material, that is to say, existing copyright works, in which case it is an analogy between the database and a generalized or specialized library. It may be a compilation of extracts of works, similar to an anthology or a documentation centre, from which relevant parts of works may be obtained. It may be a collection of material that is in the public domain, such as a list of names and addresses, prices, and reference numbers. There is here a similarity with catalogs, time tables, price lists, and other such reference material in printed form. Lastly, it may consist of the electronic publishing of a single but voluminous work, such as an encyclopedia. Green Paper on Copyright and the Challenge of Technology, The Commission of the European Communities, COM (88) 172 Final (1988).

Means a collection of data in a form capable of being processed and operated on by a computer. U.S. D.O.D. Directive and D.O.D. F.A.R. Supplement, Federal Register, Vol. 53, No. 209 43698.

A collection of data recorded in a form capable of, and for the purpose of, being stored in, processed, and operated on by a computer. The term does not include computer software. Federal Acquisition Regulation (FAR): Rights in Technical Data (Proposed Rules), Federal Register, Vol. 55, No. 199.

Database means a collection of data, works or other materials arranged, stored and accessed by electronic means, and the materials necessary for the operation of the database such as its thesaurus, index or system for obtaining or presenting information; it shall not apply to any computer program used in the making or operation of the database. Amended Proposal for a Council Directive on the Legal Protection of Databases, COM(93) 464 Final-SYN 393 Brussels, October 4, 1993.

A database is a set of data or information stored in an organised and structured way so that that data may be readily retrieved and manipulated. *Powerflex Services Pty Ltd. v. Data Access Corp.* (1997), 37 I.P.R. 436 (Aust. C.A.).

A database or database management system sits on top of the operating system and consists of a series of programmes that organize, manipulate and permit the access to and retrieval of different kinds of data and data files. Examples of database system are Oracle, Informix, Sybase. *Angoss II Partnership v. Trifox Inc.* (1997), [1997] O.J. No. 4969, affirmed (1999), [1999] O.J. No. 4144, leave to appeal dismissed (2000), [1999] S.C.C.A. No. 588, 2000 CarswellOnt 299, 2000 CarswellOnt 3000.

Database Directive

Directive 96/9/EC of the European Parliament and the Council of 11 March 1996 on the legal protection of databases.

Database Management System

Is a program used to store, retrieve, and manipulate data within a computer. *Infosystems Technology Inc. v. Logical Software Inc.*, Vol. 6, No. 5 C.L.R. 831 (4th Cir. 1987).

A database management system is designed to permit the user of a computer to store, update, and retrieve information in an organized and efficient fashion. *Cullinet Software Inc. v. McCormack & Dodge Corp.*, 500 N.E.2d 831 (Mass. App. Ct. 1986), reversed 511 N.E.2d 1101 (Sup. Jud. Ct. Mass. 1987).

Database Program

A program that allows the user to access within the program itself a variety of technical materials and data incorporated into the program's logic and analysis that one would otherwise have to provide on one's own or by reference to some type of data compilation. *Manufacturers Technology Inc. v. Cams Inc.*, 10 U.S.P.Q.2d 1321 (D. Conn. 1989).

Database Software

Database software gives instructions regarding the organization, storage and recovery of data in a database. *Madeley Pty Ltd. v. Touche Ross*, McGarvie, J., Aust. F.C., Dec. 21, 1989 (unreported).

Database Technology

Is used to store, cross-reference and retrieve large amounts of information. Advancing Global Electronic Commerce: Technology Solutions to Public Policy Challenges, The Computer Systems Policy Project, July 1999, available at http://www.cspp.org/projects/july99_cto_report.pdf

Datacom Services

Datacom service is printed page communications, allowing the transmitting or receiving of data or text over the switched telephone network. *Alta. Gov't Telephones v. Canada (CRTC)*, [1985] 2 F.C. 472, reversed [1986] 2 F.C. 179 (Fed. C.A.), reversed [1989] 2 S.C.R. 225.

Datapac

Datapac is a packet switching service wherein the data is broken down into individual packets and transmitted between nodes on the system in the form of the packets. *Alta. Gov't Telephones v. Canada (CRTC)*, [1985] 2 F.C. 472 (T.D.), reversed [1986] 2 F.C. 179 (C.A.), reversed [1989] 2 S.C.R. 225.

Dataspeed 40/4

The Dataspeed 40/4 is a complex of small machines with the cumulative capacity to send and receive messages from a central computer. There is a teletypewriter keyboard for entering messages, a teletypewriter printer for receiving them, and a viewing screen that displays incoming and outgoing information. Outgoing messages can be stored, reviewed, and revised prior to transmission. The Dataspeed 40/4 is more than a conventional teletypewriter, given its enhanced capabilities for storage, correction, and transmission of data, and less than a computer, in that it does not alter the substantive content of the messages typed into or received by it. *IBM v. F.C.C.*, 570 F.2d 452, cert. denied 99 S.Ct 213 (2nd Cir. 1978).

DCS

Digital Control System

DDoS

Distributed Denial of Services Attacks

DES

Data Encryption Standard. "Security Requirements for Cryptographic Modules", FIPS Pub. 140-1, Federal Information Processing Standards Publication, January 11, 1994, available at http://csrc.nist.gov/fips/fips1401.htm.

Debugging

Error removal. *Whelan Associates Inc. v. Jaslow Dental Laboratory Inc.*, 225 U.S.P.Q. 156 (E.D. Pa. 1985), affirmed 797 F.2d 1222 (3rd Cir. 1986).

"Debugging" is a term of art used in the computer software business to describe the correction of errors in a program. *Georgetown College of Science and Arts Ltd. v. Microsystems Engineering Corp.*, 2 C.L.R. 1058 (D.D.C. 1984).

The testing is generally called "debugging". The most common errors arise by reason of improper syntax, human errors in detailing the command steps, and logic. The correction of syntax and other human errors is discovered by reexamination of the computer command language previously written by the programmer. If there is a defect in the design of the system, the designer must reexamine the design and make the appropriate changes. Of interest is the fact that a programmer does not need the expertise of the designer, and need not know the innerworkings of the computer, and can do adequate work with only a general familiarity of its function and a grasp of computer language. *Pezzillo v. General Telephone & Electronics Information Systems, Inc.*, 414 F.Supp. 1257 (D.C. M.D. Tenn. 1976), affirmed 572 F.2d 1189 (6th Cir. 1978).

After the coding is finished, the programmer will run the program on the computer in order to find and correct any logical and syntactical errors. This is known as "debugging" and, once done, the program is complete. *Computer Associates International Inc. v. Altai Inc.*, 23 U.S.P.Q.2d 1241 (2d Cir. 1992); *Matrox Electronic Systems Ltd. v. Gaudreau*, [1993] R.J.Q. 2449 (C.S.).

Once the programming is completed, the system must be tested to determine if the design is effective and has been effectively implemented. In fact, the program is run through the computer using known sample material or with data which will produce a known result. The testing is generally called "debugging". The most common errors arise by reason of improper syntax, human errors in detailing the command steps, and logic in design. The correction of syntax and other human errors are discovered by re-examination of the computer command language previously written by the programmer. If there is a defect in the design of the system, the designer must re-examine the design and make the appropriate changes. Of interest is the fact that a programmer does not need the expertise of the designer, need to know the inner workings of the computer, and can do adequate work with only a general familiarity of its function and a grasp of computer language. *Pezzillo v. General Telephone & Electronics Information Systems, Inc.*, 414 F.Supp 1257 (M.D. Tenn. 1976).

Declare or Define Identifiers

In an attempt to make computer source programs more readable, symbolic descriptive names are assigned to areas of memory. These variable names (identifiers) must be unique within the program module and are usually selected so that they describe the data that they represent. For instance, if a program is working with payroll information, the source code instructions would probably "define" or "declare" areas of memory for "HOURS", "RATE" and "GROSS-PAY". These declarations would follow the syntax of the computer language being used and would allocate the memory area as well as assign a name to it. These names could then be used when referring to the memory areas and the program source code would be easier to understand. *Delrina Corp. v. Triolet Systems, Inc.* (1992), 47 C.P.R. (3d) 1 (Ont. H.C.).

Decoding

The writing of the command orders (translating the narrative from English into computer language, and sometimes referred to as "decoding") is a mechanical process and as a general rule comprises approximately 20% of a programmer's time in implementing a program. *Pezzillo v. General Telephone & Electronics Information Systems, Inc.*, 414 F.Supp. 1257 (D.C. M.D. Tenn. 1976), affirmed 572 F.2d 1189 (6th Cir. 1978).

It is generally conceded that the writing of the command orders (translating the narrative from English into computer language — sometimes referred to as decoding) is a mechanical process and as a general rule comprises approximately 20% of a programmer's time in implementing a program. The other approximately 80% is spent in debugging, i.e., discovering and correcting syntax and human errors in translating the narrative to code plus discovering design errors, calling them to the attention of the analyst, and thereafter, at his direction, correcting them. *Pezzillo v. General Telephone & Electronics Information Systems, Inc.*, 414 F.Supp 1257 (M.D. Tenn. 1976).

Decompilation

The working back from the object code of a computer program to a version of the source code. This process may involve a substantial recreation or reproduction of the source code of the original program. Decompilation is achieved using a computer program called a decompiler. Computer Software Protection: Australia, Copyright Law Review Committee 1995.

Decryption

The translation back to plaintext when the message is received by someone with an appropriate "key". *Bernstein v. United States Department of State*, 1996 W.L. 186106 (N.D. Cal. 1996).

The inverse function of encryption; to change ciphertext into plain text. A Cryptology Policy Framework for Electronic Commerce, Task Force on Electronic Commerce, Industry Canada, February 1998.

Is the reverse process of transforming the ciphertext message or document into the original plaintext. *Junger v. Secretary of Commerce*, case No. 1-96-CV-1723, (N.D. Ohio.1998).

Means the inverse function of encryption. *OECD Guidelines for Cryptography Policy*, March 27, 1997, available at *www.oecd.org*.

DeCSS (De-Content Scrambling System)

DeCSS is a software utility, or computer program, that enables users to break the CSS copy protection system and hence to view DVDs on unlicensed players and make digital copies of DVD movies. The quality of the motion pictures decrypted by DeCSS is virtually identical to that of encrypted movies on DVD. *Universal City Studios, Inc. v. Reimerdes* 55 U.S.P.Q. 2d 1873 (S. D.N.Y. 2000).

Deflection Yoke

A deflection yoke is a donut shaped device that fits over the neck of a CRT. When excited by electrical signals, the yoke causes an electron beam to be scanned across the face of the CRT to create the picture. *Motorola Inc. v. Computer Displays International Inc.*, 222 U.S.P.Q. 844 (7th Cir. 1984).

Design

In its ordinary sense, the word "design" would include the choice of hardware and software to work in combination with each other to do a particular job. *USM Corp. v. Arthur D. Little Systems, Inc.*, 546 N.E. 2d 888 (Mass. App. 1989).

Detailed Design Data

Means technical data that describes the physical configuration and performance characteristics of an item or component in sufficient detail to ensure that an item or component produced in accordance with the technical data will be essentially identical to the original item or component. U.S. D.O.D. Directive and D.O.D. F.A.R. Supplement, Federal Register, Vol. 53, No. 209 43698.

Detailed Design, Manufacturing, or Process Data

Means technical data of sufficient detail to enable the essentially identical reproduction, or manufacture, of an item, component, or the performance of process, to which the data pertains. Federal Acquisition Regulation (FAR): Rights in Technical Data (Proposed Rules), Federal Register, Vol. 55, No. 199.

Detailed Manufacturing or Process Data

Means technical data that describes the steps, sequences, and conditions of manufacturing, processing, or assembly used by the manufacturer to produce an item or component or to perform a process. U.S. D.O.D. Directive and D.O.D. F.A.R. Supplement, Federal Register Vol. 53, No. 209 43698.

Developed

Means that the item, component, or process exists and is workable. Thus the item or component must have been constructed or the process practiced. Workability is generally established when the item, component or process has been analyzed or tested sufficiently to demonstrate to reasonable people skilled in the applicable art that there is a high probability that it will operate as intended. Whether, how much, and what type of analysis or testing is required to establish workability depends on the nature of the item, component, or process, and the state of the art. To be considered "developed", the item, component, or process need not be at the stage where it could be offered for sale or sold on the commercial market, nor must the item, component, or process be actually reduced to practice within the meaning of Title 35 of the United States Code. U.S. D.O.D. Directive and D.O.D. F.A.R. Supplement, Federal Register Vol. 53, No. 209 43698.

Device

An invention or contrivance; peripheral device. *Autodesk Australia Pty Ltd. v. Dyason* (1989), 15 I.P.R. 1 (Aus. Fed. Ct.), reversed [1990] A.I.P.C. 36,446 (Aus. Fed. Ct. FC).

A computer disk encoded with a software program is a device within the meaning of 18 U.S.C. 1953. *United States of America v. Mendelsohn*, Comp. Lit. Reptr. 10,973 (9th Cir. 1990).

Diagnostic Software

These programs instruct the computer on how to locate, diagnose and even correct malfunctions. *ISC-Bunker Ramo Corporation v. Altech, Inc.*, 765 F.Supp. 1310 (N.D. Ill. 1990).

Digest

A much condensed version of a message produced by processing the message by a hash algorithm. Commonly, the digest has a fixed length and is not dependent on the length of the original message. *Cryptography's Role in Securing the Information Society*, United States National Research Council, 1996.

Digital

Information expressed in binary patterns of ones and zeros. *The Challenge of the Information Highway: Final Report of the Information Highway Advisory Council* (September 1995).

Of or pertaining to information represented by patterns made up from qualities existing in two states only, on and off, as pulses. *Autodesk Australia Pty Ltd. v. Dyason* (1989), 15 I.P.R. 1 (Aus. Fed. Ct.), reversed [1990] A.I.P.C. 36,446 (Aus. Fed. Ct. FC).

Information expressed in binary patterns of zeros and ones. Ministry of Revenue Advisory Committee, Report of the Committee On Electronic Commerce, April 30, 1998, Industry Canada.

Describes the way information, whether numbers, text, pictures or sound, is represented as strings of 0s or 1s (digital bits). Information in digital form can be distributed, copied, stored or manipulated in many different ways without loss of quality. Storage media for digital information is electronic, and includes computer memories, CD ROM, and DVD. *Digital Technology and the Copyright Act 1994: A Discussion Paper, Competition and Enterprise Branch, July 2001 (New Zealand)*.

Digital Audio and Video Production or Post Production

Digital audio and video production or post production (works are those) in which traditional cultural activities (such as the recording of music or the making of film) are rendered more precise and less costly through the addition of new technologies within the production process. Study on New Media and Copyright, *Final Report* (Nordicity Group Ltd., June 30, 1994) prepared for Industry Canada, New Media, Information Technologies Industry Branch.

Digital cash

A token-based currency that translates into equivalent real currency units that are guaranteed by a bank. Also referred to as electronic cash or e-cash. Ministry of Revenue Advisory Committee, Report of the Committee On Electronic Commerce, April 30, 1998, Industry Canada.

Digital Certificates

An electronic third party "voucher" that a message is authentic. This is conceptually similar to paper-based certificates, such as birth certificates, passports, and drivers licenses. The certificate (e.g., a driver's license) issued by a credible third party (state government) indicates that the information carried in the message (name, address, etc.) is authentic. The Emerging Digital Economy, United States Department of Commerce, http://www.ecommerce.gov.

Digital Computer (See also Computer)

A digital computer is conveniently thought of functionally as composed of five elements: Input, Storage (sometimes called Memory), Control, Logic (sometimes called Arithmetic), and Output. Control and Logic are sometimes referred to jointly as the Central Processing Unit (CPU). The function of Input is to get instructions and data, prepared in some computer-readable form, into the computer. Storage retains the data and instructions so entered, as well as the intermediate and final results of processing. Control directs the whole process, in accordance with predetermined instructions kept in Storage. Logic performs the arithmetic and logical operations. Output disgorges the requisite information in accordance with instructions. *Computer System of America v. Western Reserve Life Assurance Co. of Ohio*, 475 N.E.2d 745 (Mass. App. 1985).

A digital computer, as distinguished from an analog computer, operates on data expressed in digits, solving a problem by doing arithmetic as a person would do it by head and hand. Some of the digits are stored as components of the computer. Others are introduced into the computer in a form which it is designed to recognize. The computer operates then upon both new and previously stored data. *Gottschalk v. Benson*, 409 U.S. 63 (1972).

Digital computers . . . are machines . . . used to perform three types of functions electronically: (1) arithmetic calculations; (2) logical operations (e.g., comparing values to determine whether one is larger); and (3) storage and display of the results. Because computers can perform millions of operations of these types in a single second, they can be used to solve problems too complex, or too repetitious and boring, to be solved manually. Developments to the current state of the art have already transformed many areas of business, educational, and recreational activity, and they support speculations about more striking achievements in the future. *Lotus Development Corp. v. Paperback Software International*, 15 U.S.P.Q.2d 1577 (D. Mass. 1990).

A digital computer consists in essence of a memory and a central processing unit ("cpu"). The memory consists of storage elements each capable of holding a number of some prescribed length. This number is represented in binary form, that is, consisting of a string of 0's and 1's. Each storage element of the memory has a unique address, and may be selected by the cpu for the purpose either of copying the number stored at a particular address in to the cpu, or for transferring a number in the cpu to the selected storage element. *Cantor Fitzgerald International v. Tradition (UK) Ltd.,* [1999] I.N.L.R. No. 23 (Ch.D.).

Digital Licenses

Can be attached to software, music, video or information and can allow for limited use of the product in exchange for a fee or other agreed to terms. Advancing Global Electronic Commerce: Technology Solutions to Public Policy Challenges, The Computer Systems Policy Project, July 1999, available at http://www.cspp.org/projects/july99_cto_report.pdf.

Digital Pseudonym

A digital pseudonym is a method of identifying an individual through an alternate digital pseudo-identity, created for a particular purpose. It permits users to preserve their anonymity by concealing their true identities. While users are not "known" to service providers in the conventional sense, they are, nonetheless, known by their pseudonyms, for the purposes of conducting transactions. Privacy-Enhancing Technologies: The Path to Anonymity, Information and Privacy Commissioner/Ontario, August 1995, available at http://www.ipc.on.ca.

Is an alternative pseudo-identity that a user may choose to assume in order to engage in a particular transaction, communication or service in an anonymous manner. One can select a different pseudonym for every service provider, or for use each time that a particular service is used. The Emerging Digital Economy, United States Department of Commerce, http://www.ecommerce.gov.

Digital Radio

Microwave transmission of digital data via radio transmitters or radio broadcasting using a digital signal. *The Challenge of the Information Highway: Final Report of the Information Highway Advisory Council* (September 1995).

Digital Scanner

A device that allows users to monitor radiocommunication frequencies automatically. *The Challenge of the Information Highway: Final Report of the Information Highway Advisory Council* (September 1995).

Digital Service

The transmission of binary data signals (a continuous string of zeros and ones). Such service is used for computer-to-computer communications or for transmission of digitally encoded analog signals in telephone and digital cellular networks. *Report to the Governor in Council: Status of Competition in Canadian Telecom-*

munications Markets, Deployment/Accessibility of Advanced Telecommunications Infrastructure and Services, September, 2001.

Digital Signature

A "digital signature" is a cryptographic transformation of data which, when appended to a data unit, provides the service of origin authentication, data integrity and signer non-repudiation. Security and Electronic Authorization and Authentication Guideline, Communications Security Establishment, Government of Canada September 1995, CID/01/15.

Data appended to a part of a message that enable a recipient to verify the integrity and origin of a message. *The Challenge of the Information Highway: Final Report of the Information Highway Advisory Council* (September 1995).

A digital signature is a unique sequence of digits that is computed based on (1) the work being protected, (2) the digital signature algorithm being used, and (3) the key used in digital signature generation. National Information Infrastructure: A Preliminary Draft of the Report of the Working Group on Intellectual Property Rights, July 1994.

A cryptographic transformation of data which, when associated with a data unit (such as an electronic file), provides the services of origin authentication, data integrity, and signer non-repudiation. A Cryptology Policy Framework for Electronic Commerce, Task Force on Electronic Commerce, Industry Canada, February 1998.

A unique sequence of data appended to a message that allows a recipient to verify the integrity and origin of the message and prevents the repudiation of the message. Digital signatures are not designed to provide confidentiality. Ministry of Revenue Advisory Committee, Report of the Committee On Electronic Commerce, April 30, 1998, Industry Canada.

A digital signature is commonly interpreted as involving a mathematical summary ("Ash") of a document, encrypted by an individual's secret encryption key. (If the message is short, there is no hash: the message itself is encrypted, not for the purpose of confidentiality for the message, but for the purpose of proving who sent the message.) Generally, encryption is tied to a unique encryption key, which only one person has. If a message is encrypted with that key, it proves that the message was sent by the person who purportedly holds that key, and thus serves the same function as a signature, although it is not similar in nature to a handwritten signature. By way of contrast, a digitized signature means reproducing an electronic image of a person's handwritten signature (such as by faxing a document signed by hand). The received fax will have a digitized signature on it. *A Survey of Legal Issues Relating to the Security of Electronic Information*, Department of Justice, Canada.

Is the result of a transformation of a message by means of a cryptographic system using keys such that a person who has the initial message can determine: (a) whether the transformation was created using the key that corresponds to the signer's key; and (b) whether the message has been altered since the transformation was made. Public Key Infrastructure Management in the Government of Canada, Treasury Board of Canada Secretariat, May 27, 1999, available at http://www.tbs-sct.gc.ca/pubs_pol/ciopubs/PKI/pki1_e.html.

Means a transformation of a message using an asymmetric cryptosystem such that a person having the initial message and the signer's public key can accurately determine whether: (a) the transformation was created using the private key that corresponds to the signer's public key; and (b) the message has been altered since the transformation was made. *Utah Digital Signature Act* 46-3, available at http://www.le.state.ut.us/code/TITLE46/htm/46_03004.htm.

A non-forgeable transformation of data that allows the proof of the source (with non-repudiation) and the verification of the integrity of that data. "Security Requirements for Cryptographic Modules", FIPS Pub. 140-1, Federal Information Processing Standards Publication, January 11, 1994, available at http://csrc.nist.gov/fips/fips1401.htm.

A digital signature can be defined to mean a transformation of a record using asymmetric cryptosystem and a hash function so that a person having the initial message and the signor's public key can accurately determine (i) whether the transformation was created using the private key that corresponds to the signor's public key; and (ii) whether the initial record has been altered since the transformation was made. Electronic Commerce: Building A Legal Framework, Report of the Electronic Commerce Expert Group (Australia) to the Attorney General, 31 March, 1998.

Means a type of an electronic signature created by transforming an electronic record using a message digest function, and encrypting the resulting transformation with an asymmetric cryptosystem using the signer's private key such that any person having the initial untransformed electronic record, the encrypted transformation, and the signer's corresponding public key can accurately determine whether the transformation was created using the private key that corresponds to the signer's public key; and whether the initial electronic record has been altered since the transformation was made. A digital signature is a security procedure. *Illinois Electronic Commerce Security Act* 1998 5 Ill. Comp. Stat. 175.

A transformation of a message using an asymmetric cryptosystem such that a person having the ensured message and the ensurer's public key can accurately determine: (i) whether the transformation was created using the private key that corresponds to the signer's public key, and (ii) whether the signed message has been altered since the transformation was made. General Usage for International Digitally Insured Commerce (Guidec), International Chamber of Commerce, 1997, available at http://www.icc.wbo.org/guidec2.htm.

A digital signature is the electronic equivalent of a handwritten signature. Just as a signature or sealing wax on a document is proof of its authenticity, a digital signature provides the same, if not better, authentication. It provides the necessary assurance that only the individual who created the signature could have done so, and it permits all others to verify its authenticity. A particular type of encryption, "public key encryption," considered to be the most reliable and secure form of encryption ever developed, forms the basis for digital signatures. *Privacy-Enhancing Technologies: The Path to Anonymity, Information and Privacy Commissioner/Ontario*, August 1995, available at http://www.ipc.on.ca.

An electronic version of a signature. One of a number of signature alternative technologies, its uses cryptographic techniques to verify that the person who sent the message in fact sent the message and that the contents have not been altered since the message was sent. *The Emerging Digital Economy, United States Department of Commerce*, http://www.ecommerce.gov.

Digital signatures are the electronic equivalent of handwritten signatures. Like handwritten signatures, which are used to authenticate paper documents, digital signatures placed on electronic documents serve the same purpose. Digital signatures can protect against spoofing and message forgeries, but they offer little privacy since they are intended to identify the originating party. *Identity Theft: Who's Using Your Name?, Information and Privacy Commissioner/Ontario*, June 1997, available at http://www.ipc.on.ca.

An electronic identifier attached to an electronic document. Analogous to a handwritten signature. The term is almost always taken to mean identify or generated by using public key cryptography. The term electronic signature is used in a broader context to indicate the processes that include digital signatures. *Building Trust and Confidence in Electronic Commerce: A Framework for Electronic Authentication in Canada*, prepared by the Electronic Commerce Branch, Industry Canada, July 2000, available at *http://e-comm.ic.gc.ca* .

An electronic signature created using a Private Signature Key. *The Office of the Federal Privacy Commissioner (Australia), Consultation Paper, (June 2001).*

Digital Subscriber Loop (DSL)

A local loop equipped to allow high-speed data transmission. *Report to the Governor in Council: Status of Competition in Canadian Telecommunications Markets, Deployment/Accessibility of Advanced Telecommunications Infrastructure and Services, September, 2001.*

Digital Transmission

The transmission of information by converting it into binary form, that is a series of zeros and ones. In contrast to analog transmission. *Submission of the Director of Investigation and Research to the CRTC Re Public Notice CRTC 1994-130.*

Digital Typefont

Digital typefont is a bitmapped digital representation of an actual analog typeface design, stored in binary form on magnetic or optical media, or Read-Only Memory (ROM) mounted on a circuit board. Sometimes the ROM on the circuit board is assembled into a plastic cartridge which is inserted into a laser printer or other microprocessor-driven device. When decoded and interpreted by the "bitmapping code" software, the digital representation of the design will reproduce the appropriate character. U.S. Library of Congress, Copyright Office, 53 F.R. 38110.

Digital Wallet

Is software that resides on a user's computer and is capable of storing and dispensing electronic money. Advancing Global Electronic Commerce: Technology Solutions to Public Policy Challenges, The Computer Systems Policy Project, July 1999, available at http://www.cspp.org/projects/july99_cto_report.pdf.

Digital Watermarks

Use cryptography to embed unnoticeable marks in voice, video, and data files. The marks are virtually unremovable and can be read by a device that has the proper deciphering information. The mark can provide information on who owns the content and to whom it may have been licensed. Advancing Global Electronic Commerce: Technology Solutions to Public Policy Challenges, The Computer Systems Policy Project, July 1999, available at http://www.cspp.org/projects/july99_cto_report.pdf.

Are imperceptible bits of information embedded within audio, video or text data that can provide security and authentication. Digital Watermarks do not affect the integrity of the original data. Advancing Global Electronic Commerce: Technology Solutions to Public Policy Challenges, Computer Systems Policy Project (CSPP), available at http://www.cspp.org/projects/july99_cto_jyreport.pdf.

The embedding of code or information within a digital copy of a copyright work or other material that cannot easily be removed. It might also be undetectable to users. The information contained in a digital water-mark will usually be electronic rights management information. Water-marking technology can allow copyright owners and other rightholders to authenticate digital copies as originals, trace the source of unauthorised copies and potentially also provide information on the use made of digital works. *Digital Technology and the Copyright Act 1994: A Discussion Paper, Competition and Enterprise Branch, July 2001 (New Zealand).*

Digitization

The conversion of text, sound, images, video and other content into a common digitized format. Connection Community Content, *The Challenge of the Information Highway: Final Report of the Information Highway Advisory Council* (September 1995).

The conversion of an analog or continuous signal into a series of ones and zeros, i.e., into a digital format. *The Challenge of the Information Highway: Final Report of the Information Highway Advisory Council* (September 1995).

The conversion of an analog or continuous signal into a series of zeros and ones – that is, into a digital format. Software applications, written text, photographs, and audio and video signals are or can be digitized and transmitted over computer networks. Ministry of Revenue Advisory Committee, Report of the Committee On Electronic Commerce, April 30, 1998, Industry Canada.

Digitization is the conversion of analogue or print information (for example, sound or a graphical image) into digital form. *Digital Technology and the Copyright Act 1994: A Discussion Paper, Competition and Enterprise Branch, July 2001 (New Zealand).*

Digitizer

Is an electronic device that converts computer language into eye-readable configurations. *Gtco Corp. v. Kontron Elektronik Gmbh*, Vol. 6, No. 5 C.L.R. 838 (4th Cir. Ca.).

Diodes, Transistors and Similar Semiconductor Devices

These are semiconductor devices the operation of which depends on variations in resistivity on the application of an electric field. *An Act to Implement the Free Trade Agreement between Canada and the United States of America*, S.C. 1988, c. 65.

Disassemblers

Devices called "disassemblers" or "decompilers" "read" the electronic signals for "0" and "1" that are produced while the program is being run, store the resulting object code in computer memory, and translate the object code into source code. Both assembly and disassembly devices are commercially available, and both types of devices are widely used within the software industry. *Sega Enterprises Ltd. v. Accolade Inc.* (1992), 24 U.S.P.Q.2d 1561.

Through the use of a program called a "disassembler", it is possible to convert object code into a form of source code; but the disassembler is unable to provide the comments, variable names, link maps and other information which is included in the ... source code. *Otis Elevator Co. v. Intelligent Systems, Inc.*, 3 CCH Comp. Cas. 46,510 (Conn. S.C. 1990).

Disassembly (of a Computer Program)

Disassembly of a computer program is done by translating the machine or object code into humanly-readable assembly language. *E.F. Johnson Co. v. Uniden Corp. of America*, 623 F.Supp. 1485 (D.C. Minn. 1985).

This process involves the purchase of a commercially available article into which the program can be fed and which will then convert the programme back into its original format, a computer language called the "source code," from the machine code. *Milltronics Ltd. v. Hycontrol Ltd.*, Ch. D., Harman J., December 20, 1988 (unreported), affirmed C.A., The Times, March 2, 1989 (unreported).

The working back from object code to assembler code, i.e., a special case of decompilation. Disassembly is achieved using a computer program called a disassembler. Computer Software Protection: Australia, Copyright Law Review Committee 1995.

"Disassembly" which is a reverse engineering term that includes both disassembly and decompilation, is a procedure for translating the machine language program into an assembly language program. *Bateman v. Mnemonics Inc.,* 38 U.S.P.Q. 2d 1225 (11th Cir. 1996).

Disassembly Program

One which converts machine language code into humanly-readable assembly language. *E.F. Johnson Co. v. Uniden Corp. of America,* 623 F.Supp. 1485 (D.C. Minn. 1985).

Disclosure

Means with respect to personal information (a) the release of personal information collected from a child in identifiable form by an operator for any purpose, except where such information is provided to a person other than the operator who provides support for the internal operations of the website and does not disclose or use that information for any other purpose; and (b) making personal information collected from a child by a website or online service directed to children or with actual knowledge that such information was collected from a child, publicly available in identifiable form, by any means including by a public posting, through the Internet, or through (i) a home page of a website; (ii) a pen pal service; (iii) an electronic mail service; (iv) a message board; or (v) a chat room. *Children's Online Privacy Protection Act* of 1998.

Dish Antenna

An antenna used for receiving satellite signals. It is so called because its shape must be a parabola causing it to resemble a large dish. The parabola shape allows weak satellite signals to bounce off the inside of the antenna dish and be concentrated at a single point for pick up by an electronic receiving device. Submission of the Director of Investigation and Research to the CRTC Re Public Notice CRTC 1994-130.

Disk

A disk is a magnetic data storage device. It operates within a disk drive. *USM Corp. v. Arthur D. Little Systems, Inc.,* 546 N.E. 2d 888 (Mass. App. 1989).

Information is stored electronically on disks. The large storage of information and data, often called the memory of the computer, is made on a relatively large disk called a "hard disk". A microcomputer which operates on its own would have a hard disk incorporated in it or attached to it by a communication line. Information is stored electronically on a hard disk. Information of a particular category is stored as a unit in a particular area of the hard disk and is referred to as a "file". To retrieve stored information, a drive head moves to the precise point on the hard disk where the required item of information is stored and electronically retrieves it. The files of information constitute the database of the computer. *Madeley Pty Ltd. v. Touche Ross*, McGarvie, J., Aust. Fed. Ct., Dec. 21, 1989 (unreported).

A physical storage device that is capable of storing large volumes of data permanently. The data is stored on circular "platters" that are rotated and provide random access. These devices usually use some form of magnetic material similar to that of an audio recording tape. In some cases, the recording media is removable and may also be referred to as a disc. *Delrina Corp. v. Triolet Systems, Inc.* (1992), 47 C.P.R. (3d) 1 (Ont. H.C.).

Disk Access

The access time of a disk is the amount of time required to physically locate and retrieve stored data necessary for a program instruction (known as "disk read"), or to physically locate available, unoccupied space on the disk and write new data in that area (known as a "disk write"). Such a read or write is known as a disk access. Disk accessing is traditionally the most time consuming action performed by the computer. A calculation which is used to help predict response time is known as the disk-utilization factor. The calculation expresses the number of disk accesses required in a particular time period as a percentage of the total number of disk accesses available during that time period. *USM Corp. v. Arthur D. Little Systems, Inc.*, 546 N.E. 2d 888 (Mass. App. 1989).

Disk Address

In order to be able to store and retrieve information using any storage media, there must be a system of identifying locations within the storage media. In the case of disk storage media, the address is usually made up of the physical disk device (*ie.*, disk #1, disk #2) that contains the magnetic recording media plus a physical position on the disk media. The MPE operating system models a disk device as a list of sectors (256 character pieces) of storage. An MPE disk address would therefore be specified as a device plus a sector offset within that device. *Delrina Corp. v. Triolet Systems, Inc.* (1992), 47 C.P.R. (3d) 1 (Ont. H.C.).

Disk Controller

A controller, more formally called a disk processing unit ("DPU") controller board, is a piece of computer equipment which allows a user of a main computer to obtain information which is stored in a disk drive or to store additional information in a disk drive. *Southern Data Systems, Inc. v. Michael Greer*, reprinted in Comp. Ind. Lit. Reptr. 9887 (D.C.E.D.N. Cal. 1989).

Disk Drive

A disk drive is a unit which contains the motors and associated electronics for storing (writing) and retrieving (reading) data on a disk. A disk drive controller basically controls and evaluates the flow of information going from the Central

Processing Unit (CPU) to the disk or vice versa. While in operation, the disk rotates continuously in one direction and bits of information are read off of or are written onto the disk as it rotates. A hard disk controller performs the controller operations for hard disks. *Advanced Micro Devices, Inc. and Intel Corp.*, CCH Comp. Cases 60,218 (Arb. Award. 1990).

Diskette

A diskette is a storage medium for data. Sometimes called a "floppy disk," it is used in conjunction with computers. Computer programs are recorded on diskettes. Some diskettes are blank when sold and the buyer records thereon such computer programs as he chooses. Others are sold with computer programs already recorded thereon. *Apple Computer Inc. v. Formula International Inc.*, 594 F.Supp. 617 (C.D. Cal. 1984).

Display Monitor

A display monitor is an electronic device used to display data on the screen of a CRT ... Display monitors are used in word processing equipment and home computers. *Motorola Inc. v. Computer Displays International Inc*, 222 U.S.P.Q. 844 (7th Cir. 1984).

Distance Contract

Means any contract concerning goods or services concluded between a supplier and a consumer under an organized distance sales or service-provision scheme run by the supplier, who, for the purpose of the contract, makes exclusive use of one or more means of distance communication up to and including the moment at which the contract is concluded. *European Parliament and Council Directive on the Protection of Consumers in Respect of Distance Contracts*, May 20, 1997, Directive 97/7.

Distance Education

Education using different media such as correspondence, radio and television, but requiring little or no physical attendance at the institution offering the courses and accredited certification. *The Challenge of the Information Highway: Final Report of the Information Highway Advisory Council* (September 1995).

Distinguished Name

Is a unique, unambiguous name that the Certification Authority assigns to an external subscriber or an employee. Public Key Infrastructure Management in the Government of Canada, Treasury Board of Canada Secretariat, May 27, 1999, available at http://www.tbs-sct.gc.ca/pubs_pol/ciopubs/PKI/pki1_e.html.

A unique identifier assigned to each Key-holder, having the structure required by the Certificate Profile. *The Office of the Federal Privacy Commissioner (Australia), Consultation Paper, (June 2001).*

Distributed Computer Network

A new phenomenon . . . wherein computers and terminals are performing both data processing and communications control applications, both within the network and at the customer's premises. These networks are being constructed by common carriers and also by private entities using carrier furnished dedicated channels. Second Computer Inquiry (Tentative Decision), 72 F.C.C.2d 358 (F.C.C. 1979).

Distributed Network

One in which data processing and communications processing capabilities are distributed, to varying degrees, among a number of processing units . . . From a technical point of view, processing can be placed anywhere — within the network or outside the network interface — giving one greater flexibility in designing equipment and structuring various service offerings. Second Computer Inquiry (Supplemental Notice), 42 Fed. Reg. 13029 (F.C.C. 1977).

Distribution Undertaking

Any undertaking for the reception of broadcasting and the retransmission thereof by radio waves or other means of telecommunication to more than one permanent or temporary residence or dwelling unit or to another such undertaking. *Broadcasting Act*, S.C. 1991, c. 11.

DivX

DivX is a compression program available for download over the Internet. It compresses video files in order to minimize required storage space, often to facilitate transfer over the Internet or other networks. *Universal City Studios, Inc. v. Reimerdes,* 55 U.S.P.Q. 2d 1873 (S. D.N.Y. 2000).

Document Management

An information management system that manages the capture, distribution, maintenance, and disposal of source records of an organization in a controlled manner. National Standard of Canada, Microfilm and Electronic Images as documentary evidence, Can/CGSB-72.11-93.

Documentation

"Documentation" is the general term for the material that a programmer must give to a user to explain how the program runs. *Whelan Associates Inc. v. Jaslow Dental Laboratory Inc.*, 225 U.S.P.Q. 156 (E.D. Pa. 1985), affirmed 797 F.2d 1222 (3rd Cir. 1986).

Means manuals and other media, such as printed matter, magnetic tapes, discs, and microfiche, that have been or are developed for subject software by or for either party, on which is transferred to customers a description of, but not including, any computer program and shall include manuals that describe architectures implemented or intended to be implemented in subject software. *IBM v. Fujitsu*

Ltd., Copyright L.R. (CCH) 20,517 (Am. Arbtn. Assoc. Comm. Arbtn. Trib. 1988).

Documents

The files and programs stored on magnetic media are "documents," just as files in programs stored on paper are. The difference between them is the media and the techniques used to access that file or information. *Prism Hospital Software Inc. v. Hospital Medical Records Institute* (1987), 18 B.C.L.R. (2d) 34 (S.C.), leave to appeal to B.C.C.A. refused (1987), 21 B.C.L.R. (2d) 345 (C.A.).

Includes, unless the context requires otherwise, any record of information, however recorded or stored, whether in printed form, on film, by electronic means or otherwise. *New Brunswick Evidence Act*, C. E-11.

Domain Name

Every Internet user has a unique address consisting of one or more address components. This address is commonly referred to as the "domain" or "domain name". On the Internet, domain name serves as the primary identifier of the Internet user. *Panavision International, LP v. Toeppen*, 938 F.Supp. 616 (C.D. Cal. 1996).

In its most generic form, a fully qualified domain name consists of three elements. Taking "winslow.net66.com" as an example, the three elements are the hostname (winslow), a domain name (net 66) and a top level domain name (com). A given host looks up the IP addresses of other hosts on the Internet through a system known as "domain name service". *Intermatic Inc. v. Toeppen*, 40 U.S.P.Q. (2d) 1412 (N.D. Ill. 1996).

Domain names serve as a primary identifier of an Internet user. *Zippo Manufacturing Company v. Zippo Dot Com, Inc.*, 952 F.Supp. 1119 (W.D.Penn. 1997).

A domain name represents a record within the Domain Name System, such as Whitehouse.gov. The Emerging Digital Economy, United States Department of Commerce, http://www.ecommerce.gov.

Domain names consist of a second-level domain "simply a term or series of terms (e.g., westcoastvideo)" followed by a top-level domain, many of which describe the nature of the enterprise. Top-level domains include ".com" (commercial), ".edu" (educational), ".org" (non-profit and miscellaneous organizations), ".gov" (government), ".net" (networking provider), and ".mil" (military).... Commercial entities generally use the ".com" top-level domain, which also serves as a catch-all top-level domain. To obtain a domain name, an individual or entity files an application with Network Solutions listing the domain name the applicant wants. Because each web page must have a unique domain name, Network Solutions checks to see whether the requested domain name has already been assigned to someone else. If so, the applicant must choose a different domain name. Other than requiring an applicant to make certain representations, Network Solutions does not make an independent determination about a registrant's right to use a particular domain name. *Brookfield Communications, Inc. v. West Coast Entertainment Corporation*, 174 F. 3d 1036 (9th Cir. 1999).

The unique name that identifies an Internet site (e.g. *www.yourbusiness.ca*). *Domain Name System Reform and Related Internet Governance Issues: A Consultation Paper*, Industry Canada available at *www.strategis.gc.ca*

Internet domain names are comparable to telephone numbers, but are of greater importance, since there is no satisfactory Internet equivalent to a telephone directory. A domain name mirroring a corporate name may be a valuable corporate asset, since it facilitates communication with customers. The uniqueness of an Internet address is ensured by registration with the Internet Network Information Centre. *Haelan Products Inc. v. Beso Biological Research Inc.*, 43 U.S.P.Q. 2d 1672 (E.D. L.A. 1997).

An Internet domain name is an alias which facilitates the use of computers. *Interstellar Starship Services Limited v. Epix, Inc.*, 983 F.Supp. 1331 (D.Or. 1997).

Domain names are used to locate information on the Internet. Each computer or network linked to the Internet has a unique numerical address called, in Internet Protocol Number ("IP number"). *Academy of Motion Picture Arts and Sciences v. Network Solutions Inc.*, 45 U.S.P.Q. 2d 1463 (C.D.Cal. 1997).

The domain name also functions as a "World Wide Web" address, if proceeded by the letters www (i.e. *www.aol.com*) *Juno Online Service L.P. v. Juno Lighting Inc.*, 44 U.S.P.Q. 2d 1913 (N.D.Ill. 1997).

All subscribers to Internet obtain a "domain name" which is really an electronic address. *PEINET Inc. v. O'Brian* (1995), 61 C.P.R. (3d) 334 (PEI.S.C.).

A domain name can be likened to an address. It identifies a particular Internet site. A particular domain name will only be allocated to one company or individual. It represents that company's computer site and is the means by which that company's customers can find it on the Internet. *Pitman Training Ltd. v. Nominet UK*, CH 1997 F 1984 (Ch.D.).

A string of alpha-numeric characters that is maintained in a domain name database and refers to a physical Internet address. *Framework for the administration of the .CA domain name system*, Canadian Domain Name Consultative Committee, September 15, 1998, available at *www.cira.ca/documents.html*

Domain names are the familiar and easy to remember names used in lieu of the difficult to remember Internet Protocol (IP) address numbers. IP addresses are used to locate computers on the Internet. *Canadian Internet Registration Authority, Frequently Asked Questions*, available at *www.cira.ca*

A domain name refers to a computer, and does not refer to a particular file, such as a web page. Instead, a particular file on the Internet, such as a web page, is identified by its Uniform Resources Located ("URL"), which includes the domain name, identifies the file, indicates the protocol required to access the file. *America Online, Inc. v. Shih-hsien Huang*, 2000 U.S. Dist. LEXIS 10232 (E.D. Vir. 2000).

A domain name is an alphanumeric means of determining the appropriate IP address by way of the DNS. *America Online, Inc. vs. Shih-hsien Huang,* 2000 U.S. Dist. LEXIS 10232 (E.D. Vir. 2000).

A domain name is a means of determining a particular computer address by way of a process that includes the registry and registrar functions of NSI (and other entities with similar responsibilities), as well as the operation of DNS name servers scattered across the Internet, almost all of which are operated and controlled by entities other than NSI or any other registrar. *America Online, Inc. vs. Shih-hsien Huang,* 2000 U.S. Dist. LEXIS 10232 (E.D. Vir. 2000).

Domain name is a convenient shorthand for users of the Internet, giving Internet users the option of using readily understandable proper names to identify themselves and their communications. *America On-Line, Inc. v. The Christian Brothers et al,* 98 Civ. 8959 (DAV April 17, 2001).

A domain name, the address given to a webpage, consists of two parts: a top level domain and a secondary level domain. *Bihari v. Gross,* 56 U.S.P.Q. 2d 1489 (S.D.N.Y. 2000).

A domain name tells users where they can find a particular web page, much like a street address tells people where they can find a particular home or business. Domain names consist of two parts: the top level domain name (TLD) and secondary level domain name (SLD). The TLD is the suffix, identifying the nature of the site. The SLD is a prefix, identifying the site's owners. Thus in the domain name *Duek.edu,* ".edu" is the TLD, identifying the site as affiliated with an educational institution. "Duke" is the SLD, identifying the owner as Duke University. *Virtual Works Inc. v. Volkswagen of America Inc.,* 57 U.S.P.Q. 2d 1547 (4th Cir. 2001).

Businesses and people may secure domain names that are usually shorter than Internet Protocol Addresses and have meaning in one or more human languages ("Domain Names"). Domain Names are "mapped" to particular Internet Protocol Addresses so that an internet user can reach a particular computer. Domain Names have two key components, namely the top level domain name ("TLD") and the second level domain name ("SLD"). The TLD consists of two or three letters located at the far right of any domain name preceded by a decimal point. Examples include ".com", ".net", and ".ca". SLDs must be registered with non-governmental registrars in combination with a particular TLD. For example, a law firm Jones & Company uses the second level domain name "jones" and has registered that SLD with the .ca Domain Registrar resulting in the combined domain name "jones.ca". SLDs must be registered in conjunction with TLDs. Hence, one may register "jones.ca", "jones.com", or "jones.net". *British Columbia Automobile Assn. v. OPEIU. Local 378* (2001), 10 C.P.R. (4th) 423 (B.C.S.C.).

Domain Name Registrars

Domain Name Registrars provide previously unregistered domain names on a firstcome first-serve basis upon payment of small registration fee. *Porsche Cars North America Inc. vs. Spencer,* 55 U.S.P.Q. (2d) 1026 (E.D.Cal. 2000).

Domain Name Server

A domain name server is a host computer with software capable of responding to domain name inquiries and accessible on a full-time basis to other computers on the Internet. *Intermatic Inc. v. Toeppen*, 40 U.S.P.Q. (2d) 1412 (N.D. Ill. 1996).

Domain Name Service

Domain name service is accomplished as follows: the Internet is divided into several "top level" domains. For example, "edu" is a domain reserved for educational institutions, "gov" is a domain reserved for government entities, and "net" is reserved to networks. Although "com" is short for "commercial", it is a catchall domain and the only one generally available to the Internet users that have no special attributes *i.e.*, they are not a school or a government office or a network. Each domain name active in a given top-level domain is registered with the top level server which contains certain host name and IP address information. *Intermatic Inc. v. Toeppen*, 40 U.S.P.Q. (2d) 1412 (N.D. Ill. 1996).

Domain Name System - DNS

A globally distributed database that translates domain names into numeric Internet addresses and vice versa. *Domain Name System Reform and Related Internet Governance Issues: A Consultation Paper*, Industry Canada available at *www.strategis.gc.ca*

IP addresses function much like Social Security numbers or telephone numbers: each IP address is unique and corresponds to a specific entity connected to the Internet. Because number strings can be cumbersome and difficult to remember, the Domain Name System ("DNS") was developed to allow users to link a unique (and easier to remember) domain name with a numeric (and more difficult to remember) IP address, thereby making it more convenient for users to access particular addresses on the Internet. So, for example, a user wishing to access the website maintained by International Business Machines need only remember the domain name "IBM.com," rather than the elaborate numerical IP address of the computer on which information relating to IBM's website is maintained (for example, a typical IP address might be something like 192.168.0.10). *National A-1 Advertising, Inc. et al v. Networks Solutions, Inc.*, Civ. No. 99-033-M (D.N.Hamp. Sept. 28, 2000).

DoS

Denial-of-Service attacks

DoubleClick

DoubleClick, a Delaware corporation, is the largest provider of Internet advertising products and services in the world. Its Internet-based advertising network of over 11,000 Web publishers has enabled DoubleClick to become the market leader in delivering online advertising. DoubleClick specializes in collecting, compiling and analyzing information about Internet users through proprietary technologies and techniques, and using it to target online advertising. DoubleClick has placed billions of advertisements on its clients' behalf and its services reach the majority of Internet users in the United States. *DoubleClick Inc. Privacy Litigation*, Civ.0641 (N.R.V.) (S.D.N.Y. Mar. 28, 2001).

Downloading

The process of transferring files, programs, or other computer-stored information from a remote computer to one's own computer. *United States v. Riggs*, 2 CCH Comp. Cas. 43,316 (N.D. Ill. 1990).

Third party users can also retrieve information from the electronic bulletin board to their own computer memories by a process known as "downloading". *Sega Enterprises Ltd. v. Maphia*, 30 U.S.P.Q. (2d) 1921 (N.D. Cal. 1994).

The transfer of files or software from a remote computer to your computer. Cyberspeak — Learning the Language, the Federal Trade Commission and the National Association of Attorneys General,available at http://www.ftc.gov/bcp/conline/pubs/online/sitesee/index.html.

To download means to receive information, typically a file, from another computer to your's via your modem. . . .the opposite term is upload, which means to send a file to another computer. *A & M Records Inc. v. Napster Inc.*, 57 U.S.P.Q. 2d 1729 (9th Cir.2001).

Copying of information (such as a computer program or MP3 file) across an electronic network (such as the Internet) for storage on a local computer system. *Digital Technology and the Copyright Act 1994: A Discussion Paper, Competition and Enterprise Branch, July 2001 (New Zealand).*

Downtime

Meaning the time that the machine is not working due to its own failure. *Public Utilities Commn. (Waterloo) v. Burroughs Business Machines Ltd.* (1973), 34 D.L.R. (3d) 320 (Ont. H.C.), affirmed (1974), 6 O.R. (2d) 257 (Ont. C.A.).

DRAMs — Dynamic Random Access Memories

A DRAM is a type of semiconductor RAM in which the presence or absence of a capacitive charge represents the state of a binary storage element. The charge must be periodically refreshed. Information is stored in a DRAM in the form of binary numbers. A single cell of a DRAM can hold one binary digit, or "bit". DRAMs are sometimes classified by storage capacity measured in "K" bits, where K 1,024 bits. A 16K DRAM stores 65,536 bits; a 256K DRAM stores 262,144 bits; a one-megabit (1 Meg) DRAM stores in excess of one million bits; and a four-megabit (4 Meg) DRAM stores in excess of four million bits. The steps necessary to produce a DRAM or SRAM include (1) product design, (2) manufacturing process development, (3) growing crystal ingot and slicing into wafers, (4) fabricating DRAM or SRAM devices on a wafer (wafer fabrication), (5) encapsulation and (6) final testing. *Digital Equipment Corp. v. Systems Industries Inc.*, CCH Computer L Reptr. 46,229 (D.C.Mass. 1990).

DRMS

Digital Rights Management Systems

DRS

The letters "DRS" have an extensive acronymic significance in the electronics and data processing fields. For example: Data Reaction System and Data Reduction System, Data Rate Selector, Data Receiving Station, Data Recording Set, Data Recording System, and Data Retrieval System. *Re Application by Siemens Aktiengesellschaft* (1983), 1 I.P.R. 1 (Aus. Pat. Office).

DSL

Digital Subscriber Line

DTH (Direct-To-Home)

TV signal broadcast by satellite received directly in a subscriber's home via a small dish antenna. *The Challenge of the Information Highway: Final Report of the Information Highway Advisory Council* (September 1995).

Dumb Terminals

With mainframe and minicomputers, the VDUs are referred to as "dumb terminals" in the sense that while they request, receive and display information, they do no processing. *Madeley Pty Ltd. v. Touche Ross*, McGarvie, J., Aust. Fed. Ct., Dec. 21, 1989 (unreported).

Durable Medium

Means any instrument enabling the consumer to store information, without himself having to record this information, and in particular floppy disks, CD ROM's, and the hard drive of the consumer's computer on which electronic mail is stored. *European Commission Proposal for a Directive of the European Parliament and of the Council Concerning the Distance Marketing of Consumer Financial Services*, COM (1998) 468 Final, dated November 19, 1998.

DVD (Digital Video, or Versatile Disk)

DVDs are five-inch wide disks capable of storing more than 4.7 GB of data. In the application relevant here, they are used to hold full-length motion pictures in digital form. They are the latest technology for private home viewing of recorded motion pictures and result in drastically improved audio and visual clarity and quality of motion pictures shown on televisions or computer screens. *Universal City Studios, Inc. v. Reimerdes,* 55 U.S.P.Q. 2d 1873 (S. D.N.Y. 2000).

A 118 mm plastic disk, very similar in most respects to a CD ROM but capable of storing up to 17 Gigabytes of digital information (about 20 times that on a CD ROM). *Digital Technology and the Copyright Act 1994: A Discussion Paper, Competition and Enterprise Branch, July 2001 (New Zealand).*

It is said that, contrary to what might be a common perception, the term *"DVD"* is not an acronym. It may be that the term was originally an acronym of *"Digital Video Disc"* or *"Digital Versatile Disc"*. Whether it is or is not an acronym, the term *"DVD"* is now applied to a system whereby material, both video and audio, is stored on a disc in digital form and is capable of being retrieved by a device such that the material can be converted either into moving images on a screen accompanied by sound or merely into sound. *Australian Video Retailers Assn. Ltd. v Warner Home Video Pty Ltd.* (2001), 53 I.P.R. 242 (Aust. F.C.).

DVD-Audio

Just as in the case of DVD-Video, the DVD-Audio disc contains the digital representation of the content, the major part of which represents the pure audio content. However, the DVD-Audio specification also allows for the presence of related text, image and video content along with the audio data. The DVD-Audio specification defines file structures and the layout of the DVD-Audio content, and includes a simplified set of navigational instructions designed to provide such options as play/pause, jump to the next group of tracks and track access. In most cases the digitized audio signal is not compressed. After being read from the disc it is simply converted to analogue form suitable for output to the audio amplifiers and speaker system. *Australian Video Retailers Assn. Ltd. v. Warner Home Video Pty Ltd.* (2001), 53 I.P.R. 242 (Aust. F.C.)

DVD-Disc

A DVD disc contains the entirety of the information required to present and play its contents. The information carried by the disc consists of the content, such as the motion picture and audio, together with the program instructions that control the presentation of that content, and without which, the content could not be played as intended by the content owner. The program instructions present the consumer with a set of viewing options and choices that are determined by the creator of the DVD disc during the creative design phase. The options and choices are presented to the consumer as a direct result of the program instructions embedded, along with the content, on the DVD disc. Thus, the consumer is able to choose his or her viewing experience according to the options made available by the creator of the DVD disc, from which the consumer may select. The consumer choices are transmitted to the player by way of a remote control (if the DVD is played on a DVD player) or by way of a computer mouse (if the DVD is played using a computer). All the information on a DVD disc is arranged into a specific logical structure that is called the DVD file system. The file system of a DVD disc organizes the information into files and subdirectories, which in turn are organized, for the purpose of accessing, into a tree-like structure. *Australian*

Video Retailers Association Ltd. v. Warner Home Video Pty Ltd. (2001), 53 I.P.R. 242 (Aust. F.C.)

DVD Formats

Information in a DVD system is digitized and stored as binary code (1's and 0's) on DVD disc substrates using a modulation code that allows strings of digital bits to be represented by the length and sequence of pits moulded into the surface of the substrate. The pits are read by a laser within a DVD player or the DVD-ROM drive of a computer. The signal derived from that laser reading is processed by the electronics of the DVD player or computer to reproduce the original digital information. A DVD disc is formed from two 0.6 mm substrates bonded together. Since optical distortions of the laser's read out beam, caused by the DVD substrate, are decreased as against CDs, and since DVD modulation and error correction schemes are advanced over CDs, the information density of DVD's can be several times greater than CDs. That increased pit density means that a double-sided DVD disc has a storage capacity approximately fifteen times greater than a CD. There are several different DVD formats, including DVD-ROM, DVD-Videob and DVD-Audio. DVD-ROM is the base format, which determines the way in which information, that is to say programming and data, is laid out on the disc, both physically and logically, ensuring that compliant readers can reliably recover the information. DVD-Audio and DVD-Video are application formats that employ DVD physical format and DVD-ROM logical formats, with the addition of specific sorts of programming and data to convey audio, video, navigation and related functions. I shall say something about each of those formats. *Australian Video Retailers Assn. Ltd. v. Warner Home Video Pty Ltd.* (2001), 53 I.P.R. 242 (Aust. F.C.).

DVD-ROM

A DVD disc can carry any sort of digital information. A disc in DVD-ROM format has two parts. The first part defines the physical parameters of the disc as well as the physical layout and geometry of the information bearing pits. The second part defines the file system specifications for the logical structures of the information contained on the disc. If digital data is laid out in accordance with the DVD-ROM physical and logical specifications then any DVD-ROM drive, either in a computer or a DVD player, should, on playback, be able to recover reliably all of the data contained in the disc. *Australian Video Retailers Assn. Ltd. v. Warner Home Video Pty Ltd.* (2001), 53 I.P.R. 242 (Aust. F.C.).

DVD-Video

A single frame of digital video consists of a matrix of picture elements, called "pixels". The total number of pixels defined for each frame of a moving picture, and the precision with which the colour values are expressed, determines the degree of fidelity and detail in the rendered image. The number of pixels in each frame depends on the format of the video signal. In DVD-video, the original film based content is first of all optically scanned to produce a digital video signal in the desired format. The digital signal is then encoded, or compressed, before it is embedded in the disc, in order to reduce the total amount of information required to be stored on the disc. The compression of information is achieved using a standardized video compression scheme developed by the Moving Picture Experts Group *("MPEG")*. There are several different video compression schemes such as MPEG1, MPEG2 and MPEG4. Major film studios use variable bit rate MPEG2 for motion picture DVD discs. The encoded (or compressed) material is formatted as part of a DVD-video bit stream, along with audio, subtitles, navigation information and related instructions. The bit stream includes information for the decompression module, to aid the image reconstruction process. The compressed video delivered on a DVD disc is decompressed on playback. The pixel information is reconstructed *"block by block"* within a frame, and successively, frame by frame, on the basis of the bits, presentation instructions and motion prediction algorithms that convey to the decoder and display system what to represent, and where and when to represent the image information. *Australian Video Retailers Assn. Ltd. v. Warner Home Video Pty Ltd.* (2001), 53 I.P.R. 242 (Aust. F.C.)

"E"

To anyone remotely familiar with the internet and with e-mail, the prefix "e" is a shorthand for electronic, and refers to the internet. *eFax.com v. Oglesby,* Parker J., 25 January 2000 (Eng.Ch.D) (unreported).

"EDI" Electronic Data Interchange

Electronic preparation, communication and processing of business transactions in a predefined, structured format using computers and telecommunications. *The Challenge of the Information Highway: Final Report of the Information Highway Advisory Council* (September 1995).

Electronic Data Interchange or EDI is the computer-to-computer transmission of business transactions in proprietary or standard formats. *Comprehensive Technologies International Inc. v. Software Artisans Inc.*, 3F. 3d 370 (4th Cir. 1993).

The term "EDI" is derived from the name Electronic Data Interchange, and involves computer to computer transmissions of business transactions in standard or proprietary formats. *Comprehensive Technologies Int. Inc. v. Software Artisans, Inc. et al*, Civil Action No. 90-1143-A (E.D. Vir. 1992 unreported), aff'd F.3d 370 (4th Cir. 1993).

Is a standard for compiling and transmitting information between computers, often over private communications networks called value-added networks (VANs). The Emerging Digital Economy, United States Department of Commerce, http://www.ecommerce.gov.

Is the abbreviation for "electronic data interchange", which means a computer-to-computer exchange of electronic documents between trading partners. GST Memorandum 500-1-2 (Books and Records -Computerized Records), May 26, 1993.

EDL

Event Driven Language. *Whelan Associates Inc. v. Jaslow Dental Laboratory Inc.*, 225 U.S.P.Q. 156 (E.D. Pa. 1985), affirmed 797 F.2d 1222 (3rd Cir. 1986).

EDP

Is the abbreviation for electronic data processing, which means data processing performed by electronic machines and the methods and techniques associated with such processing. Revenue Canada, Customs and Excise, Books and Records, Memorandum ET 102, February 24, 1989.

Is the abbreviation for "electronic data processing", which means data processing performed by electronic machines and methods, and techniques associated with such processing. GST Memorandum 500-1-2 (Books and Records - Computerized Records), May 26, 1993.

.edu

The generic Top Level Domain (gTLD) reserved for universities and four-year colleges. *Domain Name System Reform and Related Internet Governance Issues: A Consultation Paper*, Industry Canada available at *www.strategis.gc.ca*

Edutainment

Combining education with entertainment. Monopolies and Mergers Commission — Video Games: A report on the supply of video games in the UK (LONDON: HMSO Cm2781).

EEPROM

Electrically Erasable Programmable Read Only Memory is used to hold information that may change, such as the card holder's address. Smart Cards: Implications for Privacy, Privacy Commissioner, Australia, December 1995.

eFax

The word "eFax" is essentially descriptive in its nature and . . . is already used widely on the internet to denote a "unified messaging service", to use the jargon, combining fax with e-mail. *eFax.com v. Oglesby,* Parker J., 25 January 2000 (Eng.Ch.D) (unreported)

EFT-POS

Electronic Funds Transfer-Point of Sale. *Databank Systems Ltd. v. Commnr. of Inland Revenue*, [1987] N.Z.L.R. 312 (H.C. Wellington).

Electronic Funds Transfer at Point of Sale. Smart Cards: Implications for Privacy, Privacy Commissioner, Australia, December 1995.

EGA

Enhanced graphics array. *Princeton Graphics Operating, L.P. v. Nec Home Electronics (U.S.A.), Inc.*, Comp. Ind. Lit. Reptr. 11,126 (S.D.N.Y. 1990).

Enhanced Graphics Adaptor, a type of monitor display. Monopolies and Mergers Commission — Video Games: A report on the supply of video games in the UK (LONDON: HMSO Cm2781).

EIM

Acronym for "Electronic Image Management". National Standard of Canada, Microfilm and Electronic Images as documentary evidence, Can/CGSB-72.11-93.

Electric

"Electric" means "actuated by electric, magnetic, electro-magnetic, electro-chemical or electro-mechanical energy," and "in electronic form" means "in a form usable only by electronic means." *Copyright, Designs, and Patents Act 1988,* 1988, c. 48.

Electro-Magnetic, Acoustic, Mechanical or Other Device

Any device or apparatus that is used or is capable of being used to intercept a private communication, but does not include a hearing aid used to correct subnormal hearing of the user to not better than normal hearing. *Criminal Code* (Canada), R.S.C. 1985, c. C-46, s. 183.

Electromagnetic Compatibility (EMC)

The ability of electronic systems to operate in their intended environments without suffering an unacceptable degradation of the performance as a result of unintentional electromagnetic radiation or response. "Security Requirements for Cryptographic Modules", FIPS Pub. 140-1, Federal Information Processing Standards Publication, January 11, 1994, available at http://csrc.nist.gov/fips/fips1401.htm.

Electromagnetic Interference (EMI)

Electromagnetic phenomena which either directly or indirectly can contribute to a degradation in the performance of an electronic system. "Security Requirements for Cryptographic Modules", FIPS Pub. 140-1, Federal Information Processing Standards Publication, January 11, 1994, available at http://csrc.nist.gov/fips/fips1401.htm.

Electromagnetic Spectrum

The spectrum of electromagnetic radiation comprising all frequencies from the highest (gamma and X-rays) to the lowest (radio waves). All the various rays and waves which make up the electromagnetic spectrum share a property with visible light — the speed at which it travels. The spectrum is like land in that it is natural, finite and cannot be duplicated, hence the basis for the legal rationale for the regulation of spectrum use. Frequencies must be assigned on a non-overlapping basis to television and radio stations to prevent interferences of various kinds. Only certain portions of the spectrum are suitable for broadcasting purposes. Submission of the Director of Investigation and Research to the CRTC Re Public Notice CRTC 1994-130.

Electronic

Means relating to technology having electrical, digital, magnetic, wireless, optical, electromagnetic, or similar capabilities. *Uniform Electronic Transactions Act*, National Conference of Commissioners on Uniform State Laws, July 29, 1999.

Includes electrical, digital, magnetic, optical, electromagnetic, or any other form of technology that entails capabilities similar to these technologies. *Illinois Electronic Commerce Security Act*, 1998 5 Ill. Comp. Stat. 175.

Includes created, recorded, transmitted or stored in digital form or by electronic, magnetic or optical means or by any other intangible means that has capabilities for creation, recording, transmission or storage similar to those means and "electronically" has a corresponding meaning. *Uniform Electronic Commerce Act*, Uniform Law Conference Canada.

Includes electrical, analog, digital, magnetic, optical or electromagnetic and any other form based on a similar technology. *B.C. Land Title Amendment Act*, 1999 (Bill 93-1999).

Relating to or using devices operating by principles of electronics. The branch of physics that studies the behaviour and applies the effects of the flow of electrons in vacuum tubes, gases and semiconductors. *Canada Post Corp. v. EPost Innovations Inc.*, [1999] F.C.J. No. 1297 (Fed.T.D.)

The term "electronic" means relating to technology having electrical, digital, magnetic, wireless, optical, electromagnetic, or similar capabilities. *Electronic Signatures in Global and National Commerce Act.*

Electronic includes created, recorded, transmitted or stored in digital or other intangible form by electronic, magnetic, optical or any similar means. *Electronic Commerce and Information, Consumer Protection Amendment and Manitoba Evidence Amendment Act*, C.C.S.M. c.E5S.

"Electronic" includes created, recorded, transmitted or stored in digital form or in other intangible form by electronic, magnetic or optical means or by any other means that has capabilities for creation, recording, transmission or storage similar to those means and "electronically" has a corresponding meaning. *PEI Electronic Commerce Act*, S.P.E.I. 2001, c. 31.

Caused or operated by electric, magnetic, electro-magnetic, electro-chemical, or electro-mechanical energy. "Electronic" is sometimes used interchangeably with "digital". Most forms of electronic storage will be digital, but electronic storage can also be analogue (for example, some forms of electro-magnetic or magnetic storing data). *Digital Technology and the Copyright Act 1994: A Discussion Paper, Competition and Enterprise Branch, July 2001 (New Zealand).*

Electronic Agent

Means a computer program or an electronic or other automated means used to initiate an action or respond to electronic records or performances in whole or in part without review by an individual at the time of the action or response.*Uniform Computer Information Transactions Act*, National Conference of Commissioners on Uniform State Laws, available at http://www.law.upenn.u/bll/ulc/ucita/ci-tim99.htm.

The term "electronic agent" means a computer program or an electronic or other automated means used independently to initiate an action or respond to electronic records or performances in whole or in part without review or action by an individual at the time of the action or response. *Electronic Signatures in Global and National Commerce Act.*

Electronic Authentication (See also Authentication)

Electronic authentication is the process by which an electronic authorization is verified to ensure, before further processing, that the authorizer can be positively identified, that the integrity of the authorized data was preserved and that the data are original. Security and Electronic Authorization and Authentication Guideline, Communications Security Establishment, Government of Canada September 1995, CID/01/15.

Electronic authorization is the process by which a digital signature is linked to a transaction to signify that a person with delegated authority has effectively authorized the further processing of that data. Security and Electronic Authorization and Authentication Guideline, Communications Security Establishment, Government of Canada September 1995, CID/01/15.

Electronic Authentication can be understood to encompass any method of verifying some piece of information in an electronic environment, whether it is the identity of a sender of a message (or author of the text), the authority of a person to enter into a particular kind of transaction, the security attributes or hardware or software device, etc. *Building Trust and Confidence in Electronic Commerce: A Framework for Electronic Authentication in Canada*, prepared by the Electronic Commerce Branch, Industry Canada, July 2000, available at *http://e-comm.ic.gc.ca.*

Electronic Bulletin Board (See also Bulletin Board)

An electronic messaging system and an information storage area board shared by several users, each having access to all messages left or posted in that area. *The Challenge of the Information Highway: Final Report of the Information Highway Advisory Council* (September 1995).

An electronic bulletin board consists of electronic storage media, such as computer memories or hard disks, which is attached to telephone lines via modem devices, and controlled by a computer. *Sega Enterprises Ltd. v. Maphia*, 30 U.S.P.Q. (2d) 1921 (N.D. Cal. 1994).

A storage media, e.g., computer memories or hard disks, connected to telephone lines via devices known as modems and controlled by a computer. *Lunney v. Prodigy Services Company*, 99 N.Y. Int. 0165 (Ct. App. N.Y. December 2, 1999), available at *http://legal.web.aol.com/decisions/dldefam/lunneyappeal.html*.

Also referred to as newsgroups (i.e. bulletin boards about particular topics) or message boards. As its name implies, an electronic bulletin board is analogous to its physical counterpart, and is accessible to any member of the public with a personal computer and Internet access. *Technical Committees' Internet Task Force Report*, International Organization of Securities Commissioners, September 13, 1998.

Electronic Cheque

The equivalent of a paper-based cheque, initiated during an onscreen dialogue that results in a payment transaction. Ministry of Revenue Advisory Committee, Report of the Committee On Electronic Commerce, April 30, 1998, Industry Canada.

Electronic Commerce (E-Commerce)

Consumer and business transactions conducted over a network, using computers and telecommunications. *The Challenge of the Information Highway: Final Report of the Information Highway Advisory Council* (September 1995).

Broadly, the delivery of information, products, services, or payments by telephone, computer, or other automated media. More narrowly, business-to-consumer and business-to-business transactions conducted over computer networks, whether public (such as the Internet) or private. Ministry of Revenue Advisory Committee, Report of the Committee On Electronic Commerce, April 30, 1998, Industry Canada.

Electronic commerce, which is at the heart of the information economy, is the conduct of commercial activities and transactions by means of computer-based information and communications technologies. It generally involves the processing and transmission of digitized information. Examples of electronic commerce range from the exchange of vast amounts of financial assets between financial institutions, to electronic data interchange between wholesalers and retailers, to telephone backing, and to the purchase of products and services on the Internet. The Protection of Personal Information: Building Canada's Information Economy and Society, Industry Canada, Task Force on Electronic Commerce, January 1998.

Buying and selling goods and services over the Internet. *Domain Name System Reform and Related Internet Governance Issues: A Consultation Paper*, Industry Canada available at *www.strategis.gc.ca*

The conduct of commercial activities between vendors and consumers and the solicitation of donations from consumers over open networks, including the Internet. *Principles of Consumer Protection for Electronic Commerce: A Canadian Framework*, July 8, 1999, available at *http://strategis.ic.gc.ca/SSG/ca01180e.html.*

A broad concept that covers any trade or commercial transaction that is effected using electronic means; such as facsimile, telex, EDI, Internet, and the telephone. UNCITRAL Report of the Working Group on Electronic Commerce, September 18-29, 2000, A/CN. 94/483.

"E-commerce" is defined as 'commercial activity that takes place by means of connected computers. Electronic commerce can occur between a user and a vendor through an online information service on the internet, or a BBS, or between vendor and customer computers through electronic data interchange ("EDI"). *American Eyewear, Inc. v. Peeper's Sunglasses and Accessories, Inc.*, 2000 U.S. Dist. LEXIS 6875 (D. Tex. May 16, 2000)

Electronic Commerce Activities

All activities, types of communication and transactions with a commercial purpose or background that are carried out electronically. *The Netherlands Code of Conduct for Electronic Commerce*, O.E.C.D., October 13, 1999 available at *www.ecp.nl/virtrouwen.*

Electronic Commerce Directive

Directive 2000/31/EC of the European Parliament and the Council of 8 June 2000 on certain legal aspects of information society services, in particular electronic commerce, in the Internal Market, 17 July 2000.

Electronic Communication

Any transfer of signs, signals, writing, images, sounds, data, or intelligence of any nature transmitted in whole or in part by a wire, radio. *United States of America v. Morris*, 2 CCH Comp. Cas. 46,419 (2nd Cir. 1991). 18 U.S.C. section 2510 ss. 12.

Means any transfer of signs, signals, writing, images, sounds, data, or intelligence of any nature transmitted in whole or in part by a wire, radio, electromagnetic, photoelectronic or photooptical system that affects interstate or foreign commerce, but does not include (a) the radio portion of a cordless telephone communication that is transmitted between the cordless telephone handset and the base unit; (b) any wire or oral communication; (c) any communication made through a tone-only paging device, or (d) any communication from a tracking device (as defined in Section 3117 of this title). *Electronic Communications Privacy Act* of 1986, Pub. L. 89-508 (1986).

Electronic Communication Service

Means any service which provides to users thereof the ability to send or receive wire or electronic communications. *Electronic Communications Privacy Act* of 1986, Pub. L. 89-508 (1986).

Means any wire, radio, electromagnetic, photooptical or photoelectronic facilities for the transmission of electronic communications, and any computer facilities or related electronic equipment for the electronic storage of such communication. *Electronic Communications Privacy Act* of 1986, Pub. L. 89-508 (1986).

Electronic Communication System

Means any wire, radio, electromagnetic, photooptical or photoelectronic facilities for the transmission of electronic communications, and any computer facilities or related electronic equipment for the electronic storage of such communication. *Electronic Communications Privacy Act* of 1986, Pub. L. 89-508 (1986).

Electronic Database (See also Database)

An organised collection of information stored in a computer system (usually in a database management system or DBMS) which allows the content to be retrieved readily. *Digital Technology and the Copyright Act 1994: A Discussion Paper, Competition and Enterprise Branch, July 2001 (New Zealand).*

Electronic Data Interchange (EDI)

The computer-to-computer exchange of business information using a standardized data format. EDI messages are based on common business documents such as invoices, bills of lading, and purchase orders and are sent from one computer to another over telecommunications links without human intervention or interpretation. Ministry of Revenue Advisory Committee, Report of the Committee On Electronic Commerce, April 30, 1998, Industry Canada.

Electronic data interchange and electronic commerce are terms that refer to electronic transactions and contracts. Generally, EDI involves sending purchase requests and payment invoices electronically, but electronic transactions can cover many other kinds of transactions, such as filing income tax returns, applying for licences, paying ticket. Frequently, there will be a signed, paper agreement between the parties setting out how the electronic transactions will occur (Trading Partner Agreements). *A Survey of Legal Issues Relating to the Security of Electronic Information*, Department of Justice, Canada.

Means the electronic transfer from computer to computer of information using an agreed standard to structure the information. UNCITRAL Model Law On Electronic Commerce (1996).

A system allowing for inter-corporate commerce by the automated electronic exchange of structured business information. UNCITRAL Report of the Working Group on Electronic Commerce, September 18-29, 2000, A/CN. 94/483.

Means the electronic transfer from computer to computer of information using an agreed standard to structure the information. *UNCITRAL, Working Group IV (Electronic Commerce), Thirty-ninth session New York, 11-15 March, 2002.*

Electronic Document

An "electronic document" is any collection of information stored electronically which has been logically grouped together. Examples include, but are not limited to, the files output from wordprocessors, the transactions used in transaction processing systems, electronic mail, X.400 Messages and EDI messages. Security and Electronic Authorization and Authentication Guideline, Communications Security Establishment, Government of Canada September 1995, CID/01/15.

Means data that is recorded or stored on any medium in or by a computer system or other similar device and that can be read or perceived by a person or a computer system or other similar device. It includes a display, printout or other output of that data. *Personal Information Protection and Electronic Documents Act*, S.C. 2000 C.5.

Means information that (a) is electronically recorded or stored in or by an information system, and (b) can be read or perceived by a person or by an information system. *Electronic Commerce and Information, Consumer Protection Amendment and Manitoba Evidence Amendment Act, C.C.S.M.c.E5S.*

Electronic Document System

Includes a computer system or other similar device by or in which data is recorded or stored and any procedures related to the recording or storage of electronic documents. *Personal Information Protection and Electronic Documents Act*, S.C. 2000 C.5.

Includes a computer system or other similar device by or in which data is recorded or stored, and any procedures related to the recording or storage of electronic documents. *Electronic Commerce and Information, Consumer Protection Amendment and Manitoba Evidence Amendment Act, C.C.S.M.c.E5S.*

Electronic Event

Means an electronic authentication, display, message, record, or performance. *Uniform Computer Information Transactions Act*, National Conference of Commissioners on Uniform State Laws, available at http://www.law.upenn.u/bll/ulc/ucita/citim99.htm.

Electronic Integrated Circuits and Microassemblies

These refer to:

(a) Monolithic integrated circuits in which the circuit elements (diodes, transistors, resistors, capacitors, interconnections, etc.) are created in the mass (essentially) and on the surface of a semiconductor material (doped silicon, for example) and are inseparably associated;

(b) Hybrid integrated circuits in which passive elements (resistors, capacitors, interconnections, etc.), obtained by thin- or thick-film technology, and active elements (diodes, transistors, monolithic integrated circuits, etc.) obtained by semiconductor technology, are combined to all intents and purposes indivisibly, on a single insulating substrate (glass, ceramic, etc.). These circuits may also include discrete components;

(c) Microassemblies of the moulded module, micromodule or similar types, consisting of discrete, active or both active and passive, components which are combined and interconnected.

An Act to Implement the Free Trade Agreement between Canada and the United States of America, S.C. 1988, c. 65.

Electronic Instrument

Means an instrument in electronic format and includes the electronic form of any document that is required or permitted to be filed, lodged or deposited in the land title office under this Act. *B.C. Land Title Amendment Act*, 1999 (Bill 93-1999).

Electronic Mail (See also E-mail)

Electronic mail, often referred to as e-mail, is a paperless form of communication which allows messages to be sent from one computer user to another. Within and between organizations, e-mail can be an effective tool that helps break down barriers to communication and promotes the free exchange of information and ideas. Privacy Protection Principles for Electronic Mail Systems, Information and Privacy Commissioner/Ontario, February 1994, available at http://www.ipc.on.ca.

Another service typically offered on the Internet is electronic mail (e-mail). It normally consists of alphanumeric text and may have other files attached to the message. The e-mail may be sent to one recipient or a group of recipients. An e-mail sent to an IAP's subscriber is received at a server (known as the Post Office Protocol or POP server) operated by the IAP. The subscriber may then use his/her mail reader program to download the e-mail from the server. *Public Performance of Musical Works* 1996-1998 (Tariff 22) (1999), 1 C.P.R. (4th) 417 (Copyright Board).

An e-mail is an electronic message, similar to a letter or fax, that is directed to a particular addressee. E-mail messages, like mass mailings, can be sent to a vast number of addresses. The contents of an e-mail message, in principle, are available only to the particular addressees. However, there are several ways for e-mail messages to be read or altered by someone other than the intended recipient. *Technical Committees' Internet Task Force Report*, International Organization of Securities Commissioners, September 13, 1998.

A message stored in digital form and intended for transmission over a computing system or network to another user of the system or network. *Digital Technology and the Copyright Act 1994: A Discussion Paper, Competition and Enterprise Branch, July 2001 (New Zealand).*

One to one messaging. Security and Electronic Authorization and Authentication Guideline, Communications Security Establishment, Government of Canada September 1995, CID/01/15.

E-mail allows computer network users to send messages to each other which are received at an electronic mail box identified by the recipients' unique user name and address. *CompuServe Inc. v. Patterson*, 39 U.S.P.Q. (2d) 1502 (6 Cir. 1996).

E-mail is, simply, electronic mail. Users have computer addresses to where messages can be sent. Thus, e-mail does not differ substantially from other recognizable forms of communication, such as traditional mail or phone calls, where one person has an address or phone number to reach another person. *Edias Software International, Inc. v. Basis International Ltd.*, 947 F.Supp. 413 (D. Ariz. 1996).

Computer-to-computer messages between one or more individuals via the Internet. Cyberspeak — Learning the Language, the Federal Trade Commission and the National Association of Attorneys General, available at http://www.ftc.gov/bcp/conline/pubs/online/sitesee/index.html.

E-mail is a personal communication sent directly from one user to another. United States v. Maxwell 45 M.J. 406 (Ca. Armed Forces. 1996).

Electronic Mail Address

Electronic Mail Address means the destination, commonly expressed as a string of characters, to which electronic mail may be sent or delivered. *State of Washington v. Jason Heckle doing business as Natural Instincts*, No. 69416-8 (Wash. Sup. Ct. June 7, 2001).

Electronic Mail Service Provider

Means any person who (i) is an intermediary in sending or receiving electronic mail and (ii) provides to end-users of electronic mail services the ability to send or receive electronic mail. Virginia Computer Crimes Act; (Va. Code Ann. § 18.2-152.2 et seq.) (amended effective July 1, 1999).

Electronic, Mechanical or Electronic Storage

Means (a) any temporary, intermediate storage of a wire or electronic communication incidental to the electronic transmission thereof; and (b) any storage of such communication by an electronic communication service for purposes of backup protection of such communication. *Electronic Communications Privacy Act* of 1986, Pub. L. 89-508 (1986).

Electronic Message

Means a record or display stored, generated, or transmitted by electronic means for the purposes of communication to another person or electronic agent. *Uniform*

Computer Information Transactions Act, National Conference of Commissioners on Uniform State Laws, available at http://www.law.upenn.u/bll/ulc/ucita/citim99.htm.

Electronic Payment

Internet shoppers in e-commerce households who made an online payment for at least one of their transactions. *Statistics Canada Household Shopping on the Internet, 1999, 2000 and 2001.*

Electronic Publishing

The provision of any information which a provider or publisher has, or has caused to be originated, authored, compiled, collected, or edited, or in which he has a direct or indirect financial or proprietary interest, and which is disseminated to an unaffiliated person through some electronic means. *U.S. v. American Telephone & Telegraph Co.*, 552 F.Supp. 131 (D.D.C. 1982), affirmed 103 S.Ct. 1240 (1983).

Electronic Purse

This is for small amounts of money to be paid from the card for transactions. The sums involved are small enough that no PIN is necessary. "Smart Cards", Information and Privacy Commissioner/Ontario, April 1993, available at http://www.ipc.on.ca..

Electronic Record

Means a record created, generated, sent, communicated, received, or stored by electronic means. *Uniform Electronic Transactions Act*, National Conference of Commissioners on Uniform State Laws, July 29, 1999.

Means data that is recorded or preserved on any medium in or by a computer system or other similar device, that can be read or perceived by a person or a computer system or other similar device. It includes a display, printout or other output of that data. *Uniform Electronic Evidence Act*, adopted by the ULCC (August 1998), available at http://www.law.ualberta.ca/alri/ulc/current/eueea.htm.

The term "electronic record" means a contract or other record created, generated, sent, communicated, received, or stored by electronic means. *Electronic Signatures in Global and National Commerce Act.*

Electronic Records System

Includes the computer system or other similar device by or in which data is recorded or preserved, and any procedures related to the recording and preservation of electronic records. *Uniform Electronic Evidence Act*, adopted by the ULCC (August 1998), available at http://www.law.ualberta.ca/alri/ulc/current/eueea.htm.

Electronic Serial Number (ESN)

A unique numerical code embedded in each cellular telephone by the manufacturer identifying that particular instrument. Two digits of the eight-digit ESN code identifies the manufacturer. *United States v. Brady*, 820 F.Supp. 1346 (C.D. Utah 1993).

Electronic Rights Management Information

(a) information attached to, or embodied in, a copy of a work or other subject-matter that: (i) identifies the work or subject-matter, and its author or copyright owner; or (ii) identifies or indicates some or all of the terms and conditions on which the work or subject-matter may be used, or indicates that the use of the work or subject-matter is subject to terms or conditions; or (b) any numbers or codes that represent such information in electronic form. *Copyright Amendment (Digital Agenda) Act 2000 Australia.*

Electronic Rights Management Information Systems

Electronic information that can identify the copyright owner, creator or other rightholder in relation to a work or information about the terms and conditions of the work under which a copy is sold to inform consumers and users. Such information can also appear in connection with the communication to the public or making available of works to the public. Digital water-marking technology also allows to be embedded in the work copyright owners to authenticate digital copies and to trace the source of unauthorised copies. In the future, the inclusion of electronic rights management in copyright works might allow for automatic rights clearance and the collection of copyright royalties. *Digital Technology and the Copyright Act 1994: A Discussion Paper, Competition and Enterprise Branch, July 2001 (New Zealand).*

Electronic Signature

Means an electronic sound, symbol, or process attached to or logically associated with an electronic record and executed or adopted by a person with the intent to sign the electronic record. *Uniform Electronic Transactions Act*, National Conference of Commissioners on Uniform State Laws, July 29, 1999.

Means information in electronic form that is in, attached to or associated with a document and that a person creates or adopts in order to sign the document. *Uniform Electronic Commerce Act*, Uniform Law Conference Canada — www.law.ualberta.ca/alri/ulc/acts/eueca-a.htm.

Means a signature in electronic format that is (a) created by a subscriber using a private cryptographic key under the control of the subscriber that corresponds to a public cryptographic key contained in a certificate, and (b) incorporated into (i) electronic applications and electronic instruments under this Part, and (ii) electronic returns under the *Property Transfer Tax Act. B.C. Land Title Amendment Act*, 1999 (Bill 93-1999).

Means [data in electronic form in, affixed to, or logically associated with, a data message, and] [any method in relation to a data message] that may be used to identify the signature holder in relation to the data message and indicate the signature holder's approval of the information contained in the data message. Draft Uniform Rules on Electronic Signatures, UNCITRAL, 29 June 1999.

Means a signature in electronic form attached to or logically associated with an electronic record. *Illinois Electronic Commerce Security Act* 1998 5 Ill. Comp. Stat. 175.

"Electronic signatures" can be defined as any similar method executed or adopted by a party with the present intention to be bound by or to authenticate a record, accomplished by electronic means. Electronic Commerce: Building A Legal Framework, Report of the Electronic Commerce Expert Group (Australia) to the Attorney General, 31 March, 1998.

Means a signature that consists of one or more letters, characters, numbers or other symbols in digital form incorporated in, attached to or associated with an electronic document. *Personal Information Protection and Electronic Documents Act*, S.C. 2000 C.5.

Means a signature in digital form in, or attached to, or logically associated with, data which is used by a signatory to indicate his approval of the content of that data and meets the following requirements: (a) it is uniquely linked to the signatory, (b) it is capable of identifying the signatory, (c) it is created using means that the signatory can maintain under his sole control, and (d) it is linked to the data to which it relates in such a manner that any subsequent alteration of the data is revealed. Proposal for A European Parliament and Council Directive on a Common Framework for Electronic Signatures, COM (1998) 297 Final.

Data in electronic form, attached to, or logically associated with, other electronic data and which serves as a method of authentication, as if it were a handwritten signature. *The Netherlands Code of Conduct for Electronic Commerce*, O.E.C.D., October 13, 1999 available at *www.ecp.nl/virtrouwen*.

The term "electronic signature" means an electronic sound, symbol, or process, attached to or logically associated with a contract or other record and executed or adopted by a person with the intent to sign the record. *Electronic Signatures in Global and National Commerce Act*.

Any symbol or method executed or adopted by a party with present intention to be bound by or to authenticate a record accomplished by electronic means. Digital signatures are a type of electronic signature. UNCITRAL Report of the Working Group on Electronic Commerce, September 18-29, 2000, A/CN. 94/483.

"Electronic Signature" means information in electronic form that a person has created or adopted in order to sign a document and that is in, attached to or associated with the document, and has the following characteristics: (i) it is uniquely linked to the signatory; (ii) it is capable of identifying the signatory; (iii) it is created using means that the signatory can maintain under his sole control; and (iv) it is linked to the data to which it relates in such a manner that any subsequent change of the data is detectable. *PEI Electronic Commerce Act, S.P.E.I. 2001, c. 31.*

A data element associated with a message that identifies a person and indicates their approval of the contents of the message. *The Office of the Federal Privacy Commissioner (Australia), Consultation Paper, (June 2001).*

Means data in electronic form in, affixed to, or logically associated with, a data message, which may be used to identify the person holding the signature creation data in relation to the data message and indicate that person's approval of the information contained in the data message. *UNCITRAL, Working Group IV (Electronic Commerce), Thirty-ninth session New York, 11-15 March, 2002.*

Electronic Signatures Directive

Directive 1999/93/EC of the European Parliament and of the Council of 13 December 1999 on a Community framework for electronic signatures.

Electronic Signature Product

Means hardware or software, or relevant components thereof, which are intended to be used by a certification service provider for the provision of electronic signature services. Proposal for A European Parliament and Council Directive on a Common Framework for Electronic Signatures, COM (1998) 297 Final.

Electronic Token

This is a prepaid entitlement to particular services such as transport, pay telephones, film admissions or car parking. "Smart Cards", Information and Privacy Commissioner/Ontario, April 1993, available at http://www.ipc.on.ca.

Electronic Trading

The chief purpose of electronic trading is to give the customer a process whereby orders for trades and securities may be processed and completed more rapidly than through a "full service" broker. The customer obtains the closest thing to a direct electronic contact with the market as has yet been devised. *Robet v. Versus Brokerage Services Inc.*, [2001] O.J. No. 1341 (Ont. S.C.J.).

Electronic Wallet

A software application or a smart card that can include digital cash, electronic cheques, or other data. Some wallets allow users to lock and unlock smart cards, change PINs, and view transaction information. Ministry of Revenue Advisory Committee, Report of the Committee On Electronic Commerce, April 30, 1998, Industry Canada.

This involves amounts of money being transferred between the purchaser and the retailer through the card; the sums are large enough to require the security of using the cardholder's PIN. "Smart Cards", Information and Privacy Commissioner/Ontario, April 1993.

Electronic Wire Transfers

Electronic wire transfers are similar to regular bank transfers. The originating bank transmits the wire transfer charge electronically to the Federal Reserve Bank or to a private automated clearing house. The Federal Reserve credits the transmitting bank's account and debits the customer's bank account with the bank. *Resolution Trust Corporation v. First of America Bank*, 796 F.Supp. 1333.

Enables an individual to send an electronic message - generally akin to a note or letter - to another individual or to a group of addresses. *Cyberspace Communications, Inc. et al. v. Engler*, 55 F. Supp. 2d 737 (E.D. F. Ch. 1999).

Is the day's evolutionary hybrid of traditional telephone line communications and regular postal service mail. *Lunney v. Prodigy Services Company*, 99 N.Y. Int. 0165 (Ct. App. N.Y. December 2, 1999), available at *http://legal.web.aol.com/decisions/dldefam/lunneyappeal.html*.

Email is normally electronic mailing of a message from one sender to one recipient. The sender makes a connection to his own local ISP to whom he transmits his Email message. The sender's ISP transmits the message via the Internet to the recipient's ISP. At the recipient's request his local ISP sends the message to the recipient. *Godfrey v. Demon Internet Ltd.*, [1999], E.W.J. No. 1226 (Q.B.D.).

Email consists of text messages sent electronically from one computer user to another over the Internet. *America On-Line, Inc. v. The Christian Brothers et al*, 98 Civ. 8959 (DAV April 17, 2001).

Encrypted

Treated electronically or otherwise for the purpose of preventing intelligible reception. *Broadcasting Act*, S.C. 1991, c. 11; *Radiocommunication Act*, R.S.C. 1985, c. R-2, as amended.

Encrypted Key (Ciphertext Key)

A cryptographic key that has been encrypted with a key encrypting key, a PIN or a password in order to disguise the value of the underlying plaintext key. "Security Requirements for Cryptographic Modules", FIPS Pub. 140-1, Federal Information Processing Standards Publication, January 11, 1994, available at http://csrc.nist.gov/fips/fips1401.htm.

Encrypted Program-Carrying Satellite Signal

Means a program-carrying satellite signal that is transmitted in a form whereby the aural or visual characteristics, or both, are modified or altered for the purpose of preventing the unauthorized reception, by persons without the authorized equipment that is designed to eliminate the effects of such modification or alteration, of a program carried in that signal. North American Free Trade Agreement between Canada, Mexico and the United States, Article 1721.

Encryption

The coding of data for privacy protection or security considerations when trans-mitted over telecommunications links, so that only the person to whom it is sent can read it. *The Challenge of the Information Highway: Final Report of the Information Highway Advisory Council* (September 1995).

Basically involves running a readable message known as "plaintext" through a computer that translates the message according to an equation or algorithm into unreadable "ciphertext". *Bernstein v. United States Department of State*, 1996 W.L. 186106 (N.D. Cal. 1996).

In its most basic form, encryption amounts to a "scrambling" of data using mathematical principles that can be followed in reverse to "unscramble" the data. Encryption technologies can be used to deny access to the work in a usable form. File encryption simply converts a file from a manipulatable file format (e.g., a word processor document or a picture file that opened or viewed by appropriate general purpose packages) to a scrambled format. Authorization in the form of possession of an appropriate password or "key" is required to "decrypt" the file and restore it to its manipulatable format. Encryption techniques use "keys" to control access to data that has been "encrypted." Encryption keys are actually numbers that are plugged into a mathematical algorithm and used to scramble data using that algorithm. Scrambling simply means that the original sequence of binary digits (i.e., the 1s and 0s that make up a digital file) is transformed using a mathematical algorithm into a new sequence of binary digits (i.e., a new string of 1s and 0s). The result is a new sequence of digital data that represents the "encrypted" work. Anyone with the key (i.e., the number used to scramble the data according to the specified mathematical algorithm) can decrypt a work by plugging the number into a program that applies the mathematical algorithm in reverse to yield the original sequence of digital signals. Although perhaps most commonly thought of as a tool for works transmitted via computer networks, encryption can be and is used with virtually all information delivery technologies, including telephone, satellite and cable communications. Of course, once the work is decrypted by someone with the key, there may be no technological protection for the work if it is stored and subsequently distributed in its "de-crypted" or original format. National Information Infrastructure: A Preliminary Draft of the Report of the Working Group on Intellectual Property Rights, July 1994.

The encoding of information for privacy protection or security considerations when transmitted over telecommunications links. Only the person to whom the encrypted information is sent can decrypt and read it. Ministry of Revenue Advisory Committee, Report of the Committee On Electronic Commerce, April 30, 1998, Industry Canada.

Encryption means transforming plain text into text which is unintelligible to anyone who does not have the "key" (or "code") which explains the relationships between the plain text characters and the cipher text characters. *A Survey of Legal*

Issues Relating to the Security of Electronic Information, Department of Justice, Canada.

To change plaintext into ciphertext. The word encryption is often used to mean specifically the transformation of data by the use of cryptography to produce unintelligible data (encrypted data) to ensure its confidentiality. *A Cryptology Policy Framework for Electronic Commerce, Task Force on Electronic Commerce, Industry Canada, February 1998.*

A technology that encodes a message before it is sent and decodes it when it is received. Encryption used to protect a message from unauthorized viewing and alteration. *The Emerging Digital Economy*, United States Department of Commerce, http://www.ecommerce.gov.

Basically involves running a readable message known as "plaintext" through a computer program that translates the message according to an equation or algorithm into unreadable "ciphertext." Decryption is the translation back to plaintext when the message is received by someone with an appropriate "key." *Bernstein v. Department of State*, No. 97-16686 (9th Cir. Mar. 6th, 1999).

Means the transformation of data by the use of cryptography to produce unintelligible data (encrypted data) to ensure its confidentiality. *OECD Guidelines for Cryptography Policy*, March 27, 1997, available at *www.oecd.org*.

Is the process by which the original, "human-readable" text of a message or document (also known as "plaintext") is transformed into a text (known as "ciphertext") that the sender and recipient intend third parties not to understand. *Junger v. Secretary of Commerce,* case No. 1-96-CV-1723, (N.D. Ohio.1998).

Means of encoding a message so that only those with a particular piece of information known as a key can access and decode the information. Modern computer-based encryption systems are such that encrypted information may be practically impossible (at least with present technology) to decode without the key. *Digital Technology and the Copyright Act 1994: A Discussion Paper, Competition and Enterprise Branch, July 2001 (New Zealand).*

End Entity

An entity, which uses Keys and Certificates for creating or verifying digital signatures or for confidentiality. Eng Entities are Key-holders, Organizations or Relying Parties. *The Office of the Federal Privacy Commissioner (Australia), Consultation Paper, (June 2001).*

End-User Interface (Application Program Interface)

In general, this is the information that the program's vendor provides to customers to install and use the program and to write programs that use the program's services which shall be clearly differentiated from other information about the program available from the vendor, and the information necessary to allow user-written programs that use only those interfaces to execute on a party's programs after compilation, assembly, pre-processing or link-editing by the other party's programs. *IBM v. Fujitsu Ltd.*, Copyright L.R. (CCH) 20,517 (Am. Arbtn. Assoc. Comm. Arbtn. Trib. 1988).

Enhanced Non-Voice Service

An "enhanced non-voice service" is any non-voice service which is more than the "basic" service, where computer processing applications are used to act on the form, content, code, protocol, etc., of the inputted information. Second Computer Inquiry (Tentative Decision), 72 F.C.C.2d 358 (F.C.C. 1979).

Enhanced Service

The confluence of telecommunications and computer processing technology that has increasingly taken place over the past several years has created the potential for a substantial new range of services in which ordinary telecommunications services can be combined with the provision of information storage, information processing or information creation services. The new range of services is generally referred to as enhanced services. Enhanced Services, Telecom, Decision CRTC 84-18 (July 12, 1984), 9 C.R.T. 486.

An enhanced service is any offering over the telecommunications network which is more than a basic service. In an enhanced service, for example, computer processing applications are used to act on the content, code, protocol, and other aspects of the subscriber's information. In these services, additional, different or restructured information may be provided the subscriber through various processing applications performed on the transmitted information, or other actions, such as editing or formatting, can be taken by either the vendor or the subscriber based on the content of the information transmitted. Moreover, in an enhanced service, the content of the information need not be changed and may involve subscriber interaction with stored information. Many enhanced services feature voice or data storage and retrieval applications, such as in a "mail box" service. This is particularly applicable in time-sharing services where the computer facilities are structured in a manner such that the customer or vendor can write its own customized programs and, in effect, use the time-sharing network for a variety of electronic message service applications. Thus, the kinds of enhanced store and forward services that can be offered are many and varied. Enhanced Services, Telecom, Decision CRTC 84-18 (July 12, 1984), 9 C.R.T. 486.

Means any service offering over the basic telecommunications transport network which is more than a basic telecommunications transport service as defined and classified by measures of the regulator having jurisdiction. *An Act to Implement the Free Trade Agreement between Canada and the United States of America*, S.C. 1988, c. 65.

Services offered over common carrier transmission facilities used in interstate communications, which employ computer processing applications that act on the format, content, code, protocol or similar aspects of the subscriber's transmitted information, provide the subscriber additional, different, or restructured information, or involve subscriber interaction with stored information. Second Computer Inquiry (Final Decision), 77 F.C.C.2d 384 (F.C.C. 1980).

An enhanced service is any offering over the telecommunications network which is more than a basic transmission service. In an enhanced service, for example, computer processing applications are used to act on the content, code, protocol, and other aspects of the subscriber's information. In these services additional, different, or restructured information may be provided the subscriber through various processing applications performed on the transmitted information, or other actions can be taken by either the vendor or the subscriber based on the content of the information transmitted or other actions can be taken by either the vendor or the subscriber based on the content of the information transmitted through editing, formatting, etc. Moreover, in an enhanced service the content of the information need not be changed and may simply involve subscriber interaction with stored information. Many enhanced services feature voice or data storage and retrieval applications, such as in a "mailbox" service. Second Computer Inquiry (Final Decision), 77 F.C.C.2d 384 (F.C.C. 1980).

Enhanced or Value-Added Services

Means those telecommunications services employing computer processing applications that:
    (a) act on the format, content, code, protocol or similar aspects of a customer's transmitted information;
    (b) provide a customer with additional, different or restructured information; or
    (c) involve customer interaction with stored information.

North American Free Trade Agreement between Canada, Mexico and the United States, Article 1310.

Enhancements

Changes or refinements made to an existing computer program. *Compendium of Copyright Offices Practices*, Copyright Office, Washington D.C., 1984.

(A) change or refinement to an existing computer programme. *Geac J & E Systems Ltd. v. Craig Erickson Systems Inc.* (1993), 46 C.P.R. (3d) 25 (Ont. Gen. Div.).

Ensure

To record or adopt a digital seal or symbol associated with a message, with the present intention of identifying oneself with the message. General Usage for International Digitally Insured Commerce (Guidec), International Chamber of Commerce, 1997, available at http://www.icc.wbo.org/guidec2.htm.

Envoy 100

Is a text communications service that provides for the storing and forwarding of messages using electronic switching equipment. *Alta. Gov't Telephones v. Can-*

ada (CRTC), [1985] 2 F.C. 472 (Fed. T.D.), rev'd [1986] 2 F.C. 179 (Fed. C.A.), rev'd [1989] 2 S.C.R. 225.

EOI

Evidence of Identity. *The Office of the Federal Privacy Commissioner (Australia), Consultation Paper, (June 2001).*

EPROM (Eraseable Programmable Read-Only Memory)

EPROMs are nonvolatile memory chips that are programmed after they are manufactured. . . EPROMs differ from PROMs [Programmable Read Only Memory] in that they can be erased, generally by removing a protective cover from the top of the chip package and exposing the semiconductor material to ultraviolet light, and can be reprogrammed after having been erased." *United States v. Brady*, 820 F.Supp. 1346 (C.D. Utah 1993).

An EPROM is an electronic chip that is programmable, the most important constituent of it being a piece of silicon which has a certain number of memory locations, that is, bits. This chip, when programmed, is then used by being plugged directly into the main board of a computer, incorporated into a cartridge of the type used with a video game unit, or in a piece of prototype hardware. It is a piece of industrial equipment roughly equivalent to an industrial video copying machine in the video industry. It is typically used by manufacturers of computers and computer programs and research and development organizations and software houses. *Elan Digital Systems Ltd. v. Elan Computers Ltd.*, [1984] F.S.R. 373 (C.A.).

Acronym for Erasable Programmable Read-Only Memory. A microchip on which data can be stored, and which may be erased and reprogrammed. *E.F. Johnson Co. v. Uniden Corp. of America*, 623 F.Supp. 1485 (D. Minn. 1985).

EPROMS are generic chips that anyone with a simple device, known as an EPROM burner, can program. *Apple Computer Inc. v. 115778 Can. Inc.* (1988), 23 C.P.R. (3d) 22 (Fed. T.D.).

Erasable, programmable, read-only memory: a type of computer chip, to serve as a storage device for a set of digits. *Autodesk Australia Pty Ltd. v. Dyason* (1992), A.I.P.C. 90,855 (Aust. H.C.).

EPROMS are similar to OTPROMS, save that a program loaded into a EPROM can be erased so that the EPROM can be re-used indefinitely. *Avel Pty Ltd. v. Jonathan Wells*, (1992), 22 I.P.R. 305 (Aust. H.C.).

EPROM Programmer

A EPROM programmer is a piece of equipment that enables the operator to set the bits of a Eprom on or off electrically so that the EPROM will contain a computer program in object code, that is, in its binary form. *Elan Digital Systems Ltd. v. Elan Computers Ltd.*, [1984] F.S.R. 373 (C.A.).

Equipment

"Equipment" includes all equipment used to deliver the service to the customer, including the main computer, the terminal lines, and the terminal. *Telerate Systems Inc. v. Marshal Caro*, 689 F.Supp. 221 (S.D.N.Y. 1988).

Errata

By any conventional standards, a customer thinks of an errata as a defect. *Advanced Micro Devices, Inc. and Intel Corp.*, CCH Comp. Cases 60,218 (Arb. Award. 1990).

Error Analysis

The sorting and presentation of the information collected through the error logger into a more coherent and comprehensive form. *DPCE (U.K.) Ltd. v. International Computers Ltd.*, Q.B.D., Saville J., July 31, 1985 (unreported).

Error Logger

Software that causes a permanent record to be made of incidents where the operation of the computer equipment has fallen below a set standard. *DPCE (U.K.) Ltd. v. International Computers Ltd.*, Q.B.D., Saville J., July 31, 1985 (unreported).

Ethernet

Ethernet is a proprietary form of hardware and software used in local area networks. *Madeley Pty Ltd. v. Touche Ross*, McGarvie, J., Aust. Fed. Ct., Dec. 21, 1989 (unreported).

European Convention of Human Rights

Convention for the Protection of Human Rights and Fundamental Freedoms, agreed by the council of Europe at Rome on 4th November 1950.

Exchange

A basic geographical area for the administration and provision of telephone service by an ILEC, which normally encompasses a city, town or village and adjacent areas. *Report to the Governor in Council: Status of Competition in Canadian Telecommunications Markets, Deployment/Accessibility of Advanced Telecommunications Infrastructure and Services, September, 2001.*

Exchange Access

The term "exchange access" means the offering of access to telephone exchange services or facilities for the purpose of the origination or termination of telephone toll services. United States Telecommunications Act of 1996.

Exempt Transmission Apparatus

Means any apparatus whose functions are limited to one or more of the following: (a) the switching of telecommunications, (b) the input, capture, storage, organizations, modification, retrieval, output or other processing of intelligence, or (c) control of the speed, code, protocol, content, format, routing or similar aspects of the transmission of intelligence. *Telecommunications Act*, S.C. 1993, c. 38.

Expert Systems

Expert systems — the most important artifical intelligence category from the viewpoint of existing practical application — have at their disposal, in their memory, comprehensive knowledge (expertise) in a certain field and a mechanism that enables them to answer questions and solve problems. Expert systems can also explain the solutions offered and the means by which those solutions were reached. Expert systems consist of two main elements: a knowledge base, and a so-called "inference engine" which uses the rules of logic to process and manipulate the knowledge base. As a rule, expert systems are accompanied by two other elements: a "knowledge editor," which assists the loading of the knowledge base with information; and, an "explanation facility," which can demonstrate how the system has arrived at an answer to a given problem. The inference engine, the knowledge editor, and the explanation facility are together called the "shell" of an expert system (as opposed to the knowledge that the "shell" contains). It is on the basis of the knowledge included in them and by means of their inference engines (which may be considered specific computer programs) that expert systems can solve problems and answer questions. For example, expert systems can determine the cause of the failure of a machine, identify an illness on the basis of certain symptoms, or describe the legal issues in a case on the basis of the facts input. Committee of Experts on a Possible Protocol to the Berne Convention for the Protection of Literary and Artistic Works.

External Information

A term related to the interface information that is normally provided to customers so that they can use programming material. *IBM v. Fujitsu Ltd.*, Copyright L.R. (CCH) 20,517 (Am. Arbtn. Assoc. Comm. Arbtn. Trib. 1988).

Facilities

"Facilities" has a broad meaning, and that, even if it shall be said to be used more often of a system, it can also mean a single plug-in appliance: something designed to service a specific function affording a convenience or service . . . Telephone and telegraph terminals do qualify as "facilities". *CNCP Telecommunications v. Can. Business Equipment Mfrs. Assn.*, [1985] 1 F.C. 623 (Fed. C.A.).

Facilities-based Carrier

A carrier that provides telecommunications services, using, in part, their own switching and transmission facilities. *Report to the Governor in Council: Status of Competition in Canadian Telecommunications Markets, Deployment/Accessibility of Advanced Telecommunications Infrastructure and Services, September, 2001.*

Facsimile

A form of telegraphy for the transmission of fixed images, with or without halftones, with a view to their reproduction in a permanent form. International Telecommunication Union, Radio Regulations (1982 Edition, Revised).

A visual equivalent that contains all significant details from the source record and is a substitute for the source record for all purposes for which it was created or maintained. National Standard of Canada, Microfilm and Electronic Images as documentary evidence, CAN/CGSB-72.11-93.

Facsimile Machines

In general, facsimile machines are devices that transmit and receive printed or pictorial matter on documents from one location to another, typically over telephone lines. *Secure Services Technology Inc. v. Time and Space Processing Inc.,* 772 F.Supp. 1354 (E.D.Va. 1989).

These machines have been around for many years, but recently they have become so sophisticated and user-friendly that they have become overwhelmingly the method of choice for the transmission of documents in today's world. Indeed their use has become so widespread that business stationery now commonly carries a "fax" telephone number in addition to an ordinary one, and, in common usage, "fax" has been converted into a verb as well as an adjective and noun. At the sending end, an operator phones the intended recipient's machine. If the recipient's machine does not give a busy signal, the document is then transmitted and comes out of the recipient's machine in much the same manner as with a copy machine. It then remains in a tray or other container along with prior and subsequent transmissions until picked up by the recipient. *Calabress v. Springer Personnel of New York,* 200 N.Y.L.J. No. 86, p. 22 (N.Y.S.Ct. 1988).

Fault-Tolerant Computers

Computers that are able to continue functioning even when a part of the system breaks down. Often associated with the term "continuous processing" computers. *Stratus Computers Inc. v. NCR Corp.,* 2 U.S.P.Q.2d 1375 (D. Mass. 1987).

Fax

The word "fax" is now a word in everyday use as referring to a message received in what is now termed hardcopy by means of transmission down a telephone line. eFax.com v. Oglesby, Parker J., 25 January 2000 (Eng.Ch.D) (unreported).

Fiber Optic(s)

A means of transmitting light beams along optical fibres. Fibre optic technology involves the conveyance of information through the use of thin strands of glass or other transparent material with dozens or hundreds of strands in a single cable. A single fibre-optic channel in the electromagnetic spectrum can carry significantly more information than most other means of information transmission such as conventional copper wire technology. A single fibre can carry the equivalent of 100,000 telephone conversations. Fibre optic cables can replace traditional copper wire and coaxial cables in many applications. Submission of the Director of Investigation and Research to the CRTC Re Public Notice CRTC 1994-130.

A modern transmission technology using lasers to produce a beam of light that can be modulated to carry large amounts of information through fine glass or acrylic fibres. *The Challenge of the Information Highway: Final Report of the Information Highway Advisory Council* (September 1995).

A transmission technology in which beams of light are modulated to carry large amounts of data through fine glass or acrylic fibres; superior in carrying capacity and speed to copper-based transmission technology. Ministry of Revenue Advisory Committee, Report of the Committee On Electronic Commerce, April 30, 1998, Industry Canada.

A broadband transmission facility, which uses a beam of light to transmit a digital signal through a glass strand. *Report to the Governor in Council: Status of Competition in Canadian Telecommunications Markets, Deployment/Accessibility of Advanced Telecommunications Infrastructure and Services, September, 2001.*

Fibre optic cable

A cable consisting of a bundle of glass fibres with a strong steel core used for the transmission of information in the form of light signals. *Digital Technology and the Copyright Act 1994: A Discussion Paper, Competition and Enterprise Branch, July 2001 (New Zealand).*

Fibre Optic Network

A network made of glass or plastic cables that employs pulses of light to transport large quantities of information. Submission of the Director of Investigation and Research to the CRTC Re Public Notice CRTC 1994-130.

Field

A field is a specific area within a record for storing particular information concerning the subject. *Dickerman Associates Inc. v. Tiverton Bottled Gas Co.*, 594 F.Supp. 30 (D. Mass. 1984).

A field is a data element. *Dental Office Computer Systems Inc. v. Glutting*, No. CV-86-5613DT (Mich. App. filed August 13, 1987).

File

Anything held on a computer disk, whether data, information, text, electronic mail, records, programs or other material is known as a "file". *R. v. Whiteley*, [1993] F.S.R. 168.

A file is the physical area on a magnetic disc where information is stored. *Dickerman Associates Inc. v. Tiverton Bottled Gas Co.*, 594 F.Supp. 30 (D. Mass. 1984).

A group of records is called a file. *Dental Office Computer Systems Inc. v. Glutting*, No. CV-86-5613DT (Mich. App. filed August 13, 1987).

A storage place for data like a manila folder that contains all the data on a particular subject category in a computer. *Whelan Associates Inc. v. Jaslow Dental Laboratory Inc.*, 225 U.S.P.Q. 156 (E.D. Pa. 1985), affirmed 797 F.2d 1222 (3rd Cir. 1986).

A file is a group of related records that represent ASCII text (text files) or binary data (such as executable code). Every file must have a file name so that the user can access the file's contents. A place to store related information about a subject. For instance, all information about the employees of a company might be stored in an "employee file". This file might be a paper file contained in a file folder or it may be a computerized file that is given a unique name and stored magnetically on a disk or tape. The source code for a program is also a file (or files) containing the source instructions for the program. The executable code for a program is stored in a "program" file or "object code" file. *Delrina Corp. v. Triolet Systems, Inc.* (1992), 47 C.P.R. (3d) 1 (Ont. H.C.).

Collections of digital information for storage on a computer. Under the Microsoft Windows operating system, types of information are distinguished by a three letter file name extension, such as .txt (text), .doc (Microsoft Word document) or .mp3 (one form of musical or audio information). Note that file naming conventions under other operating systems do not necessarily use this form of name. *Digital Technology and the Copyright Act 1994: A Discussion Paper, Competition and Enterprise Branch, July 2001 (New Zealand).*

File Dump

A file dump is a report that discloses significant aspects of the file structure from the file layout and the data file as well as information that concerns the source code. It can be obtained by running a utility programme called "U". The file dump document discloses the order of the fields, the size and type of fields, the key structure, the maximum number of records and maximum record size., i.e., some essential information from the file layout. *Geac J & E Systems Ltd. v. Craig Erickson Systems Inc.* (1993), 46 C.P.R. (3d) 25 (Ont. Gen. Div.).

File Layout Document

A file layout document sets out the design or file structure of data files. *Geac J & E Systems Ltd. v. Craig Erickson Systems Inc.* (1993), 46 C.P.R. (3d) 25 (Ont. Gen. Div.).

File Layouts

(F)ile layouts are part of application software. File layouts describe the design or file structure of data files. Thus, both file layouts and data files contain the file structure information which is created and owned by the software developer. Customer's data is entered into data files. *Geac J & E Systems Ltd. v. Craig Erickson Systems Inc.* (1993), 46 C.P.R. (3d) 25 (Ont. Gen. Div.).

A file layout contains information which is used by the programmer in generating the source code, i.e., it concerns the source code. *Geac J & E Systems Ltd. v. Craig Erickson Systems Inc.* (1993), 46 C.P.R. (3d) 25 (Ont. Gen. Div.).

File Locking

The computer is programmed so that only one user can access a particular file on the database at the one time. It is a matter of first come first served. The second user who seeks access to the file will have to wait until the first user has finished using it. An effective system of file locking, or the locking of some other unit of information storage, is necessary where the database is not confined to a single user but is the database of a multiuser system. *Madeley Pty Ltd. v. Touche Ross*, McGarvie, J., Aust. Fed. Ct., Dec. 21, 1989 (unreported).

File Name

A file name on an MPE system, is a string of up to eight characters used to identify a file. The file name is assigned to the file when it is saved. Files stored on disk within a computer system must have unique names that can be used to identify them. In some circumstances, a program may be attempting to create a file and want to dynamically determine a unique file name for it so that it can be distinguished from other files within the computer system. This is usually done by using a pattern that includes a sequentially assigned number possibly combined with the current date and time. *Delrina Corp. v. Triolet Systems, Inc.* (1992), 47 C.P.R. (3d) 1 (Ont. H.C.).

File server

A computer that stores information for access by users of a network, including the Internet. Ministry of Revenue Advisory Committee, Report of the Committee On Electronic Commerce, April 30, 1998, Industry Canada.

File Structure

File structure is the logical organization of the data file and the records in it, i.e., the way the data is represented. The file structure is described in the file layout. When one looks at a file layout, one sees in hard copy its file structure and how the data is going to be stored. File structure can be called the design of the data file. It includes the file name and information, including order of fields in each record, field sizes, type of data, key and other items as dictated by the file layout. The file structure can be gleaned from the file layout, the file dump and the programme which uses the file. File structure or design is created by the software programmer and owned by his employer. It is part of the software. Users generally have no knowledge or interest in the file structure. *Geac J & E Systems Ltd. v. Craig Erickson Systems Inc.* (1993), 46 C.P.R. (3d) 25 (Ont. Gen. Div.).

File Transfer Protocol (FTP)

One type of software which "implements" a set of conventions for copying files from a host computer. *Shea v. Reno*, 1996 U.S. Dist. LEXIS 10720 (S.D.N.Y. 1996).

(File transfer protocol), allows one to transfer files to and from any computer linked to the Internet. *A Survey of Legal Issues Relating to the Security of Electronic Information*, Department of Justice, Canada.

FTP allows files (not messages) to be sent from one computer to another. FTP is particularly useful for software distribution and the "downloading" of files containing public domain software and computer programs. *Technical Committees' Internet Task Force Report*, International Organization of Securities Commissioners, September 13, 1998.

Filter

Software you can buy that lets you block access to web sites and content that you may find unsuitable. Cyberspeak — Learning the Language, the Federal Trade Commission and the National Association of Attorneys General, available at http://www.ftc.gov/bcp/conline/pubs/online/sitesee/index.html.

Filtering Software

Is placed on a user's computer or Internet access device and prevents the downloading of Web site pages that contain undesirable content (based on keywords) as determined by the filter owner. Advancing Global Electronic Commerce: Technology Solutions to Public Policy Challenges, The Computer Systems Policy Project, July 1999, available at http://www.cspp.org/projects/july99_cto_report.pdf.

Firewall

A system in place between networks that filters data passing through it and removes unauthorized traffic, thereby enhancing the security of the network. Ministry of Revenue Advisory Committee, Report of the Committee On Electronic Commerce, April 30, 1998, Industry Canada.

Basically, a firewall is an access control, which controls who on a given network is permitted to send information to other networks, and who from the outside world is permitted to send information to that given network. *A Survey of Legal Issues Relating to the Security of Electronic Information*, Department of Justice, Canada.

Firmware

"Firmware" is a term of art in the computer field and refers to microinstructions permanently embodied in hardware elements. *In Re Bradley*, 600 F.2d 807 (Cust. & Pat. App. 1979), affirmed 450 U.S. 381 (1981).

The programs and data (i.e., software) permanently stored in hardware (e.g., in ROM, PROM, or EPROM) such that the programs and data cannot be dynamically written or modified during execution. "Security Requirements for Cryptographic Modules", FIPS Pub. 140-1, Federal Information Processing Standards Publication, January 11, 1994, available at http://csrc.nist.gov/fips/fips1401.htm.

Flat-rate Pricing

Means pricing on the basis of a fixed charge per period of time regardless of the amount of use. North American Free Trade Agreement between Canada, Mexico and the United States, Article 1310.

Floppy Disk

An auxiliary memory device consisting of a flexible magnetic disk resembling a phonograph record, which can be inserted into the computer and from which data or instructions can be read. *Apple Computer Inc. v. Franklin Computer Corp.*, 215 U.S.P.Q. 935 (E.D.Pa. 1982), reversed 714 F.2d 1240 (3rd Cir. 1983), cert. dismissed 104 S.Ct. 690 (1984).

A disk is a thin, circular piece of synthetic material, not unlike a 45 r.p.m. record, on which computer programs are stored electronically. When one wishes to use a program, the disk is inserted into a mechanism called a disk drive, and the computer is instructed to transfer the program from the disk into its memory. *Micro-Sparc Inc. v. Amtype Corp.*, 592 F.Supp. 33 (D. Mass. 1984).

Floppy diskettes serve as a medium upon which computer companies place their software programs. To use a program, a purchaser loads the diskette into the disk drive of a computer, thereby allowing the computer to read the program into memory. The purchaser can then remove the diskette from the disk drive and operate the program from the computer's memory. This process is repeated each time a program is used. *Vault Corp. v. Quaid Software Ltd.*, 847 F.2d 255 (5th Cir. 1988).

An information storage device. *Perry Engineering Ltd. v. Farrage* (1989), 28 C.P.R. (3d) 221 (B.C. S.C.).

The floppy disk is a type of flexible magnetic recording medium used to record and store digitally encoded computer information for access by a floppy disk drive. The disk serves as a system memory device for computers and data processing equipment. A disk consists of a piece of circular magnetic media, or "cookie" encased in a protective covering. Three sizes of flexible disks are currently available for use in conjunction with personal computers: 8" and 5.25" diskettes, and 3.5" microdisks. *International Trade Commission Determination re 3.5-Inch Microdisks*, 1 CCH Comp. Cases 60,024 (ITC Inv. No. 731-Ta-389).

Small disks, called "floppy disks" whether they are floppy or not, containing instructions and information may be inserted into the computer for the purpose of it carrying out a particular function or operation. Typically a program (or software) remains upon a floppy disk or is placed or "loaded" on to the hard disk.

Madeley Pty Ltd. v. Touche Ross, McGarvie, J., Aust. Fed. Ct., Dec. 21, 1989 (unreported).

Floppy disks are a common form of magnetic storage media used with computer disk drives. The tape backups are the end product produced by backing up hard disk drives to a tape drive dissimilar to a cassette tape recorder. *Prism Hospital Software Inc. v. Hospital Medical Records Institute* (1987), 18 B.C.L.R. (2d) 34 (S.C.), leave to appeal to B.C.C.A. refused (1987), 21 B.C.L.R. (2d) 345 (C.A.).

Flowchart

A flowchart is a graphic representation of the fundamental idea for solving a problem; it is the first expression of the programmer's ideas, and breaks down a given problem by determining the sequence in which the data is to be operated upon by the computer. The fundamental idea represented by the flowchart is known as an algorithm and is capable of being expressed in differing forms and by differing symbolizations. The flowchart is not literally a computer program, but a diagram of the logical operations that will be performed by the computer. *Paine, Webber, Jackson & Curtis Inc. v. Merrill Lynch, Pierce, Finner & Smith Inc.*, 564 F.Supp. 1358 (D. Del. 1983).

A schematic representation of the program's logic. It sets forth the watchful steps involved in solving a given problem. *Data Cash Systems Inc. v. J.S.& A. Group Inc.*, 480 F.Supp. 1063 (N.D. Ill. 1979), affirmed 628 F.2d 1038 (7th Cir. Ill. 1980).

A partly literal and partly pictorial manifestation of a computer program, still farther removed from direct use with the computer, is the flowchart. A flowchart is a graphic representation of a computer program that is written in symbols, rather than in bits or symbolic names, and with a syntax that is graphic rather than grammatical . . . A flow chart can be thought of as a kind of symbolic outline or schematic representation of a computer program's logic, which is written by a programmer once he or she has a conceptualization of the goals of the program. Creating a flowchart (at least, an early draft) is thus, typically, an early phase in the development of a software system, which is followed by the translation of the flowchart into source code. *Lotus Development Corp. v. Paperback Software International*, 15 U.S.P.Q.2d 1577 (D. Mass. 1990).

"Flow Charts" map the interactions between modules that achieve the program's end goal. *Matrox Electronic Systems Ltd. v. Gaudreau*, [1993] R.J.Q. 2449 (C.S.).

F.M. Station

A station that broadcasts in the F.M. frequency band of 88 to 108 MHz, but does not include a carrier current undertaking or a transmitter that only rebroadcasts the radiocommunications of another station. Cable Television Regulations, 1986, SOR/86-831.

Footprint

The term "footprint" refers to the area occupied by a video terminal, such as on a desk. *Digital Equipment Corp. v. C. Itoh & Co. (Can.) Ltd.* (1985), 6 C.P.R. (3d) 511 (Fed. T.D.).

Foreign Exchange Service (FX)

Gives a customer a 'local' telephone number in a distant location. CNCP Tele-communications: Interconnection with Bell Canada, CRTC Decision 79-11 (May 1979).

Foreign exchange service is a form of "switched" service, which allows a businessman located in one state to, in effect, maintain a local phone within another state. Under Foreign Exchange service, a businessman can be reached by customers in a different state and can himself reach another state through a telephone line which has the appearance to those customers of being a local telephone in their city. *MCI Communications Corp. v. AT&T*, 4 C.L.S.R. 1119 (E.D.Pa. 1973).

Forged Spamming

The practice called forged spamming, is becoming a common tactic among purveyors of the maligned marketing ploy. By routing the returns to another e-mail address, spammers can get their message out while avoiding the often arrayed backlash that can clog computer systems and shut down operations. *Seidl v. Greentree Mortgage Company,* 30 F.Supp. 2d 1292 (D.Col. 1998).

Form, Fit and Function Data

Means data relating to items, components, or processes or computer programs that are sufficient to enable physical and functional interchangeability, as well as data identifying source(s), size, configuration, mating and attachment characteristics, functional characteristics, and performance requirements. Federal Acquisition Regulation (FAR): Rights in Technical Data (Proposed Rules), Federal Register, Vol. 55, No. 199.

Format shifting

Copying of information (often music) from one form of storage to another. Thus music stored in an analogue format might be converted to and stored in a digital format or music stored as digital information might be copied from one format to another (for example, from a CD to an MP3 player (or the reverse)). *Digital Technology and the Copyright Act 1994: A Discussion Paper, Competition and Enterprise Branch, July 2001 (New Zealand).*

Fortran (Formula Translation)

A high-level programming language widely used for scientific computation and having a notation strongly reminiscent of algebra. *Eurodynamic Systems Plc v. General Automation Ltd.*, Q.B.D., Steyn J., September 6, 1988 (unreported).

Fraudulent Data Base

A computerized database application listing ESN and MIN combinations for cellular telephones which, e.g., have been reported as stolen. *United States v. Brady*, 820 F.Supp. 1346 (C.D. Utah 1993).

FreeNet

Non-profit community organization that provides free access to electronic mail and information services and to computer networks such as the Internet. *The Challenge of the Information Highway: Final Report of the Information Highway Advisory Council* (September 1995).

Free-Net

A community-based, volunteer-build network. Free-net's are springing up in cities around the world, as citizens work to provide free access to selected network resources, and to make local information available on-line. *Vancouver Regional FREENET Association v. Canada (Minister of National Revenue - M.N.R.)*, [1996] 3 F.C. 880 (Fed. C.A.).

The Free-Net movement is a visionary community-based initiative which drives to fulfil a demand for affordable and universal access to the information highway. *Vancouver Regional FREENET Association v. Canada (Minister of National Revenue - M.N.R.)*, [1996] 3 F.C. 880 (Fed. C.A.).

Free-Riding

Use of a cellular telephone which has been programmed to avoid or defeat access or billing to an individual customer account, e.g., by "tumbling" the ESN and/or MIN. *United States v. Brady*, 820 F.Supp. 1346 (C.D. Utah 1993).

Free Standing System

A free-standing system is a computer having the ability to perform computing functions on its own as opposed to a hookup with another computer. As one witness stated, it is a computer having the capability to perform computing functions on its own — to do a specific job from start to finish. *In Re Honeywell Inc.*, 1 C.L.S.R. 810.

Frequency

The number of waves or oscillations per unit of time. For purposes of electronics, expressed in cycles per second or Hertz. Submission of the Director of Investigation and Research to the CRTC Re Public Notice CRTC 1994-130.

Full-Motion Video

Video that is perceived to provide smooth, continuous motion. *The Challenge of the Information Highway: Final Report of the Information Highway Advisory Council* (September 1995).

Full-Service Network

A vertically integrated telecommunications network for the transmission, switching and storage of voice messages, data, and video images for use by business, residential and mobile customers. Such networks might prospectively combine different forms of technology like wireless, fibre optics, cable networks and conventional local telephone networks. Submission of the Director of Investigation and Research to the CRTC Re Public Notice CRTC 1994-130.

Fully Automatic

[A] machine [that] is designed to and substantially performs its job without human intervention as part of the process. *Master Pallentizer Systems, Inc. v. T.S. Ragsdale Co., Inc.*, 725 F.Supp. 1525 (D.Colo. 1989).

Function

Any basic computer operation. *Autodesk Australia Pty Ltd. v. Dyason* (1989), 15 I.P.R. 1 (Aus. Fed. Ct.), reversed [1990] A.I.P.C. 36,446 (Aus. Fed. Ct. FC)

Function Keys

Function keys present an additional way for the user to communicate with, and operate, the programmed computer. *Lotus Development Corp. v. Paperback Software International*, 15 U.S.P.Q.2d 1577 (D. Mass. 1990).

The keyboard to a computer has, in addition to the ordinary keys found on a typewriter, a number of keys called "function keys", generally positioned at the top of the keyboard and labelled 'F1', 'F2', 'F3' and so on. A computer program can be so written as to assign various "meanings" or "functions" to these keys so that when, for example, the key F1 is depressed that initiates a function such as "Help", ie the provision of assistance. *Powerflex Services Pty Ltd. v. Data Access Corp.* (1997), 37 I.P.R. 436 (Aust. C.A.).

Functional Specification

A functional specification is a description of how a computer system will function in the normal day to day environment. As its name indicates, it specifies the functions of the system. *Madeley Pty Ltd. v. Touche Ross*, McGarvie, J., Aust. Fed. Ct., Dec. 21, 1989 (unreported).

Game boy

The "game boy" product developed by Nintendo is a high quality advanced design video game system that utilizes a hand-held console unit. *I.J.E. Inc. v. Timely Publications, Inc.*, 610 So.2d 1296 (Fla. App. 1992).

General Program

A general program is a type of program that can be used by many clients without special adaptation. An example would be a program on accounts receivable.

Management Data Systems, Inc. v. Sta-Fed Computer Tax, Inc., 330 N.W. 2d 247 (Ct. App. Wisc. 1982).

General Purpose Computer

The general purpose computer is designed to perform operations under many different programs. *Gottschalk v. Benson*, 409 U.S. 63 (1972).

General Purpose Hardware

General purpose hardware is, as the name would suggest, hardware that is designed to perform data processing functions in addition to banking, financial and economic. *Association of Data Processing Service Organizations, Inc. v. Board of Governors of the Federal Reserve System*, Comp. Ind. Lit. Reptr. 1,1643 (Crt. App. D.C. 1984).

Geographic Data

Geographic data refers to spatial data in terms of their position with respect to a known co-ordinate system, their attributes (which are unrelated to their position) and their spatial inter-relationships with one another. Geographic Information Systems, Information and Privacy Commissioner/Ontario, April 1997, available at http://www.ipc.on.ca.

Geographic Information Systems (GIS)

A GIS is a computer system specifically designed to store, retrieve, and analyze geographically referenced information. Geographic Information Systems, Information and Privacy Commissioner/Ontario, April 1997, available at http://www.ipc.on.ca.

A GIS is a database management system that facilitates the storage, retrieval, manipulation and analysis of spatial and temporal data and its display in the form of maps, tables and figures. The information in a GIS describes entities that have a physical location and extent in some spatial region of interest, while queries involve identifying these entities based on their spatial and temporal attributes and relationships between entities. Geographic Information Systems, Information and Privacy Commissioner/Ontario, April 1997, available at http://www.ipc.on.ca.

GIF Tag

GIF Tags are the size of a single pixel and are invisible to users. Unseen, they record the users' movements throughout [a] website. . . to learn what information the user sought and viewed. *DoubleClick Inc. Privacy Litigation* Civ.0641 (N.R.V.) (S.D.N.Y. Mar. 28, 2001).

GII (Global Information Infrastructure)

A global information highway initiative put forward by the United States to G7 countries. *The Challenge of the Information Highway: Final Report of the Information Highway Advisory Council* (September 1995).

Gopher Server

A "gopher server" presents information in a set of menus, enabling a user who gains access to the server to select a series of increasingly detailed menu items before locating a desired file that can be displayed on or copied to the user's computer. *Shea v. Reno*, 1996 U.S. Dist. LEXIS 10720 (S.D.N.Y. 1996).

.gov

The generic Top Level Domain (gTLD) reserved for U.S. Federal government agencies. *Domain Name System Reform and Related Internet Governance Issues: A Consultation Paper*, Industry Canada available at *www.strategis.gc.ca*

Government of Canada Public Key Infrastructure

Is a public key infrastructure for use by departments within the Government of Canada and which operates in accordance with operational standards and directions of the Policy Management Authority. Public Key Infrastructure Management in the Government of Canada, Treasury Board of Canada Secretariat, May 27, 1999, available at http://www.tbs-sct.gc.ca/pubs_pol/ciopubs/PKI/pki1_e.html.

Government Purpose Rights

Means the rights of the government to use, duplicate and disclose detailed design, manufacturing, and process data and computer software by or on behalf of the government, including disclosure outside government for any government purpose. Federal Acquisition Regulation (FAR): Rights in Technical Data (Proposed Rules), Federal Register, Vol. 55, No. 199.

GPU

Graphics Processing Unit, which may consist of one or more *chips*. Monopolies and Mergers Commission — Video Games: A report on the supply of video games in the UK (LONDON: HMSO Cm2781).

Graphic Image Files (GIFs)

A GIF is created by scanning a photograph to create digital data that can be run through a computer. *Playboy Enterprises, Inc. v. Hardenburgh, Inc.*, 982 F.Supp. 503 (N.D. Ohio, 1997).

Graphical User Interface (GUI)

When a computer's visual displays incorporate significant graphic elements, as does the Macintosh, it is referred to as a graphical user interface (GUI or, in the argot of the trade, "gooey"). *Apple Computer Inc. v. Microsoft Corp.*, 1992 U.S. Dist. LEXIS 12219 (N.D. Cal. 1992).

Enables users to adjust the size and positions of each window through use of a mouse. Windows can be minimized in size and replaced by an icon to make more screen space available. *Re Microsoft Corporation*, Comp. Ind. Lit. Reptr. 16,485 (U.S. P.T.O. 1993).

[An interface] such as the one supported by the Apple Macintosh or M5-Windows, enables you to set the dimensions and position of each window by moving the mouse and clicking appropriate buttons. Windows can be arranged so that they do not overlap (tiled windows) or so they do overlap (overlaid windows). Overlaid windows (also called cascading windows) resemble a stack of pieces of paper lying on top of one another; only the topmost window is displayed in full. You can move a window to the top of the stack by positioning the pointer in the portion of the window that is visible and clicking the mouse buttons. This is known as popping. You can expand a window to fill the entire screen by selecting the window's zoom box. Philip E. Margolis, *The Random House Personal Computer Dictionary*, quoted in *Re Microsoft Corporation*, Comp. Ind. Lit. Reptr. 16,485 (U.S. P.T.O. 1993).

gTLD – Generic Top Level Domain Names

The group of TLDs that included .com, .org, .net, .edu, .mil, .int, .gov . *Domain Name System Reform and Related Internet Governance Issues: A Consultation Paper*, Industry Canada available at *www.strategis.gc.ca*

Hacker

A "hacker" is an individual who accesses another's computer system without authority. *Steve Jackson Games, Inc. v. United States Secret Service*, 816 F.Supp. 432 (W.D. Texas 1993).

We use the term "hacker" in this opinion to designate people who use computers for illegal activity. The term can also be used to describe legitimate computer users. *United States v. Riggs*, 967 F.2d 561 (11th Cir. 1992).

One who gains unauthorized, usually non-fraudulent access to another's computer system. The term "hackers" has also been understood to encompass both those who obtain unauthorized access to computer systems and those who simply enjoy using computers and experimenting with their capabilities as "innocent" hobbyists. *United States v. Riggs*, 2 CCH Comp. Cas. 43,316 (N.D. Ill. 1990).

"Computer hackers are hobbyists with intense interest in exploring the capabilities of computers and communications and causing these systems to perform to their limits. . . Hackers exhibit a spectrum of behaviour from benign to malicious. . . The word hacker has two very different meanings. The people I knew who call themselves hackers were software wizards who . . . knew all the nooks and crannies of the operating system . . . but in common usage, a hacker is someone who breaks into computers." *United States v. Riggs*, 2 CCH Comp. Cas. 43,316 (N.D. Ill. 1990).

Any person who attempts to enter a computer or communications network without authorization is known as a hacker. *A Survey of Legal Issues Relating to the Security of Electronic Information*, Department of Justice, Canada.

One who gains unauthorized, usually, illegal access to another's computer system. *In re Inuit Privacy Litigation*, 2001 U.S. Dist. LEXIS 5828 (C.D. Cal. 2001).

Hacking

Intentional misuse of authorized system access and unauthorized system access for the purposes of mischief, vandalism, sabotage, fraud or theft. Guidelines for the Security of Information Systems, O.E.C.D., November 26, 1992, available at http://www.oecd.org.dsti/sti/it/secur/prod/e_secur.htm.

Hard Disk

A hard disk drive is one of the primary types of media for storing and retrieving computer data. They are characterized by a fast access time and a fixed storage capacity. *United States of America v. Brown*, 2 CCH Comp. Cas. 46,414 (10th Cir. 1991).

Is a storage device which has been integrated with the computer hardware and allows the operator of the computer to leave the instructions from the floppy disk on the hard disk . . . thus obviating the necessity of inserting the floppy disk each time the operator wishes to start up the . . . system. *Perry Engineering Ltd. v. Farrage* (1989), 28 C.P.R. (3d) 221 (B.C. S.C.).

Hardware

The physical components of a system or device as opposed to the procedures required for its operation. *Chequecheck Services Ltd. v. Min. of Finance* (1980), 24 B.C.L.R. 217 (B.C. S.C.), reversed [1982] 5 W.W.R. 340 (B.C. C.A.).

Refers to the machine itself with all its component parts. *Clarke Irwin & Co. v. Singer Co. of Can.*, Ont. Div. Ct., Keith J., December 3, 1979, summarized at [1979] 3 A.C.W.S. 807.

Physical parts of the computer and ancillary equipment. *DPCE (U.K.) Ltd. v. International Computers Ltd.*, Q.B.D., Saville J., July 31, 1985 (unreported).

Is used to cover all those physical parts of the system which produce the desired results eventually in a printed or processed form when the program has been processed. *Han-Shan Tang Ltd. v. Macro-Micro Systems*, Q.B.D., Hoosen J., May 3, 1983 (unreported).

Hardware is the actual dealing in computers themselves or dealing in the rental by various businesses and organizations of computer time. *Digital Methods Ltd. v. Alphatext Ltd.*, Ont. H.C., Garrett J., June 30, 1978, summarized at [1978] 2 A.C.W.S. 376.

Refers to the naked, tangible parts of the machinery itself. *Honeywell Inc. v. Lithonia Lightning Inc.*, 317 F.Supp. 406 (N.D. Ga. 1970).

Any electronic or mechanical equipment used in association with data processing. *In Re Graphics Technology Corp.*, 222 U.S.P.Q. 179 (T.T.A.B. 1984).

The difference between computer hardware and computer software is well known. The hardware may be likened to the machinery which produces the results. To take a very crude analogy in the field of photography, the camera, the software is the product introduced into the machine by which some desired result is going to be achieved, again on that very crude analogy, the film. *CSS International U.K. Ltd. v. Immediate Business Systems Plc*, Ch. D., Whitford J., July 13, 1983 (unreported).

"Hardware" refers to the physical components of a computer, the machine itself, whereas "software" refers to the programs and systems used by the hardware. *Universal Computers (Systems) Ltd. v. Datamedia Corp.*, 653 F.Supp. 518 (D.N.J. 1987).

Hardware is a word in common use to describe the physical articles, being the computer, its fittings, and the physical articles which enable the computer to operate . . . disks or hardware. *Autodesk Australia Pty Ltd. v. Dyason* (1989), 15 I.P.R. 1 (Aus. Fed. Ct.), reversed [1990] A.I.P.C. 36,446 (Aus. Fed. Ct. FC).

Hardware refers to the physical computer equipment. *Computer Sciences Corp. v. Commissioner of Internal Revenue*, 63 T.C. 327 (U.S. Tax. Crt. 1974).

Hardware is the equipment used in data processing systems, such as the mainframe computer, terminals, printers, memory devices and the like. *Assn. of Data Processing Service Organizations, Inc. v. Board of Governors of the Federal Reserve System*, Comp. Ind. Lit. Reptr. 1,1643 (Crt. App. D.C. 1984).

Hardware is in the computer machinery, its electronic circuitry and peripheral items such as keyboards, readers, scanners and printers. *Advent Systems Ltd. v. Unisys Corp.*, 925 F.2d 670 (3rd Cir. 1991).

Hardware refers to the physical components of a computer system, i.e., the computer itself and its input and output devices. *Geac J & E Systems Ltd. v. Craig Erickson Systems Inc.* (1993), 46 C.P.R. (3d) 25 (Ont. Gen. Div.).

The physical equipment used to process programs and data in a cryptographic module. "Security Requirements for Cryptographic Modules", FIPS Pub. 140-1, Federal Information Processing Standards Publication, January 11, 1994, available at http://csrc.nist.gov/fips/fips1401.htm.

Electronic and other physical componentry making up a computer system or other type of electronic device. *Digital Technology and the Copyright Act 1994: A Discussion Paper, Competition and Enterprise Branch, July 2001 (New Zealand)*.

Hash

A mathematical function which maps from a large (possibly very large) domain into a smaller range. It may be used to reduce a potentially long message into a "hash value" or "message digest" which is sufficiently compact to be used as an input into a digital signature algorithm. A Cryptology Policy Framework for Electronic Commerce, Task Force on Electronic Commerce, Industry Canada, February 1998.

Hash Function

A function which maps a bit string of arbitrary length to a fixed-length bit string and satisfies the following properties: (1) It is computationally infeasible to find any input that maps to any pre-specified output. (2) It is computationally infeasible to find any two distinct inputs that map to the same output. A Cryptology Policy Framework for Electronic Commerce, Task Force on Electronic Commerce, Industry Canada, February 1998.

The term "hash function" describes a function that transforms an input into a unique output of fixed (and usually smaller) size that is dependent on the input. For some purposes (e.g. error checking, digital signatures), it is desirable that it be impossible to derive the input data given only the hash function's output—this type of function is known as a "one-way hash function." Hash functions have many uses in cryptography and computer science, and numerous one-way hash functions are widely known. *Bernstein v. Department of State*, No. 97-16686 (9th Cir. Mar. 6th, 1999).

Hashing Algorithm

A "hashing algorithm" is an algorithm which maps (compresses) an input string of arbitrary length to an output string of fixed length so that it is computationaly infeasible to find: two distinct inputs that map to the same output; for a given output, an input which is mapped to that output; or for a given input a second input which is mapped to the same output. Security and Electronic Authorization and Authentication Guideline, Communications Security Establishment, Government of Canada September 1995, CID/01/15.

Hague Conference

Special Commission of the Hague Conference on Private International Law

HDTV (High-Definition Television)

Television with greater resolution than the current 525-line television standard. *The Challenge of the Information Highway: Final Report of the Information Highway Advisory Council* (September 1995).

Headend

The installation where television signals are received by cable companies from outside sources like satellites and terrestrial transmitters. Submission of the Director of Investigation and Research to the CRTC Re Public Notice CRTC 1994-130.

Header

A "header" is a section of a digital work where information, data, codes and instructions may be embedded. National Information Infrastructure: A Preliminary Draft of the Report of the Working Group on Intellectual Property Rights, July 1994.

Header Files

Header files are repositories of common definitions and declarations. If a programmer knows that an operating system contains a certain header file, then the programmer can simply refer to the header file and avoid reproducing all of the definitions and declarations. Of course, such a program can only run with an operating system having the proper header file. *Unix System Laboratories, Inc. v. Berkeley Software Design, Inc.*, 27 U.S.P.Q. 2d 1721 (D. New Jer. 1993).

Help Screens

Help screens are an electronic form of operating manual for those using (a) computer system. *Madeley Pty Ltd. v. Touche Ross*, McGarvie, J., Aust. Fed. Ct., Dec. 21, 1989 (unreported).

Hertz

A unit of frequency designating one cycle per second. *The Challenge of the Information Highway: Final Report of the Information Highway Advisory Council* (September 1995).

Hexadecimal Notation

Hexadecimal notation is based on a number system having a base 16. It is merely a shorthand way of writing the binary code. It is used because it uses less characters and is therefore less cumbersome than binary. *Apple Computer Inc. v. Mackintosh Computers Ltd.* (1986), 28 D.L.R. (4th) 178 (Fed. T.D.).

A base 16 numbering system used as a shorthand representation of a string of binary instructions. *E.F. Johnson Co. v. Uniden Corp. of America*, 623 F.Supp. 1485 (D. Minn. 1985).

Instructions denoted by using a system in which 16 characters are used (in this case the numbers from 0 to 9 together with the letters from A to F). *IBM Corp. v. Ordinateurs Spirales Inc.* (1984), 2 C.I.P.R. 56 (Fed. T.D.).

H-Matrix

An H-Matrix is a series of 1's and 0's arranged in rows and columns in a matrix format. *E.F. Johnson Co. v. Uniden Corp. of America*, 623 F.Supp. 1485 (D. Minn. 1985).

HP3000

This is a computer system manufactured by Hewlett-Packard. Its intended use is for applications to solve business oriented data processing problems as opposed to engineering type problems. *Delrina Corp. v. Triolet Systems, Inc.* (1992), 47 C.P.R. (3d) 1 (Ont. H.C.).

High Definition Television (HDTV)

HDTV is designed to enhance the quality of existing television programming services, but offers the promise of a leap into new markets. Study on New Media and Copyright, *Final Report* (Nordicity Group Ltd., June 30, 1994) prepared for Industry Canada, New Media, Information Technologies Industry Branch.

High Level Languages

While assembler language has advantages over machine code it still requires many instructions to be written in order to achieve the simplest tasks. A variety of so-called high level languages has been devised in order to simplify the task of the programmer. These high level languages have been given names. They include such languages as Basic and derivatives of it, Fortran, Cobol and Pascal. The use of these languages enables the programmer to write a program in terms which more nearly resemble ordinary English than those used in lower level languages. They also permit what is, for the computer, quite a complex operation to be directed by a relatively compact command. Like assembler language, high level languages have to be translated into machine code before they can be understood and acted upon by a computer. The programs which have been devised to achieve this are called compilers. As with assembler language, the translation process is usually possible in one direction only. It is not generally possible to recreate a program in its higher language form from its translation into machine code. *John Richardson Computers Ltd. v. Flanders*, [1993] F.S.R. 497 (Ch.D.).

Hit

An instance of someone or something (*e.g.*, a Webcrawler application) accessing a Web page. The number of hits a Web site receives is therefore a function of both the number of visitors to the site and the number of pages each visitor accesses at the site. Ministry of Revenue Advisory Committee, Report of the Committee On Electronic Commerce, April 30, 1998, Industry Canada.

A hit is the transfer of a single file from a web site to a computer user. *Hardrock Café International (US), Inc. v. Morton 1999 U.S.*, Dist. LEXIS 8340 (S.D.N.Y. 1999).

Hold a Private Key

To use or be able to use a private key. General Usage for International Digitally Insured Commerce (Guidec), International Chamber of Commerce, 1997, available at http://www.icc.wbo.org/guidec2.htm.

Home Page

A home page is the first page or screen presented at a site on the World Wide Web. It acts like a table of contents for the Web site, offering direct links to the different parts of the site. The usual address for a Web site is the home page address, although you can enter the address (URL) of any page and have that page sent to you. The Internet: A Guide For Ontario Government Organizations, Information and Privacy Commissioner/Ontario, May 1998, available at http://www.ipc.on.ca.

Typically, one page on each Web site is the "home page", or the first access point to the site. The home page is usually a hypertext document that presents an overview of the site and hyperlinks to the other pages comprising the site. *United States of America v. Microsoft Corporation*, Civil Action No. 98-1232 (D. Col. Nov. 1999).

A home page is "one page on each Web site. . .[that typically serves as] the first access point to the site. The home page is usually a hypertext document that presents an overview of the site and hyperlinks to the other pages comprising the site." *Universal City Studios, Inc. v. Reimerdes,* 55 U.S.P.Q. 2d 1873 (S. D.N.Y. 2000).

A "homepage" is the "front door" of the website. *British Columbia Automobile Assn. v. OPEIU. Local 378* (2001), 10 C.P.R. (4th) 423 (B.C.S.C.).

Host

A computer or device that is attached to the Internet is often referred to as a "host". In order to facilitate communications between hosts, each host has a numerical IP (Internet Protocol) address. *Intermatic Inc. v. Toeppen,* 40 U.S.P.Q. (2d) 1412 (N.D. Ill. 1996).

A host is a computer that is connected to the Internet that has a unique Internet Protocol (IP) address. The Emerging Digital Economy, United States Department of Commerce, http://www.ecommerce.gov.

A device in a network that accepts and transmits data. Examples include computers, printers, servers, terminals. *Domain Name System Reform and Related Internet Governance Issues: A Consultation Paper,* Industry Canada available at *www.strategis.gc.ca*

Hosts actually possess to fungible addresses: a numeric "IP" address such as 123,456.123.12, and a alphanumeric "domain name" such as microsoft.com, with greater mnemonic potential. Internet domain names are similar to telephone number mnemonics, but they are of greater importance, since there is no satisfactory Internet equivalent to a telephone company or a white pages or directory assistance, and domain names can often be guessed. A domain name mirroring a corporate name may be a valuable corporate asset, as it facilitates communication with a customer base. *TV Networks v. Curry,* 867 F.Supp. 202 (S.D.N.Y. 1994).

Host Server

A 'host server' is a computer that is connected to a network, which provides data and services to other computers. Such services may include data storage, file transfer, data processing, email, bulletin board services, world wide web, etc. *Amberson Holdings LLC v. Westside Storey Newspaper* 56 U.S.P.Q. 2d 1847 (D.N.J. 2000)

HTML

Hypertext markup language; an open, evolving standard for coding content to be displayed in browsers; the language of the World Wide Web. HTML allows data, text, graphics, video, and audio files to be linked so that a user can move easily from one collection of information to another. HTML is an application of SGML (standard generalized markup language, ISO 8879), a text-coding standard employed in publishing. Ministry of Revenue Advisory Committee, Report of the Committee On Electronic Commerce, April 30, 1998, Industry Canada.

This is an acronym for HyperText Markup Language. HTML is the computer language used to create hypertext or linked documents. It creates the structure around the text, images, and other parts of a Web page so that the file can be read by a browser. The Internet: A Guide For Ontario Government Organizations, Information and Privacy Commissioner/Ontario, May 1998, available at http://www.ipc.on.ca..

HTTP

Hypertext Transfer Protocol. *Intermatic Inc. v. Toeppen*, 40 U.S.P.Q. (2d) 1412 (N.D. Ill. 1996).

HTTP stands for HyperText Transfer Protocol and is the method by which hypertext files are transferred across the Net. HTTP means that everyone using the Web to transfer hypertext files is doing it the same way. HTTP is the standard and exclusive protocol of the Web. When the URL begins with "http://", the file will be displayed as hypertext with working links. The Internet: A Guide For Ontario Government Organizations, Information and Privacy Commissioner/Ontario, May 1998, available at http://www.ipc.on.ca.

Huffman Compression

Huffman compression is a method, named after the person who invented it, of storing data in a smaller amount of space than would otherwise be possible by encoding characters in variable length bit strings. Normally each of the possible 256 characters is encoded in exactly 8 bits, but in Huffman encoding, common characters are encoded using short strings (less than 8 bits), and uncommon characters are encoded using longer strings (more than 8 bits). The net effect is ... a saving of up to 50% of the storage space. The actual saving depends upon the relative frequency of occurrence of each of the characters in the data actually stored. *Powerflex Services Pty Ltd. v. Data Access Corp.* (1997), 37 I.P.R. 436 (Aust. C.A.).

Human-Readable Form

A presentation of a digital message such that it can be perceived by human beings. General Usage for International Digitally Insured Commerce (Guidec), International Chamber of Commerce, 1997, available at http://www.icc.wbo.org/guidec2.htm.

Hybrid Communication Service

Is a hybrid service offering wherein the data processing capability is incidental to the message-switching function or purpose. Computer Inquiry (Final Decision), 28 F.C.C.2d 267 (F.C.C. 1971).

Hybrid Data Processing Service

Is an offering of a data processing service utilizing common carrier communications facilities for the transmission of data between remote computers and customer terminals. Second Computer Inquiry (Tentative Decision), 72 F.C.C.2d 358 (F.C.C. 1979).

Is a hybrid service offering wherein the message-switching capability is incidental to the data process function or purpose. Computer Inquiry (Final Decision), 28 F.C.C.2d 267 (F.C.C. 1971).

Hybrid Service

Is an offering of service which combines Remote Access data processing and message-switching to form a single integrated service. Computer Inquiry (Final Decision), 28 F.C.C.2d 267 (F.C.C. 1971).

HyperLink (See also Link)

A "hyperlink" is highlighted text or images that, when selected by the user, permit him to view another, related Web document. With these links a user can move seamlessly between documents, regardless of their location; when a user viewing the document located on one server selects a link to a document located elsewhere, the browser will automatically connect the second server and display the document. *Bensusan Restaurant Corporation v. King*, 1996 WL 509 716 (S.D.N.Y. 1996)

A hyperlink is a link from one site on the Internet to a second site on the Internet. "Clicking" on a designated space on the initial page which references the subsequent site by a picture, by some highlighted text or by some other indication will take a person viewing the initial page to a second page. In addition to their use in indexes, hyperlinks are commonly placed on the existing web pages, thus allowing Internet users to move from web page to web page at the click of a button, without having to type in URLs. *Intermatic Inc. v. Toeppen*, 40 U.S.P.Q. (2d) 1412 (N.D. Ill. 1996).

A hypertext link allows a user to move directly from one web location to another by using the mouse to click twice on the coloured link. *Cybersell Inc. v. Cybersell Inc.*, 44 U.S.P.Q. 2d 1928 (9th Cir. 1997).

A "hyperlink" allows Internet users to move directly from one website to another by clicking on the second website's address, which is presented in coloured text on the first website. *Origin Instruments Corp. v. Adaptive Computer Systems, Inc*, 1999 WL 76794 (N.D. Tex. 1999).

Hyperlinks can be automatic links or user-activated. A link is automatic when a code is embedded in the Web page which instructs the browser, upon obtaining access to the first site, to automatically download a file from the second site. The information from the second site is pulled without the need for further action on the part of the user. A link is user-activated when the user must click the mouse button over the hyperlink in order to obtain access to the information from the second site. If the linked files are located on another server, the user's browser makes a direct connection to the second server. The user-activated hyperlink may be made to the home page or a subpage located on the second site, in which case, the end user may have to take further action to access a particular file at that site. The link may also be made directly to a specific file, in which case the user will receive the content represented by that file without the need for further action. *Public Performance of Musical Works* 1996-1998 (Tariff 22) (1999), 1 C.P.R. (4th) 417 (Copyright Board).

Links are often graphics or logos which, if "clicked on" by the user with a computer mouse, will transport the user to a different web page covering a new topic of information. *American Civil Liberties Union et al. v. Johnson*, 4 F.Supp. 2d 1029 (D.N. Mex. 1998).

Almost all Web documents contain "links", which are short sections of text or image that refer and link to another Web document. When selected by the user, the "linked" document is automatically displayed, wherever in the world it is actually stored. "The Web is thus comparable to both a vast library including millions of readily available and indexed publications and a sprawling mall offering goods and services." *Cyberspace Communications, Inc. et al. v. Engler*, 55 F. Supp. 2d 737 (E.D. F. Ch. 1999).

Through a "hyperlink" a browser may connect to another website by clicking on the highlighted text or images on the initial website. *Blumenthal v. Drudge*, 1992 F. Supp. 44 (D.D.C. 1998).

Any page on a Web site may contain one or more hyperlinks to pages on the same or other Web sites, located on the same or different servers from the one that hosts the linking site. The files at the other site normally are under the control of another entity. However, hyperlinks may be made either with or without a business relationship with the owners of the sites to which links are made. *Public Performance of Musical Works* 1996-1998 (Tariff 22) (1999), 1 C.P.R. (4th) 417 (Copyright Board).

Programming a particular point on a screen to transfer the user to another web page when the point, referred to as a hyperlink, is clicked is called linking. *Universal City Studios, Inc. v. Reimerdes*, 55 U.S.P.Q. 2d 1873 (S. D.N.Y. 2000).

A means of jumping from one electronic document on the Web to another. The linking information is in the form of coding that includes the URL of the second document. *Digital Technology and the Copyright Act 1994: A Discussion Paper, Competition and Enterprise Branch, July 2001 (New Zealand).*

Can be used as cross-references within a single document, between documents on the same site, or between documents on different sites. *United States of America v. Microsoft Corporation*, Civil Action No. 98-1232 (D. Col. Nov. 1999).

Hyperlink is highlighted text or images that, when selected by the user, permits him to view another related Web Document. *Jeri-Joe Knitwear, Inc. vs. Club Italia,* Inc. 2000 U.S. Dist. LEXIS 4891 (S.D.N.Y. 2000).

A hyperlink or link, connects one website to another, so that a user can move directly from one website to a second. *The Putman Pit, Inc. v. City of Cookeville*, 2000 FED. App. 0235P (6th Cir. July 19, 2000).

A hyperlink is highlighted text or images that, when selected by the user, permit[s] [her] to view another, related Web document. *Bihari v. Gross,* 56 U.S.P.Q. 2d 1489 (S.D.N.Y. 2000).

A final feature of the internet of some relevance to this appeal is these hyperlinks to give access from one website page to others on the same site, or to pages on other sites located on the same or another server. When a hyperlink is imbedded in a Website Page, access to other pages is automatic, in the sense that, having gained access to the first page, the end user need take no further action in order to gain access to a linked pages. *Society of Composers, Authors & Music Publishers of Canada v. Canadian Association of Internet Providers* (2002), 19 C.P.R. (4th) 289 (Fed.C.A.).

Hypermedia

Hypermedia links not only text but graphics, sound and video from various sources and ways which are multidimensional and cross-linked rather than linear. Study on New Media and Copyright, *Final Report* (Nordicity Group Ltd., June 30, 1994) prepared for Industry Canada, New Media, Information Technologies Industry Branch.

Use of data, text, graphics, video and voice as elements in a hypertext system. All the forms of information are linked together, so that a user can easily move from one form to another. *The Challenge of the Information Highway: Final Report of the Information Highway Advisory Council* (September 1995).

Hypertext

Hypertext allows a user to jump from topic to related topic with internally cross-referenced written information. Study on New Media and Copyright, *Final Report* (Nordicity Group Ltd., June 30, 1994) prepared for Industry Canada, New Media, Information Technologies Industry Branch.

Text that contains embedded links to other documents or information. *The Challenge of the Information Highway: Final Report of the Information Highway Advisory Council* (September 1995).

Text that contains embedded links to other documents. Ministry of Revenue Advisory Committee, Report of the Committee On Electronic Commerce, April 30, 1998, Industry Canada.

Most Web pages are in the form of "hypertext"; that is, they contain annotated references, or "hyperlinks", to other Web pages. *United States of America v. Microsoft Corporation*, Civil Action No. 98-1232 (D. Col. Nov. 1999).

Text that includes linking information (on the Internet, in the form of hyperlinks) to other, usually related, documents. *Digital Technology and the Copyright Act 1994: A Discussion Paper, Competition and Enterprise Branch, July 2001 (New Zealand).*

The programming language used to create the content, design and overall layout of individual webpages is known as "HyperText Markup Language" or "HTML". *British Columbia Automobile Assn. v. OPEIU. Local 378* (2001), 10 C.P.R. (4th) 423 (B.C.S.C.).

ICANN

Internet Corporation for Assigned Names and Numbers

Icons

Graphical representations of objects. *Xerox Corp. v. Apple Computer Inc.*, Comp. Ind. Lit. Reptr. 11,155 (N.D.Cal. 1990).

Graphic displays of the computer's functions. *In re Apple Computer Securities Litigation*, 886 F.2d 1109 (9th Cir. 1989).

[Icons are] small pictures that represent commands, files, or windows. By moving the pointer to the icon and pressing a mouse button, you can execute a command or convert the icon into a window. Philip E. Margolis, *The Random House Personal Computer Dictionary*, quoted in *Re Microsoft Corporation*, Comp. Ind. Lit. Reptr. 16,485 (U.S. P.T.O. 1993).

ICQ (the Messaging Service)

I Seek You. *America Online, Inc. vs. Shih-hsien Huang*, 2000 U.S. Dist. LEXIS 10232 (E.D. Vir. 2000).

Identity Theft

Identity theft involves acquiring key pieces of someone's identifying information in order to impersonate them and commit various crimes in that person's name. Identity Theft: Who's Using Your Name?, Information and Privacy Commissioner/Ontario, June 1997, available at http://www.ipc.on.ca.

Identity Protector

An identity protector may be viewed as an element of the system that controls the release of an individual's true identity to various processes within the information system. Its effect is to cordon off certain areas of the system which do not require access to true identity. The identity protector works in such a way as to protect the interests of the user. One of its most important functions is to convert a user's actual identity into a pseudo-identity — an alternate (digital) identity that the user may adopt when using the system. Privacy-Enhancing Technologies: The Path to Anonymity, Information and Privacy Commissioner/Ontario, August 1995, available at http://www.ipc.on.ca.

Identity protectors, such as blind signatures and digital pseudonyms, are mathematical sequences based on encryption techniques that enable users to conduct electronic transactions in an anonymous manner, while at the same time, allowing the service provider to verify the user's authenticity and eligibility for benefits and services. Identity Theft: Who's Using Your Name?, Information and Privacy Commissioner/Ontario, June 1997, available at http://www.ipc.on.ca.

IETF

Internet Engineering Task Force

IFPI

International Federation of Phonographic Industries

Image

The representation of a source record that can be used to generate an intelligible reproduction of that record, or the reproduction itself, where:

[el3]a. The reproduction is made with the intention of standing in place of the source record;

[el3]b. The interpretation of the reproduction, for the purposes for which it is being used, yields the same information as the source record; and

[el3]c. The limitations of the reproduction (e.g., resolution, tonal or hues) are well defined and do not obscure significant details.

[el3]The source record may be subject to disposal for the purpose of constituting the image as the permanent record. National Standard of Canada, Microfilm and Electronic Images as documentary evidence, Can/CGSB-72.11-93.

Image Management Program

An authorized program following strict control guidelines to achieve specific objectives in the capture, storage, and retrieval of images (including photographic and electronic capture). This may also include the disposal of source records. National Standard of Canada, Microfilm and Electronic Images as documentary evidence, CAN/CGSB-72.11-93.

Image Management System

A system of procedures and technological components that operate in an integrated manner to capture, store, index, retrieve, distribute, insert, erase and modify images. National Standard of Canada, Microfilm and Electronic Images as documentary evidence, CAN/CGSB-72.11-93.

Impairment

In relation to electronic communication to or from a computer, includes: (a) the prevention of any such communication; and (b) the impairment of any such communication on an electronic link or network used by the computer, but does not include a mere interception of any such communication. *Property Damage and Computer Offences Act 2002 (Australia).*

Incumbent Local Exchange Carrier (ILEC):

A company that, prior to the introduction of competition, provided monopoly local telephone service. *Report to the Governor in Council: Status of Competition in Canadian Telecommunications Markets, Deployment/Accessibility of Advanced Telecommunications Infrastructure and Services, September, 2001.*

Information

The word "information" has a very wide connotation. An instruction or a set of instructions are comprehended as constituting information. *Autodesk Australia Pty Ltd. v. Dyason*, (1989), 15 I.P.R. 1 (Aus. Fed. Ct.), reversed [1990] A.I.P.C. 36,446 (Aus. Fed. Ct. FC).

Is the meaning assigned to data by means of conventions applied to that data. O.E.C.D. Guildines from the Security of Information Systems adopted November 26, 1992, available at http://www.oecd.org/dsti/sdi/it/secur/prod/e_secur.htm.

Means data, text, images, sounds, codes, computer programs, software, databases, or the like. *Uniform Computer Information Transactions Act*, National Conference of Commissioners on Uniform State Laws, available at http://www.law.upenn.u/bll/ulc/ucita/citim99.htm.

Information Certifier

Means a person or entity which, in the course of its business, engages in [providing identification services] [certifying information] which [are][is] used to support the use of [enhanced] electronic signatures. Draft Uniform Rules on Electronic Signatures, UNCITRAL, 29 June 1999.

Information Highway

The term flows from the convergence of once-separated communications and computing systems into a single global network of networks. It also refers to the content carried on these electronic networks. Finally, as an integrated part of the Information Highway, the software intelligence available will enable users to navigate pathways to a whole universe of information. Connection Community Content, *The Challenge of the Information Highway: Final Report of the Information Highway Advisory Council, (September 1995).*

The term "Information Highway" describes a network of networks that will link Canadian homes, businesses and institutions to a wide range of services. The Information Highway will provide the necessary infrastructure for Canada's emerging knowledge-based economy and, therefore, development of the highway will be critical to the competitiveness of all sectors of the economy. Order in Council P.C. 1994-1105.

The Information Highway is more than cable and copper wire; it is a metaphor for the promise and uncertainty surrounding the emergence of a world-wide communications network driven by innovation, competition and technology. The highway links past achievements in communications to future aspirations, binds economy and culture in ways that harness the creative energies of Canadians, and opens gateways to the global trade and information products and services. Competition and Culture on Canada's Information Highway: Managing the Realities of Transition, CRTC (the "Convergence Report"), May 19, 1995.

The information highway will encompass a variety of terrestrial and wireless distribution technologies and service providers connected in ways that serve the increasing demands of Canadian businesses and institutions, as well as individual consumers — at home, in the office or on the road. Competition and Culture on Canada's Information Highway: Managing the Realities of Transition, CRTC (the "Convergence Report"), May 19, 1995.

The popular phrase "information highway" has been used here as a convenient term to refer to the vast electronic networks that will be able to carry information through voice, data and video services. A key feature will be the interactive nature of these networks, in that they will allow users to both receive and provide information. The Information Highway: Access and Privacy Principles, Information and Privacy Commissioner/Ontario, December 1994, available at http://www.ipc.on.ca.

Information Privacy

Is defined as the right of individuals to determine when, how and to what extent they will share personal information about themselves with others. Privacy: The Protection of Personal Information, Task Force on Electronic Commerce, Industry Canada at "http://e-comm.ic.gc.ca/English/privacy/632d4.htm".

Refers to an individual's claim to control the terms under which "Personal Information" - information that can be linked to an individual or distinct group of individuals (e.g., a household) is acquired, disclosed, and used. Privacy and the NII: US Department of Congress, October 19, 1995.

Information Processing System

Means an electronic system for creating, generating, sending, receiving, storing, displaying, or processing information. *Uniform Computer Information Transactions Act*, National Conference of Commissioners on Uniform State Laws, available at http://www.law.upenn.u/bll/ulc/ucita/citim99.htm.

Information Publishing Service

Provision to any unaffiliated person of any information (a) which the publisher has (or has caused to be) authored, originated, gathered, collected, produced, compiled, edited, categorized, or indexed; or (b) in which the publisher has a direct or indirect financial or proprietary interest. *U.S. v. American Telephone & Telegraph Co.*, 552 F.Supp. 131 (D.D.C. 1982), affirmed 103 S.Ct. 1240 (1983).

Information Services

The term "information service" means the offering of a capability of generating, acquiring, storing, transforming, processing, retrieving, utilizing, or making available information via telecommunications, and includes electronic publishing, but does not include any use of any such capability for the management, control, or operation of a telecommunications system or the management of a telecommunications service. United States Telecommunications Act of 1996.

The offering of a capability for generating, acquiring, storing, transforming, processing, retrieving, using or making available information which may be conveyed via telecommunications. *U.S. v. American Telephone & Telegraph Co.*, 552 F.Supp. 131 (D.D.C. 1982), affirmed 103 S.Ct. 1240 (1983).

Information Systems

An information system is broadly defined as a system which provides organizations with the information required to conduct various activities. There are generally three types of information systems: transaction-processing systems, programmed decision-making systems, and decision-support systems. Privacy-Enhancing Technologies: The Path to Anonymity, Information and Privacy Commissioner/Ontario, August 1995, available at http://www.ipc.on.ca.

Means computers, communication facilities, computer and communication networks and data and information that may be stored, processed, retrieved or transmitted by them, including programs, specifications and procedures for their operation, use and maintenance. O.E.C.D. Guildines from the Security of Information Systems adopted November 26, 1992, available at http://www.oecd.org/dsti/sdi/it/secur/prod/e_secur.htm.

Means a system for generating, sending, receiving, storing or otherwise processing data messages. UNCITRAL Model Law On Electronic Commerce (1996).

Means a system for generating, sending, receiving, storing or otherwise processing data messages. *UNCITRAL, Working Group IV (Electronic Commerce), Thirty-ninth session New York, 11-15 March, 2002.*

Information Technology Business

Information Technology Business means it [the business] provides computer-based systems and related data processing services to various commercial and governmental customers. *Computer Associates Int., Inc. c. Electronic Data Systems Corp.*, 816 F.Supp. (E.D.N.Y. 1993).

Informational Content

Means information that is intended to be communicated to or perceived by an individual in the ordinary use of the information, or the equivalent of that information. The term does not include computer instructions that control the inter-action of a computer program with other computer programs or with a machine or device. *Uniform Computer Information Transactions Act*, National Conference of Commissioners on Uniform State Laws, available at http://www.law.upenn.u/bll/ulc/ucita/citim99.htm.

Informational Rights

Include all rights in information created under laws governing patents, copyrights, mask works, trade secrets, trademarks, publicity rights, or any other law that gives a person, independently of contract, a right to control or preclude another person's use of or access to the information on the basis of the rights holder's interest in the information. *Uniform Computer Information Transactions Act*, National Con-ference of Commissioners on Uniform State Laws, available at http://www.law.upenn.u/bll/ulc/ucita/citim99.htm.

Input

Input refers to data capture, e.g., keypunching, optical character recognition, and the entry of data into the system in machine readable form. *United States v. Jones*, 553 F.2d 351 (4th 1977).

Input/Output Processing

Comprises the uses of a computer capability resident in a carrier network facility for the purpose of making disparate computers and terminals compatible with each other. Typical functions are the formatting, editing, and buffering of data to make it compatible with the electrical characteristics of different transmission media. Second Computer Inquiry (Notice of Inquiry), 5 C.L.S.R. 1381 (F.C.C. 1976).

Comprises the uses of processing capability resident in a carrier network facility for the purpose of making disparate information sources and receptors compatible with the transmission system and with each other. Such processing activities include those necessary for formatting, editing, and buffering of information to make it compatible with the electrical characteristics of different transmission media. Second Computer Inquiry (Supplemental Notice), 42 Fed. Reg. 13029 (F.C.C. 1977).

The process of, or equipment used in transmitting information to or from the computer. The input of data to a program and the output of processed data from a program. Input of data occurs from some external device such as a keyboard, disk file or magnetic tape. The output of processed data is to an external device such as a terminal screen, printer, disk file or magnetic tape. *Delrina Corp. v. Triolet Systems, Inc.* (1992), 47 C.P.R. (3d) 1 (Ont. H.C.).

Instruction

An expression in a program or routine, or a sequence of characters in a machine language, which specifies in operation (especially in basis operation) and frequency also of one or more operands, and results in its performance by the computer. *Autodesk Australia Pty Ltd. v. Dyason* (1989), 15 I.P.R. 1 (Aus. Fed. Ct.), reversed [1990] A.I.P.C. 36,446 (Aus. Fed. Ct. FC).

A number or symbol which causes a computer to perform some specified action. *Autodesk Australia Pty Ltd. v. Dyason*, supra.

Code instructions embody and implement the programmer's solution to a programming problem — a solution that directly determines how well or how poorly the program runs. *Unix System Laboratories, Inc. v. Berkeley Software Design, Inc.*, 27 U.S.P.Q. 2d 1721 (D. New Jer. 1993).

Instrument

Any disc, tape, sound track or other device on or in which information is recorded or stored by mechanical, electronic or other means. . . Forgery and Counterfeiting Act, 1981, U.K.

.int

The generic Top Level Domain (gTLD) for organizations established by international treaties, or international databases. *Domain Name System Reform and Related Internet Governance Issues: A Consultation Paper*, Industry Canada available at *www.strategis.gc.ca*

Integrated Circuit

Is a product, in its final form or an intermediate form, at least one of the elements of which is an active element, and some or all of the interconnections of which are integrally formed in and/or on a piece of material, and which is intended to perform an electronic function. World Intellectual Property Organization, Treaty on Intellectual Property in Respect of Integrated Circuits.

Means a product, in a final or intermediate form, that is intended to perform an electronic function and in which the elements, at least one of which is an active element, and some or all of the interconnections, are integrally formed in or on, or both in and on, a piece of material. *Integrated Circuit Topography Act*, S.C. 1990, c. 37.

A single "chip" the size of a small fingernail contains multiple layers of silicon or germanium and thousands of intricate circuits measured and fabricated to molecular width and capable of millions of separate operations per second, and more often than not, costing millions of dollars in capital investment from concept to market. These products are created by a company for multiple uses, from running traffic signals, to space craft, or from the simplest task of ordering the retrieval of information, to the enormously complex task of "painting" a complex design on a screen and changing it instantly at the command of the operator (the QPDM type graphics chip exemplifies this result). Because a vertically integrated semi-conductor manufacturer has many customers whose demands may vary, it must have a product line of many chips for various uses. It will be immediately recognized, therefore, that the business requires lots of research and development for many chips for a complete product line. *Advanced Micro Devices, Inc. and Intel Corp.*, CCH Comp. Cases 60,218 (Arb. Award. 1990).

An integrated circuit or chip as understood in the science of electronics is a complex of minuscule switches joined by "wires" etched from extremely thin films of metal; the etching process is generally accomplished by "masks" or stencils used to etch a given pattern of circuiting upon the chip. *Avel Pty Ltd. v. Jonathan Wells* (1992), 22 I.P.R. 305 (Aust. H.C.).

Integrated Circuit Memory Devices

Video games are but one example of the uses to which integrated circuit memory devices are put in a wide range of items. They are also used in such things as cash registers, washing machines, television sets, mobile phones, word processors and printers, and cardiac monitors and pacemakers. *Avel Pty Ltd. v. Jonathan Wells* (1992), 22 I.P.R. 305 (Aust. H.C.).

Integrated Networks

Integrated networks provide the capacity to carry voice, video and data on the same facilities. Competition and Culture on Canada's Information Highway: Managing the Realities of Transition, CRTC (the "Convergence Report"), May 19, 1995

Integrity

Integrity of information means the information is accurate, complete and dependable. *A Survey of Legal Issues Relating to the Security of Electronic Information, Department of Justice, Canada.*

Means the characteristic of data and information being accurate and complete and the preservation of accuracy and completeness. O.E.C.D. Guildines from the Security of Information Systems adopted November 26, 1992, available at http://www.oecd.org/dsti/sdi/it/secur/prod/ e_secur.htm.

The property that sensitive data has not been modified or deleted in an unauthorized and undetected manner. "Security Requirements for Cryptographic Modules", FIPS Pub. 140-1, Federal Information Processing Standards Publication, January 11, 1994, available at http://csrc.nist.gov/fips/fips1401.htm.

Means the property that data or information has not been modified or altered in an unauthorised manner. *OECD Guidelines for Cryptography Policy*, March 27, 1997, available at *www.oecd.org*.

The property that data or information has not been modified or altered in an unauthorized manner. UNCITRAL Report of the Working Group on Electronic Commerce, September 18-29, 2000, A/CN. 94/483.

The property that data has not been changed, destroyed, or lost in an unauthorized or accidental manner. A simple checksum can provide integrity from incidental changes in the data; message authentication is similar but also protects against an active attack to alter the data whereby a change in the checksum is introduced so as to match the change in the data. *XML-Signature Syntax and Processing, W3C Recommendation 12 February 2002.*

Integrity Check

A quantity derived algorithmically from the running digital stream of a message and appended to it for transmission, or from the entire contents of a stored data file and appended to it. Some integrity checks are not cryptographically based (e.g., cyclic redundancy checks), but others are. *Cryptography's Role in Securing the Information Society*, United States National Research Council, 1996.

Intel Corp.

Intel is the quintessential high technology company. It invented the micro-processor; it is heavily into scientific research; and it has few if any equals in the design and production of innovative and successful integrated circuits for mass markets with relatively low profit margins but wide appeal. *Advanced Micro Devices, Inc. and Intel Corp.*, CCH Comp. Cases 60,218 (Arb. Award. 1990).

Intelligence

Means signs, signals, writing, images, sounds or intelligence of any nature. *Telecommunications Act*, S.C. 1993, c. 38.

Intelligent Modem

"Intelligent modem" describes a type of modem that possesses added or enhanced features as compared to a standard modem. The term "intelligent" is commonly used in the data processing and data communications field in an adjectival sense to describe an advanced-type modem having sophisticated features and to distinguish said products from standard 'dumb' modems with the advanced features. *Hayes Microcomputer Products Inc. v. Business Computer Corp.*, 219 U.S.P.Q. 634 (T.T.A.B. 1983).

Intelligent Transportation System (ITS)

ITS refers to a wide variety of advanced and emerging technology applications designed mainly to reduce traffic congestion and emissions, and to improve highway efficiency, safety, and convenience. ITS may be applied to or involve: all types of vehicles, including private cars, taxis, trucks, buses, and trains; all aspects of the surface transportation system, including urban and rural roads, freeways, transit stations, and ports; a variety of information devices, such as computers, signs, dash-board monitors, hand-held equipment, and kiosks. Eyes on the Road: Intelligent Transportation Systems and Your Privacy, Information and Privacy Commissioner/Ontario, March 1995, available at http://www.ipc.on.ca.

Interactive

Description of a computer or network system that responds in some way to information provided to it by a user. Thus an interactive program is one which can accept information and modify its behaviour while it is being run, for example a computer game. Similarly an interactive website is one where it is possible to enter information, such as credit card details in order to make a purchase, or where it is possible to select from a menu of options. *Digital Technology and the Copyright Act 1994: A Discussion Paper, Competition and Enterprise Branch, July 2001 (New Zealand).*

Interactive Computer Service

The term encompasses means of making content available to multiple users both on the vast web of linked networks popularly known as "the Internet" and other information systems (such as electronic bulletin boards maintained by educational institutions or non-profit organizations) not physically linked to the internet. *Shea v. Reno,* 1996 U.S. Dist. LEXIS 10720 (S.D.N.Y. 1996).

Interactive Program

In an interactive program the user controls the direction of the computer program. *Softel Inc. v. Dragon Medical and Scientific Communications, Inc.,* 1992 U.S. Dist. LEXIS 9502 (S.D.N.Y. 1992).

Interactivity

A service or system that allows the user to interact with the service provider by sending back data, voice or video messages, instructions or choices. Submission of the Director of Investigation and Research to the CRTC Re Public Notice CRTC 1994-130.

Intercept

Includes listen to, record or acquire a communication or acquire the substance, meaning or purport thereof. *Criminal Code* (Canada), R.S.C. 1985, c. C-46, s. 183.

The aural or other acquisition of the contents of any wire, electronic, or oral communication through the use of any electronic, mechanical, or other device. 18 U.S.C.S. 2510(4). *Steve Jackson Games, Inc. v. United States Secret Service,* 816 F.Supp. 432 (W.D. Texas 1993).

Means the aural or other acquisition of the contents of any wire, electronic, or oral communication through the use of any electronic, mechanical, or other device. *Electronic Communications Privacy Act* of 1986, Pub. L. 89-508 (1986).

Interconnection

The linkage of one telecommunications network to another. For example, the linkage of an interexchange carrier to a local exchange carrier in order to complete a long-distance call. Submission of the Director of Investigation and Research to the CRTC Re Public Notice CRTC 1994-130.

Interexchange Service

Means a service configured to operate between any two exchanges for which Message Toll Service charges would apply. Tariff Revisions Related to Resale and Sharing, Telecom Decision CRTC 87-2 (Feb. 12, 1987).

Interface

A unit needed to make communications between two computers. In *Re Honeywell, Inc.*, 1 C.L.S.R. 810.

A logical section of a cryptographic module that defines a set of entry or exit points that provide access to the module, including information flow or physical access. "Security Requirements for Cryptographic Modules", FIPS Pub. 140-1, Federal Information Processing Standards Publication, January 11, 1994, available at http://csrc.nist.gov/fips/fips1401.htm.

The computer hardware, operating system, application software, and user communicate with each other across "interfaces." The system communicates with the user through the "user interface," which consists of images on the monitor as well as the keyboard, mouse, etc. The interfaces between the application program, operating system, and hardware are internal, and thus are invisible to the user. *Bateman v. Mnemonics Inc.*, 38 U.S.P.Q. 2d 1225 (11th Cir. 1996).

Interface Information

This information essentially describes what a program does, but not how it does it. It is rather like giving the specifications for all the holes and plugs on the back of a stereo amplifier so that you can put compatible stereo components together. Interface information gives the same sort of specifications. *IBM v. Fujitsu Ltd.*, Copyright L.R. (CCH) 20,517 (Am. Arbtn. Assoc. Comm. Arbtn. Trib. 1988).

Interface Specifications

The description of the logical and physical interconnection and interaction which allows a hardware or computer program product to interact as intended with other hardware, computer program(s) or users. Computer Software Protection: Australia, Copyright Law Review Committee 1995.

Interface Standards

Interface standards set out criteria for evaluating whether a given program can be considered to differentiate clearly programming service interfaces from other information about the program. *IBM v. Fujitsu Ltd.*, Copyright L.R. (CCH) 20,517 (Am. Arbt. Assoc. Comm. Arbtn. Trib. 1988).

Interlata Service

The term "interlata service" means telecommunications between a point located in a local access and transport area and a point located outside such area. United States Telecommunications Act of 1996.

Intermediary

With respect to a particular data message, means a person who, on behalf of another person, sends, receives or stores that data message or provides other services with respect to that data message; UNCITRAL Model Law On Electronic Commerce (1996).

International Business Machines (IBM)

IBM is by far the largest supplier in the world of main frame computers. *Systems Reliability Holdings Plc v. Smith*, [1990] I.R.L.R. 377 (Ch.D.).

IBM requires little introduction. It is a massive, multi-national corporation which distributes, among other things, large business computers. *IBM Corp. v. Medlantic Healthcare Group*, 1 CCH Comp. Cas. 46,032 (D.C. Columbia 1989).

Internet

The internet is really a series of computer networks with a single point of access that connects the user to an electronic information system spanning the globe. The user can retrieve scientific information, explore "chat groups", find movie clips, listen to songs, view pictures from a museum, read a book, sell a report, choose a ski vacation or preview the newest cars. The practical-and commercial-uses of the internet are enormous and increasing daily. Connection Community Content, *The Challenge of the Information Highway: Final Report of the Information Highway Advisory Council, (September 1995)*.

The internet today is a worldwide entity whose nature cannot be easily or simply defined. From a technical definition, the Internet is the set of all Interconnected Together Networks — the collection of several thousand local, regional and global computer networks interconnected in real time via the TCP/IP Internetworking C Protocol suite. *Religious Technology Center v. Netcom On-Line*, 37 U.S.P.Q. 2d 1545 (N.D. Cal. 1995).

A collection of thousands of local, regional, and global Internet Protocol networks. What it means in practical terms is that millions of computers in schools, universities, corporations, and other organizations are tied together via telephone lines. The internet enables users to share files, search for information, send electronic mail and log onto remote computers, but it isn't the program or even a particular computer resource. It remains only a means to link computer users together. *Religious Technology Center v. Netcom On-Line*, 37 U.S.P.Q. 2d 1545 (N.D. Cal. 1995).

The internet is not a physical or tangible entity, but rather a giant network which interconnects innumerable smaller groups of linked computer networks. It is thus a network of networks. *American Civil Liberties Union v. Reno*, 929 F.Supp. 824 (E.D. Pa. 1996).

What we now refer to as "the Internet" grew out of an experimental project of the Department of Defense's Advanced Research Projects Administration (ARPA) designed to provide researchers with direct access to super computers at a few key laboratories and to facilitate the reliable transmission of vital communications. *Shea v. Reno*, 1996 U.S. Dist. LEXIS 10720 (S.D.N.Y. 1996).

What we know as the Internet today is the series of linked, overlapping networks that gradually supplanted ARPANET. *Shea v. Reno*, 1996 U.S. Dist. LEXIS 10720 (S.D.N.Y. 1996).

A vast international network of networks that enables computers of all kinds to share services and communicate directly. *The Challenge of the Information Highway: Final Report of the Information Highway Advisory Council* (September 1995).

A group of national networks that connect university, governmental, and military computers around the country. The network permits communication and transfer of information between computers on the network. *United States of America v. Morris*, 2 CCH Comp. Cas. 46,419 (2nd Cir. 1991).

The word "Internet" covers a bewildering variety of services, technologies and administrative arrangements. Among the distinct services available on the Internet, the most familiar is probably e-mail. In addition, one can access programs available on a distant computer and interact with these programs (give them commands and read their output) by using telenet. One can also send files to or retrieve files from a remote host by using FTP (i.e., "file transfer protocol"; some host sites permit this to be done "anonymously"). There are also a variety of automated tools for browsing and searching directories (e.g., ARCHIE, GOPHER, WAIS). World-Wide Web sites provide access to hypertext documents, allowing you to follow a link — a word concept or image — from one place in the file to another point either in that file or some other document that could be stored on the same computer or on a machine half-way around the world. *Illegal and Offensive Content on the Information Highway, A Background Paper*, Industry Canada (June 19, 1995).

The Internet is essentially a term that describes the interconnection of all these computers to the other. It is also referred to as "the information superhighway". The connections of these computers are completed through the use of telephone lines, which electronically transmit information from one computer to another. The Internet has created tremendous global means of rapid exchange of information by the government, academic institutions, and commercial entities. *Maritz, Inc. v. Cybergold, Inc.* 40 U.S.P.Q. (2d) 1729 (E.D.Miss. 1996).

The Internet is a giant network which interconnects in numeral smaller groups of linked computer networks. *Malarkey-Taylor Associates, Inc. v. Communications NOW, Inc.*, 929 F.Supp. 473 (D. Col. 1996).

The Internet is the world's largest computer network, often described as a "network of networks". *CompuServe Inc. v. Patterson*, 39 U.S.P.Q. (2d) 1502 (6 Cir. 1996).

The Internet is the world's largest computer network (a network consisting of two or more computers linked together to share electronic mail and files). The Internet is actually a network of thousands of independent networks, containing several million "host" computers that provide information services. An estimated twenty-five million individuals have some form of Internet access, and this audience is doubling each year. The Internet is a co-operative venture, owned by no one, but regulated by several volunteer agencies. *Bensusan Restaurant Corporation v. King*, 1996 WL 509 716 (S.D.N.Y. 1996).

The Internet is a network of thousands of independent networks, containing millions of host computers that provide information services. Further, the Internet is not owned or controlled by a private company or the government. *It's In The Cards, Inc. v. Fuschetto*, 535 N.W. (2d) 11 (Ct. App. Wisc. 1995).

The Internet is an international computer "super-network" of over fifteen thousand computer networks used by about thirty million individuals, corporations, organizations, and educational institutions worldwide. In recent years, businesses have begun to use the Internet to provide information and products to consumers and other businesses. *Panavision International, LP v. Toeppen*, 938 F.Supp. 616 (C.D. Cal. 1996).

The Internet is a giant network which allows people, institutions, corporations and governments around the globe to exchange information via computer almost instantaneously. *Playboy Enterprises, Inc. v. Chuckleberry Publishing, Inc.*, 39 U.S.P.Q. (2d) 1746, motion for reconsideration denied, 39 U.S.P.Q. (2d) 1846 (S.D.N.Y. 1996).

Today, of course, the Internet can be seen as its own thriving city, where citizens meet to exchange thoughts and ideas, where merchants buy and sell their wares, and where visitors take virtual tours of entire cities and buildings such as the White House and the Louvre. *Playboy Enterprises, Inc. v. Chuckleberry Publishing, Inc.*, 39 U.S.P.Q. (2d) 1746, motion for reconsideration denied, 39 U.S.P.Q. (2d) 1846 (S.D.N.Y. 1996).

In general, the Internet is a giant network which allows people, institutions, corporations and governments around the globe to exchange information via computer almost instantaneously. *Playboy Enterprises, Inc. v. Chuckleberry Publishing, Inc.*, 939 F.Supp. 1032 (S.D.N.Y. 1996).

The Internet is a vast and expanding network of computers and other devices linked together by various telecommunications media, enabling all the computers and other devices on the Internet to exchange and share data. The Internet provides information about a myriad of corporations and products, as well as educational, research and entertainment information and services. An estimated thirty million people worldwide use the Internet with one hundred million predicted to be on the "net" in a matter of years. *Intermatic Inc. v. Toeppen*, 40 U.S.P.Q. (2d) 1412 (N.D. Ill. 1996).

The Internet is a vast world-wide computer network. Anyone with a personal computer, a telephone modem, an appropriate computer software may gain access to the Internet. Once connected, a user may view "home pages" which provide information about almost anything one can imagine. An Internet user may retrieve the score of a recent Washington Redskins game from the Sports Illustrated home page, listen to excerpts of a popular rap song from the MTV home page, or browse the University of Michigan's law school course catalogue on-line. Internet users may also order products, participate in surveys, play games, or communicate with the host of a particular home page by e-mail. At least twenty-five million people have access to the Internet. *Heroes Inc. v. Heroes Foundation*, 41 U.S.P.Q. (2d) 1513 (D.C. 1996).

The Internet can be described by a number of different metaphors, all fitting for different features and services that it provides. For example, the Internet resembles a highway, consisting of many streets leading to places where a user can find information. The metaphor of the Internet as a shopping mall or supermarket, on the other hand, aptly describes the Internet as a place where the user can shop for goods, information, and services. Finally, the Internet also can be viewed as a telephone system for computers by which data bases of information can be down-loaded to the user, as if all the information existed in the user's computer's disc drive. The highway metaphor highlights the expansiveness of the Internet--the ability for a user to reach another person or database instantly despite great physical distances. The shopping mall metaphor reveals the newly developed commercial feature of the Internet as a place to go to purchase needed items or services. Finally, the Internet as a telephone line describes the technology that allows people and computers to "talk" to each other and access information. Today, approximately 25 million people have access to this incredible network of information and services. *Edias Software International, Inc. v. Basis International Ltd.*, 947 F.Supp. 413 (D. Ariz. 1996).

The Internet is a worldwide electronic system for the exchange of information. Such information may include advertising material. Information is accessed through computers in conjunction with the telephone system. Persons wishing to impart information or to advertise on the Internet can do so by establishing for themselves a "Web site". Access to the information available at a Web site is gained by callers accessing a "relative Web address". *Shetland Times Ltd. v. Wills*, 1996 37 I.P.R. 71 (Scot. Ct. Sess.).

Internet means the international computer network commonly known by that name. *Bill C-396*, An Act to Restrict the Use of the Internet to Distribute Pornographic Material involving Children.

A global, public network of computers over which digital information and products can be distributed. Access to the Internet, by means of communications protocols and addressing schemes, is open to anyone with telecommunications equipment (*e.g.*, a modem and a telephone line) and appropriate computer hardware and software. Ministry of Revenue Advisory Committee, Report of the Committee On Electronic Commerce, April 30, 1998, Industry Canada.

In general terms, the Internet consists of a large number of computers throughout the world which are connected to each other, either directly through communication links or indirectly through other computers and communication links. The computers which are directly linked in this way are known as Internet hosts. Some Internet hosts, sch as universities or large companies, only allow users within their organisations to connect to the Internet. Other Internet hosts, called Internet Service Providers (ISP), allow members of the public to connect to the Internet through the provider's computer. The individual user connects to the Internet by using a modem in conjunction with his or her computer. The modem provides the user with a telephone dial-in link to the chosen ISP who will usually charge a fee for providing access in this way. *Trumpet Software Pty Ltd. v. OzEmail Pty Ltd.* (1996), 34 I.P.R. 481 (Aust. F.C.).

Means collectively the myriad of computer and telecommunications facilities, including equipment and operating software, which comprise the interconnected world-wide network of networks that employ the Transmission Control Protocol/ Internet Protocol, or any predecessor or successor protocols to such protocol, to communicate information of all kinds by wire or radio. *Children's Online Privacy Protection Act* of 1998

The Internet is a global matrix of interconnected computer networks using the Internet Protocol (IP) to communicate with each other. For simplicity, the term "Internet" . . . encompass all such data networks and hundreds of applications such as the World Wide Web and e-mail that run on those networks, even though some electronic commerce activities may take place on proprietary or other networks that are not technically part of the Internet. The Emerging Digital Economy, United States Department of Commerce, http://www.ecommerce.gov.

The universal network that allows computers to talk to other computers in words, text, graphics, and sound, anywhere in the world. Cyberspeak — Learning the Language, the Federal Trade Commission and the National Association of Attorneys General, availableat http://www.ftc.gov/bcp/conline/pubs/online/sitesee/index.html.

Generally called a "network of networks," it is a loose confederation of networks around the world. The networks that make up the Net are connected through several backbone networks. The Net grew out of a U.S. Government project, and is specifically designed to have no central governing authority or location. The Internet: A Guide For Ontario Government Organizations, Information and Privacy Commissioner/Ontario, May 1998, available at http://www.ipc.on.ca.

The term "Internet" generally refers to an informal, worldwide network of computers linking millions of computers. Although the information disseminated over the Internet may be no different from the information disseminated by telephone and fax machine, the Internet provides several new methods of communication. Each of these new methods of communication provides for ease, immediacy and low cost in the dissemination of information, "interactivity", hyperlinks, decentralization, anonymity and flexibility. *Technical Committees' Internet Task Force Report*, International Organization of Securities Commissioners, September 13, 1998.

The Internet is a global communications network linked principally by modems which transmit electronic data. *Haelan Products Inc. v. Beso Biological Research Inc.*, 43 U.S.P.Q. 2d 1672 (E.D. Louis 1997).

The Internet is a network of computers and computer networks designed to receive and forward bytes of data grouped into packets between end nodes (the source and destination computers). It supports a range of user-visible, high-level services or applications, depending on what software is loaded on the end nodes. The basic communication service of the Internet consists of two components: the addressing structure and the delivery model. *Public Performance of Musical Works* 1996-1998 (Tariff 22) (1999), 1 C.P.R. (4th) 417 (Copyright Board).

The Internet is a decentralized, global medium of communication that links people, institutions, corporations and governments around the world. It is a giant computer network that interconnects innumerable smaller groups of linked computer networks and individual computers. *American Civil Liberties Union et al. v. Johnson*, 4 F. Supp. 2d 1029 (D.N. Mex. 1998).

The term "Internet" means the International Computer Network of both federal and non-federal interoperable packet switched data networks. The Internet is not a physical or tangible entity, but rather a giant network which interconnects innumerable smaller groups of linked computer networks. *Blumenthal v. Drudge*, 1992 F. Supp. 44 (D.D.C. 1998).

The Internet is a world wide computer network. Three facilities (amongst others) are provided via the Internet: email, the World Wide Web and Usenet. This case is primarily concerned with Usenet. *Godfrey v. Demon Internet Ltd.*, [1999], E.W.J. No. 1226 (Q.B.D.)

The Internet is a global network of interconnected computers which allows individuals and organizations around the world to communicate and share information with one another. *GoTo,com v. Walt Disney* Co., 53 U.S.P.Q. 2d 1652 (9th Cir. 2000).

The Internet is a global network of interconnected computers which allows individuals and organizations around the world to communicate and to share information with one another. *Brookfield Communications, Inc. v. West Coast Entertainment Corporation*, 174 F. 3d 1036 (9th Cir. 1999).

A global electronic network, consisting of smaller, interconnected networks, which allows millions of computers to exchange information over telephone wires, dedicated data cables, and wireless links. The Internet links PCs by means of servers, which run specialized operating systems and applications designed for servicing a network environment. *United States of America v. Microsoft Corporation*, Civil Action No. 98-1232 (D. Col. Nov. 1999).

178

The Internet is a giant electronic network which connects to smaller networks of the world. The Internet was developed by the Department of Defence's Advanced Researched Project Agency twenty-five years ago in order to link the computer systems of universities, government agencies, and other research organizations. Since then, the activity generated by the Internet, as well as the size of the Internet itself, has grown exponentially. *Hasbro, Inc. v. Clue Computing, Inc.*, 45 U.S.P.Q. 2d 1170 (D. Mass. 1997).

The Internet is a giant computer "network of networks" which interconnects innumerable smaller groups of linked computer networks and individual computers offering a range of digital information including text, images, sound and video. *Cyberspace Communications, Inc. et al. v. Engler*, 55 F. Supp. 2d 737 (E.D. F. Ch. 1999).

The Internet is a decentralized, global communications medium that links people, institutions, corporations and governments around the world. *Cyberspace Communications, Inc. et al. v. Engler*, 55 F. Supp. 2d 737 (E.D. F. Ch. 1999).

The Internet (or "world wide web") is a network of computers that allows a user to gain information stored on any other computer on the network. Information on the Internet is lodged on files called web pages, which can include printed matter, sound, pictures and links to other web pages. An Internet user can move from one page to another with just the click of a mouse. *Sporty's Farm L.L.C., v. Sportman's Market, Inc.* 202 F. 3d 489 (2d. Cir. 2000).

The Internet is a vast and expanding network of computers and other devices linked together by various telecommunications media, enabling all the computers and other devices on the Internet to exchange and share data. *Snap-On Tools Company v. C/Net, Inc.*, 1997 U.S.Dist. LEXIS 14501 (N.D.Ill. 1997).

The Internet is the world's largest computer network (a network consisting of two or more computers linked together to share electronic mail and files). The Internet is actually a network of thousands of independent networks, containing several million "host" computers that provide information services. An estimated 25 million individuals have some form of Internet access, and this audience is doubling each year. The Internet is a cooperative venture, owned by no one, but regulated by several volunteer agencies. *MTV Networks v. Curry*, 867 F.Supp. 202 (S.D.N.Y. 1994).

Internet is a world wide computer network. *PEINET Inc. v. O'Brian* (1995) 61 C.P.R. (3d) 334 (P.E.I.S.C.)

The Internet is a network of computer networks. *Pitman Training Limited v. Nominet UK*, CH 1997 F 1984 (Ch.D.).

Internet is a collection of computers which are connected through the telephone network to communicate with each other. *British Telecommunications PLC v. One In A Million Ltd.,* [1999] R.P.C. 1 (Eng. C.A.).

At a high level of abstraction, the Internet is simply a medium by which computers or computer networks, otherwise isolated from one another, may interact. *America Online, Inc. vs. Shih-hsien Huang*, 2000 U.S. Dist. LEXIS 10232 (E.D. Vir. 2000).

The word "internetwork" or "internet" is a computer science term of art that refers to "a network formed by connecting two or more networks together." *America Online, Inc. vs. Shih-hsien Huang*, 2000 U.S. Dist. LEXIS 10232 (E.D. Vir. 2000).

The Internet, in reality a network of networks, has created a whole new territory independent of conventional geography. The conceptual location of this electronic interactivity available to us through our computers is oft referred to as "cyberspace". Unlike a "real" territory with fixed boarders, the internet is constantly growing and at a phenomenal rate. *Pro-C Limited vs. Computer City, Inc.* (2000), 7 C.P.R. (4th) 193 (Ont. S.C.J.).

The Internet is a network of networks accessible by computer. It is sometimes referred to as the World Wide Web or simply the "web". *Pro-C Limited vs. Computer City, Inc.* (2000), 7 C.P.R. (4th) 193 (Ont. S.C.J.).

The Internet is a world wide network of computers that enables various individuals and organizations to share information. The Internet allows computer users to access millions of websites and web pages. *Porsche Cars North* America *Inc. v. Spencer*, 55 U.S.P.Q. (2d) 1026 (E.D.Cal. 2000).

The internet is a unique and wholly new medium of world wide telecommunication. *Playboy Enterprises, Inc. vs. Netscape Communications Corp.* SA CV 99-320 A.H.S. (C.D.Cal. July 27, 1999).

Means the open and decentralized global network connecting networks of computers and similar devices to each other for the electronic exchange of information using standardized communication protocols. *Electronic Commerce and Information, Consumer Protection Amendment and Manitoba Evidence Amendment Act, C.C.S.M.c.E5S.*

Means the decentralized global network connecting networks of computers and similar devices to each other for the electronic exchange of information using standardized communication protocols. *Internet Sales Contract Harmonization Template, May 29, 2001* available at http://strategis.ic.gc.ca.

Internet means the open and decentralized global network connecting networks of computers with similar devices to each other for the electronic exchange of information using standardized communication protocols. *Consumer Protection Act, C.C.S.M.C., see 200, amended. Section 127.*

The Internet is a global electronic network, consisting of smaller, interconnected networks, which allows millions of computers to exchange information over telephone wires, dedicated data cables, and wireless links. The Internet links PCs by means of servers, which run specialized operating systems and applications designed for servicing a network environment. *Universal City Studios, Inc. v. Reimerdes*, 55 U.S.P.Q. 2d 1873 (S. D.N.Y. 2000).

A network of computer systems interconnected using the Transmission Control Protocol/Internet Protocol (TCP/IP) set of communication standards. The Internet runs over virtually all telecommunications technologies. It has no central authority, control, or ownership, and its continued functioning depends on co-operation between peer network operators. *Digital Technology and the Copyright Act 1994:*

A Discussion Paper, Competition and Enterprise Branch, July 2001 (New Zealand).

The Internet is accurately described as a "network of networks." Computer networks are interconnected individual computers that share information. Anytime two or more computer networks connect, they form an "internet." The "Internet" is a shorthand name for the vast collection of interconnected computer networks that evolved from the Advanced Research Projects Agency Network ("ARPA-Net") developed by the United States Defense Department in the 1960's and 1970's. Today, the Internet spans the globe and connects hundreds of thousands of independent networks. *DoubleClick Inc. Privacy Litigation,* Civ.0641 (N.R.V.) (S.D.N.Y. Mar. 28, 2001).

The internet is an international network of computers that communicate with each other according to certain protocols. Every computer participating in the internet is assigned a particular alpha-numerical address that has no other meaning in any human language (an "Internet Protocol Address"). *British Columbia Automobile Assn. v. OPEIU. Local 378* (2001), 10 C.P.R. (4th) 423 (B.C.S.C.).

The Internet is essentially a network of computer networks. It grew out of work conducted by two relatively small groups of research-oriented governmental, academic, and corporate entities. The first group was engaged in networking research and it developed and used what was known as the ARPANET. *National A-1 Advertising, Inc. et al v. Networks Solutions, Inc.,* Civ. No. 99-033-M (D.N.Hamp. Sept. 28, 2000).

The Internet itself is a global network of networks—the "information superhighway". It includes numerous avenues for a through which users can disseminate information, engage in discussions, or post opinions, including, for example, USENET newsgroups, mail exploders (also known as "listservs"), and chat rooms. *National A-1 Advertising, Inc. et al v. Networks Solutions, Inc.,* Civ. No. 99-033-M (D.N.Hamp. Sept. 28, 2000).

Commonly known as "World Wide Web", a worldwide computer network. *Report to the Governor in Council: Status of Competition in Canadian Telecommunications Markets, Deployment/Accessibility of Advanced Telecommunications Infrastructure and Services, September, 2001.*

Means collectively the myriad of computer and telecommunications facilities, including equipment and operating software, which comprise the interconnected world-wide network of networks that employ the Transmission Control Protocol/ Internet Protocol, or any predecessor or successor protocols to such protocol, to communicate information of all kinds by wire, radio, or other methods of transmission. *United States Children's On-Line Privacy Protection Rule, Federal Trade Commission, 16 CFR part 312.*

Means the combination of computer facilities and electromagnetic transmission media, and related equipment and software, comprising the interconnected worldwide network of computer networks that employ the Transmission Control Protocol/ Internet Protocol or any successor protocol to transmit information. *Child Online Protection Act (United States).*

The Internet comprises a network of computers and a network of computer networks that enable those connected to them to gain access to data stored on computers around the world that are themselves connected to the internet and have an intranet protocol (IP) address in which they can be located. *Society of Composers, Authors & Music Publishers of Canada v. Canadian Association of Internet Providers (2002), 19 C.P.R. (4th) 289 (Fed.C.A.)*

Internet Access Provider (IAP)

An access service provided by a Local Exchange Carrier (LEC) to an ISP which allows calls to be originated from or terminated to the Public Switched Telephone Network (PSTN). IAP's typically connect to a "gateway" or server which provides the functionality to connect a caller to the Internet. Telecom Order CRTC 98-929, September 17, 1998

The IAPs include both Internet Service Providers, which offer consumers internet access, and Online Services ("OLSs '') such as America Online ("AOL ''),which offer proprietary content in addition to internet access and other services. *United States of America v. Microsoft Corporation,* No. 00-5212 (D.C. Cir. June 28, 2001).

Internet Access Service

Means a service that enables users to access content, information, electronic mail, or other services offered over the Internet, and may also include access to proprietary content, information, and other services as part of a package of services offered to consumers. Such term does not include telecommunications services. *Child Online Protection Act (United States).*

Internet Address

Internet addresses . . . typically include a final extension to their "uniform resource locator" ("URL"). To United States users of the Internet, the most familiar URL extensions are ".com" (indicating that the access computer is commercial); ".edu" (educational); ".org" (non-profit organization); ".gov" (government agency); and ".net" (networking organization). *Playboy Enterprises, Inc. v. Chuckleberry Publishing, Inc.,* 39 U.S.P.Q. (2d) 1746, motion for reconsideration denied, 39 U.S.P.Q. (2d) 1846 (S.D.N.Y. 1996).

Internet addresses . . . typically include a final extension to their "uniform resource locator" ("URL"). *Playboy Enterprises, Inc. v. Chuckleberry Publishing, Inc.,* 939 F.Supp. 1032 (S.D.N.Y. 1996).

IANA — Internet Assigned Numbers Authority

IANA allocates IP address blocks to the regional IP registries (ARIN, RIPE, APNIC). *Domain Name System Reform and Related Internet Governance Issues: A Consultation Paper*, Industry Canada available at *www.strategis.gc.ca*

Internet Content

Internet content is somewhat analogous to newspaper stories or magazine articles, but can include other information such as stock quotes, sports scores and weather. *Snap-On Tools Company v. C/Net, Inc.* 1997 U.S.Dist. LEXIS 14501 (N.D.Ill. 1997).

Internet Content Providers ("ICPs")

Are the individuals and organizations that have established a presence, or "site", on the Web by publishing a collection of Web pages. *United States of America v. Microsoft Corp.*, Civil Action No. 98-1232 (D. Col. Nov. 1999).

Internet Information Location Tool

Means a service that refers or links users to an online location on the World Wide Web. Such term includes directories, indices, references, pointers, and hypertext links. *Child Online Protection Act (United States)*.

Internet Protocol (IP)

Refers to the manner of carriage of Internet Services between Internet gateways, servers or routers, but not to carriage on access lines to or from the PSTN.

A computer or device that is attached to the Internet is often referred to as a "host". In order to facilitate communications between hosts, each has a numerical IP (Internet Protocol) address. The IP address is comprised of four groups of numbers separated by decimals. . . . Each host also has a unique "fully qualified domain name.". The "fully qualified domain name" may not be repeated in the Internet. *Intermatic Inc. v. Toeppen*, 40 U.S.P.Q. (2d) 1412 (N.D. Ill. 1996).

Internet protocol address (IP Address)

An Internet protocol address is a string of integer numbers separated by periods, for example, <129.137.84.101>. For ease of recall and use, a user relies on a "domain-name combination" to reach a given web site. *Avery Dennison v. Sumpton*, Case No. 98-555810 (9th Cir. August 23, 1999).

Numerical 32-bit addresses expressed as four numbers between 0 and 255 separated by periods (e.g. 198.41.0.52) used to identify hosts that are connected to the Internet. *Domain Name System Reform and Related Internet Governance Issues: A Consultation Paper*, Industry Canada available at *www.strategis.gc.ca*

IP number

An IP number is four groups of digits separated by decimal points, for example, "013.917.114.41.". These IP numbers are converted into a more user-friendly, letter based format called a "domain name" by specialized computers called "domain name servers". A typical domain name would appear as follows: winesap.apples.net. *Academy of Motion Picture Arts and Sciences v. Network Solutions Inc.*, 45 U.S.P.Q. 2d 1463 (C.D.Cal. 1997).

Internet Relay Chat ("IRC")

Is a system that enables individuals connected to the Internet to participate in live typed discussions. Participation in an IRC discussion requires an IRC software program, which sends messages via the Internet to the IRC server, which in turn broadcasts the messages to all participants. The IRC system is capable of supporting many separate discussions at once. *Universal City Studios, Inc. v. Reimerdes*, 55 U.S.P.Q. 2d 1873 (S. D.N.Y. 2000).

Internet Service Provider (ISP)

Internet Service Provider means a person who provides a service that facilitates access to the Internet, whether the service is provided free or for a charge. Bill C-396, *An Act to Restrict the Use of the Internet to Distribute Pornographic Material involving Children.*

A service provider who provides dial access capability to connect customers to the Internet via and Internet gateway or server. Telecom Order CRTC 98-929, September 17, 1998.

An organization that provides individuals and businesses with access to the Internet. ISPs may be wholesalers or retailers or both. Wholesalers usually resell bandwidth and other services to smaller ISPs who act as retailers. The amount of bandwidth purchased is the most significant component of the sale price. Report of the Committee On Electronic Commerce, April 30, 1998, Industry Canada.

A service that allows you to connect to the Internet. Cyberspeak — Learning the Language, the Federal Trade Commission and the National Association of Attorneys General, available at http://www.ftc.gov/bcp/conline/pubs/online/sitesee/index.html.

The IAPs include both Internet Service Providers, which offer consumers internet access, and Online Services ("OLSs ") such as America Online ("AOL "),which offer proprietary content in addition to internet access and other services. *United States of America v. Microsoft Corporation*, No. 00-5212 (D.C. Cir. June 28, 2001).

Entities that provide connectivity to subscribers. *Public Performance of Musical Works* 1996-1998 (Tariff 22) (1999), 1 C.P.R. (4th) 417 (Copyright Board).

PCs typically connect to the Internet through the services of Internet access providers ("IAPs"), which generally charge subscription fees to their customers in the United States. There are two types of IAPs. Online services ("OLSs") such as America Online ("AOL"), Prodigy, and the Microsoft Network ("MSN") offer, in addition to Internet access, various services and an array of proprietary content. Internet service providers ("ISPs") such as MindSpring and Netcom, on the other hand, offer few services apart from Internet access and relatively little of their own content. *United States of America v. Microsoft Corporation*, Civil Action No. 98-1232 (D. Col. Nov. 1999).

Companies that provide customers with access to Internet services. *Report to the Governor in Council: Status of Competition in Canadian Telecommunications Markets, Deployment/Accessibility of Advanced Telecommunications Infrastructure and Services, September, 2001.*

Internet Sales Contract

Means a consumer transactions formed by text-based internet communications. *Internet Sales Contract Harmonization Template, May 29,2001* available at http://strategis.ic.gc.ca.

Internet Service Provider (ISP)

An organization that provides users with access to the Internet. Sometimes called Internet access provider (IAP). *Domain Name System Reform and Related Internet Governance Issues: A Consultation Paper*, Industry Canada available at *www.strategis.gc.ca*

Internet shoppers

Regular-use households that engaged either in window shopping or electronic commerce. *Statistics Canada Household shopping on the Internet, 1999, 2000 and 2001.*

Inter NIC — (Internet Network Information Centre)

The organization that provides domain name registration services for the top level domains .com, .net, .org and .edu. It comprises two distinct services partially funded by the NSF: Directory and Databases Services managed by AT&T and Registration services managed by Network Solutions, Inc. *Domain Name System Reform and Related Internet Governance Issues: A Consultation Paper,* Industry Canada available at *www.strategis.gc.ca*

Internet Site

A "site" is an Internet address which permits users to exchange digital information with a particular host. *Bensusan Restaurant Corporation v. King*, 1996 WL 509 716 (S.D.N.Y. 1996).

Interoperability

The ability of computer systems to exchange information and mutually to use the information which has been exchanged. Computer Software Protection: Australia, Copyright Law Review Committee 1995.

Refers to the connection of networks that allows traffic to move efficiently from one network to another. Competition and Culture on Canada's Information Highway: Managing the Realities of Transition, CRTC (the "Convergence Report"), May 19, 1995.

Interoperability of cryptographic methods means the technical ability of multiple cryptographic methods to function together. *OECD Guidelines for Cryptography Policy*, March 27, 1997, available at *www.oecd.org*.

Interpretation

The process whereby a source code program is translated "on the run" one instruction at a time into machine code or object code. Computer Software Protection: Australia, Copyright Law Review Committee 1995.

Interpreter Program

A program that enables a user to communicate with the computer in a high-level language. *Apple Computer Inc. v. Mackintosh Computers Ltd.* (1986), 28 D.L.R. (4th) 178 (Fed. T.D.).

An "interpreter" progam is a simultaneous translator that works in conjunction with the application program every time the application program is run, carrying out the instructions of the program one step at a time. *Lotus Development Corp. v. Paperback Software International*, 15 U.S.P.Q.2d 1577 (D. Mass. 1990).

Intracorporate Communications

Means telecommunications through which an enterprise communicates: (a) internally or with or among its subsidiaries, branches or affiliates, as defined by each party, or (b) on a non-commercial basis with other persons that are fundamental to the economic activity of the enterprise and that have a continuing contractual relationship with it, but does not include telecommunications services provided to persons other than those described herein. North American Free Trade Agreement between Canada, Mexico and the United States, Article 1310.

Intranet

A computer network that is internal to an organization. Only users within the organization have access to the Intranet; typically, they also have access to the Internet, but outside access to the Intranet is prevented by a firewall. Ministry of Revenue Advisory Committee, Report of the Committee On Electronic Commerce, April 30, 1998, Industry Canada.

A section of the Web which is only accessible to a closed group, such as within an organization. *Digital Technology and the Copyright Act 1994: A Discussion Paper, Competition and Enterprise Branch, July 2001 (New Zealand)*.

Inverse H-Matrix

An H-Matrix in which the rows of the matrix have been interchanged. *E.F. Johnson Co. v. Uniden Corp. of America*, 623 F.Supp. 1485 (D. Minn. 1985).

IP

Internet Protocol

IP Internet Protocol

The software rules that enable hosts to exchange data packets over the Internet. *Domain Name System Reform and Related Internet Governance Issues: A Consultation Paper*, Industry Canada available at *www.strategis.gc.ca*

IPP

Information Privacy Principles. *The Office of the Federal Privacy Commissioner (Australia), Consultation Paper, (June 2001).*

ISDN (Integrated Services Digital Network)

A set of digital telecommunications network standards. *The Challenge of the Information Highway: Final Report of the Information Highway Advisory Council* (September 1995).

ISO

International Organization for Standardization. "Security Requirements for Cryptographic Modules", FIPS Pub. 140-1, Federal Information Processing Standards Publication, January 11, 1994, available at http://csrc.nist.gov/fips/fips1401.htm.

ISP

Internet Service Provider

Issue a Certificate

The process by which a certifier creates a certificate and gives notice to the subscriber listed in the certificate of its contents. General Usage for International Digitally Insured Commerce (Guidec), International Chamber of Commerce, 1997, available at http://www.icc.wbo.org/guidec2.htm.

ISV

Independent software vendors. *United States of America v. Microsoft Corporation*, 87 F.Supp. 2d 30 (D.D.C. 2000).

IT

Information Technology

ITU

International Telecommunications Union

Java

Java, a set of technologies developed by Sun Microsystems, is another type of middleware posing a potential threat to Windows 'position as the ubiquitous platform for software development. The Java technologies include: (1) a programming language; (2) a set of programs written in that language, called the "Java class libraries," which expose APIs; (3) a compiler, which translates code written by a developer into "bytecode"; and (4) a Java Virtual Machine ("JVM"), which translates bytecode into instructions to the operating system. Programs calling upon the Java APIs will run on any machine with a "Java run time environment," that is, Java class libraries and a JVM. technologies. *United States of America v. Microsoft Corp.,* No. 00-5212 (D.C. Cir. June 28, 2001).

Joystick

Add-on device for *hardware*, used to control a character or object in a game. Monopolies and Mergers Commission — Video Games: A report on the supply of video games in the UK (LONDON: HMSO Cm2781).

Jughead Server

A "jughead server" is an aptly named tool for searching menus only on a single server. *Shea v. Reno,* 1996 U.S. Dist. LEXIS 10720 (S.D.N.Y. 1996).

Junk E-Mail (See also SPAM)

Unsolicited commercial e-mail; also known as "spam." Usually junk e-mail doesn't contain the recipient's address on the "To" line. Instead, the addressee is a made-up name, such as "friend
public.com." Or the address on the "To" line is identical to the one on the "From" line. Cyberspeak — Learning the Language, the Federal Trade Commission and the National Association of Attorneys General, available at http://www.ftc.gov/bcp/conline/pubs/online/sitesee/index.html.

Key

Key is the information used with a cryptographic algorithm to generate or verify a digital signature. Security and Electronic Authorization and Authentication Guideline, Communications Security Establishment, Government of Canada September 1995, CID/01/15.

Is a sequence of symbols that controls digital signature and encryption processes. Public Key Infrastructure Management in the Government of Canada, Treasury Board of Canada Secretariat, May 27, 1999, available at http://www.tbs-sct.gc.ca/pubs_pol/ciopubs/PKI/pki1_e.html.

A data element used to encrypt or decrypt a message - includes both Public Keys and Private Keys. *The Office of the Federal Privacy Commissioner (Australia), Consultation Paper, (June 2001).*

Key Encapsulation

A technique by which a session key is "wrapped" (*i.e.* the session key is encrypted) by another key belonging to a third party (such as a key recovery agent). In E-mail applications, the "wrapped" key is typically stored in a message's header. In real-time communications, the "wrapped" key may be transmitted in the initial "handshake" that establishes the secure connection. A Cryptology Policy Framework for Electronic Commerce, Task Force on Electronic Commerce, Industry Canada, February 1998.

Key Encrypting Key

A cryptographic key that is used for the encryption or decryption of other keys. "Security Requirements for Cryptographic Modules", FIPS Pub. 140-1, Federal Information Processing Standards Publication, January 11, 1994, available at http://csrc.nist.gov/fips/fips1401.htm.

Key Escrow

A key escrow cryptography system (or simply escrowed cryptography system) is a cryptography system with a backup decryption capability which, under certain specified prescribed conditions, allows authorised persons (users, officers of an organisation, and government officials) to decrypt ciphertext with the help of information supplied by or more trusted parties who hold special data recovery keys. These keys are not normally those used to encrypt and decrypt the data, but rather provide a means of determining the data encryption/decryption keys. Business - To Consumer Electronic Commerce: Survey of Status and Issues, OECD/gd (97) 219.

Key Escrow Policy

Refers to a United States policy concerning the technology that has been developed to address the concern that widespread use of encryption would make lawfully authorized electronic surveillance more difficult. Involves granting designated third parties special keys needed for law enforcement agencies to gain access, under court warrant, to encrypted communications or transactions. *The Challenge of the Information Highway: Final Report of the Information Highway Advisory Council* (September 1995).

Key Management

The activities involving the handling of cryptographic keys and other related security parameters (e.g., IVs, counters) during the entire life cycle of the keys, including their generation, storage, distribution, entry and use, deletion or destruction, and archiving. "Security Requirements for Cryptographic Modules", FIPS Pub. 140-1, Federal Information Processing Standards Publication, January11, 1994, available at http://csrc.nist.gov/fips/fips1401.htm.

Means a system for generation, storage, distribution, revocation, deletion, archiving, certification or application of cryptographic keys. *OECD Guidelines for Cryptography Policy*, March 27, 1997, available at *www.oecd.org*.

Key Pair

Means, in an asymmetric cryptosystem, two mathematically related keys, referred to as a private key and a public key, having the properties that (i) one key (the private key) can encrypt a message which only the other key (the pubic key) can decrypt, and (ii) even knowing one key (the public key), it is computationally infeasible to discover the other key (the private key). *Illinois Electronic Commerce Security Act* 1998 5 Ill. Comp. Stat. 175.

Means a private key and its corresponding public key in an asymmetric cryptosystem, keys which have the property that the public key can verify a digital signature that the private key creates. *Utah Digital Signature Act* 46-3, available at http://www.le.state.ut.us/code/TITLE46/htm/46_03004.htm.

Key Recovery

A broad range of techniques permitting the recovery of plaintext from encrypted data when the decryption key is not in the possession of the decrypting party (*e.g.* the key is lost; the password encrypting the key has been forgotten; court-authorized agents who otherwise would not have access to the cryptographic key). This could include: (1) retrieving an entity's long-term encryption key, which had been stored in a secondary location (sometimes called "commercial key back-up" or "key escrow" depending on who controls the backed-up keys); (2) key encapsulation; or (3) key derivation techniques which allow for the confidential key to be regenerated from either end of the communication by the trusted third parties who provided the original mathematical elements used in generating the key. A Cryptology Policy Framework for Electronic Commerce, Task Force on Electronic Commerce, Industry Canada, February 1998.

Keyboard

Interface between the human operator and the computer takes place through a keyboard. Depression of a key sends a string of impulses to the computer which the computer is programmed to recognise. *Powerflex Services Pty Ltd. v. Data Access Corp.* (1997), 37 I.P.R. 436 (Aust. C.A.).

Keyholder

Means an individual or entity in possession or control of cryptographic keys. A keyholder is not necessarily a user of the key. *OECD Guidelines for Cryptography Policy*, March 27, 1997, available at *www.oecd.org*.

An individual who holds and uses Keys and certificates on behalf of an Organization, including an Authorized Officer. *The Office of the Federal Privacy Commissioner (Australia), Consultation Paper, (June 2001).*

Key Pair

A pair of asymmetric cryptographic Keys (i.e. one decrypts messages which have been encrypted using the other) consisting of a Public Key and a Private Key. *The Office of the Federal Privacy Commissioner (Australia), Consultation Paper, (June 2001).*

Keystroke Sequence

Keystroke sequence refers to a sequence of keystroke entries that a user may invoke. Keystroke sequences may be generated as one navigates the menu command hierarchy performing sequential spreadsheet operations. *Lotus Development Corporation v. Borland International Inc.*, 788 F.Supp. 78 (D.C. Mass. 1992).

Keyword

A word you enter into a search engine to begin the search for specific information or web sites. Cyberspeak — Learning the Language, the Federal Trade Commissionand the National Association of Attorneys General,available at http://www.ftc.gov/bcp/conline/pubs/online/sitesee/index.html.

Know-How

Factual knowledge not capable of precise, separate description, but which, when used in an accumulated form, after being acquired as a result of trial and error, gives the one acquiring it an ability to produce something that he otherwise would not have known how to produce with the same accuracy or precision found necessary for commercial success. *Mycalex v. Pemco Corp.*, 64 F.Supp. 420 (D. Md. 1946).

Practical knowledge of how to do something. *Beecham Group Ltd. v. Bristol Laboratories International S.A.*, [1978] R.P.C. 521 (H.L.).

Knowledge Seeker

KnowledgeSeeker is a statistical analysis package, typically used by companies to analyze statistics on data and from such analysis to determine trends or patterns or relationships. *Angoss II Partnership v. Trifox Inc.* (1997), [1997] O.J. No. 4969 (Gen. Div.), affirmed (1999), [1999] O.J. No. 4144, 1999 CarswellOnt 3474 (C.A.), leave to appeal dismissed (2000), [1999] S.C.C.A. No. 588, 2000 CarswellOnt 2999.

Label

A label is a name for a section of code. One needs labels for a variety of purposes: for instance one might have a command GOTO X, where X is the label. Then the computer when running the program will at this point go to the label X and start doing whatever X requires. *IBCOS Computers Ltd. v. Barclay's Mercantile Highland Finance Ltd.*, [1994] F.S.R. 275 (Ch.D.).

Are data inserted into the coding of a Web site and detectable by agent software designed to determine whether the site meets the user's standards. (e.g. for privacy or con-tent purposes). *Advancing Global Electronic Commerce: Technology Solutions to Public Policy Challenges, The Computer Systems Policy Project, July 1999*, available at http://www.cspp.org/projects/july99_cto_report.pdf.

When inserted into the presentation of information, allow users to protect their privacy and shield themselves from content that they do not wish to receive. Labels can work in isolation or in conjunction with filtering or blocking software, smart agents or e-chips. *Advancing Global Electronic Commerce: Technology Solutions to Public Policy Challenges, Computer Systems Policy Project (CSPP)*, available at http://www.cspp.org/projects/july99_cto_report.pdf.

LANs (Local Area Network)

Local Area Network systems. *Digital Microsystems Ltd. v. Datascope Microsystems Ltd.*, Ch. D., Falconer J., April 11, 1984 (unreported).

Several minicomputers in the one office or building may be coupled by a piece of coaxial cable, commonly called an Ethernet cable, so as to form a local area network ("LAN"). The computers in a local area network may share the use of a particular facility. The computers could share the use of the information or data stored on a hard disk. One of the computers would have a hard disk incorporated in it, or attached to it by a communication line a hard disk housed in a box. All the computers in the local area network could use the information stored in the one hard disk. The microcomputer which is directly linked to the hard disk and performs the function of placing information in the files of the disk and retrieving information from those files is called a "file server". A file server may provide the other computers in the local area network not only with access to disk storage but with access to a printer or to shared programs. *Madeley Pty Ltd. v. Touche Ross*, McGarvie, J., Aust. Fed. Ct., Dec. 21, 1989 (unreported).

A private data network in which serial transmission is used without store and forward techniques for direct data communication among stations located within the user's premises. *The Challenge of the Information Highway: Final Report of the Information Highway Advisory Council* (September 1995).

Laser DISC

"Laser disc" is used in the electronics field to describe both video and audio discs, where both the recording and the reading process is performed by lasers. The words "laser discs" are used in the trade as a generic term for video or compact or digital discs, the latter descriptions indicating the more specific functions of a laser-recorded and read disk. *Re Application by Pioneer Kabushiki Kaisha* (1985), 5 I.P.R. 285 (Aus. Pat. Office).

Lawful Access

Means access by third party individuals or entities, including governments, to plaintext, or cryptographic keys, of encrypted data, in accordance with law. *OECD Guidelines for Cryptography Policy*, March 27, 1997, available at *www.oecd.org*.

Legacy System

A computer system using old technology which, for some reason, cannot immediately be updated or replaced. *A Survey of Legal Issues Relating to the Security of Electronic Information*, Department of Justice, Canada.

Legal Recognition

Information, records, and signatures shall not be denied legal effect, validity, or enforceability solely on the grounds that they are in electronic form. *Illinois Electronic Commerce Security Act* 1998 5 Ill. Comp. Stat. 175.

License

Means a contract that authorizes access to, use of, distribution, display, performance, modification, or reproduction of information, or use of informational rights, and expressly limits the contractual rights, permissions, or uses granted, expressly prohibits some uses, or expressly grants less than all rights in the information. A contract may be a license whether or not the transferee has title to a licensed copy. The term includes an access contract and a consignment of a copy. The term does not include a reservation or creation of a security interest. *Uniform Computer Information Transactions Act*, National Conference of Commissioners on Uniform State Laws, available at http://www.law.upenn.u/bll/ulc/ucita/citim99.htm.

Line Draw

Line draw is that function of a graphics chip which does just what the name implies, i.e. it draws a line on the screen. This is accomplished by inserting in a horizontal line of pixels, the designated dark or light or colored pixels which, when associated with the similarly designated pixels in the lines above or below, will draw a line, either vertically, horizontally, arced or curved. The speed, measured in billionths of a second (nano-seconds) at which it puts a pixel on the screen, is line draw speed. *Advanced Micro Devices, Inc. and Intel Corp.*, CCH Computer Cases 60,218 (Arb. Award. 1990).

Linear Programming

"Linear programming" means the control of digital data-processing machines to find solutions of sets of simultaneous linear equations or inequalities, or mixtures of both. *Re Slee and Harris' Application*, [1966] R.P.C. 194.

Link (See also Hyperlink)

This term generally refers to any highlighted words, phrases or graphics in a hypertext document that allow you to "jump" to another section of the same document or to another document on the World Wide Web. A browser usually displays a link in some distinguishing way, for example, in a different colour, font or style. When you place the cursor on a link, the URL of the linked page will appear at the bottom of your screen. When you activate a link, usually by clicking on it with the mouse, the browser will initiate the link. *The Internet: A Guide For Ontario Government Organizations, Information and Privacy Commissioner/Ontario, May 1998*, available at http://www.ipc.on.ca.

Highlighted words on a web site that allow you to connect to other parts of the same web site or to other web sites. *Cyberspeak — Learning the Language, the Federal Trade Commission and the National Association of Attorneys General*, available at http://www.ftc.gov/bcp/conline/pubs/online/sitesee/index.html.

A link is an image or short section of text referring to another document on the Web. A user interested in accessing the referenced document, selects the link, causing the document to be displayed automatically along with a new set of links that the user may follow. *Lockheed Martin Corp. v. Network Solutions Inc.,* 44 U.S.P.Q. 2d 1865 (C.D.Cal. 1997).

Link is defined as (1) in communication, a line, channel or circuit over which data is transmitted. . ., (3) in programming, a call to another program or subroutine. *3Com Corp.* 56 U.S.P.Q. 2d 1060 (T.T.A.B.2000).

A connection between computers, devices, programs, or files over which data is transmitted. *3Com Corp.* 56 U.S.P.Q. 2d 1060 (T.T.A.B.2000).

Linking

"Linking" is the process of combining all of the parts of the computer program into the "executable" code which runs the program. *Softel Inc. v. Dragon Medical and Scientific Communications, Inc.,* 1992 U.S. Dist. LEXIS 9502 (S.D.N.Y.1992).

Linux

Linux, which was and continues to be developed through the open source model of software development, also is an operating system. It can be run on a PC as an alternative to Windows, although the extent to which it is so used is limited. Linux is more widely used on servers. *Universal City Studios, Inc. v. Reimerdes,* 55 U.S.P.Q. 2d 1873 (S. D.N.Y. 2000).

ListServe

One to many messaging. *Security and Electronic Authorization and Authentication Guideline, Communications Security Establishment, Government of Canada September 1995, CID/01/15.*

An online mailing list that allows individuals or organizations to send e-mail to groups of people at one time. *Cyberspeak — Learning the Language, the Federal Trade Commission and the National Association of Attorneys General,* available at http://www.ftc.gov/bcp/conline/pubs/online/sitesee/index.html.

Literal Similarity

Literal similarity refers to similarity at the code level; that is, there is a verbatim copying of part or whole of the source or object codes of the computer program. *Bateman v. Mnemonics Inc.*, 38 U.S.P.Q. 2d 1225 (11th Cir. 1996).

Local Access Loop

The local access loop is the dedicated line between a telephone company switching centre and a subscriber's premises. Competition and Culture on Canada's Information Highway: Managing the Realities of Transition, CRTC (the "Convergence Report"), May 19, 1995.

Local Computer Bulletin Board

A local computer bulletin board is a computer information sharing system with modem access. *R. v. Hurtubise*, [1997] B.C.J. No. 40 (B.C.S.C.).

Local Data Processing Service

Is an offering of data processing wherein communications facilities are not involved in serving the customer. Computer Inquiry (Final Decision), 28 F.C.C.2d 267 (F.C.C. 1971).

Local Loop

Designates the part of a communications circuit between the subscriber's equipment and the line termination equipment in the exchange facility. *The Challenge of the Information Highway: Final Report of the Information Highway Advisory Council* (September 1995).

Typically called the "last mile", the physical connection between the customer premise and the Central Office. *Report to the Governor in Council: Status of Competition in Canadian Telecommunications Markets, Deployment/Accessibility of Advanced Telecommunications Infrastructure and Services, September, 2001.*

Local Multichannel Distribution Service (LMDS)

A system of distributing television signals over the air at relatively high radio frequencies (28GHz) within cells a few miles in radius. This is in contrast to wireless cable, which uses lower frequencies (2GHz) to broadcast over a radius of 30 miles or so. Submission of the Director of Investigation and Research to the CRTC Re Public Notice CRTC 1994-130

Local Number Portability (LNP)

The ability for customers to retain their telephone numbers when they change local service provider. *Report to the Governor in Council: Status of Competition in Canadian Telecommunications Markets, Deployment/Accessibility of Advanced Telecommunications Infrastructure and Services, September, 2001.*

Locking

Where an operating system permits two processes which are running concurrently to change the contents of a particular part of memory, there is a risk that they will both try to change that part of memory simultaneously, either may be interrupted at any time, and its continued execution delayed. *Cantor Fitzgerald International v. Tradition (UK) Ltd,.* [1999] I.N.L.R. No. 23 (Ch.D.).

Logic Bombs

A computer program that triggers an unauthorized act when particular circumstances on the system occur. *A Survey of Legal Issues Relating to the Security of Electronic Information*, Department of Justice, Canada.

Long Distance Selling Directive

Directive 97/7/EEC of the European Parliament and of the Council of 20 May 1997 on the protection of consumers in respect of distance contracts.

Long Prompt

Long prompt refers to a displayed multi-word English language description of a "highlighted" menu command. A "highlighted" menu command appears on the computer monitor as a block of inverse video — that is, on a monochrome monitor with a black background on which characters are lit, a highlighted word appears as black letters within a lit block. *Lotus Development Corporation v. Borland International Inc.*, 788 F.Supp. 78 (D.C. Mass. 1992).

Long-term Encryption Key

In public key cryptography, a long-term encryption key would be associated with an entity (*e.g.* an individual, agent, or automated process) for an extended period of time, perhaps one or two years. Possession of such a key enables access to all data encrypted with that key for the lifetime of its use. A long-term encryption key can be contrasted with a session key. A Cryptology Policy Framework for Electronic Commerce, Task Force on Electronic Commerce, Industry Canada, February 1998.

Low Level Computer Language

When one speaks of the "lowest level" computer language, therefore, one is talking of the machine language which is executed directly by the computer. Modern computer programmers typically write computer programs in a higher level language or source code. Common examples include FORTRAN, COBOL, Pascal, BASIC or C. Such languages are not specific to a particular make or model of computer but are universal to practically all computers. A program written in source code must be translated into the appropriate object code for execution. This translation, which may involve more than one layer of recoding, is achieved by an interpreter program known as a computer program. *Powerflex Services Pty Ltd. v. Data Access Corp.* (1997), 37 I.P.R. 436 (Aust. C.A.).

Low Level Documentation

Is a phrase used to describe the technical documentation which provides instructions to the programmers on how to build and install the product or object code. *Angoss II Partnership v. Trifox Inc.* (1997), [1997] O.J. No. 4969 (Gen. Div.), affirmed (1999), [1999] O.J. No. 4144, 1999 CarswellOnt 3474 (C.A.) leave to appeal dismissed (2000), [1999] S.C.C.A. No. 588, 2000 CarswellOnt 299.

Machine Code or Object Code

The program in its electrical code form. *Apple Computer Inc. v. Mackintosh Computers Ltd.* (1986), 28 D.L.R. (4th) 178 (Fed. T.D.).

Computer programs expressed as sequences of 1's and 0's, readable only by machines. *E.F. Johnson Co. v. Uniden Corp. of America*, 623 F.Supp. 1485 (D. Minn. 1985).

Object code is simply a form of the source code that can be read and acted upon by the microprocessor(s) or the central processing unit (CPU) of the computer. Object code is thus expressed in machine-readable form and consists of a series of electrical impulses. These impulses comprise a series of electronically on and electronically off states that can be represented by binary notation. Object code is merely a sequence of electrical impulses that may be embodied in static circuitry. These electrical impulses may be represented in writing in binary notation to correspond to the on/off pulses. *IBM Corp. v. Computer Imports Ltd.*, N.Z. H.C., Smellie J., March 21, 1989 (unreported).

Object code is the representation of the program in machine language (*e.g.*, using binary coding 0's and 1's or hexadecimal coding using letters and numbers or octal code using 0 and 7) which the computer executes. *Manufacturers Technology Inc. v. Cams Inc.*, 10 U.S.P.Q.2d 1321 (D. Conn. 1989).

When a computer runs a program, what it does is follow a series of machine code instructions, but these are not the instructions which the programmer wrote. The machine code instructions are generated by a computer program from the computer language instructions prepared by the programmer. Such a program is known as a compiler. Compilers exist for a range of computer languages. *Saphena Computing Ltd. v. Allied Collection Agencies Ltd.*, Ch. D., Recorder, July 22, 1988 (unreported), affirmed C.A., May 3, 1989 (unreported).

The class of computer languages which can be interpreted directly by computers (machines) without a translation process. Computer Software Protection: Australia, Copyright Law Review Committee 1995.

See also Binary Code.

Machine Language

The "lowest"-level computer progamming language is machine language, which is a binary language written in "bits" (*BI*nary digi*TS*). Each bit is equal to one binary decision — that is, to the designation of one of two possible and equally likely values, such as an "on" — "off" or "yes" — "no" choice. These binary decisions, the only kind that a typical computer can understand directly, are commonly represented by 0's and 1's. A sequence of eight bits (which allows 256 unique combinations of bits) is commonly called a "byte" ("by eight"), and 1024 bytes form a "kilobyte" (commonly referred to as "K," e.g., sixty-four kilobytes is "64K"). Machine language may also be represented in hexadecimal form, rather than in binary form, by the characters 0-9 and A-F, where "A" represents 10, "B" represents 11, and so on through "F," which represents "15." In hexadecimal machine language, only two rather than eight characters are required to allow for 256 unique combinations (e.g., 37 instead of 00110111, each of which represents the 55th of 256 combinations; 7B instead of 01111011, each of which represents the 123rd of 256 combinations; EA instead of 11101010, each of which represents the 234th of 256 combinations). The computer is able to translate these hexadecimal instructions into binary form. Other versions of machine language are represented in decimal (0-9) and octal (0-7) form. *Lotus Development Corp. v. Paperback Software International*, 15 U.S.P.Q.2d 1577 (D. Mass. 1990).

A sequence of binary instructions is known as "machine language" or "object code." *Softel Inc. v. Dragon Medical and Scientific Communications, Inc.*, 1992 U.S. Dist. LEXIS 9502 (S.D.N.Y.1992).

In order for a computer to be given the appropriate instructions it is necessary to communicate with it in some way. The only instructions which a computer can understand are those which consist of a series of 0's and 1's. Instructions set out in this way are said to be written in "machine language" or "machine code." (This may represent something of an oversimplification. I gather that at least in some cases the machine code which is fed into the computer will be translated by the machine into a more elaborate series of 0's and 1's. However this description will suffice for present purposes.) The machine code for one type of computer will usually be different from that for another type, although there may, of course, be compatibility between different manufacturers' products. *John Richardson Computers Ltd. v. Flanders*, [1993] F.S.R. 497 (Ch.D.).

Machine Sensible

Means data recorded in such a way that it can be sensed or read by an automatic data processing machine. Revenue Canada, Customs and Excise, Books and Records, Memorandum ET 102, February 24, 1989.

In relation to data, means recorded in such a way as to be sensed or read by an automatic data processing machine. GST Memorandum 500-1-2 (Books and Records -Computerized Records), May 26, 1993.

Macro

A macro is a single instruction that initiates a sequence of operations or module interactions within the program. Very often the user will accompany a macro with an instruction from the parameter list to refine the instruction. *Computer Asso-*

ciates International Inc. v. Altai Inc., 23 U.S.P.Q.2d 1241 (2d Cir. 1992); *Matrox Electronic Systems Ltd. v. Gaudreau*, [1993] R.J.Q. 2449 (C.S.).

Macro Language

Macro language refers to a feature by which a user may define a very short keystroke sequence as equivalent to a longer keystroke sequence. Thus, a user may invoke the short keystroke sequence (a "macro") as a substitute for the longer keystroke sequence. In stating this definition, I omit a sophisticated programming capability available in 1-2-3 through its macro language feature that Lotus, as I understand its submissions, does not contend is involved in its claim of infringement in this action. Having stated the definitions of the components of the user interface that I will use in this Memorandum, I now state additional points that I conclude are not in dispute about the relations among these definitions and associated matters. *Lotus Development Corporation v. Borland International Inc.*, 788 F.Supp. 78 (D.C. Mass. 1992).

Magnetic Ink Character Recognition (MICR)

The method of processing cheques now in universal use in the United States, Magnetic Ink Character Recognition (MICR) was first adopted by the American Bankers Association in 1956, and has been in common use since the mid-1960s. The form of each blank cheque is preprinted with magnetic characters, along the bottom of the cheque, toward the left-hand side. These characters designate the bank upon which the cheque is drawn, and the account number of the maker. When a cheque is presented to another bank (the "depository bank"), that bank adds additional magnetic encoding at the lower right-hand side of the cheque, specifying the amount. From that point on, the cheque works its way through the bank clearing system to the bank on which the cheque is drawn (the "payor" bank) and is charged against the maker's account, all without further human intervention. *The First National Bank of Boston v. Fidelity Bank*, 724 F.Supp. 1168 (E.D. Pa. 1989).

Magnetic Memory Core

These devices are used in the manufacture of electronic computers. The magnetic memory core is the device which essentially performs the function of storing information. This is accomplished by passing electrical signals or impulses through specific combinations of the wires upon which the cores have been connected. The electrical signal magnetizes the selected core. *Sperry Rand Corp. v. Pentronix Inc.*, 311 F.Supp. 910 (E.D. Pa. 1970).

See also Core.

Magnetic Stripe Card

The magnetic stripe card is undoubtedly the most recognizable ACT. Anyone who uses a credit card or an automated teller banking card is using a magnetic stripe card. This type of card is distinguishable by the dark stripe of magnetic material which is placed on one side of the card. The magnetic stripe is capable of storing 400 bytes (characters) of information. Its very limited information storage capabilities require that systems utilizing this technology store only essential information, such as cardholder identification codes to the card. Although the magnetic stripe card has gained massive acceptance throughout the world, it is widely recognized that its limited data storage capability and the data's susceptibility to fraudulent alternation will severely limit the future uses of the technology. *A Survey of Legal Issues Relating to the Security of Electronic Information*, Department of Justice, Canada.

A card with one or more magnetic stripes. Smart, Optical and Other Advanced Cards: How to Do a Privacy Assessment, Information and Privacy Commissioner/ Ontario Canada, available at http://www.itc.on.ca.

Magnetic Tape

The data to be processed by a computer is frequently stored on magnetic tapes. Typically, data is stored on tape in physically separate blocks, containing a few to many thousand characters of information. The organization of a tape is analogous to a long-playing record with small bands of unrecorded area separating each song. Splitting this tape into physically separate blocks permits the computer to process them one at a time with the tape recorder coming to a standstill, if desired, between each block. Computer users realized long ago that it was desirable to place on magnetic tape not only data, but label blocks, which identify or derive the data contained therein. These label blocks can be used to separate the beginning and the end of the logical collections of data blocks. A label block at the beginning of the tape can name the data set, record the date on which the tape was written and provide information such as the length of each data block and the structure of individual data items within a block. *United Software Corp. v. Sperry Rand Corp.*, 5 C.L.S.R. 1492 (E.D. Pa. 1974).

Mail Exploder

A program such as a list serve running on the server on which the list resides that automatically (i.e., without human intervention) responds to a user's request to be added to or removed from the list of subscribers and retransmits messages posted by a subscriber to others on the mailing list. *Shea v. Reno*, 1996 U.S. Dist. LEXIS 10720 (S.D.N.Y. 1996).

Mail exploders, also called mailing lists, allow online users to subscribe to automated mailing lists that disseminate information on particular subjects. Subscribers send an e-mail message to the "list," and the mail exploder automatically and simultaneously sends the message to all of the other subscribers on the list. Subscribers can reply to the message by sending a response to the list. Users of mailing lists typically can add or remove their names from the list automatically, with no direct human involvement. *Cyberspace Communications, Inc. et al. v. Engler*, 55 F. Supp. 2d 737 (E.D. F. Ch. 1999).

Mail-Box Service

In a typical mail-box application, Party A, who wished to send a message to Party B, would compose a message at his terminal, and, over a communications line, direct the message to a computer memory location having the address "Party B". Party B can periodically communicate with the computer using his terminal, and withdraw the contents of his memory location for display at the terminal. This is, in effect, a store and forward communications service in which the information content of the originating message is not changed. Second Computer Inquiry (Tentative Decision), 72 F.C.C.2d 358 (F.C.C. 1979).

Mainframe Computers

In the early 1960's computers were large mainframe computers. These consisted of numbers of visual display units ("VDUs") which resembled a television screen, with a keyboard attached, linked to the central processing unit ("CPU"), which did all the processing. The central computer could have occupied a whole room. *Madeley Pty Ltd. v. Touche Ross*, McGarvie, J., Aust. Fed. Ct., Dec. 21, 1989 (unreported).

Maintenance

Maintenance means changes to an existing system, namely, to have it perform new or advanced functions or correct defects. *Computer Associates International, Inc. v. Bryan*, 3 CCH Comp. Cases 46,619 (E.D. N.Y. 1992).

Makefile

A "makefile" is a file which contains the rules used to build an executable program. Makefiles are sometimes referred to as the "recipe for building the programs." *Angoss II Partnership v. Trifox Inc.* (19997), [1997] O.J. No. 4969, 1997 CarswellOnt 4888 (Gen. Div.), affirmed (1999), [1999] O.J. No. 4144, 1999 CarswellOnt 3474 (C.A.) leave to appeal dismissed (2000), [1999] S.C.C.A. No. 588.

Make Available

The "posting" or storage of material or information on a computer or server connected to the World-Wide-Web or connection of a computer containing material or information for access using the Internet or an intranet. The making available to the public of material or information refers to situations where the material can be accessed by anyone with Internet services available to them - as opposed to a computer or server that might only be available to a select group of people over either a LAN or where Internet access is restricted using some form of encryption or access-protection. *Digital Technology and the Copyright Act 1994: A Discussion Paper, Competition and Enterprise Branch, July 2001 (New Zealand).*

Make Compatible

Means bring different standards-related measures of the same scope approved by different standardizing bodies to a level such that they are either identical, equivalent or have the effect of permitting goods or services to be used in place of one another or fulfil the same purpose. North American Free Trade Agreement between Canada, Mexico and the United States, Article 915.

Manual Key Distribution

The distribution of cryptographic keys, often in a plaintext form requiring physical protection, but using a non-electronic means, such as a bonded courier. "Security Requirements for Cryptographic Modules", FIPS Pub. 140-1, Federal Information Processing Standards Publication, January 11, 1994, available at http://csrc.nist.gov/fips/fips1401.htm.

Manual Key Entry

The entry of cryptographic keys into a cryptographic module from a printed form, using devices such as buttons, thumb wheels or a keyboard. "Security Requirements for Cryptographic Modules", FIPS Pub. 140-1, Federal Information Processing Standards Publication, January 11, 1994, available at http://csrc.nist.gov/fips/fips1401.htm.

Manuals and Instructional Materials

Means data necessary for the installation, operation, maintenance and repair, or training, with respect to any item, component, process, or computer software. Federal Acquisition Regulation (FAR): Rights in Technical Data (Proposed Rules), Federal Register, Vol. 55, No. 199.

Mask Works

See also Topography.

"Mask works" are defined in the Act (United States Semi-Conductor Chip Protection Act) as a series of related images, however fixed or encoded, (1) having or representing the pre-determined three-dimensional pattern of metallic, insulating, or semiconductor material or removed from the layers of a semiconductor chip product; (2) in which series the relation of the images to one another is that each image has the pattern of the surface of one form of the semi-conductor chip product. United States Copyright Act, 17 U.S.C. 101, c. 9.

Mass-Market License

Means a standard form that is prepared for and used in a mass-market transaction. *Uniform Computer Information Transactions Act*, National Conference of Commissioners on Uniform State Laws, available at http://www.law.upenn.u/bll/ulc/ucita/citim99.htm.

Material Form

In relation to a work or an adaptation of a work, includes any form (whether visible or not) of storage from which the work or adaptation, or a substantial part of the work or adaptation, can be reproduced. *Autodesk Australia Pty Ltd. v. Dyason* (1989), 15 I.P.R. 1 (Aus. Fed. Ct.), reversed [1990] A.I.P.C. 36,446 (Aus. Fed. Ct. FC).

Includes such methods of fixation or storage as reproduction on magnetic tape, read only or random access computer memory, magnetic or laser disks, bubble memories and other forms of storage which will doubtless be developed. *Autodesk Australia Pty Ltd. v. Dyason*, supra.

Means of Distance Communication

Means any means which, without the simultaneous physical presence of the supplier and the consumer, may be used for the conclusion of a contract between those parties. *European Parliament and Council Directive on the Protection of Consumers in Respect of Distance Contracts*, May 20, 1997, Directive 97/7.

Measurement Interface [MI]

This is a facility provided within the MPE operating system that gathers and accumulates statistics relating to the activities within various components of the computer system as it is being used. This information is divided into several basic categories. The "Global" category of data reflects the activities within the computer system as a whole including how busy the CPU actually is, how often the CPU is idle and how much memory management activity is occurring. The "Process" category provides data collected for each individual process within the system and includes similar information to that at the global level but charged individually to the various processes. The third category of data is "I/O" and includes data reflecting the activity of the various peripheral devices including discs, tapes and printers. *Delrina Corp. v. Triolet Systems, Inc.* (1992), 47 C.P.R. (3d) 1 (Ont. H.C.).

Memory

An area of the computer's circuitry that holds applications and any data generated with those applications. Information held in Random Access Memory (RAM) is erased whenever the computer is turned off. Information held in Read Only Memory (ROM) is retained even when the computer is off. Memory usually refers to the high speed semiconductor storage within a computer that is used to temporarily store data while it is being processed or examined. The term "memory" is also generically extended to refer to data that is stored externally on disks and tapes. *Delrina Corp. v. Triolet Systems, Inc.* (1992), 47 C.P.R. (3d) 1 (Ont. H.C.).

[t]here are three types of memory device containing computer programs which are fitted to the PCBs. These are known respectively as ROMs, EPROMs and OTPROMs. Each of these is an integrated circuit device, commonly referred to

as a "memory chip". The electrical interconnection between the various integrated circuit devices is achieved by mounting them on the PCBs. *Avel Pty Ltd. v. Wells* (1992), 23 I.P.R. 353 (Aust. Fed. C.A.).

Menu

Menu refers to a display on the computer monitor of a limited number of commands available to the user at a given moment. *Lotus Development Corporation v. Borland International Inc.*, 788 F.Supp. 78 (D.C. Mass. 1992).

Menus are employed in graphical user interfaces to store information or functions of the computers in a place that is convenient to reach, but saves screen space for other images. *Apple Computer Inc. v. Microsoft Corp.*, 1992 U.S. Dist. LEXIS 12219 (N.D. Cal. 1992).

Menus may mean the visual screen displays that present a computer operator with a limited number of commands available at a given stage in the computer programs operation. *Gates Rubber Co. v. Bando American Inc.*, 28 U.S.P.Q. 2d 1503 (10th Cir. 1993).

A menu, in computer parlance, is a graphical user interface employed to store information or functions of the computers in a place that is convenient to reach, but saves screen space for other images. *MiTek Holdings Inc. v. Arce Engineering Inc.*, 39 U.S.P.Q. 2d 1609 (11th Cir. 1996).

Menu Command

Menu command refers to a command that appears in a menu. In Lotus 1-2-3, a menu command is ordinarily a single English word. In rare instances, it is instead a representation of an English pronunciation (such as "Xtract"). Menu commands are displayed on the computer monitor by the 1-2-3 program in a succession of menus. The menus communicate to the user, in sequence, the spreadsheet operations available to the user. *Lotus Development Corporation v. Borland International Inc.*, 788 F.Supp. 78 (D.C. Mass. 1992).

Menu Program

Is one which displays on a computer screen a selection of options, each representing a specific function and a separate program, from which the user may choose a program. *Northern Office Micro Computers Ltd. v. Rosenstein*, [1982] F.S.R. 124 (S.C. S.Africa).

Message Digest Function

Means an algorithm that maps or translates the sequence of bits comprising an electronic record into another, generally smaller, set of bits (the message digest), without requiring the use of any secret information such as a key, such that an electronic record yields the same message digest every time the algorithm is executed using such record as input and it is computationally unfeasible that any two electronic records can be found or deliberately generated that would produce the same message digest using the algorithm unless the two records are precisely identical. *Illinois Electronic Commerce Security Act* 1998 5 Ill. Comp. Stat. 175.

Message Service (Computer)

A data processing system for store and forward message services. Second Computer Inquiry (Tentative Decision), 72 F.C.C.2d 358 (F.C.C. 1979).

Message-Switching

The transmission of messages between two or more points, via communication facilities, wherein the content of the information remains unaltered. Second Computer Inquiry (Tentative Decision), 72 F.C.C.2d 358 (F.C.C. 1979).

Message-switching essentially involves the sending of a message by a device, e.g., a teletypewriter, through common carrier lines to a computer where it is stored until an appropriate line is available for forwarding the message to the receiving station; the content of the message remains unaltered. *GTE Service Corp. v. F.C.C.*, 3 C.L.S.R. 592 (2nd Cir. 1973).

Is the computer-controlled transmission of messages, between two or more points, via communications facilities, wherein the content of the message remains unaltered. Computer Inquiry (Final Decision), 28 F.C.C.2d 267 (F.C.C. 1971).

Message-switching is, in essence, an operation which is inherent in the process of transmitting, by wire or radio, intelligence of data from point of origin to point of destination. As in the case of remote access data processing, user terminals are linked to the central computer by communications channels. Thus, it is possible for users not only to have on-line communication with the computer for data processing purposes, but it is also possible for such users to communicate with each other when the computer is programmed to switch messages of one to another. Unlike data processing, however, the computer, when and if used for message-switching, does not alter the content of the intelligence transmitted. It simply performs the function of storage and either immediate or delayed forwarding of the message to its addressed destination. In this respect the computer takes the place of those manual or electro-mechanical switching or relay operations which typically involved in the transmission of intelligence for hire by communications common carriers. Computer Inquiry (Tentative Decision), 28 F.C.C.2d 291 (F.C.C. 1970).

The computer-controlled transmission of messages between two or more points via communications facilities, wherein the content of the message remains unaltered. Message-switching should be distinguished from circuit switching notwithstanding the fact that both functions involve the interconnection or transfer of electric signals from one channel to another. Historically, circuit-switching, typified by the telephone industry, involved a carrier's providing its customer with exclusive use of an open channel for direct electrical connection between two or more points. Message-switching, typified by the telegraph industry, involved a carrier's transmission over its facilities of a customer's set message at a charge based upon the information sent. Connection was indirect in the sense that there occurred a temporary storage or delay of signals prior to forwarding the message to its ultimate destination. In effect, message-switching is essentially a "store and forward" function with respect to pre-determined information; circuit-switching, on the other hand, involves the establishment of a completed transmission path prior to the communication of any information. The computer, because of its great speed, has so reduced time delay with respect to message-switching that historical distinctions in switching have become blurred. However, the role of the computer in circuit-switching still remains distinct from that of a computer in message-switching. Although it serves as the "control" element in basic functions, in a circuit-switched network, the actual information is through a switching matrix from terminal points must necessarily pass through and undergo some processing by the computer mainframe. Computer Inquiry (Tentative Decision), 28 F.C.C.2d 291 (F.C.C. 1970).

META description (See Metatags)

"Meta description" refers to words that identify an Internet site. *Niton Corp. v. Radiation Monitoring Devices, Inc.*, 27 F.Supp. 2d. 104 (D.Mass. 1998).

META key words (See Metatags)

META key words refers to key words that are listed by the web page creator when creating a web site. An Internet user then uses a web search engine that searches the "META" key words and identifies a match or a "hit". *Niton Corp. v. Radiation Monitoring Devices, Inc.*, 27 F.Supp. 2d. 104 (D.Mass. 1998).

Metatags

Metatags are HTML code intended to describe the contents of the web site. There are different types of metatags, but those of principal concern to us are the "description " and "keyword" metatags. The description metatags are intended to describe the web site; the keyword metatags, at least in theory, contain keywords relating to the contents of the web site. The more often a term appears in the metatags and in the text of the web page, the more likely it is that the web page will be "hit" in a search for that keyword and the higher on the list of "hits" the web page will appear. *Brookfield Communications, Inc. v. West Coast Entertainment Corp.*, 174 F. 3d 1036 (9th Cir. 1999).

Some search engines look in particular for words that are invisible to the user but are nonetheless embedded in the sites as software code so that the site may be picked up by search engines. Such words are called metatags. *Playboy Enterprises, Inc. v. Netscape Communications,* Corp. SA CV 99-320 A.H.S. (C.D.Cal. July 27, 1999).

A metatag is a specific word programmed within a website. Internet search engines look for meta-tags and direct consumers to websites which contain meta-tags corresponding to the consumer's server terms. *Ty Inc. v. Baby Me, Inc.*, 2001 U.S. Dist. LEXIS 5761 (N.D. Ill 2001).

A metatag is part of a website not automatically displayed on the user's computer screen in the normal course of viewing a website. A meta tag is put on the website by the website owner to provide key information about the website. Through the use of meta tags, a website creator can describe what is available at that particular site or insert any other information. A meta tag is written in HTML. When search engines gather information they seek out and obtain the information in the meta tags. Meta tags are used by most search engines and directories to gather information, index a website and match the website to the key words in a user's query. This generates search results corresponding to the user's query. It is common to use meta tags to specify key words that will be matched to key words entered by someone conducting a search. *British Columbia Automobile Assn. v. OPEIU. Local 378* (2001), 10 C.P.R. (4th) 423 (B.C.S.C.).

In order to increase the likelihood that their pages will be returned as a "hit" by the various search engines, Web page designers embed key words in their Web Pages, known as "meta-tags". Although normally invisible to the Internet user, meta-tags are detected by search engines and increase the likelihood that a user searching for a particular topic will be directed to that Web designer's page. So, for example, the homepage of General Motors' website contains the following meta-tags: "General Motors, GM. Buick, Cadillac, Chevrolet, EV1, GMC, Holden, Isuzu, Oldsmobile, Opel, Pontiac, Saab, Saturn, Vauxhall, Detroit, Car, Cars, Truck, Trucks, river, Drivers, Driving, Driving experience, Innovations, Vehicle, Vehicles, Automobile, Automobiles, Automotives". General Motors Home Page (visited September 13, 2000) <*http://www.GM.com*>. By embedding those "invisible" meta-tags in its home page, General Motors increases the likelihood that a user employing a search engine to locate websites containing information on General Motors' products (or automotive products in general) will be directed to the GM website. *National A-1 Advertising, Inc. et al v. Networks Solutions, Inc.*, Civ. No. 99-033-M (D.N.Hamp. Sept. 28, 2000).

A metatag is hypertext markup language ("HTML") code, invisible to the Internet user that permits web designers to describe their web pages. There are two different types of metatags: keyword and description. The keyword metatag permits designers to identify search terms for use by search engines. Description metatags allow designers to briefly describe the contents of their pages. This description appears as sentence fragments beneath the webpages's listing in a search result. *Bihari v. Gross*, 56 U.S.P.Q. 2d 1489 (S.D.N.Y. 2000).

MFLOPS

Million floating operations per second. Protest of Stellar Computer, Inc., CCH Comp. L.R. 60,139 (G.S.B.C.A. 1990).

Microcode

A very low level machine code used to write programs that define machine instructions to perform specific machine operational functions, e.g., moving or examining data. Computer Software Protection: Australia, Copyright Law Review Committee 1995.

A microcode consists of a series of instructions that tell a microprocessor which of its thousands of transistors to actuate in order to perform the tasks directed by the macroinstruction set. *NEC Corp. v. Intel Corp.*, 10 U.S.P.Q.2d 1177 (N.D. Cal. 1989).

Microcode is a set of encoded instructions . . . that controls the fine details of the execution of one or more primitive functions of a computer. Microcode serves as a substitute for certain elements of the hardware circuitry that had previously controlled that function. *Lotus Development Corp. v. Paperback Software International*, 15 U.S.P.Q.2d 1577 (D. Mass. 1990).

The elementary computer instructions that correspond to an executable program instruction. "Security Requirements for Cryptographic Modules", FIPS Pub. 140-1, Federal Information Processing Standards Publication, January 11, 1994, available at http://csrc.nist.gov/fips/fips1401.htm.

Microcomputer

A microcomputer is one that utilizes a microprocessor as its central control and arithmetic element. Microprocessors are the product of the vast improvements in the technology for fabricating integrated circuits which, beginning in the 1950s, made possible construction of huge numbers of transistors on a single chip, now usually made from silicon. *Apple Computer Inc. v. Microsoft Corp.*, 1992 U.S. Dist. LEXIS 12219 (N.D. Cal. 1992).

A computer system that uses a microprocessor as its processing unit. Computer Software Protection: Australia, Copyright Law Review Committee 1995.

Microdisk

The term "microdisk" refers generally to the class of floppy disks smaller than 5.25 inches. *International Trade Commission Determination re 3.5-Inch Microdisks*, 1 CCH Comp. Cases 60,024 (ITC Inv. No. 731-Ta-389).

Microfilm

Microfilm is 16 or 35 mm high-resolution photographic film used to store images of documents.

Microfiche

Microfiche consists of transparent cards with miniaturised photographic document images arranged in a grid of rows and columns so that they can be read on a Microfiche viewer. *Digital Technology and the Copyright Act 1994: A Discussion Paper, Competition and Enterprise Branch, July 2001 (New Zealand).*

Micropayments

Enable the electronic transferal of small sums of money (often less than $.01) between two parties. Advancing Global Electronic Commerce: Technology Solutions to Public Policy Challenges, The Computer Systems Policy Project, July 1999, available at http://www.cspp.org/projects/july99_cto_report.pdf.

Microprocessor

A small, integrated circuit. A microprocessor forms the heart of desktop computers. Submission of the Director of Investigation and Research to the CRTC Re Public Notice CRTC 1994-130.

A miniature computer placed on a single microchip which is capable of performing arithmetic, logic, and control functions. *E.F. Johnson Co. v. Uniden Corp. of America*, 623 F.Supp. 1485 (D.C. Minn. 1985).

The development of the microprocessor has led to the circumstance where such devices can be produced on a production line basis as essentially identical units, and at dramatically low costs. These extremely compact devices can then be adapted at any specific application by the addition of a unique program of coded instructions which is stored in an ancillary read-only memory (ROM). Thus microprocessors can be programmed to perform: (a) traditional computer data processing functions (as in today's pocket calculators) or (b) various control, logic, and buffering functions which were previously performed by hard-wired arrays of discrete components. Dataspeed 40/4, 52 F.C.C.2d 21 (F.C.C. 1977).

An integrated circuit that performs the function of the central processor of a computer. It carries out the arithmetic, logic, and control functions. Computer Software Protection: Australia, Copyright Law Review Committee 1995.

Microsoft Windows ("Windows")

A windowing environment and application user interface (API) for DOS that brings to IBM-format computing some of the graphical user interface features of the Macintosh, such as pull-down menus, multiple typefaces, desk accessories (a clock, calculator, calendar and notepad, for example), and the capability of moving text and graphics from one program to another via a clipboard. *Que's Computer User's Dictionary*, Que Corporation (1990), quoted in *Re Microsoft Corporation*, Comp. Ind. Lit. Reptr. 16,485 (U.S. P.T.O. 1993).

Microsoft Windows ("Windows") is an operating system released by Microsoft Corp. It is the most widely used operating system for PCs in the United States, and its versions include Windows 95, Windows 98, Windows NT and Windows 2000. *Universal City Studios, Inc. v. Reimerdes,* 55 U.S.P.Q. 2d 1873 (S. D.N.Y. 2000).

Middleware

Operating systems are not the only software programs that expose APIs to application developers. The Netscape Web browser and Sun Microsystems, Inc.'s Java class libraries are examples of non-operating system software that do likewise. Such software is often called "middleware" because it relies on the interfaces provided by the underlying operating system while simultaneously exposing its own APIs to developers. *United States of America v. Microsoft Corporation*, 87 F.Supp. 2d 30 (D.D.C. 2000).

.mil

The generic Top Level Domain (gTLD) used by the U.S. military. *Domain Name System Reform and Related Internet Governance Issues: A Consultation Paper*, Industry Canada available at *www.strategis.gc.ca*

Minicomputers

In the late 1960's, minicomputers which were smaller and cheaper versions of mainframe computers, were produced. They were powerful to act as a central computer. The central computer was typically about the size of a large filing cabinet. While one hundred VDUs might be attached, a mainframe of about ten might be attached to a minicomputer. *Madeley Pty Ltd. v. Touche Ross*, McGarvie, J., Aust. Fed. Ct., Dec. 21, 1989 (unreported).

Mirror

A mirror site is a copy of a primary website. The mirror site may exist to provide continuity and reliability of access, or to spread loading caused by heavy use of the primary site. Normally a mirror site is updated by copying from the primary site continuously or at regular intervals, a process known as mirroring. *Digital Technology and the Copyright Act 1994: A Discussion Paper, Competition and Enterprise Branch, July 2001 (New Zealand).*

Mirror Site

A "mirror site" involves an arrangement in which the owner of a Web site allows another entity to copy the content of that site onto another server. That server will be closer to a segment of users, who may obtain access to the materials without going back to the original site. *Public Performance of Musical Works* 1996-1998 (Tariff 22) (1999), 1 C.P.R. (4th) 417 (Copyright Board).

Mobile Identification Number (MIN)

A ten-digit numerical telephone number (area code + seven-digit telephone number) assigned to each cellular telephone customer, usually identical to the customer's home telephone number. *United States v. Brady*, 820 F.Supp. 1346 (C.D. Utah 1993).

Mobility

Mobility of cryptographic methods only means the technical ability to function in multiple countries or information and communications infrastructures. *OECD Guidelines for Cryptography Policy*, March 27, 1997, available at *www.oecd.org*.

Mobile Services

Wireless services including analog and digital cellular (e.g. Personal Communications Services or PCS). *Report to the Governor in Council: Status of Competition in Canadian Telecommunications Markets, Deployment/Accessibility of Advanced Telecommunications Infrastructure and Services, September, 2001.*

Modem

The term is a contraction of "*mo*dulator-*dem*odulator". A modem is generally any device that modulates signals to adapt them for use in two different types of equipment. However, the term most commonly refers to the device that allows computers to communicate over telephone lines or coax cables. For example, modems transmit digital information from a computer into analog information which can be fed over telephone lines. At the receiving end, the process is reversed. Submission of the Director of Investigation and Research to the CRTC Re Public Notice CRTC 1994-130.

A modem (a contraction of "*mo*dulator" and "*dem*odulator") is a device that translates digital information into a signal for transmission over a telephone line (modulation) and translates a signal received over a telephone line into digital information (demodulation). *Shea v. Reno*, 1996 U.S. Dist. LEXIS 10720 (S.D.N.Y. 1996).

Modems, widely used in the data processing and data communications fields, provide a communication link between a signal generator, such as a computer terminal which generates discreet voltage levels to represent data, and a telephone distribution network. The modem modulates the discreet voltage level signal to produce a signal which can be transmitted over a telephone line. An identical or similar modem at the receiving end of the telephone line demodulates the signal to produce a discreet voltage level form signal which is compatible with a data receiver. *Hayes Microcomputer Products Inc. v. Business Computer Corp.*, 219 U.S.P.Q. 634 (T.T.A.B. 1983).

The function of a modem is to enable data (ones and zeroes) to be transmitted over telephone lines. The ordinary telephone line transmits only analog signals — for example: "on" or "off". Data comes in ones and zeroes from the computer. It is then translated by a modem into an analog signal and transmitted over the telephone line to a receiving modem which takes the analog signal, re-translates it into digital data and sends it to the receiving computer. Thus, two modems enable two computers, which talk in digital language, to communicate with each other over a telephone line which cannot handle digital signals. *Advanced Micro Devices, Inc. and Intel Corp.*, CCH Comp. Cases 60,218 (Arb. Award. 1990).

A contraction of "mo(dulator)" and "dem(odulator)": an accessory that allows computers and terminal equipment to communicate through telephone lines or cable; converts analog data into the digital language of computers. *The Challenge of the Information Highway: Final Report of the Information Highway Advisory Council* (September 1995).

A "modem" is a device attached to, or inside of, a computer which enables one computer to "communicate" with another computer via telephone lines. *United States v. Johnson*, summarized in Comp. Ind. Lit. Reptr. 21,494.

A contraction of "*modu*lator" and "*demo*dulator"; a piece of equipment that digitizes analog data and enables computers to communicate through telephone lines or cable. Ministry of Revenue Advisory Committee, Report of the Committee On Electronic Commerce, April 30, 1998, Industry Canada.

(Modulator/Demodulator) electronic device used to carry out conversion of data from *digital* to *analogue* form (and the reverse) for transmission over a telecommunications link. *Digital Technology and the Copyright Act 1994: A Discussion Paper, Competition and Enterprise Branch, July 2001 (New Zealand).*

Modification

In relation to data held in a computer, means –(a) the alternation or removal of the data; or (b) an addition to the data. *Property Damage and Computer Offences Act 2002 (Australia).*

Module

Most programs of any size will be divided into a series of smaller parts that contain the instructions for handling some part of the total processing task. This is done to break up the total problem into a number of smaller, more manageable problems that can each be dealt with separately. In many cases, these pieces form solutions for general purpose processing and will be re-used by many programs in which case they will be stored in a centralized library. *Delrina Corp. v. Triolet Systems, Inc.* (1992), 47 C.P.R. (3d) 1 (Ont. H.C.).

A module is a relatively short sequence of instructions which performs a specific sub-task in the computer program. *Softel Inc. v. Dragon Medical and Scientific Communications, Inc.*, 1992 U.S. Dist. LEXIS 9502 (S.D.N.Y. 1992).

A module typically consists of two components: operations and data types. *Gates Rubber Co. v. Bando American Inc.*, 28 U.S.P.Q. 2d 1503 (10th Cir. 1993).

Moral rights

Rights provided to authors and directors of copyright works under copyright law that are independent of the economic rights that might exist in a work. Moral rights are granted to authors and directors to protect their personal interests in relation to their creations. Unlike economic rights granted under copyright, moral rights cannot be sold. *Digital Technology and the Copyright Act 1994: A Discussion Paper, Competition and Enterprise Branch, July 2001 (New Zealand).*

Morphing

Graphics effect where one object changes flawlessly into another on the screen. Monopolies and Mergers Commission — Video Games: A report on the supply of video games in the UK (LONDON: HMSO Cm2781).

Mouse

Handheld device. *Xerox Corp. v. Apple Computer Inc.*, Comp. Ind. Lit. Reptr. 11,155 (N.D. Cal. 1990).

A hand-held device which allows the operator to communicate with the computer without using the keyboard. *In re Apple Computer Securities Litigation*, 886 F.2d 1109 (9th Cir. 1989).

Device used to input information into a computer. Monopolies and Mergers Commission — Video Games: A report on the supply of video games in the UK (LONDON: HMSO Cm2781).

Mousetrapped

Means that [visitors to a website] were unable to exit without clicking on a succession of advertisements. *Shields v. Zuccarini,* case no. 00-2236 (3rd. Cir. June 15, 2001).

When a potential or existing online customer, attempting to access EB's website, mistakenly types one of Mr. Zucccarini's domain misspellings, he is "mousetrapped" in a barrage of advertising windows, featuring a variety of products, including credit cards, internet answering machines, games, and music. The Internet user cannot exit the Internet without clicking on the succession of advertisements that appears. Simply clicking on the "X" in the top right-hand corner of the screen, a common way to close a web browser window, will not allow the user to exit. *Electronics Boutique Holdings Corp. v. Zuccarini,* 56 U.S.P.Q. 2d 1705 (E.D.P. 2000).

MPE

This is the operating system that is an integral part of the HP3000 computer system and is unique and proprietary to that family of computer systems. *Delrina Corp. v. Triolet Systems, Inc.* (1992), 47 C.P.R. (3d) 1 (Ont. H.C.).

MPEG

Motion Picture Experts Group. Name given to a data compression technique which makes possible Full Motion Video (FMV) playback. Monopolies and Mergers Commission — Video Games: A report on the supply of video games in the UK (LONDON: HMSO Cm2781).

MP3

A standard file format for the storage of audio recordings in a digital format called MPEG-3, abbreviated as MP3. *A & M Records Inc. v. Napster Inc.*, 57 U.S.P.Q. 2d 1729 (9th Cir.2001).

Strictly, a three-letter Microsoft Windows file name extension. It is more generally used to stand for MPEG (Moving Picture Experts Group) audio layer 3, which is a standard for compression of audio signals for efficient storage and transmission over the Internet. *Digital Technology and the Copyright Act 1994: A Discussion Paper, Competition and Enterprise Branch, July 2001 (New Zealand).*

MS-DOS

An operating system that has become popular since its adoption by IBM on its personal computers. *IBM Corp. v. Computer Imports Ltd.*, N.Z. H.C., Smellie J., March 21, 1989 (unreported).

MS-DOS was the standard operating system for IBM and compatible personal computers. *Step-Saver Data Systems, Inc. v. Wise Technology*, 1990 W.L. 158151 (E.D. Pa. 1990).

MTS

Message Telecommunication Service. *MCI Communications Corp. v. AT&T*, 4 C.L.S.R. 1119 (E.D. Pa. 1973).

Message Toll Service. American Trucking Association, Inc./Resale and Shared Use, 47 F.C.C.2d 644 (U.S. Fed. Coom. Comm. 1974).

Multicasting

Multicasting occurs when a computer sends out a single set of packets which are replicated at a certain point in the network and then distributed to a number of recipients. The destination address for packets sent by multicast consists of a multicast group identifier. Any person who sends a message to join the group becomes part of a distribution tree to which the packets are distributed. *Public Performance of Musical Works* 1996-1998 (Tariff 22) (1999), 1 C.P.R. (4th) 417 (Copyright Board).

Multimedia

Multimedia is an important subset of new media, and, indeed, the term can be used, in many ways, as its surrogate. However, to be precise, multimedia is a technology which integrates two or more existing or new media forms, such as audio, full-motion video, still photographs, graphics, animation, text and data, on a single form. New media is broader since it encompasses enrichment of traditional media, and includes entirely new areas, such as hypermedia and virtual reality. Study on New Media and Copyright, *Final Report* (Nordicity Group Ltd., June 30, 1994) prepared for Industry Canada, New Media, Information Technologies Industry Branch.

Multimedia is a collection of heterogenous technologies which will enable information providers and users to process information in a variety of novel ways. Study on New Media and Copyright, *Final Report* (Nordicity Group Ltd., June 30, 1994) prepared for Industry Canada, New Media, Information Technologies Industry Branch.

A term which generally refers to the communication of messages or information through the combined use of text, graphics, animation, audio and motion video.

It is also used as a synonym for convergence, in that any product, system, venture, agreement or technology that brings together components of more than one previously distinct sector of the media industry can be described as "multimedia". For example, computer touchscreen TV and laserdisk. Submission of the Director of Investigation and Research to the CRTC Re Public Notice CRTC 1994-130.

Machines offering the possibility of interacting with a wide variety of *software* applications, such as games, films, music and books. Monopolies and Mergers Commission — Video Games: A report on the supply of video games in the UK (LONDON: HMSO Cm2781).

Is a digitized interactive application involving more than one medium (video, text, graphics, sound). Its major uses range from entertainment education (these are often combined to form "edutainment") to conveying information, to corporate applications. The Economic and Social Impact of Electronic Commerce: Preliminary Findings and Research Agenda, OECD August 7, 1998.

Digital representation of different types of information such as text, graphics, audio and video, so that all of these can be stored in a common medium (such as CD ROM or computer storage). *Digital Technology and the Copyright Act 1994: A Discussion Paper, Competition and Enterprise Branch, July 2001 (New Zealand).*

Multimedia Works

The very premise of a so-called "multimedia work" is that it combines several different elements or types of works (e.g., text (literary works), sound (sound recording), still images (pictorial works), and moving images (audio visual works)) into a *single medium* (e.g., a CD ROM) — not multiple media. Intellectual Property and the National Information Infrastructure, *The Report of the Working Group on Intellectual Property Rights* (September 1995).

Multiplexed Programming

Programming broadcast by a pay television service that is distributed on two or more channels. Cable Television Regulations, 1986, SOR/86-831.

Multiplexing

The combining of two or more distinct signals on one channel or frequency. Submission of the Director of Investigation and Research to the CRTC Re Public Notice CRTC 1994-130.

Multipoint Distribution System (MDS)

Sometimes referred to as MMDS for "Multipoint *Mulitchannel* Distribution System". This is a wireless distribution technology whose basic function, similar to that of cable distribution, is to package a number of channels and services and distribute them to local subscribers for a fee, only using microwave transmission instead of cables. Submission of the Director of Investigation and Research to the CRTC Re Public Notice CRTC 1994-130.

Multiprogrammed Format

A multiprogrammed format is one in which the computer is capable of executing more than one program, and thus perform more than one application at the same time, without the need to reprogram the computer for each task it must perform. *In Re Bradley*, 600 F.2d 807 (Cust. & Pat. App. 1979), affirmed 450 U.S. 381 (1981).

Multi-User Relational Database

A multi-user relational database system is suitable for use where the one database is used by a number of computers. *Madeley Pty Ltd. v. Touche Ross*, McGarvie, J., Aust. Fed. Ct., Dec. 21, 1989 (unreported).

Multi-Vendor Interoperability

An ability to communicate between systems, and, to a reasonable degree, share data between systems; the first category describes the information necessary for the maintenance of networking and communication between networks. The second category describes the information necessary for the maintenance of data sharing between systems. *IBM v. Fujitsu Ltd.*, Copyright L.R. (CCH) 20,517 (Am. Arbtn. Assoc. Comm. Arbtn. Trib. 1988).

Name of Items

In an attempt to make computer source programs more readable, symbolic descriptive names are usually assigned to areas (items) of memory. These variable (item) names must be unique within the module and are usually selected so that they describe the data that they represent. For instance, if a program is working with payroll information, the source code instructions would probably "define" or "declare" (name) areas of memory (items) for "HOURS", "RATE" and "GROSS-PAY". These declarations would follow the syntax of the computer language being used and would allocate the memory area as well as assign a name to it. These names could then be used when referring to the memory areas and the program source code would be easier to understand. *Delrina Corp. v. Triolet Systems, Inc.* (1992), 47 C.P.R. (3d) 1 (Ont. H.C.).

Nano-Seconds

This refers to speed, measured in billionths of a second. *Advanced Micro Devices, Inc. and Intel Corp.*, CCH Comp. Cases 60,218 (Arb. Award. 1990).

Narrative

A narrative has been defined as a running account of the logical operations occurring in any segment of a program. *Pezzillo v. General Telephone & Electronics Information Systems, Inc.*, 414 F.Supp 1257 (M.D. Tenn. 1976).

Narrowband

Transmission speeds of less than 64kbps such has traditional telephone copper wire. Submission of the Director of Investigation and Research to the CRTC Re Public Notice CRTC 1994-130.

A relatively restricted frequency band normally used for a single purpose or made available to a single user. *The Challenge of the Information Highway: Final Report of the Information Highway Advisory Council* (September 1995).

Narrowband Services

A service enabling the two-way transmission of voice or data communications with speed in either direction not exceeding 64 Kbps. *Report to the Governor in Council: Status of Competition in Canadian Telecommunications Markets, Deployment/Accessibility of Advanced Telecommunications Infrastructure and Services, September, 2001.*

Narrowcasting

A television service that differs from broadcasting in one or more ways having to do with content, audience or technology. For example, pay or specialty channels which provide only one type of programming like movie pay TV or ethnic channels. These services are referred to as "narrowcast" because they are not transmitted over the air but rather made available for a fee to a subgroup of the general television audience. Submission of the Director of Investigation and Research to the CRTC Re Public Notice CRTC 1994-130.

National Automated Clearing House Association (NACHA)

A nation-wide electronics payment system used by participating financial institutions. *Resolution Trust Corporation v. First of America Bank*, 796 F.Supp. 1333.

Neighbouring Rights

Rights that are related to or neighbour on copyright. Examples are: performers rights, the rights of phonogram producers, publishers' rights in typographical arrangements and the rights of broadcasting organisations in relation to their broadcasts. In New Zealand, related or neighbouring rights are provided through the Copyright Act, although in some countries they are provided through legislation separate from copyright. *Digital Technology and the Copyright Act 1994: A Discussion Paper, Competition and Enterprise Branch, July 2001 (New Zealand).*

Nesting

Sub-structure or nesting describes the inner structure of a module whereby one module is subsumed within another and performs part of the second modules task. *Gates Rubber Co. v. Bando American Inc.*, 28 U.S.P.Q. 2d 1503 (10th Cir. 1993).

.net

The generic Top Level Domain (gTLD) intended for organizations that administer or provide network connection services. *Domain Name System Reform and Related Internet Governance Issues: A Consultation Paper*, Industry Canada available at *www.strategis.gc.ca*

Net List

A net list is a list of all the components in a circuit and in relation to each component what other components it is connected to and, if necessary, where. These days one can feed a net list into a computer and it will produce a circuit diagram and probably also a scheme for making a printed circuit board. *Anacon Corp. Ltd. v. Environmental Research Technology*, [1994] F.S.R. 659 (Ch.D.).

Netiquette

The growing body of a acceptable, though as yet largely unwritten, etiquette with respect to conduct by users of the internet. *1267623 Ontario Inc. v. NEXX On-Line Inc.* [1999] O.J. No. 2246 (Ont. S.C.).

Network

Includes any operation where control over all or any part of the programs or program schedules of one or more broadcasting undertakings is delegated to another undertaking or person. *Broadcasting Act*, S.C. 1991, c. 11.

Network Computer System (sometimes called a "thin client")

Typically contains central processing components with basic capabilities, certain key peripheral devices (such as a monitor, a keyboard, and a mouse), an operating system, and a browser. The system contains no mass storage, however, and it processes little if any data locally. Instead, the system receives processed data and software as needed from a server across a network. A network computer system lacks the hardware resources to support an Intel-compatible PC operating system. *United States of America v. Microsoft Corporation*, 87 F.Supp. 2d 30 (D.D.C. 2000).

Network Control and Routing

Applications include: Message and circuit switching, speed and code conversion, pulse format conversion, error detection and correction, analog to digital and digital to analog conversion, signal processing, and time division multiplexing. Second Computer Inquiry (Notice of Inquiry), 5 C.L.S.R. 1381 (F.C.C. 1976).

Applications include: message and circuit switching, speed and code conversion, pulse format conversion, transmission error detection and correction, analog to digital and digital to analog conversion, signal processing, and time division multiplexing. Second Computer Inquiry (Supplemental Notice), 42 Fed. Reg. 13029 (F.C.C. 1977).

Network Effect (Positive Network Effect)

In markets characterised by network effects, one product or standard tends towards dominance, because 'the utility that a user drives from assumption of a good increases with a number of other agents consuming the goods. *United States of America v. Microsoft Corp.,* No. 00-5212 (D.C. Cir. June 28, 2001).

A phenomenon by which the attractiveness of a product increases with the number of people using it. *United States of America v. Microsoft Corp.*, 87 F.Supp. 2d 30 (D.D.C. 2000).

Network Element

The term "network element" means a facility or equipment used in the provision of a telecommunications service. Such term also includes features, functions, and capabilities that are provided by means of such facility or equipment, including subscriber numbers, databases, signaling systems, and information sufficient for billing and collection or used in the transmission, routing, or other provision of a telecommunications service. United States Telecommunications Act of 1996.

Network Feed

Means any radiocommunication that is transmitted
    (a) by a network operation to its affiliates,
    (b) to a network operation for retransmission by it to its affiliates, or
    (c) by a lawful distributor to a programming undertaking. *Radiocommunication Act*, R.S.C. 1985, c. R-2, as amended.

Network Manager

Network Manager means any person offering to customers access or services in connection with a network. Statement of Proposed Royalties to be Collected by SODRAC for the Reproduction, in Canada, of Musical Works in the Exploitation of an Electronic Network for the Years 1999 and 2000.

Network Solutions, Inc. (NSI)

Network Solutions, Inc. is a private company which performs the function of registering Internet domain names. It is currently under contract with the National Science Foundation (NSF) and is the leading registrar of domain names. It is the only organization which is permitted to register domain names ending in ".com", ".org", ".net", ".edu" or ".gov". It registers over 100,000 new domain names each month approximately 1 every 20 seconds. *Academy of Motion Picture Arts and Sciences v. Network Solutions Inc.,* 45 U.S.P.Q. 2d 1463 (C.D.Cal. 1997).

Network System

This is a telecommunications network comprising terminals, terminal controllers, lines and modems (which convert digital information so it can be carried by Telecom's voice grade lines) linked via a communications computer to the main computer. *Databank Systems Ltd. v. Commnr. of Inland Revenue*, [1987] N.Z.L.R. 312 (H.C. Wellington).

Network Termination Point

Means the final demarcation of the public telecommunications transport network at the customer's premises. North American Free Trade Agreement between Canada, Mexico and the United States, Article 1310.

Networking Software

Networking software enables the microcomputers cabled together in a local area network to share resources such as access to the hard disk and the printer. *Madeley Pty Ltd. v. Touche Ross*, McGarvie, J., Aust. Fed. Ct., Dec. 21, 1989 (unreported).

New Media

New media consists of high breeds of print and/or electronic media in which the content can include text, sound, graphics and audio-visual programming. It encompasses enrichment of traditional media (e.g., digital audio broadcasting), combinations of previously separate media (e.g., multimedia) and creation of entirely new ones (e.g., hypermedia). Study on New Media and Copyright, *Final Report* (Nordicity Group Ltd., June 30, 1994) prepared for Industry Canada, New Media, Information Technologies Industry Branch.

New Media Retransmitter

Means a person whose retransmission is lawful under the *Broadcasting Act* only by reason of the *Exemption Order for New Media Broadcasting Undertakings* issued by the Canadian Radio-television and Telecommunications Commission as Appendix A to Public Notice CRTC 1999-197, as amended from time to time. *Bill C-48, An Act to Amend the Copyright Act*, June 18, 2002.

New Product

A new product may be something out of the blue, entirely original, or it may be a "derivative" or "superset" of the old product, incorporating some functions of the old product, proceeding either in parallel or departing in a new direction to give the market something new. There are many hallmarks of a new product; fresh database tape, different target market, lack of backward pin compatibility, added and/or improved function, independent development plan and market analysis with management authorization as new product. *Advanced Micro Devices, Inc. and Intel Corp.*, CCH Comp. Cases 60,218 (Arb. Award. 1990).

New Versions

Most applications programs undergo a more or less continuous process of organic growth. Individual programs are updated, features are added or modified and so on. Large software houses issue new versions of their programs from time to time.

Sometimes the upgrade is given a new number: lesser modifications tend to be given an old number with a new decimal place. A small house is likely to be less systematic in its numbering system, as was the case here. *IBCOS Computers Ltd. v. Barclay's Mercantile Highland Finance Ltd.*, [1994] F.S.R. 275 (Ch.D.).

News Group

A news group is an electronic discussion group, serving as a bulletin board for users to post universally accessible messages, and to read and apply to those from others. *Religious Technology Center v. F.A.C.T.Net, Inc.*, 36 U.S.P.Q. 2d 1690 (D. Col. 1995).

Node

A computer system that is connected to a communications network and participates in the routing of messages within that network. Networks are usually described as a collection of nodes that are connected by communications links. *Cryptography's Role in Securing the Information Society*, United States National Research Council, 1996.

Non-Literal Aspects (of a Computer Program)

Those aspects that are not reduced to written code. *Computer Associates International Inc. v. Altai Inc.*, 23 U.S.P.Q.2d 1241 (2d Cir. 1992).

Non Literal Similarity

Non literal similarity is where the fundamental essence or structure of one work is duplicated in another. Thus, non literal similarity can be thought of as paraphrasing or copying the essence or a structure of a work just short of literal copying. *Bateman v. Mnemonics Inc.*, 38 U.S.P.Q. 2d 1225 (11th Cir. 1996).

Non-repudiation

Proof that a message was sent by a particular person at a time, without being altered since being sent. *A Survey of Legal Issues Relating to the Security of Electronic Information*, Department of Justice, Canada.

Means a property achieved through cryptographic methods, which prevents an individual or entity from denying having performed a particular action related to data (such as mechanisms for non-rejection of authority (origin); for proof of obligation, intent, or commitment; or for proof of ownership). *OECD Guidelines for Cryptography Policy*, March 27, 1997, available at *www.oecd.org*.

Proof that a transaction occurred or that a message was sent or received (so that parties cannot deny that the exchange occurred). *Building Trust and Confidence in Electronic Commerce: A Framework for Electronic Authentication in Canada*, prepared by the Electronic Commerce Branch, Industry Canada, July 2000, available at *http://e-comm.ic.gc.ca* .

Notation

The process or method of representing numbers, quantities, etc. by a set or design of sign; hence, any set of symbols or characters. To denote things or relations in order to facilitate the recording or considering of them. *Autodesk Australia Pty Ltd. v. Dyason* (1989), 15 I.P.R. 1 (Aus. Fed. Ct.), reversed [1990] A.I.P.C. 36,446 (Aus. Fed. Ct. FC).

Number Portability

Ability to maintain the same user number when transferring among various networks and service providers. *The Challenge of the Information Highway: Final Report of the Information Highway Advisory Council* (September 1995).

The term "number portability" means the ability of users of telecommunications services to retain, at the same location, existing telecommunications numbers without impairment of quality, reliability, or convenience when switching from one telecommunications carrier to another. United States Telecommunications Act of 1996.

Numerical Control

Numerical control involves automatically moving a machine tool under the control of a prerecorded part program for precisely cutting a particular workpiece or part. *White Consolidated Industries Inc. v. Vega Servo-Control Inc.*, 214 U.S.P.Q 796 (S.D. Mich. 1982), affirmed 218 U.S.P.Q. 961 (Fed. Cir. 1983).

Object

An XML Signature element wherein arbitrary (non-core) data may be placed. An Object element is merely one type of digital data (or document) that can be signed via a Reference. *XML-Signature Syntax and Processing, W3C Recommendation 12 February 2002.*

Object Code

See Machine Code.

An object program, or object code, is a program written in machine language that can be executed directly by the computer's CPU without need for translation. For example, in the machine language of a certain computer, the instructions to divide the value in "B" by the value in "C" and add that number to the value in "A" may be represented by the following sequence of instructions (in binary form): 0010000000010001; 1000000011010010; 1101000000010000. *Lotus Development Corp. v. Paperback Software International*, 15 U.S.P.Q.2d 1577 (D. Mass. 1990).

The program as compiled in machine code, not easily read and understood and exceptionally difficult to modify, except for the most trivial changes. *Saphena Computing Ltd. v. Allied Collection Agencies Ltd.*, Ch. D. Recorder, July 22, 1988 (unreported), affirmed, C.A., May 3, 1989 (unreported).

The object code is the engineer's instructions translated into a language that only the computer hardware can "read" to become a functioning machine. It is an essential part of the machine in that sense. *In Re Bedford Computer Corporation*, 62 Bank. Rep. 555 (Bky. Crt. 1986).

The object code is a file that contains the actual computer code, consisting of a series of zeroes and ones, that runs the computer. *Stenograph Corporation v. Microcat Corporation*, 1990 U.S. Dist. Lexis 12945 (N.D. Ill. 1990).

Object code is machine readable, binary code, represented on paper as a series of ones and zeros. In actuality, those ones and zeros represent "on" and "off" states of switches on a computer chip. *Atari Games Corp. and Tengen Inc. v. Nintendo of America Inc.*, 18 U.S.P.Q.2d 1935 (N.D. Cal. 1991).

Each program consisted of object codes (binary, machine-readable only codes). *William E. Hill v. Xyquad Inc.*, 2 CCH Comp. Cases 46,500 (8th Cir. 1991).

Object code is the binary language comprised of zeros and ones through which the computer directly receives its instructions. *Computer Associates International Inc. v. Altai Inc.*, 23 U.S.P.Q.2d 1241 (2d Cir. 1992).

Object code appears as a series of zeros and ones, representing the magnetic polarization of the "bits" that are read by the computer. *Computer Associates International Inc. v. Altai Inc.*, 775 F.Supp. 544 (E.D.N.Y. 1991), affirmed 23 U.S.P.Q.2d 1241 (2d Cir. 1992).

Object code uses only two symbols: "0" and "1" in combinations which represent the alphanumeric characters of the source code. A program written in source code is translated into object code using a computer program called an "assembler" or "compiler," and then imprinted into a silicon chip for commercial distribution. Devices called "disassemblers" or "decompilers" can reverse this process by "reading" the electronic signals for "0" and "1" that are produced while the program is being run, storing the resulting object code in computer memory, and translating the object code into source code. Both assembly and disassembly devices are commercially available, and both types of devices are widely used within the software industry. *Sega Enterprises Ltd. v. Accolade Inc.* (1992), 24 U.S.P.Q.2d 1561.

Object code is the binary language comprised of zeros and ones through which the computer directly receives its instructions. *Trandes Corp. v. Atkinson Co.*, 27 U.S.P.Q. 2d 1014 (4th Cir. 1993).

Object code is simply the source code translated into the form recognized by computer hardware, a binary sequence of 0s and 1s. Although readable by computers, sequences of 0s and 1s are generally inscrutable to humans. *Unix System Laboratories, Inc. v. Berkeley Software Design, Inc.*, 27 U.S.P.Q. 2d 1721 (D. New Jer. 1993).

[The] machine readable form of the program is called object code. *Delrina Corp. v. Triolet Systems, Inc.* (1992), 47 C.P.R. (3d) 1 (Ont. H.C.).

. . .consists of a series of zeros and ones that are understand by the computer. *Otis Elevator Co. v. Intelligent Systems, Inc.* 3 CCH Comp. Cases 46,510 (Conn. S.C. 1990).

The instructions required to define the processing required to be performed expressed in a format that the computer can directly interpret. This format of code is not readily understandable by humans but can be interpreted very efficiently by the computer. *Delrina Corp. v. Triolet Systems, Inc.* (1992), 47 C.P.R. (3d) 1 (Ont. H.C.).

A binary program code is called an "object code" or, more graphically, "machine code". *IBCOS Computers Ltd. v. Barclay's Mercantile Highland Finance Ltd.*, [1994] F.S.R. 275 (Ch.D.).

Object code is the literal text of a computer program written in a binary language through which the computer directly receives its instructions. *Gates Rubber Co. v. Bando American Inc.*, 28 U.S.P.Q. 2d 1503 (10th Cir. 1993).

The class of computer programs expressed in machine code which contain additional information necessary to ensure correct loading of the program. Computer Software Protection: Australia, Copyright Law Review Committee 1995.

Object code refers to programs that are in a form that a computer can understand. Object code is a set of instructions able to be interpreted by computers. Generally the object code cannot be understood by people, even skilled programmers. Programs are originally written in semi-English language, called source code. These source code instructions are then converted into object code (or "compiled") by a special device known as a compiler. The file in which the resulting object code is stored is known as a compiled file. The object code is what the customer usually receives when software is purchased or licensed. *Ni-Tech Pty Ltd. v. Bruce Peter Parker & Ors,* [1998] 484 FCA (27 April 1998) (Aust. F.C.).

Obsolete (in relation to computer hardware)

Refers to the lessee's technical or functional requirements; the equipment, or some part of it (becoming) technologically outmoded or no longer capable of handling the lessee's day-to-day business needs. *Computer System of America v. Western Reserve Life Assurance Co. of Ohio*, 475 N.E.2d 745 (Mass. App. 1985), quoting from *Computer Law: Evidence and Procedure*, 2.02 at 2-7 (1983).

OECD

Organization for Economic Cooperation and Development

OEM (Original Equipment Manufacturer)

An OEM is a company that purchases hardware (the physical elements in the computer, such as integrated circuits, wires, and terminals) and systems software (machine-readable instructions in written and electromagnetic form which enable a computer system to function) from a vendor and adds value, in the form of applications software or other components, and then re-sells both the hardware and software at a mark-up to end users. OEM is thus a type of middleman in the computer business. *Accusystems Inc. v. Honeywell Information Systems Inc.*, 580 F.Supp. 474 (S.D.N.Y. 1984).

An OEM is a company which purchases computer hardware and enhances its value by adding software and re-selling the combined package as a complete system. *Vista Computer Systems Ltd. v. Scitex (U.K.) Ltd.*, Ch. D., Bromley J., October 15, 1985 (unreported).

Offeree

Means a natural person or legal entity that receives or retrieves an offer of goods or services. *UNCITRAL, Working Group IV (Electronic Commerce), Thirty-ninth session New York, 11-15 March, 2002.*

Offeror

Means a natural person or legal entity that offers goods or services. *UNCITRAL, Working Group IV (Electronic Commerce), Thirty-ninth session New York, 11-15 March, 2002.*

Off-Premises Extension (OPX)

Is an extension telephone in other premises which may be in a distant city. This permits the user of the extension to have access to local and long distance telephone service as if he were located in the main premises. CNCP Telecommunications: Interconnection with Bell Canada, CRTC Decision 79-11 (May 1979).

Office Machines

Machines which are used in offices, shops, factories, workshops, schools, depots, hotels, and elsewhere, for doing work concerning the writing, recording, sorting, filing, mailing of correspondence, records, accounts, forms, etc., or for doing other "office work", and which have a base for fixing or placing them on a table, desk, wall, floor, or similar place. *Apple Computer, Inc. v. U.S.*, CCH Comp.L. 46,363 (Cit. 1991).

On demand

Services which can be accessed as required and at a time determined by the consumer, as opposed to a service (such as a TV programme) which is available at a time determined by the broadcaster. *Digital Technology and the Copyright Act 1994: A Discussion Paper, Competition and Enterprise Branch, July 2001 (New Zealand).*

On Line

(1) Pertaining to a user's ability to interact with a computer. (2) Pertaining to a user's access to computer via terminal. (3) Pertaining to the operation of a functional unit that is under the continual control of a computer. The term "on line"

is also used to describe a user's access to a computer via a terminal. *In Re TBG Inc.*, 229 U.S.P.Q. 759 (T.T.A.B. 1986), quoting from *Vocabulary for Data Processing, Telecommunications and Office Systems*, 7th ed. (1981).

Services which can be accessed over a telecommunications system, especially the Internet. *Digital Technology and the Copyright Act 1994: A Discussion Paper, Competition and Enterprise Branch, July 2001 (New Zealand).*

On-Line Contact Information

Means an e-mail address or another substantially similar identifier that permits direct contact with a person online. *Children's Online Privacy Protection Act* of 1998.

Online Contact Information

Means an e-mail address or any other substantially similar identifier that permits direct contact with a person online. *United States Children's On-Line Privacy Protection Rule, Federal Trade Commission, 16 CFR part 312.*

On-Line Data Processing

On-line data processing refers to a system by which one communicates directly with the computer and obtains immediate responses from the computer via computer terminals, provided that one's communications are in a format that the computer is programmed to understand. An off-line data processing system exists where data is entered by means of punch cards or computer tapes rather than directly by a computer terminal. *Liberty Financial Management Corp. v. Beneficial Data Processing Corp.*, 670 S.W.2d 40 (Mo. Ct. App. 1984).

Online Discussion Groups

Thousands of discussion groups have been organized by individuals, institutions, and organizations on many different computer networks and cover virtually every topic imaginable — creating a new, global version of the village green. The three most common methods for online discussion are mail exploders, USENET newsgroups, and chat rooms. *Cyberspace Communications, Inc. et al. v. Engler*, 55 F. Supp. 2d 737 (E.D. F. Ch. 1999).

Open Network

Means a network which has no specific manager or controller to govern the entire system. In case of the Internet, there is no, in general, no specific qualification for joining the network other than technical and commercial requirements, such as having the necessary equipment and subscribing to the services of certain service providers. Business - To - Consumer Electronic Commerce: Survey of Status and Issues, OECD/gd (97) 219.

Operating System Program

Operating system programs are designed primarily to facilitate the operation of application programs and perform tasks common to any application program, such as reading and writing data to a disc. Without them, each application program would need to duplicate their functions. *Apple Computer Inc. v. Computermat Inc.* (1983), 1 C.I.P.R. 1 (Ont. H.C.); *Apple Computer Inc. v. MacIntosh Computers Ltd.* (1985), 3 C.I.P.R. 133 (Fed. T.D.).

This is the basic set of instructions to the computer on how it is to operate. These instructions describe how the computer is to deal with all its tasks but not with any particular task. *Continental Commercial Systems Corp. (Telecheque Can.) v. R.*, [1982] 5 W.W.R. 340 (B.C. C.A).

Programs that are designed to manage the computer system. These programs are distinguishable from application programs, which are programs that directly interact with the computer user. *Apple Computer Inc. v. Formula International Inc. (No. 2)*, 562 F.Supp. 775 (C.D. Cal. 1983), affirmed 725 F.2d 521 (9th Cir. 1984).

The operating system is the brain of the computer. It determines the computer's capability to store memory, operate peripheral items such as view terminals, and do other basic operating chores. The operating system itself is in the form of a disc or tape, and is loaded into a computer to start its operation. *Hubco Data Products Corp. v. Management Assistance Inc. (No. 2)*, 219 U.S.P.Q. 450 (D. Idaho 1983).

An operating system is an organized collection of software used to assist and in part to control the operations of a computer. Operating systems generally manage the internal functions of the computer, and, to facilitate the use of applications software (*e.g.*, accounts receivable and payroll programs), they co-ordinate the reading and writing of data between the internal memory and the external devices (*e.g.*, disc drives, keyboard, printer), perform basic housekeeping functions for the computer system, and prepare the computer to execute applications programs. Operating system programs for mainframe computers are extremely large and complex, involving hundreds of thousands (and in some cases millions) of lines of code. *IBM v. Fujitsu Ltd.*, Copyright L.R. (CCH) 20,517 (Am. Arbtn. Assoc. Comm. Arbtn. Trib. 1988).

Operating systems control the internal functioning of the computer. Green Paper on Copyright and the Challenge of Technology, The Commission of the European Communities, COM (88) 172 Final (1988).

Examples of operating systems are UNIX, OS2, DOS, Windows, Apply-Mac-Intosh, and Bax/BMS. *Angoss II Partnership v. Trifox Inc.* (1997), [1997] O.J. No. 4969, 1997 CarswellOnt 4888 (Gen. Div.), affirmed (1999), [1999] O.J. No. 4144, 1999 CarswellOnt 3474 (C.A.) leave to appeal dismissed [1999] S.C.C.A. No. 588, 2000 CarswellOnt 2999.

Operating system programs — such as DOS, XENIX, and OS/2 — are programs that control the basic functions of the computer hardware, such as the efficient utilization of memory and the starting and stopping of application programs.

Lotus Development Corp. v. Paperback Software International, 15 U.S.P.Q.2d 1577 (D. Mass. 1990).

An operating system is a term which is used to describe a certain type of program. In essence, it is characterized by a program that controls other programs. *United Software Corp. v. Sperry Rand Corp.*, 5 C.L.S.R. 1492 (E.D. Pa. 1974).

An "operating system" is itself a program that manages the resources of the computer, allocating those resources to other programs as needed. *Computer Associates International Inc. v. Altai Inc.*, 23 U.S.P.Q.2d 1241 (2d Cir. 1992).

A set of programs, usually supplied by the manufacturer of a computer system that manages the basic operation of the computer system including such things as saving and retrieving data, providing security between users and backing up the data for archival purposes. Common examples of these include MSDOS (IBM compatible PC's), MPE (HP3000), UNIX (various computers), VMS (Digital Vax). *Delrina Corp. v. Triolet Systems, Inc.* (1992), 47 C.P.R. (3d) 1 (Ont. H.C.).

Software is commonly developed to be used in layers. The basic "layer" is referred to as the "operating system". This tells the computer how to perform basic functions necessary to achieve the end results that the customer needs. *ISC-Bunker Ramo Corporation v. Altech, Inc.*, 765 F.Supp. 1310 (N.D. Ill. 1990).

Computers are given so-called "operating systems". These are a kind of basic program concerned with essential computer functions. Popular operating systems are, for instance, MS-DOS, and Unix. There are a number of others. These systems are themselves, when in the computer, in binary code. When an applications program (i.e. one which will be used for a particular application) is loaded into the computer it is loaded, as it were, on top of the operating system. The applications program speaks to the operating system which speaks to the computer. *IBCOS Computers Ltd. v. Barclay's Mercantile Highland Finance Ltd.*, [1994] F.S.R. 275 (Ch.D.).

Operating System Software

A software program that controls the allocation and use of computer resources (such as central processing unit time, main memory space, disk space, and input/output channels). The operating system also supports the functions of software programs, called "applications", that perform specific user-oriented tasks. The operating system supports the functions of applications by exposing interfaces, called "application programming interfaces," or "APIs". *United States of America v. Microsoft Corporation*, 87 F.Supp. 2d 30 (D.D.C. 2000).

An operating system is a software program that controls the allocation and use of computer resources (such as central processing unit time, main memory space, disk space, and input/output channels). The operating system also supports the functions of software programs, called 'applications', that perform specific user-oriented tasks. . . Because it supports applications while interacting more closely with the PC system's hardware, the operating system is said to serve as a 'platform'. *Universal City Studios, Inc. v. Reimerdes*, 55 U.S.P.Q. 2d 1873 (S. D.N.Y. 2000).

Any electronic computer is a complex piece of equipment. Quite apart from the memory and the CPU. . . there has to be some way of getting the data in (a keyboard) and out again (a screen) and of providing more permanent storage for programs and data (one or more disks or various types). Each of these components contains its own processing ability, and must be programmed to operate correctly. To have to program the keyboard controller to scan the keys waiting for one to be pressed, read the key pressed and so on when all the programmer wants to do is to input a number would be immensely wasteful of effort. So all computers have available large programs called operating systems which start automatically when the computer is turned on. Operating systems provide a multitude of services which absolve the programmer from worrying about how to open a file, lay out files on a hard disk, label his fields, read his keyboard, output data to the screen and so on. They also come with a number of programs sometimes called utilities. Anyone who has used a Intel-based personal computer will be familiar with the Microsoft Windows family of operating systems: Windows 3.1, Windows 95, Windows 98, Windows NT and so on. *Cantor Fitzgerald International v. Tradition (UK) Ltd.,*. [1999] I.N.L.R. No. 23 (Ch.D.).

Operating systems perform many functions, including allocating computer memory and controlling peripherals such as printers and keyboards. Operating systems also function as platforms for software applications. They do this by "exposing " — *i.e.*, making available to software developers — routines or protocols that perform certain widely-used functions. These are known as Application Programming Interfaces, or "APIs." *United States of America v. Microsoft Corp.*, No. 00-5212 (D.C. Cir. June 28, 2001).

Operating systems are the programs that manage the resources of the computer and allocate those resources to other programs that need them. For example, operating system software might perform, among others, these functions: channeling information entered at a keyboard to the proper application program; sending information from an application program to a display screen; providing blocks of memory to an application program that requires them; and allocating processing time among several application programs running on the computer at the same time. Operating system software interacts with whatever other programs are being used or "executed" by the computer to provide computer resources (such as processors, memory, disk space, printers, tape drives, etc.) for those programs that need them. These interactions are often referred to as "system calls." For such interactions to occur properly, the other programs must be compatible with the operating system software in use on the computer, i.e., they must be able to exchange information precisely and accurately with the operating system to interact with those computer resources. *Computer Associates International Inc. v. Altai Inc.*, 775 F.Supp. 544 (E.D.N.Y. 1991), affirmed 23 U.S.P.Q.2d 1241 (2d Cir. 1992).

Operation

An operation identifies a particular result or set of actions that may be performed. For example, operations in a calculated program might include adding or printing data. *Gates Rubber Co. v. Bando American Inc.*, 28 U.S.P.Q. 2d 1503 (10th Cir. 1993).

Operator

Means any person who operates a website located on the Internet or an online service and who collects or maintains personal information from or about the users of or visitors to such website or online service, or on whose behalf such information is collected or maintained, where such website or online service is operated for commercial purposes, including any person offering products or products or services for sale through that website or online service, involving commerce. Children's Online Privacy Protection Act of 1998.

Means any person who operates a website located on the Internet or an online service and who collects or maintains personal information from or about the users of or visitors to such website or online service, or on whose behalf such information is collected or maintained, where such website or online service is operated for commercial purposes, including any person offering products or services for sale through that website or online service, involving commerce: (a) Among the several States or with 1 or more foreign nations; (b) In any territory of the United States or in the District of Columbia, or between any such territory and (1) Another such territory, or (2) Any State or foreign nation; or (c) Between the District of Columbia and any State, territory, or foreign nation. This definition does not include any nonprofit entity that would otherwise be exempt from coverage under Section 5 of the Federal Trade Commission Act (15 U.S.C. 45). *United States Children's On-Line Privacy Protection Rule, Federal Trade Commission, 16 CFR part 312.*

Operator of a Means of Communication

Means any public or private natural or legal person whose trade, business or profession involves making one or more means of distance communication available to suppliers. *European Parliament and Council Directive on the Protection of Consumers in Respect of Distance Contracts*, May 20, 1997, Directive 97/7.

Optical Card

Incorporates optical data storage technology (such as high-capacity optical disks) to portable credit-card sized plastic cards. Data is stored and retrieved using laser beams in essentially the same manner as used for optical disks. *A Survey of Legal Issues Relating to the Security of Electronic Information*, Department of Justice, Canada.

Also known as laser cards, because a low-intensity laser is used to burn holes of several microns in diameter into a reflective material exposing a substrata of lower reflectivity. The presence, or absence, or a burned hole represents bits. The areas of high and low reflectivity are read using a precision light source. Smart, Optical and Other Advanced Cards: How to Do a Privacy Assessment, Information and Privacy Commissioner/Ontario Canada, available at http://www.itc.on.ca.

Optical Fibre

Optical fibre is a new signal transport medium using light to carry information by means of a fibre made of glass (silica) about the size of a thread. Actually the light signal is confined within the centre core which is only about one tenth of the fibre diameter and can only be observed under a microscope. The relatively low signal loss gives a reach of 50 kilometers without using repeaters to boost the signal, as compared with 2 kilometers for coaxial cables with a similar capacity. The idea of using silica glass for light signal transport was proposed in 1966, but it was not until 1960 that it was confirmed in a laboratory, and it took another ten years to produce the transmission to a 90% level for the fibres produced in a factory environment. By the early 1980's, there was no doubt in the telecommunication industries that this new technology would become commercially viable and eventually revolutionize the industry. Today, a single fibre, the size of a thread, carries about 8,000 voice channels simultaneously over a distance of 50 kilometers without any regenerators. Even this will be dwarfed by the next generation system, with four times the capacity in the near future. Many TV channels are now transported through optical fibres over a long distance beyond the reach of aerial broadcasting. *British Columbia Telephone Co. v. Canada*, [1991] F.C.J. No. 340 (Fed. T.D.).

Optical Fibre Transmission System

Unlike copper-based systems which use copper wires through which signals are conducted by a flow of electrons, in an optical fibre transmission system optical fibres guide photons (electromagnetic waves) in a lightwave frequency range. The optical fibre system is similar to a microwave system, in that both require equipment to convert electrical signals into electromagnetic signals which radiate to the receiver. In the case of a microwave system, electromagnetic signals emanate from an antenna and radiate through free space. In the case of an optical fibre system, the electromagnetic signals emanate from a laser and are guided through glass core optical fibres. Optical fibres now in use in the telecommunications industry are bundled together with a steel core within a protective coating. This process is called "cabling" and the result is called "fibre optic cable" or sometimes, depending upon the context, simply "cable". *British Columbia Telephone Co. v. Canada*, [1991] F.C.J. No. 340 (Fed. T.D.).

Optical Reader

An optical reader is a scanner, an electronic device, which senses the presence or absence of marks on input paper as the sheet is mechanically transported through the scanner. It is essentially a device that reads data from a printed or handwritten sheet and translates the data into machine-readable language. *Moore Business Forms Inc. v. National Computer Systems Inc.*, 211 U.S.P.Q. 909 (T.T.A.B. 1981).

.org

The generic Top Level Domain (gTLD) used by many non-governmental organizations and other associations. *Domain Name System Reform and Related Internet Governance Issues: A Consultation Paper*, Industry Canada available at *www.strategis.gc.ca*

Originator

Of a data message means a person by whom, or on whose behalf, the data message purports to have been sent or generated prior to storage, if any, but it does not include a person acting as an intermediary with respect to that data message. UNCITRAL Model Law On Electronic Commerce (1996).

Originator of a data message means a person by whom, or on whose behalf, the data message purports to have been sent or generated prior to storage, if any, but it does not include a person acting as an intermediary with respect to that data message. *UNCITRAL, Working Group IV (Electronic Commerce), Thirty-ninth session New York, 11-15 March, 2002.*

Oscilloscope

A device which makes voltage visible on a screen. *Autodesk Australia Pty Ltd. v. Dyason* (1992), A.I.P.C. 90,855 (Aust. H.C.).

OSI

Open Systems Interconnection. *IBM v. Fujitsu Ltd.*, Copyright L.R. (CCH) 20,517 (Am. Arbtn. Assoc. Comm. Arbtn. Trib. 1988).

Other Device

Means any device or apparatus which can be used to intercept a wire, oral, or electronic communication other than: (a) any telephone or telegraph instrument, equipment or facility, or any component thereof, (i) furnished to the subscriber or user by a provider of wire to electronic communication service in the ordinary course of its business and being used by the subscriber or user in the ordinary course of its business or furnished by such subscriber or user for connection to the facilities of such service and used in the ordinary course of its business; or (ii) being used by a provider or wire or electronic communication service in the ordinary course of its business, or by an investigative or law enforcement officer in the ordinary course of his duties. *Electronic Communications Privacy Act* of 1986, Pub. L. 89-508 (1986).

OTPROMS

OTPROMS and EPROMS can be used where there may be a need to modify the program in the device. The OTPROM is produced in a "blank" form; the circuit is a large matrix at the intersections of which are a number of data storage locations, usually one byte capacity. The program may then be loaded directly onto the blank device. *Avel Pty Ltd. v. Jonathan Wells* (1992), 22 I.P.R. 305 (Aust. H.C.).

OTPROM means one time programmable ROM. *Avel Pty Ltd. v. Wells* (1992), 23 I.P.R. 353 (Aust. Fed. C.A.).

Overlapping Window System

In an overlapping window system . . . open main application windows are overlapped, appearing like papers loosely stacked on a desk. The active window is automatically moved to the top of the stack. Because the open windows overlap, each window may be sized and moved independently of all other windows. When one window is opened, closed, moved, or resized, all other windows remain the same except to the extent that previously visible portions are covered and previously covered portions are revealed. *Apple Computer Inc. v. Microsoft Corp.*, Vol. 9, No. 6., Comp. Law Rep. 1043.

Packet Switching Technology

A communications network providing terminal-to-computer and computer-to-computer data communications utilizing what is known as "packet-switching technology." American Trucking Association, Inc/Resale and Shared Use, 47 F.C.C.2d 644 (U.S.Fed.Coom.Comm. 1974).

The Internet utilizes a technology called "packet switching" to carry data. Packet switching works as follows. The computer wishing to send a document ("originating computer"), such as a music file or digital image, cuts the document up into many small "packets" of information. Each packet contains the Internet Protocol ("IP") address of the destination Web site, a small portion of data from the original document, and an indication of the data's place in the original document. *DoubleClick Inc. Privacy Litigation,* Civ.0641 (N.R.V.) (S.D.N.Y. Mar. 28, 2001).

Paddle

Type of controller for game playing with circular control of motion. Monopolies and Mergers Commission — Video Games: A report on the supply of video games in the UK (LONDON: HMSO Cm2781).

Paint-and-draw Computer Programs

Paint-and-draw computer programs enable the user to create graphic images on a computer screen. *Softel Inc. v. Dragon Medical and Scientific Communications, Inc.*, 1992 U.S. Dist. LEXIS 9502 (S.D.N.Y.1992).

Palette

The range of colours a video games machine has available. Monopolies and Mergers Commission — Video Games: A report on the supply of video games in the UK (LONDON: HMSO Cm2781).

Parallax scrolling

The movement of foreground and background scenery in relation to one another, to preserve perspective. Monopolies and Mergers Commission — Video Games: A report on the supply of video games in the UK (LONDON: HMSO Cm2781).

Parameter

In the context of programming, this refers to a variable that is passed to a procedure and is used to qualify or customize the processing done within the procedure. For instance, in a procedure to calculate GST you would normally pass two parameters, one representing the amount for which the tax is to be calculated and the second to receive the result of the tax calculation. *Delrina Corp. v. Triolet Systems, Inc.* (1992), 47 C.P.R. (3d) 1 (Ont. H.C.).

Parameter List

Parameter list refers to the form in which information is passed between modules and the information's actual content. *Computer Associates International Inc. v. Altai Inc.*, 23 U.S.P.Q.2d 1241 (2d Cir. 1992).

A parameter list is the information sent to and received from a subroutine. The term "parameter list" refers to the form in which information is passed between modules. With respect to form, interacting modules must share similar parameter lists so that they are capable of exchanging information. *Matrox Electronic Systems Ltd. v. Gaudreau*, [1993] R.J.Q. 2449 (C.S.).

Parameters

Possible or accessible variables that can be used by operators to condition the execution of a program; quantitive information specific to each plant or to conditions at a given time, for example the percentage of humidity contained in sand exposed to outdoor weather conditions. Physical dimensions that cannot be effectively embodied in a software package are intended to have a general application for all concrete batching plants. They allow the software to be adapted to specific conditions. *Systèmes Informatisés Solartronix c. CÉGEP de Jonquière* (1988), 22 C.I.P.R. 101 (C.S. Qué).

Variables such as the range of cells and number of decimal places, for which values must be input each time an operation is to be performed, are called "parameters." *Lotus Development Corporation v. Borland International Inc.*, 788 F.Supp. 78 (D.C. Mass. 1992).

PARC

Palo Alto Research Centre. *Xerox Corp. v. Apple Computer Inc.*, Comp. Ind. Lit. Reptr. 11,155 (N.D.Cal. 1990).

Password

A string of characters used to authenticate an identity or to verify access authorization. "Security Requirements for Cryptographic Modules", FIPS Pub. 140-1, Federal Information Processing Standards Publication, January 11, 1994, available at http://csrc.nist.gov/fips/fips1401.htm.

Are secret combinations of letters, numbers and/or symbols that provide a user with access to a system. Advancing Global Electronic Commerce: Technology Solutions to Public Policy Challenges, The Computer Systems Policy Project, July 1999, available at http://www.cspp.org/projects/july99_cto_report.pdf.

Patch

Segments of program code (individual statements or routines) added to the body of a completed computer program to enhance or amend the program. *Compendium of Copyright Offices Practices*, Copyright Office, Washington D.C., 1984.

Pay-per-view

A service offering programs for viewing on a pay per order rather than an ongoing basis like a regular cable service. Viewers pay to watch a particular movie or event such as a concert or fight. The services are typically available through participating cable companies. Submission of the Director of Investigation and Research to the CRTC Re Public Notice CRTC 1994-130.

Pay-TV

A special channel or service for which subscribers pay by the month. These are typically services like a movie channel and are discretionary in that they are purchased separately from basic cable. Submission of the Director of Investigation and Research to the CRTC Re Public Notice CRTC 1994-130.

Pay Television Service

A programming service provided pursuant to an agreement between a licensee and a person licensed to carry on a pay television programming undertaking or a pay television network. Cable Television Regulations, 1986, SOR/86-831.

PC Voice

"Real Time" voice communication via the Internet using a personal computer (PC) or other terminal equipment which is equipped with a modem, and the hardware and software required to perform voice compression and conversion to a form which can be transmitted to or from an ISP over IALs. At the IAL, PC Voice communication is effectively indistinguishable from other forms of communication between a modem-equipped PC and an ISP. Telecom Order CRTC 98-929, September 17, 1998.

PCB

Printed Circuit Board. *Avel Pty Ltd. v. Jonathan Wells* (1992), 22 I.P.R. 305 (Aust. H.C.).

PC-DOS (Personal Computer Disk Operating System)

A CP/M-like operating system for the IBM Personal Computer, developed by IBM and Microsoft. *In Re Digital Research Inc.*, 4 U.S.P.Q.2d 1242 (T.T.A.B. 1987).

The operating system PC-DOS is the software that gives the basic instructions to the computer such as: read the data, load the information into the memory, print or move from one procedure to another; e.g. drop out of Crossalk and enter Dataflex. It is the program that makes the computer perform its basic functions at the lowest level; i.e. work as a computer. *Madeley Pty Ltd. v. Touche Ross*, McGarvie, J., Aust. Fed. Ct., Dec. 21, 1989 (unreported).

PCMCIA

A standard which describes the physical requirements, electrical specifications and software architecture for PC cards. *A Survey of Legal Issues Relating to the Security of Electronic Information*, Department of Justice, Canada.

PCS (Personal Communications Services)

A family of radio-communications services provided through personal user radio terminals operating in a mobile or portable mode. *The Challenge of the Information Highway: Final Report of the Information Highway Advisory Council* (September 1995).

Pen Register

The pen register is a device attached to a given telephone line which records all numbers dialled on that line. The device is installed by connecting it with the line at a point where the line makes an "appearance" in the terminal near the telephone number under investigation. *United States v. Mountain States Telephone & Telegraph Co.*, 7 C.L.S.R. 1612 (9th 1980).

A pen register is a device that identifies all local and long distance numbers dialled, whether the call is completed or not. Although a pen register does not intercept spoken words, it does record an exchange of information — the dialling from one telephone number to another. A pen register is thus comparable in impact to electronic eavesdropping devices in that it may affect other persons and can involve multiple invasions of privacy. *State of Washington v. Riley*, 846 P.2d 1365 (Sup. Ct. Wash. 1993).

Means a device which records or decodes electronic or other impulses which identify the numbers dialed or otherwise transmitted on the telephone line to which such device is attached, but such term does not include any device used by a provider or customer of a wire communication service for cost accounting or other like purposes in the ordinary course of its business. *Electronic Communications Privacy Act* of 1986, Pub. L. 89-508 (1986).

Personal Computer

A personal computer system consists of hardware and software. The hardware includes the central processing unit ("CPU"), which contains the electronic circuits that control the computer and perform the arithmetic and logical functions, the internal memory of the computer ("random access memory," or "RAM"), input devices such as a keyboard and mouse, output devices such as a display screen and printer, and storage devices such as hard and floppy disk drives. The software includes one or more computer programs, usually stored magnetically on hard or floppy disks, along with such items as instruction manuals and "templates," which are pieces of plastic that fit around the function keys on the keyboard, identifying the specifc functions or commands that can be invoked by those keys. A personal computer system can also include "firmware," or "microcode". *Lotus Development Corp. v. Paperback Software International*, 15 U.S.P.Q.2d 1577 (D. Mass. 1990).

The development of the silicon chip in the 1970's and 1980's lead to the development of much smaller computers called micro-computers or personal computers ("PCs"). It is possible to join PCs together so that they share disks. A PC is not a dumb terminal but is capable of doing processing work. A typical micro-computer or personal computer consists of a screen, a central processing unit and a keyboard. At the relevant time it was common for the screen to be like a television screen which sat on top of the central processing unit. Below, or level with the bottom of the central processing unit and protruding forward was the keyboard. A keyboard is arranged similarly to that of a typewriter with some extra function keys. The operator uses the keyboard to operate the computer. The striking of a key sends a code to the central processing unit which may place the correspondence character on the screen and may also perform some other function. The central processing unit does the processing or computing work. It also acts as the interchange point which may be regarded as performing a function similar to that of a telephone exchange. When instructions known to the computer are typed, the central processing unit performs the function as instructed. *Madeley Pty Ltd. v. Touche Ross*, McGarvie, J., Aust. Fed. Ct., Dec. 21, 1989 (unreported).

A personal computer ["PC"] consists of both hardware and software. The hardware includes the central processing unit, which controls the computer's functions; the internal memory; input devices such as a keyboard, mouse or touchscreen; output devices, such as a display screen and printer; and storage devices such as hard and floppy disc drives. *Softel Inc. v. Dragon Medical and Scientific Communications, Inc.*, 1992 U.S. Dist. LEXIS 9502 (S.D.N.Y.1992).

A general purpose computer designed for operation and use by one person at a time. Computer Software Protection: Australia, Copyright Law Review Committee 1995.

A digital information processing device designed for use by one person at a time. A typical PC consists of central processing components (*e.g.*, a microprocessor and main memory) and mass data storage (such as a hard disk). A typical PC system consists of a PC, certain peripheral input/output devices (including a monitor, a keyboard, a mouse, and a printer), and an operating system. PC systems, which include desktop and laptop models, can be distinguished from more powerful, more expensive computer systems known as "servers", which are designed to provide data, services, and functionality through a digital network to multiple users. *United States of America v. Microsoft Corp.*, 87 F.Supp. 2d 30 (D.D.C. 2000).

Personal computers ("PCs") are computers designed for use by one person at a time. "[M]ore powerful, more expensive computer systems known as 'servers'. . . are designed to provide data, services, and functionality through a digital network to multiple users." *Universal City Studios, Inc. v. Reimerdes*, 55 U.S.P.Q. 2d 1873 (S. D.N.Y. 2000).

Personal Data

Means any information relating to an identified or identifiable individual ("data subject"). Council of Europe: Convention for the Protection of Individuals with Regard to Automatic Processing of Personal Data.

Shall mean any information relating to an identified or identifiable natural person ("data subject"); and identifiable person is one who can be identified, directly or indirectly, in particular by reference to an identification number or to one or more factors specific to his physical, physiological, mental, economic, cultural or social identity. European Union Data Protection Directive.

Means any information related to an identified or identifiable individual ("data subject"). OECD Guidelines on the Protection of Privacy and Transborder Flows of Personal Data, dated September 23, 1980, available at http://www.oecd.org// dsti/sti/it/secur/prod/privacyguide.htm.

Means any information relating to an identified or identifiable individual. *OECD Guidelines for Cryptography Policy*, March 27, 1997, available at *www.oecd.org*.

Personal Data Filing System

Shall mean any structured set of personal data which are accessible according to specific criteria, whether centralized, decentralized or dispersed on a functional or geographical basis. European Union Data Protection Directive.

Personal Identification Number (PIN)

A 4 to 12 character alphanumeric code or password used to authenticate an identity, commonly used in banking applications. "Security Requirements for

Cryptographic Modules", FIPS Pub. 140-1, Federal Information Processing Standards Publication, January 11, 1994, available at http://csrc.nist.gov/fips/fips1401.htm.

Personal Information

Information about an identifiable individual that is recorded in any form. *Personal Information Protection and Electronics Documents Act, S.C. 2000 C.5.*

Means individually identifiable information about an individual collected online, including (a) a first and last name; (b) a home or other physical address including street name and name of a city or town; (c) an e-mail address; (d) a telephone number; (e) a Social Security number; (f) any other identifier that the Commission determines permits the physical or online contacting of a specific individual; or (g) information concerning the child or the parents of that child that the website collects online from the child and combines with an identifier described in this paragraph. *Children's Online Privacy Protection Act of 1998.*

Was defined to include to two broad information categories: information that can be used to identify consumers, such as name, postal or e-mail address (person identifying information); and demographic and preference information (such as age, gender, income level, hobbies, or interests) that can be used either in the aggregate, non-identifying form for purposes such as market analysis, or in conjunction with personal identifying information to create detailed personal profiles of consumers. *Privacy on Line: A Report to Congress, Federal Trade Commission June 1998.*

Information about an identifiable individual that is recorded in any form. *Principles of Consumer Protection for Electronic Commerce: A Canadian Framework, July 8, 1999, available at http://strategis.ic.gc.ca/SSG/ca01180e.html.*

Means individually identifiable information about an individual collected online, including: (a) A first and last name; (b) A home or other physical address including street name and name of a city or town; (c) An e-mail address or other online contact information, including but not limited to an instant messaging user identifier, or a screen name that reveals an individual's e-mail address; (d) A telephone number; (e) A Social Security number; (f) A persistent identifier, such as a customer number held in a cookie or a processor serial number, where such identifier is associated with individually identifiable information; or a combination of a last name or photograph of the individual with other information such that the combination permits physical or online contacting; or (g) Information concerning the child or the parents of that child that the operator collects online from the child and combines with an identifier described in this definition. *United States Children's On-Line Privacy Protection Rule, Federal Trade Commission, 16 CFR part 312.*

Means information about an identifiable individual; and includes information contained in any register of deaths kept under the Births and Deaths Registration Act 1951. *Privacy Act 1993, New Zealand.*

Means information or an opinion (including information or an opinion forming part of a database), whether true or not, and whether recorded in a material form or not, about an individual whose identity is apparent, or can reasonably be ascertained, from the information or opinion. *Privacy Act 1988, amended Australia.*

PGA/PGC

Professional graphics array. *Princeton Graphics Operating, L.P. v. Nec Home Electronics (U.S.A.), Inc.*, Comp. Ind. Lit. Reptr. 11,126 (S.D.N.Y. 1990).

PGP

Pretty Good Privacy

Physical Tokens

Allow users to store important information in a portable format like a credit card that they can use to authenticate identity. Advancing Global Electronic Commerce: Technology Solutions to Public Policy Challenges, Computer Systems Policy Project (CSPP), available at http://www.cspp.org/projects/july99_cto_report.pdf.

PIN

Personal Identification Number *Databank Systems Ltd. v. Commnr. of Inland Revenue*, [1987] N.Z.L.R. 312 (H.C. Wellington).

Personal Identification Number. Smart Cards: Implications for Privacy, Privacy Commissioner, Australia, December 1995.

Ping

Pings are generated by a software program and are designed to be used by Internet users to check network connections. These "pings" are also used illegitimately to disable computers attached to the Internet by flooding them with repeated information requests. *Cyberpromotions, Inc. v. Apex Global Information Services, Inc.*, No. 97-5931 (E.D. Penn. September 30, 1997).

PIPEDA

Personal Information Protection and Electronic Document Act (Canada)

Piracy

Theft of *IPRs* through unlawful copying. Monopolies and Mergers Commission — Video Games: A report on the supply of video games in the UK (LONDON: HMSO Cm2781).

Pixel

A pixel is a point of light (sometimes coloured) on a cathode ray tube. The basic TV or computer screen is "painted" by pixels serially in lines starting at the upper left hand corner and then horizontally, then starting again from the left hand side and across until the whole screen has been "painted". The process then is started again at the upper left hand corner as the previous pixels fade from the screen. This entire process takes place 65 times or more per second. The eye cannot discern the "painting" nor the dissolution of the image and the renewal of the same by the next "painting". Depending on the size of the screen, there can be a million pixels or more on the screen at one time. *Advanced Micro Devices, Inc. and Intel Corp.*, CCH Comp. Cases 60,218 (Arb. Award. 1990).

PKI Service Provider

Any entity, which has roles, functions, obligations or rights under the CP other than an End Entity. PKI Service Providers include the RCA, Specification Administration Organizations, the CA and Subordinate Entities. *The Office of the Federal Privacy Commissioner (Australia), Consultation Paper, (June 2001).*

Place of Business

Means any place of operations where a person carries out a non-transitory activity with human means and goods or services. *UNCITRAL, Working Group IV (Electronic Commerce), Thirty-ninth session New York, 11-15 March, 2002.*

Plaintext

Intelligible data. A Cryptology Policy Framework for Electronic Commerce, Task Force on Electronic Commerce, Industry Canada, February 1998.

Means intelligible data. *OECD Guidelines for Cryptography Policy*, March 27, 1997, available at *www.oecd.org.*

Plaintext Key

An unencrypted cryptographic key which is used in its current form. "Security Requirements for Cryptographic Modules", FIPS Pub. 140-1, Federal Information Processing Standards Publication, January 11, 1994, available at http://csrc.nist.gov/fips/fips1401.htm.

Plantronics Board

A Plantronics board is a colour graphics card which expanded the range of colours on a PC from four to sixteen. *Softel Inc. v. Dragon Medical and Scientific Communications, Inc.*, 1992 U.S. Dist. LEXIS 9502 (S.D.N.Y.1992).

Platform

Is the combination of the computer hardware system plus the basic operating system which drives the essential computer functions. *Angoss II Partnership v. Trifox Inc.* (1997), [1997] O.J. No. 4969, 1997 CarswellOnt 488 (Gen. Div.), affirmed (1999), [1999] O.J. No. 4144, 1999 CarswellOnt 3474 (C.A.) leave to appeal dismissed (2000), [1999] S.C.C.A. No. 588, 2000 CarswellOnt 2999.

Play Mode (in relation to video games)

"Play mode" refers to the audio-visual effects displayed during the actual play of the game, when the game symbols move and interact on the screen, and the player controls the movement of one of the symbols. *Williams Electronics Inc. v. Artic International Inc.*, 685 F.2d 870 (3rd Cir. 1982).

"Play mode" refers to the audio-visual display seen and heard by a person playing the game. *Stern Electronics Inc. v. Kaufman*, 669 F.2d 852 (2nd Cir. 1982).

Plotter

A plotter makes its pictures or follows what the computer tells it to do by simply attaching points together as you might with, say, taking a ruler and laying it down and drawing a line between the points. If you have a starting point and an ending point, and draw a line between those two, that is substantially what the plotter does. *Apple Computer, Inc. v. U.S.*, CCH Comp. L. 46,363 (Cit. 1991).

Point of Sale Terminal Systems (POS)

In the use of POS's, funds are electronically transferred directly from the customer's account to the retailer's account without the use of cash or cheques. *Independent Bankers Association of New York State, Inc. v. Marine Midland Bank*, Comp. Ind. Lit. Reptr. 2,390 (2nd Cir. 1985).

Point of Sale Transactions (POS or EFT-POS)

These transactions, often referred to as EFT-POS (Electronic Funds Transfer-Point of Sale) transactions, are similar to ATM transactions in that they are card initiated. They are used soley for sale transactions so that each transaction results in a debit to the customer's account and a credit to the merchant's account. The authorization procedure is the same for ATM's. *Databank Systems Ltd. v. Commnr. of Inland Revenue*, [1987] N.Z.L.R. 312 (H.C. Wellington).

Point of Sale Systems (POS)

Systems which function from the cash register, as each sale is made. *Lalesc Enterprises Inc. v. Arete Technologies Inc.* (1994) 59 C.P.R. (3d) 438 (B.C.S.C.), additional reasons at (1994), 59 C.P.R. (3d) 438 at 448 (B.C.S.C.).

Poke

Put new data into a memory location. Monopolies and Mergers Commission — Video Games: A report on the supply of video games in the UK (LONDON: HMSO Cm2781).

Port

A functional unit of a cryptographic module through which data or signals can enter or exit the module. Physically separate ports do not share the same physical pin or wire. "Security Requirements for Cryptographic Modules", FIPS Pub. 140-

1, Federal Information Processing Standards Publication, January 11, 1994, available at http://csrc.nist.gov/fips/fips1401.htm.

Portability

Portability of cryptographic methods means the technical ability to be adapted and function in multiple systems. *OECD Guidelines for Cryptography Policy*, March 27, 1997, available at *www.oecd.org*.

Portals

Web sites that aggregate a large number of variety of content and services in order to attract visitors. *Domain Name System Reform and Related Internet Governance Issues: A Consultation Paper*, Industry Canada available at *www.strategis.gc.ca*

Porting

Making the arrangements necessary so that a computer program that runs on one computer is able to run on a differently configured computer. This generally involves modification of the original program. Computer Software Protection: Australia, Copyright Law Review Committee 1995.

Positive Roamer Verification (PRV)

A computer-based system used to verify valid cellular telephone ESN/MIN combinations assigned to authorized customers on any participating system. If the PRV identifies a particular combination as valid, the local cellular telephone system will permit telephone calls to be placed using that combination. If the combination is not identified as valid, the local system will deny service to a telephone using that combination. *United States v. Brady*, 820 F.Supp. 1346 (C.D. Utah 1993).

Postmarks

Electronically stamped e-mail with an unalterable time and date that it is sent. Advancing Global Electronic Commerce: Technology Solutions to Public Policy Challenges, The Computer Systems Policy Project, July 1999, available at http://www.cspp.org/projects/july99_cto_report.pdf.

Power Transformer

A power transformer is the component through which electrical power is brought to the monitor. *Motorola Inc. v. Computer Displays International Inc*, 222 U.S.P.Q. 844 (7th. Cir. 1984).

PPU

Picture Processing Unit. Monopolies and Mergers Commission — Video Games: A report on the supply of video games in the UK (LONDON: HMSO Cm2781).

Price Caps

Price caps are an alternative to traditional rate-of-return regulation. Price caps focus on price levels rather than return on investment. Price caps are intended to reward productivity and reduce concerns about unnecessary overinvestment and inappropriate cost allocations. Competition and Culture on Canada's Information Highway: Managing the Realities of Transition, CRTC (the "Convergence Report"), May 19, 1995.

Printed Circuit Assembly

Means a good consisting of one or more printed circuits, with one or more active elements assembled thereon, with or without passive elements. North American Free Trade Agreement between Canada, Mexico and the United States, Annex 401.

Printed Circuit Board (PCB)

A sheet of fiberglass or epoxy onto which a thin layer of metal has been applied, then etched away to form traces. Electronic components can then be attached to the board with molten solder, and they can exchange electronic signals via the etched traces on the board. *Apple Computer Inc. v. Mackintosh Computers Ltd.* (1986), 28 D.L.R. (4th) 178 (Fed. T.D.).

Prior Art

Prior art is defined as any relevant knowledge, acts, descriptions, and patents which pertain to, but predate, invention in question. *Infodek Inc. v. Meredith-Webb Printing Co. Inc.*, 28 U.S.P.Q. 2d 1669 (N.D. Georgia 1993).

Privacy-Enhancing Technologies

Privacy-enhancing technologies or "PETs" refer to technologies that transmit your personal information in encrypted form, or otherwise enable you to conduct electronic transactions in an anonymous manner by minimizing or eliminating the collection of personally identifying data. Identity Theft: Who's Using Your Name?, Information and Privacy Commissioner/Ontario, June 1997, available at http://www.ipc.on.ca.

Privacy Policy

A statement on a web site describing what information about you is collected by the site, and how it is used. Ideally, the policy is posted prominently and offers you options about the use of your personal information. These options are called opt-in and opt-out. An opt-in choice means the web site won't use your information unless you specifically say it's okay. An opt-out choice means the web site can use the information unless you specifically direct it not to. Cyberspeak — Learning the Language, the Federal Trade Commission and the National Association of Attorneys General, available at http://www.ftc.gov/bcp/conline/pubs/online/sitesee/index.html.

Private Communication

Any oral communication, or any telecommunication, that is made by an originator who is in Canada or is intended by the originator to be received by a person who is in Canada and that is made under circumstances in person other than the person intended by the originator to receive it, and includes any radio-based telephone communication that is treated electronically or otherwise for the purpose of preventing intelligible reception by any person other than the person intended by the originator to receive it. *Criminal Code* (Canada), R.S.C. 1985, c. C-46, s. 183.

Private Key

Private key is the key used to generate a digital signature using asymmetric cryptography. This key must be kept private by the owner. Security and Electronic Authorization and Authentication Guideline, Communications Security Establishment, Government of Canada September 1995, CID/01/15.

A cryptographic key used with a public key cryptographic algorithm, uniquely associated with an entity, and not made public. "Security Requirements for Cryptographic Modules", FIPS Pub. 140-1, Federal Information Processing Standards Publication, January 11, 1994, available at http://csrc.nist.gov/fips/fips1401.htm.

Means the key of a key pair used to create a digital signature. *Utah Digital Signature Act* 46-3, available at http://www.le.state.ut.us/code/TITLE46/htm/46 03004.htm.

The half of a Key Pair that must be kept secret to ensure confidentiality, integrity, authenticity and non-repudiation of messages. *The Office of the Federal Privacy Commissioner (Australia), Consultation Paper, (June 2001).*

Private Line Service

We believe the *sine qua non* of a private line service is that it (a) either originate or terminate at a specific location designated by the customer via a communications channel dedicated to his private use and not used or usable for public communications services; and (b) access only those distant locations (including, if appropriate, distant telephone central offices) specifically designated by the customer to meet his private communications needs. CNCP Telecommunications: Interconnection with Bell Canada, CRTC Decision 79-11 (May 1979).

Consist of custom designed intra-subscriber networks to meet specialized user requirements which vary from simple two-point circuits to complex coast-to-coast networks for voice, data or combinations thereof. Examples of such private networks provided by CNCP include air traffic control for Transport Canada; a meteorological network involving the collection of weather information and the transmission of facsimile weather charts for the Canadian meteorological Centre; an intra-police network centered around the RCMP's main computer in Ottawa; and a private line data network linking the Quebec Government's Social Affairs Department with over 150 terminal devices in regional offices throughout the province. CNCP Telecommunications: Interconnection with Bell Canada, CRTC Decision 79-11 (May 1979).

Private Line Service

A dedicated communications channel provided at flat rates between points in the same exchange. *Report to the Governor in Council: Status of Competition in Canadian Telecommunications Markets, Deployment/Accessibility of Advanced Telecommunications Infrastructure and Services, September, 2001.*

Private Network

Means a telecommunications transport network that is used exclusively for intra-corporate communications. North American Free Trade Agreement between Canada, Mexico and the United States, Article 1310.

Privileged Code

A capability assigned to accounts, groups or users allowing unrestricted memory access, access to privileged CPU instructions, and the ability to call privileged procedures. One of the tasks of any operating system is to provide integrity and security features that protect the users of the system from each other and from themselves. To do this, a protection mechanism (privileged mode) is built that prevents "normal" programs and users from performing processing that might corrupt the integrity or breach the security of one another, their data files or of the operating system itself. Because certain programs including parts of the operating system itself must be allowed unrestricted access to the system, the ability can be "given" out by the manager of the computer system under very carefully controlled circumstances. *Delrina Corp. v. Triolet Systems, Inc.* (1992), 47 C.P.R. (3d) 1 (Ont. H.C.).

Process

To manipulate (data) in order to abstract the required information. *Autodesk Australia Pty Ltd v. Dyason* (1989), 15 I.P.R. 1 (Aus. Fed. Ct.), reversed [1990] A.I.P.C. 36,446 (Aus. Fed. Ct. FC).

Process . . . a method for achieving a particular result. *Gates Rubber Co. v. Bando American Inc.*, 28 U.S.P.Q. 2d 1503 (10th Cir. 1993).

Most modern operating systems, include VAX/VMS permit more than one program to execute either apparently or actually concurrently. To take a simple example, one might have a program which displays an image of a clock face on which the hands move to tell the time. Such operating systems allow this program to be started twice. The result will be two clock faces on the computer screen, on each of which the hands move, more or less simultaneously. One program has been loaded twice, and is being executed twice. The two instances of the executing program are called processes. In the example I have given one could say that there were two clock processes running. *Cantor Fitzgerald International v. Tradition (UK) Ltd.,*. [1999] I.N.L.R. No. 23 (Ch.D.).

Process Control

Applications include the use of electronic equipment to monitor and control some process which is occurring on a continuing basis — such as nuclear-powered generating stations, an electric power distribution grid, an automatic machine tool, or a fire detection and control system. Second Computer Inquiry (Supplemental Notice), 42 Fed. Reg. 13029 (F.C.C. 1977).

Processing

Entails the use of a computer for operations upon data which include, *inter alia:* arithmetic and logical operations, storage, retrieval, and transfer. Second Computer Inquiry (Notice of Inquiry), 5 C.L.S.R. 1381 (F.C.C. 1976).

Processing of Personal Data

Shall mean any operation or set of operations which is performed upon personal data, whether or not by automatic means, such as collection, recording, organization, storage, adaptation or alteration, retrieval, consultation, use, disclosure by transmission, dissemination or otherwise making available, alignment or combination, blocking, erasure or destruction. European Union Data Protection Directive.

Processor Time (CPU Time)

The amount of time, in seconds, that a user, group, or account has used the CPU. . . . The consumption of time within a computer system is measured at two basic levels. The first is the quantity of real (wall clock) time that a user or program has been using the services of the computer. The second is the amount of time that the user or program has actually been using the CPU (processor) to perform processing. For instance, a program might have been running for 60 seconds but waiting for user input from a terminal for 59 seconds and therefore only used 1 second of CPU (processor) time to actually do useful work. *Delrina Corp. v. Triolet Systems, Inc.* (1992), 47 C.P.R. (3d) 1 (Ont. H.C.).

Program

Sounds or visual images, or a combination of sounds and visual images, that are intended to inform, enlighten or entertain, but does not include visual images, whether or not combined with sounds, that consist predominantly of alphanumeric text. *Broadcasting Act*, S.C. 1991, c. 11.

Program Flow Control Instructions

These instructions alter the content of the program counter (a 16 bit location holding the address of the next instruction to be executed) and hence after normal sequential execution of instructions into memory, for example, "branch, jump to subroutine," etc. *Apple Computer Inc. v. Mackintosh Computers Ltd.* (1986), 28 D.L.R. (4th) 178 (Fed. T.D.).

Program Listing

The set of instructions which constitute the program or suite of programs. *Northern Office Micro Computers Ltd. v. Rosenstein*, [1982] F.S.R. 124 (S.C. S.Africa).

Program Structure

The functions of the modules in a program together with each module's relationship to other modules constitute the structure of the program. Additionally, the term structure may include the category of modules referred to as "macros". *Matrox Electronic Systems Ltd. v. Gaudreau*, [1993] R.J.Q. 2449 (C.S.).

The program's architectural structure is a description of how the program operates in terms of its various functions, which are performed by discreet modules, and how each of these modules interact with each other. The architecture or structure of a program is often reduced to a flowchart, which a programmer uses visually to depict the inner workings of a program. Structure exists at nearly every level of a program and can be conceived of as including control flow, data flow, and sub-structure or nesting. *Gates Rubber Co. v. Bando American Inc.*, 28 U.S.P.Q. 2d 1503 (10th Cir. 1993).

The functions of the modules together with each modules relationships to other modules constitute the "structure" of the program. *Micro Consulting, Inc. v. Zubeldia*, 813 F.Supp. 1514 (W.D. Okla. 1993).

Programmed

Constitutes the means of preordaining a response to give input or stimulus regardless of whether that means is achieved through the use of software, hardware, firmware of fundamental equipment design. Second Computer Inquiry (Supplemental Notice), 42 Fed. Reg. 13029 (F.C.C. 1977).

Programming

To accomplish the desired result, a person with knowledge of the computer's capability must design a system for the particular information to be put into the machine, prescribe certain manipulations, and specify the desired result. This requires considerable expertise, discretion, and independent judgment free from immediate direction or supervision.

Once the designer, sometimes called an analyst, determines the system, he usually describes this system in narrative form, commonly referred to as a program narrative or specifications. To further complicate the matter there is ordinarily an overall system with numerous subsystems. At this point, there exists input of known information, a designation of certain computations or operations, and a desired result narrated by the designer. The next step is to translate the narrative, which is in the English language, into computer language. This portion of the project is referred to as programming. The programmer writes in computer language the commands to the computer to implement the narrative. (To illustrate:

Assume one were instructing a baby to eat from a bowl. Instead of placing a spoon in the hand of the baby and demonstrating, through performance, the dipping of the spoon into the bowl, carrying it to the mouth and depositing its contents into the mouth, the instructions to a computer would be more detailed. The possible commands might be: (1) Raise your right arm to table height, (2) Move your right hand forward 8", (3) Place your right hand on the spoon, (4) Curl your fingers around the spoon, (5) Raise your right arm 4", (6) Move your right arm 4" to the left, (7) Lower your right arm 4", (8) Tilt the spoon forward 30[cf11]o, (9) Move the spoon forward 1", (10) Tilt the spoon upward 30[cf11]o, (11) Raise your right arm upward 14", (12) Turn the spoon horizontally 180[cf11]o, (13) Move your right arm 4" and simultaneously open your mouth, (14) Rotate the spoon 180[cf11]o, (15) Move the spoon outward 4" and return it to the original position.) These commands, once translated into computer language, can be stored on punch cards, the use of which avoids necessity of typing the entire process on each use of the computer. *Pezzillo v. General Telephone & Electronics Information Systems, Inc.*, 414 F.Supp 1257 (M.D. Tenn. 1976).

Programming Language

Letters and other symbols as well as their systems for use as a means of expressing a program. Japanese Amended Copyright Law.

Now binary form is practically impossible for a human to read or write. Humans write programs in a particular language called a higher level language. That language must have a perfect syntax and grammar. Computers are unforgiving: there is no room for irregular verbs with them. Programming languages are a mixture of words of English and a system of a kind of algebraic instructions. There are many such languages. A popular language of some antiquity is COBOL. A variant of this usable only on Digital Computer Company's (DEC's) products is DIBOL and a later variant of DIBOL, usable on other company's machines is DBL. *IBCOS Computers Ltd. v. Barclay's Mercantile Highland Finance Ltd.*, [1994] F.S.R. 275 (Ch.D.).

It is in principle possible to program a computer by directly specifying the numbers which are to be entered into memory as a program. Such a task is extremely complex and error-prone. The task is simplified slightly if mnemonics are provided for the numbers, because words are easier for humans to understand. But the underlying programming task is very difficult. It is referred to as assembly language programming. It is machine specific (cpu's from different manufacturers use different numbers and different mnemonics) and thus cannot readily be transferred from machine to machine. Every subroutine call has to be expressly specified. From the earliest days, therefore, programmers have endeavoured to provide a more human-friendly method of programming computers. Programming languages have been designed to make it possible to program without being concerned with the detail of the particular instructions used by particular cpu's. There are hundreds of such languages. They differ widely from each other not only in their syntax, but in many other respects. *Cantor Fitzgerald International v. Tradition (UK) Ltd.,* [1999] I.N.L.R. No. 23 (Ch.D.).

Programming Service

Means any combination of images, sounds or images and sounds including a commercial message, other than an alphanumeric service, that is designed to inform or entertain the public and is

(a) transmitted to a cable head end over the air, by microwave or satellite relay or by means of a hard wire feed, or

(b) distributed by a licensee.

Cable Television Regulations, 1986, SOR/86-831.

Programming Undertaking

An undertaking for the transmission of programs, either directly by radio waves or other means of telecommunication or indirectly through a distribution undertaking, for reception by the public by means of broadcasting receiving apparatus. *Broadcasting Act*, S.C. 1991, c. 11.

PROM (Programmable Read-Only Memory)

Acronym for Programmable Read-Only Memory. A microchip-mounted program from which a computer may read instructions. Non-erasable. *E.F. Johnson Co. v. Uniden Corp. of America*, 623 F.Supp. 1485 (D. Minn. 1985).

A PROM device is a ROM memory that may be programmed in the field by the customer. *Intel Corp. v. Radiation Inc.*, 184 U.S.P.Q. 54 (T.T.A.B. 1974).

Program Read-Only Memory is memory, the contents of which can be altered once the microprocessor/card is being used. Smart Cards: Implications for Privacy, Privacy Commissioner, Australia, December 1995.

Proprietary Architecture

ISC designed what is referred to in the industry as a "proprietary architecture" computer system, which means that ISC did not make the design of its computer system available to outsiders so that they could create software to run on the system. *ISC-Bunker Ramo Corporation v. Altech, Inc.*, 765 F.Supp. 1310 (N.D. Ill. 1990).

Proprietary Network

Means owned and managed by specific service providers or network management. Use of the network is limited to the parties or participants who have rights or membership to use by agreeing upon the terms and rules for use of the network. Business - To Consumer Electronic Commerce: Survey of Status and Issues, OECD/gd (97) 219.

Proprietary Project

In the computer industry, a "proprietary project" refers to a project developed at the creator's own initiative and expense, the rights to which are retained by the creator. *Computer Sciences Corp. v. Commissioner of Internal Revenue*, 63 T.C. 327 (U.S. Tax. Crt. 1974).

Protection-Defeating Device

Any device, product or component incorporated into a device or product, the primary focus or effect of which is to circumvent any process, treatment, mechanism or system that prevents or inhibits any of the acts covered by the rights under this Treaty. WIPO Diplomatic Conference on Certain Copyright and Neighbouring Rights Questions, Geneva, December 2 - 20, 1996, August 30, 1996, C.R.N.R./DC/4.

Protocol(s)

A protocol is a series of procedures and conventions that govern communictions between a computer and various terminals linked to that computer. Put another way, the protocol tells the computer "how" as opposed to "what" to communicate. *Telerate Systems Inc. v. Marshal Caro*, 689 F.Supp. 221 (S.D.N.Y. 1988).

Computer programming software which permits two computers to communicate. *Neon Products Ltd. v. Signs of the Times Ltd.*, Ont. Dist. Ct., Doc. No. M 227240/84, 227815/84, Gibson D.C.J., February 2, 1988 (unreported).

Protocols govern the methods used for packaging the transmitted data in quanta, the rules for controlling the flow information, and the format of headers and trailers surrounding the transmitted information and the format of separate control messages. Second Computer Inquiry (Final Decision), 77 F.C.C.2d 384 (F.C.C. 1980).

Means a set of rules and formats that govern the exchange of information between two peer entities for purposes of transferring signalling or data information. North American Free Trade Agreement between Canada, Mexico and the United States, Article 1310.

Sets of technology language rules that determine how various components of communications systems interact. *The Challenge of the Information Highway: Final Report of the Information Highway Advisory Council* (September 1995).

Are common agreements between systems that allow a transaction to occur. Advancing Global Electronic Commerce: Technology Solutions to Public Policy Challenges, The Computer Systems Policy Project, July 1999, available at http://www.cspp.org/projects/july99_cto_report.pdf.

The Internet functions by means of conventions and standards (called "protocols") that are implemented in the software and other products used in the operation of the Internet and that define how information is to be processed. *Public Performance of Musical Works* 1996-1998 (Tariff 22) (1999), 1 C.P.R. (4th) 417 (Copyright Board).

A set of rules governing how data are to be transmitted and received over a computer network. *Domain Name System Reform and Related Internet Governance Issues: A Consultation Paper,* Industry Canada available at *www.strategis.gc.ca*

Protocol Analyzer

A protocol analyzer slows the transmission so that the protocol signal can be analyzed. *Secure Services Technology Inc. v. Time and Space Processing Inc.,* 772 F.Supp. 1354 (E.D.Va. 1989).

Prototype

The first full-scale model of a new type of design of furniture, machinery, or vehicle. *Fargo Machine & Tool Co. v. Kearney & Trecker Corp.,* 428 F.Supp. 364 (E.D. Mich. 1977).

Proxy Server

Proxy Server software acts as the focal point for outgoing Internet requests. Proxy Servers conserve system resources by directing all outgoing and incoming data traffic through a centralized portal. *eBay v. Bidder's Edge Inc.,* 54 U.S.P.Q. 2d 1798 (N.D. Cal. 2000).

Pseudocode

A method of describing the mechanism of a computer program by the use of statements that are written in free English text, consisting of nouns and verbs (for example, 'get employee work details'). The statements are linked together either sequentially or by simple controls (for example, 'if the employee is Claude Smith return to the main menu'). The generation of these statements is usually the final step before a computer program is written in the chosen computer language. *Admar Computers Pty v. EZY Systems Pty Ltd.,* [1997] 853 FCA (29 August, 1997) (Aust. F.C.).

Pseudonymity

Pseudonymity refers to the use of an identifier for a party to a transaction, which is not, in the normal course of events, sufficient to associate the transaction with a particular individual. To explain in more detail, data can be indirectly associated with a person through such procedures as storage of partial identifiers by two or more organizations, both of whom must provide their portions of the transaction trail in order for the identity of the individual to be constructed; storing of an indirect identifier with the transaction data; and storing separately a cross-index between the indirect identifier and the individual's real identity. Smart, Optical and Other Advanced Cards: How to Do a Privacy Assessment, Information and Privacy Commissioner/Ontario Canada, available at http://www.itc.on.ca.

Pseudonymizers

Provide the user with an alias to replace identifying information such as an e-mail address or Web site address. Advancing Global Electronic Commerce: Technology Solutions to Public Policy Challenges, The Computer Systems Policy Project, July 1999, available at http://www.cspp.org/projects/july99_cto_report.pdf.

PSS

An acronym for Packet Switching Service. *Datacall Ltd. v. The Post Office*, Ch. D., Whitford J., November 27, 1981 (unreported).

PSTN Voice

"Real Time" voice communication via the Internet to or from a telephone set or other equipment where the conversion for carriage on the Internet is performed at the service provider's (*i.e.*, the ISP's) equipment, set, without requiring the user to be equipped with a modem or a computer with special hardware or software at the terminal location. Telecom Order CRTC 98-929, September 17, 1998.

Public Domain (Computer Programs)

Programs which the copyright owner has granted the world at large a licence to reproduce. While copyright subsists in such programs the copyright owner is, however, precluded from claiming damages from anyone who reproduces the program. Computer Software Protection: Australia, Copyright Law Review Committee 1995.

Used to refer to *software* which can be made freely available but not resold for profit. Monopolies and Mergers Commission — Video Games: A report on the supply of video games in the UK (LONDON: HMSO Cm2781).

Public Key

Public key is the key used to verify a digital signature using asymmetric cryptography. This key can be freely disclosed. Security and Electronic Authorization and Authentication Guideline, Communications Security Establishment, Government of Canada September 1995, CID/01/15.

A cryptographic key used with a public key cryptographic algorithm, uniquely associated with an entity, and which may be made public. "Security Requirements for Cryptographic Modules", FIPS Pub. 140-1, Federal Information Processing Standards Publication, January 11, 1994, available at http://csrc.nist.gov/fips/fips1401.htm.

Means the key of a key pair used to verify a digital signature. *Utah Digital Signature Act* 46-3, available at http://www.le.state.ut.us/code/TITLE46/htm/46 03004.htm.

Means the key of a key pair used to verify a digital signature. *Illinois Electronic Commerce Security Act* 1998 5 Ill. Comp. Stat. 175.

The half of a Key Pair, which may be made public. *The Office of the Federal Privacy Commissioner (Australia), Consultation Paper, (June 2001).*

Public Key (Asymmetric) Cryptographic Algorithm

A cryptographic algorithm that uses two related keys, a public key and a private key; the two keys have the property that, given the public key, it is computationally infeasible to derive the private key. "Security Requirements for Cryptographic Modules", FIPS Pub. 140-1, Federal Information Processing Standards Publication, January 11, 1994, available at http://csrc.nist.gov/fips/fips1401.htm.

Public Key Certificate

Is the public key of a user, together with related information, digitally signed with the private key of the Certification Authority that issued it. The certificate format is in accordance with ITU-T Recommendation X.509. Public Key Infrastructure Management in the Government of Canada, Treasury Board of Canada Secretariat, May 27, 1999, available at http://www.tbs-sct.gc.ca/pubs_pol/ciopubs/PKI/pki1_e.html.

A set of data that unambiguously identifies an entity, contains the entity's public key, and is digitally signed by a trusted party. "Security Requirements for Cryptographic Modules", FIPS Pub. 140-1, Federal Information Processing Standards Publication, January 11, 1994, available at http://csrc.nist.gov/fips/fips1401.htm.

A certificate identifying a public key to its subscriber, corresponding to a private key held by that subscriber. General Usage for International Digitally Insured Commerce (Guidec), International Chamber of Commerce, 1997, available at http://www.icc.wbo.org/guidec2.htm.

Public Key Cryptography

A form of cryptography that utilizes a cryptographic algorithm which uses two related keys: a public key and a private key. The two keys have the property that, given the public key, it is computationally infeasible to derive the private key. A Cryptology Policy Framework for Electronic Commerce, Task Force on Electronic Commerce, Industry Canada, February 1998.

Public Key Encryption

Public key encryption transforms the work using an algorithm requiring two particular keys — a "public" key and a "private" key. The keys have complementary roles. Data encrypted using a public key can only be decrypted using a secret, private key. For instance, a copyright owner could encrypt a work using the public key of the intended recipient; then, only the intended recipient could decrypt a copy of the work with his private key. No secret (private) keys need to be exchanged in this transaction. Without the private key of the intended recipient, the work cannot be read, manipulated or otherwise deciphered by other parties. Of course, if a decrypted copy is made and shared, then others could manipulate the work unless other means are used to protect it. National Information Infrastructure: A Preliminary Draft of the Report of the Working Group on Intellectual Property Rights, July 1994.

Public Key Infrastructure (PKI)

A network of connected third-party certification authorities allowing the movement of data and information between organizations that have their own security architecture or system. *The Challenge of the Information Highway: Final Report of the Information Highway Advisory Council* (September 1995).

A system of public and private cryptography keys, used in tandem, that can be used to encrypt and decrypt documents. A PKI ensures the security of electronic communications and transactions. Ministry of Revenue Advisory Committee, Report of the Committee On Electronic Commerce, April 30, 1998, Industry Canada.

Is the entire set of policies, processes, server platforms, software, and work stations used for (the purpose of) administering certificates and keys. Public Key Infrastructure Management in the Government of Canada, Treasury Board of Canada Secretariat, May 27, 1999, available at http://www.tbs-sct.gc.ca/pubs_pol/ciopubs/PKI/pki1_e.html.

The particular implementation of Public Key Technology described in the CP and other Accredited Documents, under which Keys and Certificates are issued and used. *The Office of the Federal Privacy Commissioner (Australia), Consultation Paper, (June 2001).*

Public Key System

In a public key system, two keys are created for each individual — one private one public. The private key is known only to the individual while the public key is made widely available. When an individual encrypts a document with his or her private key, this is the equivalent of signing it by hand since the private key is unique to that individual alone. Any third party may decrypt the message using the individual's public key, which corresponds only to his/her private key. If the document is successfully decrypted, then one has the necessary assurance that it could only have been created by that individual. Otherwise, one would not have been able to decode it. Digital signatures thus provide proof of a document's authenticity — that the document originated from the sender. Privacy-Enhancing Technologies: The Path to Anonymity, Information and Privacy Commissioner/ Ontario, August 1995, available at http://www.ipc.on.ca.

Public Key Technology (PKT)

An encryption scheme, introduced by Diffie and Hellman in 1976, where each person gets a pair of keys, called the public key and the private key. Each person's public key is published while the private key is kept secret. Messages are encrypted using the intended recipient's public key and can only be decrypted using their private key. This is often used in conjunction with a digital signature. *The Office of the Federal Privacy Commissioner (Australia), Consultation Paper, (June 2001).*

Public Switched Telephone Network (PSTN)

Abbreviated as the "PSTN", it is a network that provides POTS (plain old telephone service) as well as increasingly intelligent functions like voicemail, caller recognition and so on. The PSTN is public because regulation requires that any member of the public can become a telephone subscriber at published rates and send messages without interference from the carrier. The PSTN is "switched", meaning that any subscriber can reach any other subscriber simply by dialing. Submission of the Director of Investigation and Research to the CRTC Re Public Notice CRTC 1994-130.

A telecommunication facility the primary purpose of which is to provide a land line-based telephone service to the public for compensation. *Radiocommunication Act*, R.S.C. 1985, c. R-2, as amended. *Criminal Code* (Canada), R.S.C. 1985, c. C-46, s. 183.

Public Telecommunications Transport Network

Means public telecommunications infrastructure that permits telecommunications between defined network termination points. North American Free Trade Agreement between Canada, Mexico and the United States, Article 1310.

Means public telecommunications transport networks or public telecommunications transport services. North American Free Trade Agreement between Canada, Mexico and the United States, Article 1310.

Public Telecommunications Transport Service

Means any telecommunications transport service required by a party, explicitly or in effect, to be offered to the public generally, including telegraph, telephone, telex and data transmission, that typically involves the real-time transmission of customer-supplied information between two or more points without any end-to-end change in the form or content of the customer's information. North American Free Trade Agreement between Canada, Mexico and the United States, Article 1310.

Published Informational Content

Means informational content prepared for or made available to recipients generally, or to a class of recipients, in substantially the same form. The term does not include informational content that is: (A) customized for a particular recipient by an individual or group of individuals acting as or on behalf of the licensor, using judgment or expertise; or (B) provided in a special relationship of reliance between the provider and the recipient. *Uniform Computer Information Transactions Act*, National Conference of Commissioners on Uniform State Laws, available at http://www.law.upenn.u/bll/ulc/ucita/citim99.htm.

Push Media

Allows information to be distributed to viewers automatically, without any need for the viewer to contact a particular website or bulletin board system. Rather, the information is "pushed" at individuals while they are on-line or while logging onto their computers, regardless of where they are located. *Technical Committees' Internet Task Force Report*, International Organization of Securities Commissioners, September 13, 1998.

Qualified Certificate

Means a digital attestation which links a signature verification device to a person, confirms the identity of that person and meets the requirements laid down in Annex I. Proposal for A European Parliament and Council Directive on a Common Framework for Electronic Signatures, COM (1998) 297 Final.

Quality Assured Image Record

The set of quality assured images which has associated (e.g., bibliographic and biographic) and the linkage between the image and the associated data that have been verified according to quality assurance procedures and maintained in a manner that provides confidence that the image can be retrieved allowing it to stand in place of the source record. National Standard of Canada, Microfilm and Electronic Images as documentary evidence, Can/CGSB-72.11-93.

Radio

A general term applied to the use of radio waves. International Telecommunication Union, Radio Regulations (1982 Edition, Revised).

Radio Apparatus

A device or combination of devices intended for, or capable of being used for, radiocommunication. *Radiocommunication Act*, R.S.C. 1985, c. R-2, as amended.

Radio-Based Telephone Communication

Any radiocommunication that is made over apparatus that is used primarily for connection to a public switched telephone network. *Radiocommunication Act*, R.S.C. 1985, c. R-2, as amended.

Radio or Radiocommunication

Radio communication or "radio" means any transmission, emission or reception of signs, signals, writing, images, sounds or intelligence of any nature by means of electromagnetic waves of frequencies lower than 3,000 GHz propgated in space without artificial guide. *Radiocommunication Act*, R.S.C. 1985, c. R-2, as amended.

Means any transmission, emission or reception of signs, signals, writing, images, sounds or intelligence of any nature by means of electromagnetic waves of frequencies lower than 3,000 GHz propagated in space without artificial guide. *Interpretation Act*, R.S.C. 1985, c. I-21.

Radio Waves

Electromagnetic waves of frequencies lower than 3000 GHz that are propagated in space without artificial guide. *Broadcasting Act*, S.C. 1991, c. 11.

Radiocommunication

Means any transmission, emission or reception of signs, signals, writing, images, sounds or intelligence of any nature by means of electromagnetic waves of frequencies lower than 3,000 GHz propagated in space without artificial guide. *Canadian Radio-television and Telecommunications Commission Act*, R.S.C. 1985, c. C-22.

Means any transmission, emission or reception of signs, signals, writing, images, sounds or intelligence of any nature by means of electromagnetic waves of frequencies lower than 3,000 Gigacycles per second propagated in space without artificial guide. *Capital Cities Communications Inc. v. CRTC*, [1978] 2 S.C.R. 141.

R&D

Research and Development

RAM (Random-Access Memory)

Random-Access Memory. *Intel Corp. v. Radiation Inc.*, 184 U.S.P.Q. 54 (T.T.A.B. 1974); *IBM Corp. v. Ordinateurs Spirales Inc.* (1984), 2 C.I.P.R. 56 (Fed. T.D.); *Apple Computer Inc. v. Mackintosh Computers Ltd.* (1986), 28 D.L.R. (4th) 178 (Fed. T.D.).

Every general purpose computer apparently contains what is called RAM. This is an acronym for Random-Access Memory. RAM can be simply defined as a computer component in which data and computer programs can be temporarily recorded. It is a property of RAM that when the computer is turned off, the copy of the programs recorded in RAM is lost. *Apple Computer Inc. v. Formula International Inc.*, 534 F.Supp. 617 (C.D. Cal. 1984).

A random access memory is a memory device for efficiently storing information in which the information can be randomly accessed or retrieved at a speed independent of the physical location of the information in storage. Semiconductor RAM devices are in wide use today in a variety of electronic systems. *Digital Equipment Corp. v. Systems Industries, Inc.*, CCH Comp. Law Rep. 46,229 (D.C. Mass. 1990).

Computer memory that can be accessed randomly (without reference to any neighbouring information), usually at the level of a word of memory which, depending on the type of computer, may be from 16 bits (single binary digits) upwards in length. By contrast, information stored on disks of different types can only be accessed in larger units such as records (which may be thousands of words in length) and sometimes only sequentially. *Digital Technology and the Copyright Act 1994: A Discussion Paper, Competition and Enterprise Branch, July 2001 (New Zealand).*

Rate of Return

Rate of return regulation is intended to allow a telephone company to earn a reasonable return on its rate base (which includes investments in capital and operating expenses). Competition and Culture on Canada's Information Highway: Managing the Realities of Transition, CRTC (the "Convergence Report"), May 19, 1995.

Rate Rebalancing

Process aimed at increasing prices for local telephone service subsidized by long distance revenues and reducing subsidies paid by long distance service providers. *The Challenge of the Information Highway: Final Report of the Information Highway Advisory Council* (September 1995).

Read Disk

The act of making a request to the operating system to cause information previously stored on a disk media to be transferred into a location in main memory where it can be further processed or examined. *Delrina Corp. v. Triolet Systems, Inc.* (1992), 47 C.P.R. (3d) 1 (Ont. H.C.).

Reading

"Reading" is the instruction to the computer to retrieve data from the record. The programme specifies the order of fields, type of fields and sometimes key, all of which are derived from the file layout. Thus, whenever a programme is used to write to a data file or read from a data file, the file structure from the file layout and thus the software is necessarily used. To produce a "report," the programme "reads" a record in a data file. That "read" step requires knowledge of the file layout information as described above, e.g., order of fields, type of fields. The programme then formats the data in human readable form. To do that, data which has been encoded in the data file must be decoded. Thus, the making of a report uses the file layout. It also uses the source code. *Geac J & E Systems Ltd. v. Craig Erickson Systems Inc.* (1993), 46 C.P.R. (3d) 25 (Ont. Gen. Div.).

Real Time

"Real time" means that the processing of the input to the system (of which the computer is a part) obtains a result occurring almost simultaneously with the event generating the data. *White Consolidated Industries Inc. v. Vega Servo-Control Inc.*, 214 U.S.P.Q. 796 (S.D. Mich. 1982), affirmed 218 U.S.P.Q. 961 (Fed. Cir. 1983).

Real Time Protocol (RTP)

Is used to support streaming or transmissions that simulate real-time communications. RTP can skip packets while allowing subsequent ones to be transmitted so that the work as a whole continues to be received. *Public Performance of Musical Works* 1996-1998 (Tariff 22) (1999), 1 C.P.R. (4th) 417 (Copyright Board).

Receive

Means: (A) with respect to a copy, to take delivery; or (B) with respect to a notice: (i) to come to a person's attention; or (ii) to be delivered to and available at a location or system designated by agreement for that purpose or, in the absence of an agreed location: (I) to be delivered at the person's residence, or the person's place of business through which the contract was made, or at any other place held out by the person as a place for receipt of communications of the kind; or (II) in the case of an electronic notification, to come into existence in an information processing system in a form capable of being processed by or perceived from a system of that type by a recipient, if the recipient uses, or otherwise has designated or holds out that system or address as a place for receipt of notices of the kind and the sender does not know that the notice cannot be accessed from the particular system of the recipient. *Uniform Computer Information Transactions Act*, National Conference of Commissioners on Uniform State Laws, available at http://www.law.upenn.u/bll/ulc/ucita/citim99.htm.

Reception Equipment

Means equipment whose operation, either alone or together with other equipment, enables people to hear or see a work or other subject matter that is communicated. *Copyright Amendment (Digital Agenda) Act 2000 Australia.*

Record

A record is data in a file which relates to a particular subject. *Dickerman Associates Inc. v. Tiverton Bottled Gas Co.*, 594 F.Supp. 30 (D. Mass. 1984).

A record is a collection of related fields. *Dental Office Computer Systems Inc. v. Glutting*, No. CV-86-5613DT (Mich. App. filed August 13, 1987).

Includes any correspondence, memorandum, book, plan, map, drawing, diagram, pictorial or graphic work, photograph, film, microform, sound recording, videotape, machine-readable record and any other documentary material, regardless of physical form or characteristics, and any copy of any of those things. Ministry of Revenue Advisory Committee, Report of the Committee On Electronic Commerce, April 30, 1998, Industry Canada.

Includes a book, an account, a statement, a voucher, an invoice, a letter, a telegram, an agreement and a memorandum, whether recorded in writing or in some other manner, and whether or not some process must be applied to the record to make it readily intelligible. GST Memorandum 500-1-2 (Books and Records -Computerized Records), May 26, 1993.

Means information that is inscribed on a tangible medium or that is stored in an electronic or other medium and is retrievable in perceivable form. *Uniform Computer Information Transactions Act*, National Conference of Commissioners on Uniform State Laws, available at http://www.law.upenn.u/bll/ulc/ucita/citim99.htm.

Means information that is inscribed, stored, or otherwise fixed on a tangible medium or that is stored in an electronic or other medium and is retrievable in perceivable form. *Illinois Electronic Commerce Security Act* 1998 5 Ill. Comp. Stat. 175.

The term "record" means information that is inscribed on a tangible medium or that is stored in an electronic or other medium and is retrievable in perceivable form. *Electronic Signatures in Global and National Commerce Act*.

Means a record of information in any form and includes notes, images, audiovisual recordings, x-rays, books, documents, maps, drawings, photographs, letters, vouchers and papers and any other information that is written, photographed, recorded or stored in any manner, but does not include software or any mechanism that produces records. *Alberta, Electronic Transactions Act*, Bill 21.

Record Locking

A locking device in a multiuser computer system may involve not file locking but record locking, where two users may have simultaneous access to a file but only one may have access to a particular record at a time. There is also volume locking. *Madeley Pty Ltd. v. Touche Ross*, McGarvie, J., Aust. Fed. Ct., Dec. 21, 1989 (unreported).

Registrant

A person, company or other legal entity that has registered a domain name. *Framework for the administration of the .CA domain name system*, Canadian Domain Name Consultative Committee, September 15, 1998, available at *www.cira.ca/documents.html*

Registration Authority (RA)

An Entity which registers applicants for Keys and Certificates. RAs may have other functions or obligations specified in the CP. *The Office of the Federal Privacy Commissioner (Australia), Consultation Paper, (June 2001)*.

Registry

The organization that is responsible for setting policy, managing and operating a top-level domain. *Framework for the administration of the .CA domain name system*, Canadian Domain Name Consultative Committee, September 15, 1998, available at *www.cira.ca/documents.html*

Release

A "release" is a version of a software and is subject to "upgrade", i.e., replacement by a higher-numbered, more powerful replacement. *Hosiery Corporation of America, Inc. v. International Data Processing, Inc.*, 1991 U.S. Dis. Lexis 2501 (D.C.N.J. 1991).

Reliability

The ability of a computer or an information or telecommunications system to perform consistently and precisely according to its specifications and design requirements and to do so with high confidence. *Cryptography's Role in Securing the Information Society*, United States National Research Council, 1996.

Relying Party

Is a person who acts in reliance on a Certificate signed by a Certification Authority to verify a digital signature or to encrypt communications to the certificate subject. Public Key Infrastructure Management in the Government of Canada, Treasury Board of Canada Secretariat, May 27, 1999, available at http://www.tbs-sct.gc.ca/pubs_pol/ciopubs/PKI/pki1_e.html.

The recipient of an electronic communication or other person using that communication who will rely on a certificate as part of a process of authenticating the identity of the originator of the communication. UNCITRAL Report of the Working Group on Electronic Commerce, September 18-29, 2000, A/CN. 94/483.

An individual or entity that receives a digitally signed message and wishes to rely on the contents of that message as binding the signer. *The Office of the Federal Privacy Commissioner (Australia), Consultation Paper, (June 2001).*

Remailer

A computer-based process that automatically redistributes electronic mail, often to multiple recipients. Remailers can be anonymous (i.e., they can be configured to strip off information identifying the sender of a message, while still enabling a return "path" so that recipients can reply to messages). *Cryptography's Role in Securing the Information Society*, United States National Research Council, 1996.

Remote Access Data Processing Service

An offering of data processing wherein communications facilities, linking a central computer to remote customer terminals, provide a vehicle for the transmission of data between such computer and customer terminals. Computer Inquiry (Tentative Decision), 28 F.C.C.2d 291 (F.C.C. 1970); Computer Inquiry (Final Decision), 28 F.C.C.2d 267 (F.C.C. 1971).

Remote Access Device

Devices used to access a host computer. Dataspeed 40/4, 52 F.C.C.2d 21 (F.C.C. 1977).

Remote File Access

Use of high-speed channel-to-channel data transfer interfaces. *IBM v. Fujitsu Ltd.*, Copyright L.R. (CCH) 20,517 (Am. Arbtn. Assoc. Comm. Arbtn. Trib. 1988).

Repository

Means a system for storing and retrieving certificates or other information relevant to certificates, including information relating to the status of a certificate. *Illinois Electronic Commerce Security Act* 1998 5 Ill. Comp. Stat. 175.

A computer-based system for storing and retrieving certificates and other messages relevant to ensuring a message. General Usage for International Digitally Insured Commerce (Guidec), International Chamber of Commerce, 1997, available at http://www.icc.wbo.org/guidec2.htm.

Is a system for storing and accessing certificates or other information relevant to certificates. The Government of Canada Public Key Infrastructure repository is an X.500 directory. Public Key Infrastructure Management in the Government of Canada, Treasury Board of Canada Secretariat, May 27, 1999, available at http://www.tbs-sct.gc.ca/pubs_pol/ciopubs/PKI/pki1_e.html.

Reproducing

Reproducing means routing, memorizing, storing, hosting, logging, mirroring, encoding, digitalizing, uploading, downloading, browsing and any other digital recording of a work. Statement of Proposed Royalties to be Collected by SOD-RAC for the Reproduction, in Canada, of Musical Works in the Exploitation of an Electronic Network for the Years 1999 and 2000.

Resale

Is the subsequent sale or lease on a commercial basis, with or without adding value, of communications services or facilities leased from a carrier. Interexchange Competition and Related Issues, Telecom Decision CRTC 85-19, Aug. 25, 1985 (Decision 85-19).

Research and Development Services

Include the acquisition of specialized expertise for the purposes of increasing knowledge in science; applying increased scientific knowledge or exploiting the potential of scientific discoveries and improvements in technology to advance the state of art; and systematically using increases in scientific knowledge and advances in state of art to design, develop, test, or evaluate new products or services. North American Free Trade Agreement between Canada, Mexico and the United States, Appendix 1001.1b-2-B.

Resolution

The number of dots or *pixels* used on the screen by a computer to display images. Monopolies and Mergers Commission — Video Games: A report on the supply of video games in the UK (LONDON: HMSO Cm2781).

Resource

"A resource can be anything that has identity. Familiar examples include an electronic document, an image, a service (e.g., 'today's weather report for Los Angeles'), and a collection of other resources.... The resource is the conceptual mapping to an entity or set of entities, not necessarily the entity which corresponds to that mapping at any particular instance in time. Thus, a resource can remain constant even when its content—-the entities to which it currently corresponds—-changes over time, provided that the conceptual mapping is not changed in the process." *XML-Signature Syntax and Processing, W3C Recommendation 12 February 2002.*

Response Time

The time between the last keystroke made by the operator and the first listing displayed on the CRT. *Hawaiian Telephone Co. v. Microform Data Systems Inc., 829 F.2d 919 (9th Cir. 1987).*

Response time is the amount of time between entry of a command into the system and the appearance on the screen of the requested output. *USM Corp. v. Arthur D. Little Systems, Inc., 546 N.E. 2d 888 (Mass. App. 1989).*

Retransmitter

Means a person who performs a function comparable to that of a cable retransmission system, but does not include a new media retransmitter. *Bill C-48, An Act to Amend the Copyright Act, June 18, 2002.*

Retransmission

In relation to a broadcast, means a retransmission of the broadcast, where: (a) the content of the broadcast is unaltered (even if the technique used to achieve retransmission is different to the technique used to achieve the original transmission); and (b) either: (i) in any case—the retransmission is simultaneous with the original transmission; or (ii) if the retransmission is in an area that has, wholly or partly, different local time to the area of the original transmission—the retransmission is delayed until no later than the equivalent local time. *Copyright Amendment (Digital Agenda) Act 2000 Australia.*

Reverse Engineering, Decompiling, or Disassembling

It involves starting with a known product and working backwards to discover the process by which it was developed and manufactured; in the context of the semiconductor industry, it includes the purchase of several computer chips of a competitor, stripping layers, photographing the circuitry of each layer through a microscope, dissecting the chip to discover the actual layout design and then drawing inferences about the technical process used to make the device. *People v. Gopal*, 217 Cal. Reptr. 487 (Ct. App. 1985).

Is defined as "any process by which computer software is converted from one form to another form which is more readily understandable to human beings, including without limitation, any decoding or decrypting of any computer program which has been encoded or encrypted in any manner." L.A. Rev. Stat. Ann. No. 51:1962 (3), referred to in *Vault Corp. v. Quaid Software Ltd.*, 655 F.2d 750 (E.D. L.A. 1987), affirmed 847 F.2d 255 (5th Cir. 1988).

Reverse engineering is the process of starting with a finished product and working backwards to analyze how the product operates or how it was made. *Secure Services Technology, Inc. v. Time and Space Processing Inc.*, 772 F.Supp. 1354 (E.D.Va. 1989).

Reverse engineering is the process by which a person takes a legitimately acquired item, disassembles it to learn its component parts, and from that process determines how the product is manufactured. *Motorola Inc. v. Computer Displays International Inc.*, 222 U.S.P.Q. 844 (7th Cir. 1984).

Reverse engineering is starting with a known product and working backward to find the method by which the item was developed. *Minuteman, Inc. v. L.D. Alexander, George Cash and Amity, Inc.*, 1 CCH Comp. Cases 46,024 (Sup. Crt. Wisconsin 1989).

Reverse engineering involves going backwards from a finished product and determining how the program works. One method of reverse engineering involves the use of disassemblers, which allows someone to convert object code into a form more easily read by people. *Sega Enterprises Ltd. v. Accolade Inc.*, 23 U.S.Q.D. 1440 (N.D. Cal. 1992).

Reverse engineering is simply a short hand way to describe the process of creating a new mask work based on a competitor's existing product, through a process of "substantial study and analysis", in contrast to "plagiarism accomplished without such study and analysis." *Intel Corporation v. Advanced Micro Device Inc.*, Comp.Ind.Lit.Reptr. 14,861 (N.D. Cal. 1992).

Reverse engineering . . . [is] a process of engineering backwards from the source code to reconstruct the design functions on which the code was originally based. *Prism Hospital Software Inc. v. Hospital Medical Records Institute*, 18 C.P.R. (3d) 398 (B.C.S.C.).

The study or analysis of a computer product (including a computer program) in order to reveal the underlying idea or principle on which it operates. This analysis may include an examination of relevant published documentation, study of the operation of the product and, in the case of a computer programs, their decompilation. Studying the operation of a program would involve reproduction of the program in the same way as normal use. Computer Software Protection: Australia, Copyright Law Review Committee 1995.

Revoke a Certificate

Means to permanently end the operational period of a certificate from a specified time forward. *Illinois Electronic Commerce Security Act* 1998 5 Ill. Comp. Stat. 175.

The act of a certifier in declaring a public key certificate permanently invalid from a specified time forward. General Usage for International Digitally Insured Commerce (Guidec), International Chamber of Commerce, 1997, available at http://www.icc.wbo.org/guidec2.htm.

RFP

Request for Proposal. *Mesa Business Equipment Inc. v. Ultimate Southern California Inc.*, Vol. 8, No. 1 C.L.R. 168 (U.S. Bky. Crt. 1988).

Roamer

A cellular telephone user who is a customer of a system in a market outside of the local cellular telephone system who accesses the local system while present in the area. *United States v. Brady*, 820 F.Supp. 1346 (C.D. Utah 1993).

Robot (Software Robot)

A software robot is a computer program which operates across the Internet to perform searching, copying and retrieving functions on the websites of others. A software robot is capable of executing thousands of instructions per minute, far in excess of what a human can accomplish. *eBay v. Bidder's Edge Inc.*, 54 U.S.P.Q. 2d 1798 (N.D. Cal. 2000).

Robot Exclusion Headers

A Robot Exclusion Header is a message sent to computers programmed to detect and respond to such headers that [the entity employing] does not permit unauthorized robotic activity. Programmers who wish to comply with the Robot Exclusion Standard design the robots to read a particular data file "robots.txt" and to comply with the control directives it contains. *eBay v. Bidder's Edge Inc.*, 54 U.S.P.Q. 2d 1798 (N.D. Cal. 2000).

ROM (Read-Only Memory)

Read-Only Memory. *IBM Corp. v. Ordinateurs Spirales Inc.* (1984), 2 C.I.P.R. 56 (Fed. T.D.); *Apple Computer Inc. v. Mackintosh Computers Ltd.* (1986), 28 D.L.R. (4th) 178 (Fed. T.D.).

ROM chips are permanent storage devices designed to plug into printed circuit boards within computers. The devices are generic in the sense that they are manufactured in a raw state. The raw state includes circuitry within the chip, known as decoders, designed to locate areas of memory storage therein and deliver the contents thereof to the microprocessor. ROM's, by their very name (Read-Only Memories), are specialized chips designed to act as storage media for programs or data. They are permanent in the sense that any programs and data encoded therein reside therein whether or not power is turned on or off. The programs and data contained therein are readable by computers, and the contents thereof can be displayed or printed in various languages by a computer. *Apple Computer Inc. v. Mackintosh Computers Ltd.* (1986), 28 D.L.R. (4th) 178 (Fed. T.D.).

A ROM product is a memory device in which information is permanently stored. This device is distinguishable from a RAM (Random-Access Memory) in that in a RAM the stored information may be continuously changed even as the device is in operation. In a ROM memory a fixed pattern of signals or program is placed within the device by the manufacturer and not the customer. This is sometimes referred to as mask programmed. *Intel Corp. v. Radiation Inc.*, 184 U.S.P.Q. 54 (T.T.A.B. 1974).

Is a type of memory that is permanently structured, through having been permanently etched with electric circuits, to carry a particular program, which can subsequently be read (by way of contrast with RAM or Random-Access Memory, which is erased when the power is turned off). ROM circuits consist of interconnected transistors built in and of the silicon. Their pattern cannot be discerned by the human eye except with the aid of an electron microscope. *Apple Computer Inc. v. Mackintosh Computers Ltd.* (1986), 28 D.L.R. (4th) 178 (Fed. T.D.).

Is an internal permanent memory device consisting of a semiconductor chip which is incorporated into the circuitry of the computer. *Apple Computer Inc. v. Franklin Computer Corp.*, 215 U.S.P.Q. 935 (E.D.Pa. 1982), reversed 714 F.2d 1240 (3rd Cir. 1983), cert dismissed 104 S.Ct. 690 (1984).

A silicon chip that contains thousands of connected electrical circuits. It is called a read-only memory chip because it can only be read. When one is created, the object program is recorded on the blank silicon chip in such a way that minute fusible connectors in the chip are burned out. The recording of the program in this manner is virtually irreversible. ROMs are thus a permanent storage medium that may be contrasted with RAM (Random-Access Memory) chips, in which the information stored in the chip is lost when the power is turned off. *IBM Corp. v. Computer Imports Ltd.*, N.Z. H.C., Smellie J., March 21, 1989 (unreported).

ROMS are customized chips. *Apple Computer Inc. v. 115778 Can. Inc.* (1988), 23 C.P.R. (3d) 22 (Fed. T.D.).

ROM is nothing other than a means of storage of spiritual fruit and labour of the artist who wrote the software, by means of which the work can be executed and used. The ROM is, in fact, a memory unit that facilitates the reading of the software, while serving for storage, and forms the expression of the software that was written on the paper, and enables the creator of the software to express it by means of a machine that is called a "computer." The ROM is identical to the status of a sheet of paper upon which the program is written, only that instead of inscribing it on a sheet of paper with pen and ink, it is assembled within the ROM; because it is inscribed therein in a new form of writing, our minds, apparently, find difficulty in grasping the concept. *Apple Computer Inc. v. New-Com Technologies Ltd.* (1986), 8 I.P.R. 353 (Israel Dist. Ct. Tel Aviv).

ROMS or "mask ROMS" are the cheapest type of memory storage device in integrated circuit form. The data is contained in an arrangement of the circuit layout within the ROM. The particular computer program to be encoded is delivered to a manufacturer of ROMS that then prepares a circuit layout or "mask" which incorporates the data concerned, and manufactures quantities of the mask ROM containing the particular circuit layout. Mask ROMS are generally used when the program to be stored is simple and to be utilized in mass-produced consumer products. *Avel Pty Ltd. v. Jonathan Wells* (1992), 22 I.P.R. 305 (Aust. H.C.).

A ROM ("read only memory") chip retains stored data when unpowered or even removed from the microcomputer. It is specially produced with internal link points, either connected or not, thus defining the desired pattern of stored data at the time of manufacture. Accordingly, when it was necessary to produce ROM chips for a particular game, the relevant appellant would supply details of desired data pattern to the ROM manufacturer who would incorporate this information in the manufacturing specification for that batch of ROM chips. *Avel Pty Ltd. v. Wells* (1992), 23 I.P.R. 353 (Aust. Fed. C.A.).

Root server system

The database used to match domain names to their equivalent numerical addresses in order to route data on the Internet. *Domain Name System Reform and Related Internet Governance Issues: A Consultation Paper*, Industry Canada available at *www.strategis.gc.ca*

Router

Devices used to receive and forward packets are known as routers. A router retains information for as little time as possible before forwarding it to the next router or the destination computer. *Public Performance of Musical Works* 1996-1998 (Tariff 22) (1999), 1 C.P.R. (4th) 417 (Copyright Board).

Routine or Subroutine

A routine or subroutine is a program or set of instructions with a beginning and a defined end, which can be invoked at its beginning and will always return to its end after performing a given function between those two points. An example is a square root routine which will calculate the square root of a number when it is started and will produce the answer when it returns at its end. *Jostens Inc. v. National Computer Systems Inc.*, 318 N.W.2d 691 (Minn. Sup. Ct. 1982).

A subroutine is basically a discrete part of a program with a readily identifiable task. *Pearl Systems Inc. v. Competition Electronics Inc.*, 8 U.S.P.Q.2d 1520 (U.S.D.C.S.D. Fl. 1988).

Routines are so-called program functions with a certain sequence of commands. *Amsdos*, Munich Dist. Ct., August 29, 1985, English translation in 17 IIC 691.

RPC

Regional Playback Control. Australia Copyright Law Review Committee, Copyright and Contract, October 8, 2002

RSA

RSA algorithm is an asymmetric crptographic algorithm invented by Rivest, Shamir and Adleman. Security and Electronic Authorization and Authentication Guideline, Communications Security Establishment, Government of Canada September 1995, CID/01/15.

Rule

Means a special rule on how to use, in a given program, a programming language. Japanese Amended Copyright Law.

SAM (Simultaneous-Access Memory)

Simultaneous-Access Memory. *Intel Corp. v. Radiation Inc.*, 184 U.S.P.Q. 54 (T.T.A.B. 1974).

Sampling

Where users make temporary copies of the work before purchasing. *A & M Records Inc. v. Napster Inc.*, 57 U.S.P.Q. 2d 1729 (9th Cir.2001).

Satellites

Devices used to receive transmitted signals from a site such as telephone calls or TV feeds and retransmit them to another site in some other location. Satellites perform this function using a transponder, which is a combination receiver-transmitter. Most communications satellites are of the geostationary type, meaning they appear to be in a fixed location about 36,000 km above the equator. Different satellites are designed to operate in different frequency ranges. The two most common types being used in North America are "C" band and "Ku" band satellites. C band is the most common, using a frequency of 6GHz for uplinking and 4GHz for downlinking (the frequencies must be different for each function so they don't interfere with each other) while Ku band satellites use 14GHz to uplink and 12 GHz to downlink. Satellite technology is advancing to the point where signals can be provided directly to individual homes. Satellites broadcasting directly to households are known as Direct-to-Home (DTH) satellites. Submission of the Director of Investigation and Research to the CRTC Re Public Notice CRTC 1994-130.

Satellite Master Antenna Television (SMATV)

This refers to a privately operated cable system whereby signals are taken from satellites by a large dish antenna, then distributed to a limited numbers of subscribers. A typical application would be in large apartment blocks. Submission of the Director of Investigation and Research to the CRTC Re Public Notice CRTC 1994-130.

Satellite Telecommunication System

Means a complete telecommunication system consisting of two or more commercial radio stations situated on land, water or aircraft, in this Act referred to as "earth stations", and one or more radio stations situated on a satellite in space, in this Act referred to as "satellite stations", in which at least one earth station is capable of transmitting signs, signals, writing, images, or sounds, or intelligence of any nature to a satellite station that is in turn capable of receiving or retransmitting those signs, signals, writing, images or sounds, or intelligence of any nature for reception by one or more earth stations. *Telesat Canada Act*, R.S.C. 1985, c. T-6.

Scrambling

The practice of making an electronic signal carrying television programming unintelligible except to viewers equipped with a decoding device known as a "descrambler". A descrambler uses an electronic "key" to decode the signals. The purpose is to protect the distributor's revenue by ensuring that only those who have paid for the service receive clear signals. The practice is also known as "encryption". Submission of the Director of Investigation and Research to the CRTC Re Public Notice CRTC 1994-130.

Scratchpad Register (Scratchpad Memory)

A scratchpad register is a plurality of multibit storage locations, usually located in the central processing unit (CPU) of a computer, used for temporary storage of program information, operands, and calculation results for use by the computer's arithmetic and logic unit, and other information of a temporary nature. *In Re Bradley*, 600 F.2d 807 (Cust. & Pat. App. 1979), affirmed 450 U.S. 381 (1981).

Screen Shot

A video game screen shot is a small image depicting the computer or television screen in a frozen moment during the playing of the video game. The cinematic equivalent of a screen shot would be a depiction of one single frame from a movie. *Sony Computer Entertain America v. Bleem Ltd.,* 54 U.S.P.Q. 2d 1753 (9th Cir. 2000).

Screen Name

Means the name you call yourself when you communicate online. You may want to abbreviate your name or make up a name. Your ISP may allow you to use several screen names. Federal Trade Commission and the National Association of Attorneys General -Cyberspeak - Learning the Language.

Scrolling

Scrolling is a form of switching the screen from one image to the next by adding one new line and subtracting one other at the top or bottom or at the sides of the scrolled image. *Apple Computer Inc. v. Microsoft Corp.*, 1992 U.S. Dist. LEXIS 12219 (N.D. Cal. 1992).

Search Engine

A number of "search engines", such as Yahoo, Magellan, Alta Vista, WebCrawler and Lycos, are available to help users navigate the worldwide web. *Shea v. Reno*, 1996 U.S. Dist. LEXIS 10720 (S.D.N.Y. 1996).

A function that lets you search for information and web sites. Using a search engine is like accessing the main card file in a library, only easier. A few keywords can lead you almost anywhere on the Internet. You can find search engines or a search function on many web sites. Federal Trade Commission and the National Association of Attorneys General - Cyberspeak - Learning the Language.

Because the internet contains an almost infinite number of webpages, internet search engines provide a critical tool for internet users. Without search engines, internet users would be unable to locate all but the most obvious websites. Search engines generally use algorithms to assess the relevance of websites to a search query by, among other things, looking at the words used on the site. *Playboy Enterprises, Inc. vs. Netscape Communications Corp.* SA CV 99-320 A.H.S. (C.D.Cal. July 27, 1999).

Search engines are popular Web-retrieval tools that match a search query submitted by an Internet user with the website whose content best corresponds to the submitted search terms. *Northern Light Technology, Inc. v. Northern Lights Club*, (1st Cir. Jan. 8, 2001).

A database of Web documents that are catalogued (usually by a fully automated procedure) and can be retrieved according to words in the text or other information contained within the document. Websites often include a search engine and there are many sites that specialise in automated catalogues of Web documents. *Digital Technology and the Copyright Act 1994: A Discussion Paper, Competition and Enterprise Branch, July 2001 (New Zealand).*

Search engines are databases that list most sites accessible on the Web. The user simply types a key word or words as a "search" request and the search engine then returns a list (usually in the form of hyperlinks) of various sites that contain one or more of the search terms. *National A-1 Advertising, Inc. et al v. Networks Solutions, Inc.*, Civ. No. 99-033-M (D.N.Hamp. Sept. 28, 2000).

Search Results Pages

Web pages that contain the list of websites generated by a search engine are called the "search results pages". *Playboy Enterprises, Inc. vs. Netscape Communications Corp.*, SA CV 99-320 A.H.S. (C.D.Cal. July 27, 1999).

Second Level Domain Name (SLD)

A second-level domain name is nothing more than a more convenient way for humans to navigate to the appropriate IP address of a particular entity connected to the Internet. *National A-1 Advertising, Inc. et al v. Networks Solutions, Inc.*, Civ. No. 99-033-M (D.N.Hamp. Sept. 28, 2000).

That portion of the domain name that appears immediately to the left of the top level domain. For example, the "yourbusiness" in *www.yourbusiness.ca. Domain Name System Reform and Related Internet Governance Issues: A Consultation Paper*, Industry Canada available at *www.strategis.gc.ca*

Second-Sourcing

A computer manufacturer will gamble millions in a new and untested computer to enter a fiercely competitive, ever changing market. For this the manufacturer must have a reliable supply of component parts; and this is particularly so if, for example, he or she is designing a new computer around a new micro-processor. The manufacturer is much better off if he or she has an alternate source of supply for this item. Consequently, a semi-conductor manufacturer who is seeking a "design win" for a newly developed product may well want to bolster its chances by providing a second source for the product. This idea of second-sourcing is common in the industry. In return for a negotiated royalty, a developing company will license to a non-developing company enough know-how to permit the non-developing company to produce the developing company's product to the performance specifications of the latter. Both companies are then free to sell the product in competition with each other in the market. Theoretically, everyone profits: the developing company has a second source so its customers feel more secure, the non-developing company has a new chip to sell without investing the necessary millions for its development, the customer enjoys lower prices because the competition of the two sellers, and the overall market for the product is enlarged. *Advanced Micro Devices, Inc. and Intel Corp.*, CCH Comp. Cases 60,218 (Arb. Award. 1990).

Secret Key

A cryptographic key used with a secret key cryptographic algorithm, uniquely associated with one or more entities, and which shall not be made public. The use of the term "secret" in this context does not imply a classification level, rather the term implies the need to protect the key from disclosure or substitution. "Security Requirements for Cryptographic Modules", FIPS Pub. 140-1, Federal Information Processing Standards Publication, January 11, 1994, available at http://csrc.nist.gov/fips/fips1401.htm.

A cryptographic algorithm that uses a single, secret key for both encryption and decryption. "Security Requirements for Cryptographic Modules", FIPS Pub. 140-1, Federal Information Processing Standards Publication, January 11, 1994, available at http://csrc.nist.gov/fips/fips1401.htm.

Secret Key Cryptography

A form of cryptography which uses the same key to encrypt and decrypt. Also called "symmetric cryptography". A Cryptology Policy Framework for Electronic Commerce, Task Force on Electronic Commerce, Industry Canada, February 1998.

Secure Electronic Signature

Means an electronic signature that results from the application of a technology or process prescribed by regulations made under subsection 48(1). *Personal Information Protection and Electronic Documents Act*, S.C. 2000 C.5.

Secured Facility Regime

Provides an integrated and strictly monitored preventative approach to resolving disputes with respect to the use of one party's information in the other party's software development process. *IBM v. Fujitsu Ltd.*, Copyright L.R. (CCH) 20,517 (Am. Arbtn. Assoc. Comm. Arbtn. Trib. 1988).

Secure Gateway

A secure gateway (or Trusted Guard) goes beyond the function of a firewall in that not only does it act as a firewall but has added features involving looking into each packet of information passing through it to or from an authorized user to ensure that no unauthorized information is enclosed in the packet. Current technology limits this to e-mail or EDI because specific information would reside in a specific format in a specific location. Artificial intelligence must become much more advanced before this feature would be able to address general communications packets. An unsecured gateway may be thought of simply as an access point to a computer system. *A Survey of Legal Issues Relating to the Security of Electronic Information*, Department of Justice, Canada.

Security Procedure

Means a procedure employed for the purpose of verifying that an electronic signature, record, or performance is that of a specific person or for detecting changes or errors in the information in an electronic record. The term includes a procedure that requires the use of algorithms or other codes, identifying words or numbers, encryption, or callback or other acknowledgment procedures. *Uniform Electronic Transactions Act*, National Conference of Commissioners on Uniform State Laws, July 29, 1999.

Semiconductor (Product or Integrated Circuit)

Means a circuit in which the active elements, interconnections, and any passive elements are integrally formed in and/or on a semiconductor substrate and which is intended to perform an electronic function. Draft Treaty on the Protection of Intellectual Property in respect of Integrated Circuits, WIPO Geneva, IPIC/CE/II/2, March 17, 1986.

A semiconductor is one of a class of materials (such as silicon) whose electrical conductivity falls between that of a conductor (metal) and that of an insulator. *Sperry Rand Corp. v. Rothlein*, 241 F.Supp. 549 (D. Conn. 1964).

A semiconductor chip product is the final or intermediate form of any product (a) having two or more layers of metallic, insulating, or semiconductor material, deposited or otherwise placed on, or etched away or otherwise removed from, a piece of semiconductor material in accordance with a pre-determined pattern; and (b) intended to perform electronic functions. United States Copyright Act, 17 U.S.C. 101, c. 9.

The final or an intermediate form of any product: (i) consisting of a body of material which includes a layer of semiconducting material; and (ii) having one or more other layers composed of conducting, insulating or semiconducting material, the layers being arranged in accordance with a pre-determined three-dimensional pattern; and (iii) intended to perform, exclusively or together with other functions, an electronic function. European Economic Community Council Directive 87/54/EEC (OJ No. L.24, 27.1.87).

An article the purpose, or one of the purposes, of which is the performance of an electronic function and which consists of two or more layers, at least one of which is composed of semiconducting material and in or upon one or more of which is fixed a pattern appertaining to that or another function, The Semiconductor Products (Protection of Topography) Regulations 1987 (U.K., SI 1987/1497).

Means a circuit in which the active elements, interconnections, and any passive elements are integrally formed in and/or on a semiconductor substrate and which is intended to perform an electronic function. Draft Treaty on the Protection of Intellectual Property in respect of integrated Circuits, WIPO Geneva, IPIC/CE/II/2, March 17, 1986.

Send

Means, with any costs provided for and properly addressed or directed as reasonable under the circumstances or as otherwise agreed, to (i) deposit in the mail or with a commercially reasonable carrier, (ii) deliver for transmission to or re-creation in another location or system, or (iii) take the steps necessary to initiate transmission to or re-creation in another location or system. In addition, with respect to an electronic message, the term means to initiate operations that in the ordinary course will cause the record to come into existence in an information processing system in a form capable of being processed by or perceived from a system of that type by the recipient, if the recipient uses or otherwise has designated or held out that system or address as a place for the receipt of communi-cations of the kind. Receipt within the time in which it would have arrived if properly sent has the effect of a proper sending. *Uniform Computer Information Transactions Act*, National Conference of Commissioners on Uniform State Laws, available at http://www.law.upenn.u/bll/ulc/ucita/citim99.htm.

Server

A computer whose purpose is to receive, organize and retrieve information quickly. It contains a storage system (usually a hard disk), high speed input and output connections, and a program that keeps track of information in the system. Submission of the Director of Investigation and Research to the CRTC Re Public Notice CRTC 1994-130.

A "server", short for "file server" is a "computer in a network that stores appli-cation programs and data files accessed by the other computers in the network." *American Eyewear, Inc. v. Peeper's Sunglasses and Accessories, Inc.*, 2000 U.S. Dist. LEXIS 6875 (D. Tex. May 16, 2000).

Computers known as "servers" store these documents and make them available over the Internet through "TCP/IP" (Transmission Control Protocol/Internet Pro-tocol), a set of standard operating and transmission protocols that structure the Web's operation. *DoubleClick Inc. Privacy Litigation* Civ. 0641 (N.R.V.) (S.D.N.Y. Mar. 28, 2001).

Service Bureau (Bureau Service)

A service bureau is a company that uses its own computer system to process applications for customers who do not have computer systems. *Accusystems Inc. v. Honeywell Information Systems Inc.*, 580 F.Supp. 474 (S.D.N.Y. 1984).

A computer facility maintained by someone else. *Mackenzie Patten & Co. v. British Olivetti Ltd.* (1984), 48 M.L.R. 344 (Q.B.D.).

An organization that leases or sells computer time, manpower, or other compu-tational support to the public. *Systems Development Corp. v. United States*, 531 F.2d 529 (U.S. Crt. Claims 1976).

An organization that leases or sells computer time, manpower, or other compu-tational support to the public. *Systems Development Corp. v. United States*, 531 F.2d 529 (U.S. Ct. Claims 1976).

Service Provider

Means (a) any public or private entity that provides to users of its service the ability to communicate by means of a computer system, and (b) any other entity that processes or stores computer data on behalf of such communication service or users of such service. *Committee of Experts on Crime in Cyb-Space, Draft Convention on Cyber Crime (PC-CY)*.

Means a person who owns or operates a transmission facility that is used by that person or another person to provide telecommunications services to the public in

Canada. *Lawful Access – Consultation Document, Depart. of Justice, Industry Canada, August 25, 2002.*

Session Key

An encryption key which may be used for only a single session and then destroyed; sometimes called a "transaction key." For connection-oriented protocols (such as those in real-time communications), a session key is generally used only for the length that the connection is open (unless the connection time is long enough to warrant more than one session key). A new session key is generated for each new session (for example, each time one made a secure telephone call, a different session key would be generated). In many E-mail implementations which employ both public key cryptography and secret key cryptography, the term "session key" is sometimes used to describe the symmetric key that has been generated to encrypt that specific document. In this instance, the symmetric key would likely be encrypted with the recipient's public key to facilitate key exchange. A Cryptology Policy Framework for Electronic Commerce, Task Force on Electronic Commerce, Industry Canada, February 1998.

Set

The word "set" can have very many different meanings. In the context of the definition of "computer program" and "a set of instructions" the word connotes the concept of a number or a group and in particular is used to identify such a number or group whether small or large. A computer program, of necessity, means the expression of a set of instructions. *Autodesk Australia Pty Ltd. v. Dyason* (1989), 15 I.P.R. 1 (Aus. Fed. Ct.), reversed [1990] A.I.P.C. 36,446 (Aus. Fed. Ct. FC).

A number of things customarily used together or forming a complete assortment, outfit, or collection: a set of dishes. *Autodesk Australia Pty Ltd. v. Dyason*, supra.

Shared ATM and Network

Shared ATM and Networks are relatively sophisticated businesses whose function is to deliver banking services at a variety of locations, both during and after normal banking hours, without the need for a human teller. *Plus System, Inc. v. New England Network, Inc.*, 804 F.Supp. 111 (D. Col. 1992).

Shareware

Programs which have been made available for users to reproduce and use free of charge subject to certain conditions. Typical conditions that apply to shareware are that it is freely transferable to other users provided that after a specified period the user(s) cease to use it or make a payment to the copyright owner. Computer Software Protection: Australia, Copyright Law Review Committee 1995.

Shareware is software which a user is permitted to download and use for a trial, after which the user is asked to pay a fee to the author for continued use. *Zippo*

Manufacturing Company v. Zippo Dot Com, Inc., 952 F.Supp. 1119 (W.D.Penn. 1997).

Sharing

Is the use by two or more persons, in an arrangement not involving resale, of communications services or facilities leased from a carrier. Interexchange Competition and Related Issues, Telecom Decision CRTC 85-19, Aug. 25, 1985 (Decision 85-19).

Sharing Group

Means a group of persons engaged in sharing. Tariff Revisions Related to Resale and Sharing, Telecom Decision CRTC 87-2 (Feb. 12, 1987).

Shrink-wrap license

A license concerning the use of a copyright work that includes pre-drafted terms and conditions of sale that consumers are required to agree before unpacking and using the work, usually a software product. These terms and conditions, which are almost always non-negotiable, are usually displayed on a piece of paper that can be read through shrink-wrap packaging. By breaching the shrink-wrap of the packaging, a consumer is deemed by the copyright owner to have agreed to the terms and conditions of use. *Digital Technology and the Copyright Act 1994: A Discussion Paper, Competition and Enterprise Branch, July 2001 (New Zealand).*

Shrink Wrapped

"Shrink wrapped" is a term used to describe licenses and contracts which are enclosed with prepackaged software and which contain a notice whose operative message is: "Opening this package constitutes agreement to the terms and conditions of a legally binding agreement stated below. If you do not agree to these terms and conditions, then do not open the package." National Information Infrastructure: A Preliminary Draft of the Report of the Working Group on Intellectual Property Rights, July 1994.

Shrinking

In relation to computer chips, shrinking is significantly different from "reverse engineering." Instead of the "reverse designer" making an evaluation or analysis with a view to understanding the design and then creating his own design, shrinking essentially involves a computer scaling operation and no intellectual or unique design work is carried out. When a module is shrunk from one technology (bearing in mind manufacturer's design rules and/or line widths), the betraying factor is that each transistor is still in its same location with the same connections made to it, going to the same locations. This process requires no detailed knowledge of the circuit design (though a detailed analysis could be done after the event). The practice is performed by numerous companies who design their own chips. Two reasons a company might do this are: to increase the speed of the device (shrinking the line width has the effect of increasing speed); or to make the chip from another manufacturer (the first or primary manufacturer may go out of business, or start charging too much for the chip). *Nintendo Co. Ltd. v. Centronics Systems Pty Ltd.* (1992), 23 I.P.R. 119 (Aust. Fed. Ct.).

Signalling

Signalling is the functional process of identifying and setting up calls within the telephone network. Competition and Culture on Canada's Information Highway: Managing the Realities of Transition, CRTC (the "Convergence Report"), May 19, 1995.

Signal Processing

This refers to any changes effected to electrical signals by devices such as amplifiers, TV sets, etc., in order to convey information or execute some task. Submission of the Director of Investigation and Research to the CRTC Re Public Notice CRTC 1994-130.

Comprises the use of processing operations in applications which maintain the information content of an electrical signal. These include signal detection and regeneration and the adaptive equalization of transmission channels. Second Computer Inquiry (Supplemental Notice), 42 Fed. Reg. 13029 (F.C.C. 1977).

Signal processing comprises the use of computers in applications which maintain the information content of an electrical signal. These include signal detection and regeneration, and the adaptive equalization of transmission channels. Second Computer Inquiry (Notice of Inquiry), 5 C.L.S.R. 1381 (F.C.C. 1976).

Signatory

Means a person who creates an electronic signature. Proposal for A European Parliament and Council Directive on a Common Framework for Electronic Signatures, COM (1998) 297 Final.

Signature

Formally speaking, a value generated from the application of a private key to a message via a cryptographic algorithm such that it has the properties of *integrity, message authentication* and/or *signer authentication*. A signature may be (non-exclusively) described as detached, enveloping or enveloped. *XML-Signature Syntax and Processing, W3C Recommendation 12 February 2002.*

Signature includes any method used for identifying the originator of a message and indicating that the information contained in the message is attributable to the originator. *UNCITRAL, Working Group IV (Electronic Commerce), Thirty-ninth session New York, 11-15 March, 2002.*

Signature, Application

An application that implements the MANDATORY (REQUIRED/MUST) portions of this specification; these conformance requirements are over application behavior, the structure of the Signature element type and its children (including SignatureValue) and the specified algorithms. *XML-Signature Syntax and Processing, W3C Recommendation 12 February 2002.*

Signature Creation Device

Means unique data, such as codes or private cryptographic keys, or a uniquely configured physical device which is used by the signatory in creating an electronic signature. Proposal for A European Parliament and Council Directive on a Common Framework for Electronic Signatures, COM (1998) 297 Final.

Signature, Detached

The signature is over content external to the Signature element, and can be identified via a URI or transform. Consequently, the signature is "detached" from the content it signs. This definition typically applies to separate data objects, but it also includes the instance where the Signature and data object reside within the same XML document but are sibling elements *XML-Signature Syntax and Processing, W3C Recommendation 12 February 2002.*

Signature Device

Means unique information, such as codes, algorithms, letters, numbers, private keys, or personal identification numbers (PINs), or a uniquely configured physical device, that is required, alone or in conjunction with other information or devices, in order to create an electronic signature attributable to a specific person. *Illinois Electronic Commerce Security Act* 1998 5 Ill. Comp. Stat. 175.

Signature, Enveloping

The signature is over content found within an Object element of the signature itself. The Object (or its content) is identified via a Reference (via a URI fragment identifier or transform). *XML-Signature Syntax and Processing, W3C Recommendation 12 February 2002.*

Signature, Enveloped

The signature is over the XML content that contains the signature as an element. The content provides the root XML document element. Obviously, enveloped signatures must take care not to include their own value in the calculation of the SignatureValue. *XML-Signature Syntax and Processing, W3C Recommendation 12 February 2002.*

Signature Holder

[device holder] [key holder] [subscriber] [signature device holder] [signer] [signatory] means a person by whom, or on whose behalf, an enhanced electronic signature can be created and affixed to a data message. Draft Uniform Rules on Electronic Signatures, UNCITRAL, 29 June 1999.

Signature Policy

A named set of rules for the creation and verification of an electronic signature, including any use of CSPs that is being recognized as being valid within a given legal/contractual context. "European Electronic Signature Standardization Initiative", Final Draft of the EESSI Expert Team Report, June 18, 1999.

Signature Verification Device

Means unique data, such as codes or public cryptographic keys, or a uniquely configured physical device which is used in verifying the electronic signature. Proposal for A European Parliament and Council Directive on a Common Framework for Electronic Signatures, COM (1998) 297 Final.

Signed or Signature

Includes any symbol executed or adopted, or any security procedure employed or adopted, using electronic means or otherwise, by or on behalf of a person with intent to authenticate a record. *Illinois Electronic Commerce Security Act* 1998 5 Ill. Comp. Stat. 175.

SIMM (Single-In-Line Modules)

SIMMs allow arrays of memory to be plugged into a computer's main circuit board or a plug-in-card, instead of soldering or plugging in individual memory devices. *Digital Equipment Corp. v. Systems Industries Inc.*, CCH Comp. Law Rep. 46,229 (D.C. Mass. 1990).

Simulcasting

Means simultaneously broadcasting a broadcasting service in both analog and digital form in accordance with the requirements of the *Broadcasting Services Act 1992* or of any prescribed legislative provisions relating to digital broadcasting. *Copyright Amendment (Digital Agenda) Act 2000 Australia.*

Site (See also Web Site)

A "site" is an Internet address that permits the exchange of information with a host computer. *Zippo Manufacturing Company v. Zippo Dot Com, Inc.*, 952 F.Supp. 1119 (W.D.Penn. 1997).

A site is a group of documents stored together at one location or "address" on the web. A computer user with access to the web site can view documents that are "published" or made publicly available at the site. When a computer user "visits" or connects to a site on a server, the server transmits information to the user's computer and the user may then view on his or her computer screen the transmitted information, usually in the form of a document or image. *American Network, Inc. v. Access America/Connect Atlanta, Inc.*, 975 F.Supp. 4940 (S.D.N.Y. 1997).

Skipjack

A classified symmetric key encryption algorithm that uses 80-bit keys; developed by the National Security Agency. *Cryptography's Role in Securing the Information Society*, United States National Research Council, 1996.

Small Computer System Interface (SCSI)

The SCSI chip creates a protocol permitting data to be transmitted between the system side (CPU) and the peripheral side (e.g. an HDC). A SCSI (there are two identical chips) is embedded on each side of the cable to put the signals into SCSI format and send them over the cable and receive them at the other end-much like a modem functions to transmit data over a telephone line. *Advanced Micro Devices, Inc. and Intel Corp.*, CCH Comp. Cases 60,218 (Arb. Award. 1990).

Smart Agents

Are software programs that automatically perform online operations on behalf of a specific user. Smart agents can ensure user security and privacy by acting as an intermediary for the user. Advancing Global Electronic Commerce: Technology Solutions to Public Policy Challenges, Computer Systems Policy Project (CSPP), available at http://www.cspp.org/projects/july99_cto_report.pdf.

Smart Card

A card, similar to a debit or credit card, that allows a user to pay with it without having to connect to a remote system. Smart cards can store cash-equivalent value, data such as an encryption key or a digital signature, or tradeable value such as loyalty program points. Ministry of Revenue Advisory Committee, Report of the Committee On Electronic Commerce, April 30, 1998, Industry Canada.

Is perhaps the most promising ACT of all. A smart card is a credit card sized plastic card that contains an imbedded computer chip which possesses computer logic and is capable of processing, storing and retrieving information loaded into the chip. Although memory storage capacity is currently limited to a maximum of 64 kilobytes, the smart card's microprocessor offers functionality that is not available with any other ACT. The smart card's microprocessor is able to employ sophisticated password and encryption/decryption techniques to prevent unauthorized users from accessing or modifying data stored on the card. Also, the smart card's microprocessor is capable of performing computer logic functions such as addition, subtraction, multiplication, division, conditional branching, *etc.* In fact, these functions are used by the smart card's microprocessor to monitor access attempts and to shut off the smart card when the number of incorrect access attempts reaches a predefined number. *A Survey of Legal Issues Relating to the Security of Electronic Information*, Department of Justice, Canada.

A credit card sized piece of plastic with an embedded computer chip. i.e., capable of calculation. Smart, Optical and Other Advanced Cards: How to Do a Privacy Assessment, Information and Privacy Commissioner/Ontario Canada, available at http://www.itc.on.ca.

Represent but one of a number of different types of plastic cards that fall under the umbrella term of "Advanced Card" Technologies. "Smart Cards", Information and Privacy Commissioner/Ontario April 1993.

Smart Data Terminals

Terminals which locally perform some of the functions which previously were performed by a data processing computer. Dataspeed 40/4, 5 C.L.S.R. 1323 (F.C.C. 1976).

SmartWare

SmartWare product is an office automation product which contains within several distinct products including a word processor, spreadsheet and database. *Angoss II Partnership v. Trifox Inc.* (1997), [1997] O.J. No. 4969, 1997 CarswellOnt 4888 (Gen. Div.), affirmed (1999), [1999] O.J. No. 4144, 1999 CarswellOnt 3474 (C.A.) leave to appeal dismissed (2000), [1999] S.C.C.A. No. 588, 2000 CarswellOnt 2999.

SNA

IBM's Systems Network Architecture. *IBM v. Fujitsu Ltd.*, Copyright L.R. (CCH) 20,517 (Am. Arbtn. Assoc. Comm. Arbtn. Trib. 1988).

SNI Protocols

SNI Protocols allow communications to flow across a boundary between two SNA networks. *IBM v. Fujitsu Ltd.*, Copyright L.R. (CCH) 20,517 (Am. Arbtn. Assoc. Comm. Arbtn. Trib. 1988).

SNI (SNA Network Interconnections)

SNI is simply a set of protocols that allows communications to flow across a boundary between two SNA networks. *IBM v. Fujitsu Ltd.*, Copyright L.R. (CCH) 20,517 (Am. Arbtn. Assoc. Comm. Arbtn. Trib. 1988).

Software

See also Computer Program

(1) Computer programs, routines, programming languages and systems. (2) The collection of related utility, assembly, and other programs that are desirable for properly presenting a given machine to a user. (3) Detailed procedures to be followed, whether expressed as programs for a computer or as procedures for an

operator or other person. (4) Documents, including hardware manuals and drawings, computer program listings and diagrams etc. *In Re Graphics Technology Corp.*, 222 U.S.P.Q. 179 (T.T.A.B. 1984) (quoted from the definition in the *IEEE Standard Dictionary of Electrical and Electronic Terms* (1972)).

Computer software consists of programs that operate the computer system. Software can be divided into two categories: operating system software, and application software. Operating system software is necessary for a computer to function because it provides the interface between the equipment and the operator. Application software, in contrast, consists of programs designed to perform a specific task, such as balancing an account. *Graphic Sales Inc. v. Sperry Univac Division, Sperry Corp.*, 824 F.2d 576 (7th Cir. 1987).

"Software" denotes the information loaded into the machine and the directions given to the machine (usually by card or teleprompter) as to what it is to do and upon what command. "Software" is also frequently used to include "support," that is, advice, assistance, counselling, and sometimes even expert engineering help furnished by the vendor in loading the machine for a certain program such as inventory control or preparation of payroll. *Honeywell Inc. v. Lithonia Lightning Inc.*, 317 F.Supp. 406 (N.D. Ga. 1970).

Any of the written programs, flowcharts, etc., including general subroutines, that may be included in computer programs. *In Re Graphics Technology Corp.*, 222 U.S.P.Q. 179 (T.T.A.B. 1984) (as quoted from *Random House Dictionary of The English Language*, unabridged ed. (New York: Random House, 1981)).

The instructions that you give a computer that tell the computer what it is supposed to do when you want it to do it. It includes memory tapes, punch cards and paper tapes programmed to instruct the computer what to do. *Law Research Service Inc. v. General Automation Inc.*, 494 F.2d 202 (2nd Cir. 1974).

Is the term used to describe the programs that are fed into the equipment, and this software requires skill, experience and detailed knowledge in its production. *Han-Shan Tang Ltd. v. Macro-Micro Systems*, Q.B.D., Hoosen J., May 3, 1983 (unreported).

May be very broadly defined as a collection of instructions of programs (such as assemblers, compilers, utility routines, application programs and operating systems) which are fed into a computer to tell it what to do. *Chequecheck Services Ltd. v. Min. of Finance* (1980), 24 B.C.L.R. 217 (B.C. S.C.), reversed [1982] 5 W.W.R. 340 (B.C. C.A.).

Software is a computer program encoded on punch cards, tapes, or discs or other media in machine-readable form and in written documents in human-readable form. *Kalil Bottling Co. v. Burroughs Corp.*, 619 P.2d 1055 (Ariz. Ct. App. 1980).

The collection of programs that can be used with a particular kind of computer, especially the general and routine ones not written for specific tasks and often supplied by the manufacturer. *Chequecheck Services Ltd. v. Min. of Finance* (1980), 24 B.C.L.R. 217 (B.C. S.C.), reversed [1982] 5 W.W.R. 340 (B.C. C.A.).

Software is instructions or programs recorded electronically either on magnetic tape or discs or contained in punch cards to be read into the central processing unit through peripheral devices. *Teamsters Security Fund of North Carolina Inc. v. Sperry Rand Corp.*, 6 C.L.S.R. 951 (1977).

Software refers to the programs and controls that are used in the computer. *Com-Share Inc. v. Computer Complex Inc.*, 338 F.Supp. 1229 (E.D. Mich. 1971), affirmed 458 F.2d 1341 (6th Cir. 1972).

Instructions to the hardware to perform particular functions or sets of functions for use with computers. *DPCE (U.K.) Ltd. v. International Computers Ltd.*, Q.B.D., Saville J., July 31, 1985 (unreported).

The program together with the preparatory design material constitutes the software. Green Paper on Copyright and the Challenge of Technology, The Commission of the European Communities, COM (88) 172 Final (1988).

Comprises the stages of development from the definition of the object via problem analysis, data flowchart, program flowchart, to the writing of the primary program (also called "source program") and its encoding. *Bappert und Berker v. Sud-Westdeutsche Inkasso*, Karlsruhe, February 9, 1983, summarized at [1984] 9 E.I.P.R. 253.

Software refers to the programming part of data processing as distinguished from "hardware" which is the actual computer itself. The term refers strictly to the programming instructions for the work to be performed by the computer. In *Re Honeywell, Inc.*, 1 C.L.S.R. 810.

Software is a word in common use to describe the information constituting a computer program. *Autodesk Australia Pty Ltd. v. Dyason* (1989), 15 I.P.R. 1 (Aus. Fed. Ct.), reversed [1990] A.I.P.C. 36,446 (Aus. Fed. Ct. FC).

Software has several traits that make its classification within the UCC a complicated question. Software exhibits characteristics of a good, a service, and an intangible object. Typical software transactions takes place in widely varying forms. When analysing the applicability of the UCC to software, it is useful to consider the character of the property (whether it is tangible or intangible), the character of the transaction (whether it is a good or a service), the form of the transaction (whether it is a sale, a lease or a license), and the compatibility of software transactions with the goals and effects of the UCC. Horowitz, "Computer Software As A Good Under the Uniform Commercial Code: Taking a Byte Out of the Intangibility Myth", 65 Boston University Law Review 1290164 (1985), quoted in *In Re Bedford Computer Corporation*, 1 CCH Comp. Cases 45,049, 62 Bank. Rep. 555 (Bky. Crt. 1986).

Software is an illusive concept. Generally speaking, software refers to the medium that stores input and output data as well as computer programs. The medium includes hard disks, floppy disks, and magnetic tapes. In simplistic terms, programs are codes prepared by a programmer that instruct the computer to perform certain functions. When the program is transposed onto a medium compatible with the computer's needs, it becomes software. *Advent Systems, Ltd. v. Unisys Corporation*, 925 F.2d 670 (3rd Cir. 1991).

"Software" is the generic name for a computer program, or a group of computer programs. *United Software Group v. Sperry Rand Corp.*, 5 C.L.S.R. 1492 (E.D. Pa. 1974).

Software encompasses systems programs and application programs. *Computer Sciences Corp. v. Commissioner of Internal Revenue*, 63 T.C. 327 (U.S. Tax. Crt. 1974).

Software is the coded instructions which control the way data is processed, for example, individual programs. *Association of Data Processing Service Organizations, Inc. v. Board of Governors of the Federal Reserve System*, Comp. Ind. Lit. Reptr. 1,1643 (Crt. App. D.C. 1984).

It is important to understand that both source and object codes, even when printed out in "hard-copy" form from the magnetic media, are not recognizable as "language" in the ordinary sense. The printout just produces "gibberish" of two types. The source code "gibberish" is understandable to engineers if sufficient commentary is provided. The object code "gibberish" is understandable to no one but the computer. Courts have trouble enough reading contractual and statutory language and the undersigned judge has had to take on faith the foregoing gibberish-analysis presented by the expert witnesses. As far as this court is concerned, one of the piles of gibberish looks pretty much like the other pile. *In Re Bedford Computer Corporation*, 1 CCH Comp. Cases 45,049, 62 Bank. Rep. 555 (Bky. Crt. 1986).

Is a term with no precise definition, but it is usually taken to include computer programs and associated documentation and manuals. *Broderbund Software Inc. v. Computermate Products (Australia) Pty Ltd.* (1992), 22 I.P.R. 215 (Aust. H.C.).

Programs which consist of instructions to the computer telling it what to do are generally referred to as "software". The instructions are written in different types of computer language. The most basic language is referred to as "object code" which the computer can read but which is virtually unintelligible to people. *ISC-Bunker Ramo Corporation v. Altech, Inc.* 765 F.Supp. 1310 (N.D. Ill. 1990).

The word has a broader meaning than merely "programmes" or "source code." *Geac J & E Systems Ltd. v. Craig Erickson Systems Inc.* (1993), 46 C.P.R. (3d) 25 (Ont. Gen. Div.).

Software is commonly used by programmers and customers to mean "programmes." *Geac J & E Systems Ltd. v. Craig Erickson Systems Inc.* (1993), 46 C.P.R. (3d) 25 (Ont. Gen. Div.).

The word "software" refers to all other aspects of the system that allow the hardware to work. "Software" includes "operating system software," which relates to the management of the internal functions of the computer, and "application system software," which relates to solving a problem or performing a particular type of process. *Geac J & E Systems Ltd. v. Craig Erickson Systems Inc.* (1993), 46 C.P.R. (3d) 25 (Ont. Gen. Div.).

"Software" in its normal, broad meaning includes the following:

(1) Specifications.

(2) File layouts, including the design and name of data files.

(3) Source code or computer programme listings.

(4) Manuals, including detailed procedures to be followed, whether expressed as programmes for a computer or as procedures or instructions for an operator or other person, and documents such as hardware manuals and drawings.

(5) Routines, programming languages and systems, and the collection of related utility, and other programmes that are desirable for properly presenting a given machine to a user. *Geac J & E Systems Ltd. v. Craig Erickson Systems Inc.* (1993), 46 C.P.R. (3d) 25 (Ont. Gen. Div.).

Refers to the combination of programs and procedures that serve as instructions to the computer. The term is often used in contrast with "hardware" which refers to a computer system's physical elements. *Shea v. Reno*, 1996 U.S. Dist. LEXIS 10720 (S.D.N.Y. 1996).

Means a computer program, informational content included in the program, and any supporting information provided by the licensor. *Uniform Computer Information Transactions Act*, National Conference of Commissioners on Uniform State Laws, available at http://www.law.upenn.u/bll/ulc/ucita/citim99.htm.

Any form of codified information, usually in the form of a set of instructions, which enables a computer to manipulate data/information. Software may be in the form of a program written in a human readable computer language such as Cobol, C or Java, or in a machine readable form generated (compiled) from the human readable form. *Digital Technology and the Copyright Act 1994: A Discussion Paper, Competition and Enterprise Branch, July 2001 (New Zealand).*

Software Packages

They consist of one or more pre-programmed routines or applications that go onto a computer as sort of base program. As one witness testified, "They are to a computer what a record is to a Victrola." *Honeywell Inc. v. Lithonia Lightning Inc.*, 317 F.Supp. 406 (N.D. Ga. 1970).

Software Product

Generally, it is described as software, which can find general use by a number of users, as contrasted with a particular program for a particular entity. *United Software Corp. v. Sperry Rand Corp.*, 5 C.L.S.R. 1492 (E.D. Pa. 1974).

Software Support

Software support means any set of activities that assists someone in using "software." *Geac J & E Systems Ltd. v. Craig Erickson Systems Inc.* (1993), 46 C.P.R. (3d) 25 (Ont. Gen. Div.).

Sorting Criteria

Sorting criteria would ordinarily mean the factors that determine how the data in the program is organized. *Gates Rubber Co. v. Bando American Inc.*, 28 U.S.P.Q. 2d 1503 (10th Cir. 1993).

Source Code

The source code for a computer program is the series of instructions to the computer for carrying out the various tasks which are performed by the program, expressed in a human-readable programming language. The source code serves two functions. First, it can be treated as comparable to text material, and in that respect can be printed out, read and studied, and loaded into a computer's memory, in much the same way as documents are loaded into word processing equipment. Second, the source code can be used to cause the computer to execute the program. To accomplish this, the source code is compiled. This involves an automatic process, performed by the computer under the control of a program called a compiler, which translates the source code into object code, which is very difficult to comprehend by human beings. The object code version of the program is then loaded into the computer's memory and causes the computer to carry out the program function. *SAS Institute Inc. v. S. & H. Computer Systems Inc.*, 605 F.Supp. 816 (M.D. Tenn. 1985).

Disassembled object code, expressed in humanly-readable form with accompanying comments and labels. *E.F. Johnson Co. v. Uniden Corp. of America*, 623 F.Supp. 1485 (D.C. Minn. 1985).

A program source code is the original set of programming instructions drawn up by its creator. Because source code reveals the mechanics of the program, software is rarely distributed to users in this form. *Infosystems Technology Inc. v. Logical Software Inc.*, Vol. 6, No. 5 C.L.R. 831 (4th Cir. 1987).

A source code is a computer program written in any of the several programming languages employed by computer programmers. Final Report of the National Commission of New Technological Uses of Copyrighted Works, (Contu Report).

The source program is generally regarded as the alphanumeric translation of the flowchart idea into the problem-oriented computer language, that is, Fortran, COBOL, or ALGOL, and may be punched on a deck of cards or imprinted on discs, tapes, or drums. *Paine, Webber, Jackson & Curtis, Inc. v. Merrill Lynch, Pierce, Finner & Smith Inc.*, 564 F.Supp. 1358 (D. Del. 1983).

When a computer program is brought into existence, it passes through a variety of stages. The programmer may initially produce a flowchart or flow-diagram setting out the basic logic of the program, although this is not necessary. Then the source code program will be written in computer language. The source code is essentially a series of instructions or commands that constitute the program and that can be read and understood by computer scientists. It may be written out by hand in the first instance, or else keyed directly onto the computer keyboard. The language in which it is written may be a higher-level language, corresponding more closely to ordinary mathematics and English (*e.g.*, BASIC, PASCAL, FOR-TRAN) or it may be a lower-level language, corresponding more explicitly to the operations to be performed by the computer. The source code cannot be read directly by the computer. When it is keyed into a computer it passes through a compiler or assembler program, which converts it into object code. Source code is the original program written in comprehensible form by the programmer. *IBM Corp. v. Computer Imports Ltd.*, N.Z. H.C., Smellie J., March 21, 1989 (unreported).

Source code is the computer program code as the programmer writes it, using a particular programming language, generally written in a high-level language, such as BASIC, COBOL, or FORTRAN. A program in source code must be changed into object code before the computer can execute it. *Manufacturers Technology Inc. v. Cams Inc.*, 10 U.S.P.Q.2d 1321 (D. Conn. 1989).

The source code is understandable, everyday language. The computer is unable to read source code language. It is converted by translator (compiler) into an object code written in electronic zeros and ones. The information contained in the object code is stored in silicon chips in the form of minute "bits" or in a diskette by photochemical or electrical processes . . . In order to modify or update a program, the source code must be modified. *Soft Computer Consultants, Inc. v. Lalehzarzadeh*, [1989] Copyright L. Dec. (CCH) 26,403 (E.D.N.Y. 1988).

The source code is a set of instructions to the computer, in languages such as BASIC or Fortran. The object code is the same set of instructions, but in binary code, a series of ones and zeros, which the computer reads. *Johnson Controls Inc. v. Phoenix Control Systems Inc.*, 886 F.2d 1173 (9th Cir. 1989).

During the early period of computing, "programmers" ordinarily wrote programs exclusively in machine language. Today, object code is rarely written directly by computer programmers. Rather, modern programmers typically write computer programs in a "higher"-level programming language. These programs are called source programs, or source code. Although "source code" has been defined far more broadly in some of the literature in the field, and in some of the expert testimony in this case, more commonly the term "source code" refers to a computer program written in some programming language — such as FORTRAN (*FOR*mula *TRAN*slation), COBOL (*CO*mmon *Business Oriented Language*), Pascal, BASIC, or C — that uses complex symbolic names, along with complex rules of syntax. In a typical higher-level programming language, for example, the above-described computation — that is, $(A)+(B/C)$ — might be represented as follows: $A+B/C$. Unlike machine language, which is unique to each kind of CPU and which is executed directly by the computer, source code programming languages are universal to almost all computers. As a consequence, source code is executed indirectly. Thus, a program written in source code must be translated into the appropriate object code for execution in one type of computer, and into a different object code for execution in another type of computer. The translation can be effectuated by an "interpreter" program or by a "compiler" program. *Lotus*

Development Corp. v. Paperback Software International, 15 U.S.P.Q.2d 1577 (D. Mass. 1990).

The program as written by the programmer, capable of being understood by a programmer and capable of modification. *Saphena Computing Ltd. v. Allied Collection Agencies Ltd.*, Ch. D., Recorder, July 22, 1988 (unreported), affirmed, C.A., May 3, 1989 (unreported).

A source code is a set of instructions written in the words of a computer language such as COBOL. which is a contraction of "Common Business Oriented Language". The source code is written by a programmer who understands that language and what is written would be understood by another programmer who knows the language. The source code is then translated or compiled by a prewritten program called a "compiler" into an object code or machine code in binary symbols understood by a computer. The source code is thus the source of a computer's instructions. If it were desired to alter the program of a computer, it would usually be necessary to alter the source code and recompile it. *Madeley Pty Ltd. v. Touche Ross*, McGarvie, J., Aust. Fed. Ct., Dec. 21, 1989 (unreported).

The source code is the same original set of instructions, expressed in a language that the engineers can read and deal with. Customers are almost never given the source code when they purchase a computer product. The source code is the "lifeblood" of any computer company and is rarely disclosed. *In Re Bedford Computer Corporation*, 1 CCH Computer Cases 45,049, 62 Bank. Rep. 555 (Bky. Crt. 1986).

Source code is a computer program written in either a high-level English-like language such as Pascal or Fortran or in assembly language; in any case, the source code usually includes the programmer's running commentary as to the function of a particular module or segment of code. Once the programmer develops the source code, it is compiled into the object code. *Stenograph Corporation v. Microcat Corporation*, 1990 U.S. Dist. Lexis 12945 (N.D. Ill. 1990).

The source code is the human readable form of the software, written in a recognized, high-level computer language. *Hodge Business Computer Systems Inc. v. U.S.A. Mobile Communications Inc.*, C.L.R. 106 (6th Cir. 1990).

The list of commands written by the programmer is known as source code and is typically readable by those conversant in the programming language (e.g., "C," BASIC, PASCAL, FORTRAN, etc.). The source code is converted by a program known as a compiler into the binary zeros and ones — the object code or machine language — to be run by the computer. *Brown Bag Software v. Symantec Corp.*, 22 U.S.P.Q.2d 1429 (9th Cir. 1992).

The source code is a combination of words, symbols, and numbers used by programmers to describe, or provide the basis for, the object code of a particular program. *Computer Associates International Inc. v. Altai Inc.*, 775 F.Supp. 544 (E.D.N.Y. 1991), affirmed 23 U.S.P.Q.2d 1241 (2d Cir. 1992).

The source code is a set of instructions to the computer. *Autoskills Inc. v. National Educational Support Systems Incorporated*, Comp.Ind.Lit.Reptr. 15074 (D.C. New Mex. 1992).

A source code for a computer product is the actual programming language listings of the instructions to the computer. It is readable to people. Computers basically work in numeric code. One would write something which is called the source language, a semi-English like language, and another computer program called a compiler translates into the numeric codes to get the computer to do what is required. The computer essentially speaks in one language, a numeric language. People used to write in the numeric language and it was very difficult. Now they write in source languages, which are English-like languages and let other computer programs do the work of translating into the machine language. Source code is usually kept in two forms: on magnetic media, which is on a diskette, and in a book, listing what is on the magnetic media, or it might be saved on a tape or on a disc and kept in a secure, safe area. *Computer Associates International, Inc. v. Bryan*, 3 CCH Comp. Cases 46,619 (E.D. N.Y. 1992).

[Is] a language comprised of words and symbols that resemble English. A device exists (with its own conversion "program") which automatically converts "source code" that people can work with, to "object code" that a computer can read. *ISC-Bunker Ramo Corporation v. Altech, Inc.*, 765 F.Supp. 1310 (N.D. Ill. 1990).

Is written in a language intended to be read and understood by human beings. *Otis Elevator Co. v. Intelligent Systems, Inc.*, 3 CCH Comp. Cases 46,510 (Conn. S.C. 1990).

[Source code is a set of] computer instructions that are written in a structured programming language that is human readable. The opposite of "object code". Instructions required to define the processing steps required and expressed in a format that the human programmers can more easily work with. This format of code is not readily understandable by the computer but can be interpreted more easily by the programmer. The notation used to express the instructions is referred to as a computer language. *Delrina Corp. v. Triolet Systems, Inc.* (1992), 47 C.P.R. (3d) 1 (Ont. H.C.).

Source code is comprised of rather cryptic English language expressions and readable numbers and symbols. The exact form varies with the programming languages. When the source code is loaded into a computer memory, it is "compiled" or converted into a series of symbols that are readable only to the computer hardware. *Delrina Corp. v. Triolet Systems, Inc.* (1992), 47 C.P.R. (3d) 1 (Ont. H.C.).

The program the human writes is called the "source code". After it is written it is processed by a program called a compiler into binary code. That is what the computer uses. All the words and algebraic symbols become binary numbers. *IBCOS Computers Ltd. v. Barclay's Mercantile Highland Finance Ltd.*, [1994] F.S.R. 275 (Ch.D.).

"Source code", being what humans can understand, is very important to anyone who wants to copy a program with modifications, for instance to upgrade it. It is the source code which shows the human how it all works, and he or she will also get the benefit of all the comments laid down by the original programmer. Software houses not surprisingly normally keep their source code to themselves and confidential. *IBCOS Computers Ltd. v. Barclay's Mercantile Highland Finance Ltd.*, [1994] F.S.R. 275 (Ch.D.).

"Source code" (sometimes called "programmes" or "computer programmes") is a listing of statements in a programming language to achieve a desired result in the computer. Source code is found in hard copy (paper) and magnetic medium (on the computer disk). *Geac J & E Systems Ltd. v. Craig Erickson Systems Inc.* (1993), 46 C.P.R. (3d) 25 (Ont. Gen. Div.).

In computer parlance the program as written in whatever language is used by the programmer (whether machine code, assembler language or a high level language) is known as the source code. When this is converted by an assembler or a compiler into machine code it is known as the object code. *John Richardson Computers Ltd. v. Flanders*, [1993] F.S.R. 497 (Ch.D.)

Source code is the literal text of a programs' instructions written in a particular programming language. *Gates Rubber Co. v. Bando American Inc.*, 28 U.S.P.Q. 2d 1503 (10th Cir. 1993).

Source code is what the programmer creates, it is readable by humans. Source code is then compiled (translated) into object code, the binary system of "0" and "1" that the computer reads. *NU Business Information Systems, Inc. v. The Social Secretary, Ltd.*, 4 CCH Computer Cases 46,986 (N.D. Ill. 1993).

A source code is the code from which the executables are derived. A source code is the actual language that the person or persons who is creating the code writes in. *Micro Consulting, Inc. v. Zubeldia*, 813 F.Supp. 1514 (W.D. Okla. 1993).

Source code is the programming language readable by human programmers; object code is the binary expression that controls the computer hardware. *Engineering Dynamics, Inc. v. Structural Software, Inc.*, 31 U.S.P.Q. 2d 1641 (5th Cir. 1994), as corrected, rehearing denied, 1995 U.S. App. LEXIS 3126 (5th Cir. 1995).

Source code is the actual text of a computer program — the instructions written by the programmer and translated by the computer. *Qad, Inc. v. ALN Associates Inc.*, 24 U.S.P.Q. 2d 1145 (7th Cir. 1992).

The class of computer languages expressed in human readable form and which allow a human programmer to work with instructions rather than binary or hexadecimal numbers. Computer Software Protection: Australia, Copyright Law Review Committee 1995.

Programmers often write programs in source code, also called "assembly language". This type of code contains mneumonic abbreviations for each step and can be read by expert programmers. Once a programmer has access to the source code of a program, he is able to determine the construction of the program and write his own version. For this reason, source code programs are typically compiled (and then translated) into and sold as object code or machine language, which is not discernable to even an expert programmer, but which is readily usable by the computer. *United States of America v. Brown*, 2 CCH Comp. Cas. 46,414 (10th Cir. 1991).

Source code is the text of a source program and is generally written in a high-level language that is two or more steps removed from machine language which is a low-level language. High-level languages are closer to natural language than low-level languages which direct the functioning of the computer. Source code must be translated by way of a translating program into machine language before it can be read by a computer. The object code is the output of that translation. It is possible to write a source program in high-level language without knowing about the actual functions of the computer that carry out the program. *Bernstein v. United States Department of State*, 1996 W.L. 186106 (N.D. Cal. 1996).

Is a series of instructions to a computer in programming languages such as BASIC, PERL, or FORTRAN. *Junger v. Secretary of Commerce,* Case No. 1-96-CV-1723, (N.D. Ohio.1998).

At least as currently understood by computer programmers, refers to the text of a program written in a "high-level" programming language, such as "PASCAL" or "C." The distinguishing feature of source code is that it is meant to be read and understood by humans and that it can be used to express an idea or a method. A computer, in fact, can make no direct use of source code until it has been translated ("compiled") into a "low-level" or "machine" language, resulting in computer-executable "object code." That source code is meant for human eyes and understanding, however, does not mean that an untutored layperson can understand it. Because source code is destined for the maw of an automated, ruthlessly literal translator—the compiler—a programmer must follow stringent grammatical, syntactical, formatting, and punctuation conventions. As a result, only those trained in programming can easily understand source code. *Bernstein v. Department of State*, No. 97-16686 (9th Cir. Mar. 6th, 1999), available at *http://zeus.bna.com/e-law/cases/bernstein2.html* (9th Cir. 1999).

Source code is the text-based form of a program that is written by a programmer using the commands, and the syntax (grammar), of the particular programming language employed. Source code can be interpreted or "read" by someone who is familiar with the programming language. *Ni-Tech Pty Ltd. v. Bruce Peter Parker & Ors,* [1998] 484 FCA (27 April 1998) (Aust. F.C.).

Source Record

A source record may be:

[el3]a. In relation to a record, the record itself or any facsimile intended by the author of the record to have the same effect.

[el3]b. In relation to a photograph, the negative or any print made from it.

[el3]c. In relation to a record produced by a computer system, any printout or

other intelligible output that accurately reproduces, whether in the same or a modified form, the data supplied to the computer system.

National Standard of Canada, Microfilm and Electronic Images as documentary evidence, Can/CGSB-72.11-93.

Space Shifting

Where users access a sound recording. . .that they already own in audio CD format. *A & M Records Inc. v. Napster Inc.*, 57 U.S.P.Q. 2d 1729 (9th Cir.2001).

Spam (See also Junk E-mail)

Spam is unsolicited commercial bulk e-mail akin to "junk mail" sent through the postal mail. The transmission of Spam is a practice widely condemned in the Internet community. *America Online, Inc. v. LCGM, Inc.*, Action No. 98-102-A (E.D. Vir. December 21, 1998).

Internet communications services for commercial bulk-e-mail advertising purposes. *1267623 Ontario Inc. v. NEXX On-Line Inc.* [1999] O.J. No. 2246 (Ont. S.C.).

Unsolicited commercial messages or communications in any form. *1267623 Ontario Inc. v. NEXX On-Line Inc.* [1999] O.J. No. 2246 (Ont. S.C.).

Unsolicited commercial bulk email. *America On-Line, Inc. v. The Christian Brothers et al*, 98 Civ. 8959 (DAV April 17, 2001).

A spammed email is an unsolicited email which is distributed in massive quantities to a large number of internet users. *Maxnet Holdings Inc. v. Maxnet, Inc.*, 2000 U.N. Dist. Lexis 7524 (E.D. Penn. June 2, 2000).

Spamming

Refers to the posting indiscriminately of advertisements to newsgroups on the web. Unlike crossposting, spamming individually posts the advertisement to each newsgroup, requiring the recipient to delete the message from each newsgroup to which she has subscribed. *Cybersell Inc. v. Cybersell Inc.*, 44 U.S.P.Q. 2d 1928 (9th Cir. 1997).

Specialty Channel

A special interest channel usually available only by cable service (see "Narrowcasting"). Submission of the Director of Investigation and Research to the CRTC Re Public Notice CRTC 1994-130.

Specifications

Program narrative. *Pezzillo v. General Telephone & Electronics Information Systems, Inc.*, 414 F.Supp. 1257 (D.C. M.D. Tenn. 1976), affirmed 572 F.2d 1189 (6th Cir. 1978).

A technical description of the desired behaviour of a system, as derived from its requirements. A specification is used to develop and test an implementation of a system. *Cryptography's Role in Securing the Information Society*, United States National Research Council, 1996.

Spectrum

Range of electromagnetic frequencies capable of traversing space without the benefit of physical interconnection. *The Challenge of the Information Highway: Final Report of the Information Highway Advisory Council* (September 1995).

Spider

A search engine uses specialised computer programs sometimes called "spiders" or "crawlers" to electronically visit websites, gather relevant data about those websites, and compile and index the information. *British Columbia Automobile Assn. v. OPEIU. Local 378* (2001), 10 C.P.R. (4th) 423 (B.C.S.C.).

SPLIT

Sundstrand Programming Language Internally Translated. *White Consolidated Industries Inc. v. Vega Servo-Control Inc.*, 214 U.S.P.Q 796 (S.D. Mich. 1982), affirmed 218 U.S.P.Q. 961 (Fed. Cir. 1983).

Spoofing

Illicitly masquerading as a legitimate company, party, or individual. *Cryptography's Role in Securing the Information Society*, United States National Research Council, 1996.

Sprite

A sprite involves the use of a special technique for creating mobile graphic images on a computer screen that is appropriate for animation. An increase in sophistication of sprite techniques used in the computer program will increase the graphic quality of the games' animation. *Data East Usa Inc. v. Epyx Inc.*, 862 F.2d 204 (4th Cir. 1988).

SRAMs — Static Random Access Memories

A SRAM is a type of semiconductor RAM in which there is a bistable circuit which serves a binary storage element. Unlike a DRAM, a SRAM does not require periodic refresh cycles to maintain the stored data. A SRAM stores the data for as long as power is available to the storage circuits. Like a DRAM, a SRAM stores information in the form of binary numbers. A single cell of a SRAM can hold one binary digit, or "bit". Like DRAMs, SRAMs are sometimes classified by storage capacity measured in "K" bits, where K 1,024 bits. A 2K SRAM is capable of storing 2,048 binary digits or bits; a 16K SRAM is capable of storing 16,384 binary digits or bits; a 64K SRAM stores 65,536 bits; a 256K SRAM stores 262,144 bits; and a 1 Meg SRAM stores in excess of one million bits. See also DRAM. *Digital Equipment Corp. v. Systems Industries Inc.*, CCH Comp. Law Rep. 46,229 (D.C. Mass. 1990).

Standards-Related Measure

Means a standard, technical regulation or conformity assessment procedure. North American Free Trade Agreement between Canada, Mexico and the United States, Article 1310.

State of the Art System

This is an advanced system which is right up to date. *Madeley Pty Ltd. v. Touche Ross*, McGarvie J., Aust. Fed. Ct., Dec. 21, 1989 (unreported).

Stentor

The former national alliance of incumbent telecommunication carriers.

Stock Quotation Service

The service enables a broker to query the computer's store of market data and receive the information on a print-out or visual display device. Computer Inquiry (Interim Statement), 17 F.C.C.2d 587 (F.C.C. 1969).

Stored Value Cards

Are credit card-sized cards with an embedded computer chip that stores and dispenses electronic money. Advancing Global Electronic Commerce: Technology Solutions to Public Policy Challenges, The Computer Systems Policy Project, July 1999, available at http://www.cspp.org/projects/july99_cto_report.pdf.

Streaming

A means of sending multimedia information such as sound or video over the Internet so that it is played by the recipient as it is being transmitted. Although it involves temporary storage (buffering) of limited segments of the streamed information so as to ensure continuous play, streaming avoids the need to copy and store a complete file before playback can begin. *Digital Technology and the Copyright Act 1994: A Discussion Paper, Competition and Enterprise Branch, July 2001 (New Zealand)*.

Structural separation

Refers to the setting up of a separate but affiliated company to provide a specific line of business. Structural separation is one approach to dealing with cross-subsidization or undue preference. *The Challenge of the Information Highway: Final Report of the Information Highway Advisory Council* (September 1995).

Structure

Structured design seeks to conquer the complexity of large systems by means of partitioning the system into "black boxes" and by organizing the black boxes into hierarchies suitable for computer implementation. At the most abstract level, structure can be used to describe the general way that the source code for a product is organized. For example, the organization of any operating system makes major organizational divisions between tasks associated with managing users of the system (passwords, file security, etc) and tasks related to managing the physical hardware devices connected to the system (handling conditions such as turning off the power switch on a disk drive, a printer running out of paper, etc). The use of a "monolithic" (single program) approach versus a "client-server" (multiprogram) approach would also be a characteristic of the high level structure of a product. Structure can also refer to the functional decomposition of the source code into modules or procedures. In order to manage the complexity of a program, the overall functionality is broken down into smaller parts such as gathering and displaying data and configuring the software. Each of these functions is then broken down further into tasks such as gathering global level data versus process level data. These sub functions are further broken down until each of the tasks is of a size that lends itself to a coherent implementation in source code. The term "structure" can also refer to the interconnection of the various modules within the source code. In this case, it refers to which procedures refer to (call) which other procedures and in what order. This would be using structure as a synonym for the computer science term "invocation tree". The word "structure" can also be applied to the user interface for a software product using similar points of view. At the most abstract level, the division of the data available into logically related sets displayed as individual screens can be referred to as structure. The contents and arrangement of any individual screen could be referred to as the structure of the display. The method of using commands to navigate from one display screen to another would be analogous to the "invocation tree" structure of the source code. *Delrina Corp. v. Triolet Systems, Inc.* (1992), 47 C.P.R. (3d) 1 (Ont. H.C.).

Structure, Sequence, and Organization (SSO)

The structure, sequence, and organization of a computer program consists of the manner in which the program operates, controls, and regulates the computer in receiving, assembling, calculating, retaining, correlating, and producing useful information. *Healthcare Affiliated Services Inc. v. Lippany*, 701 F.Supp. 1142 (W.D. Pa. 1988).

Submenu

A submenu is an additional set of options that relates to a prior menu selection. *MiTek Holdings Inc. v. Arce Engineering Inc.*, 39 U.S.P.Q. 2d 1609 (11th Cir. 1996).

Sub-routines

Most programs are complicated and have a history of growth. A typical applications program will in fact consist of a number of individual programs linked in various ways, accessing data held in the computer for various purposes. Sometimes there are little programs which are used by larger programs. Some of these are called "sub-routines", e.g. an instruction to print. *IBCOS Computers Ltd. v. Barclay's Mercantile Highland Finance Ltd.*, [1994] F.S.R. 275 (Ch.D.).

Any compiler for a particular programming language on a particular machine is supplied with libraries of subroutines. These routines are commonly used utility routines, and in the present case include subroutines which invoke all the system services. The programmer writes his own library routines for a particular project. *Cantor Fitzgerald International v. Tradition (U.K.) Ltd.*, [1999] I.N.L.R. No. 23 (Ch.D.).

Subscriber

A person who accesses or is contractually entitled to access the service provided by the telecommunications service in a given month. Neighbouring Rights Internet Tariff, 1999-2002.

A person who accesses or is contractually entitled to access the service provided by the telecommunication service in a given month. Tariff 22 Transmission of Musical Works to Subscribers Via a Telecommunications Service Not Covered Under Tariff Nos. 16 or 17.

Means a person who is the subject named or otherwise identified in a certificate, who controls a private key that corresponds to the public key listed in that certificate, and who is the person to whom digitally signed messages verified by reference to such certificate are to be attributed. *Illinois Electronic Commerce Security Act* 1998 5 Ill. Comp. Stat. 175.

Means an individual who is authorized by a certificate to sign (a) electronic applications and instruments under this Part, and (b) electronic returns under the *Property Transfer Tax Act. B.C. Land Title Amendment Act*, 1999 (Bill 93-1999).

A person who is the subject of a certificate. General Usage for International Digitally Insured Commerce (Guidec), International Chamber of Commerce, 1997, available at http://www.icc.wbo.org/guidec2.htm.

Is a person whose public key is certified in a certificate. In the Government of Canada Public Key Infrastructure, subscribers are employees and external subscribers. Public Key Infrastructure Management in the Government of Canada, Treasury Board of Canada Secretariat, May 27, 1999, available at http://www.tbs-sct.gc.ca/pubs_pol/ciopubs/PKI/pki1_e.html.

An individual who obtains a certificate from a certification authority. When originating an electronic communication, this person will send the certificate or refer the recipient to the certificate so the recipient can authenticate the identity of the originator of the communication. Since both consumers and merchants may have digital certificates which are used to conclude a transaction, they may both be subscribers in certain circumstances. This person may also be referred to as the signer of a digital signature or the sender of data message signed with a digital signature. UNCITRAL Report of the Working Group on Electronic Commerce, September 18-29, 2000, A/CN. 94/483.

Subscription Programming Signal

Radiocommunication that is intended for reception either directly or indirectly by the public in Canada or elsewhere on payment of subscription fee or other charge. *Radiocommunication Act*, R.S.C. 1985, c. R-2, as amended.

Sub-structure

Sub-structure or nesting describes the inner structure of a module whereby one module is subsumed within another and performs part of the second modules task. *Gates Rubber Co. v. Bando American Inc.*, 28 U.S.P.Q. 2d 1503 (10th Cir.).

Sui generis legislation

Custom-made legislation specially designed to meet a particular policy objective, regulate a particular area of activity or confer (and/or impose) specific legal rights (or obligations). *Digital Technology and the Copyright Act 1994: A Discussion Paper, Competition and Enterprise Branch, July 2001 (New Zealand).*

Support

In this context means assistance in the operation of software systems. *Eurodynamic Systems Plc v. General Automation Ltd.*, Q.B.D., Steyn J., September 6, 1988 (unreported).

Supporting Material

Means any material, other than a computer program or a program description, created for aiding the understanding or application of a computer program, such as, for example, problem descriptions and user instructions. Model Provisions on the Protection of Computer Software, World Industrial Property Organization, 1978.

Suspend a Certificate

Means to temporarily suspend the operational period of a certificate for a specified time period or from a specified time forward. *Illinois Electronic Commerce Security Act* 1998 5 Ill. Comp. Stat. 175.

The act of a certifier in declaring a public key certificate temporarily invalid for a specified time period. General Usage for International Digitally Insured Commerce (Guidec), International Chamber of Commerce, 1997, available at http://www.icc.wbo.org/guidec2.htm.

SVGA

Super Video Graphics Array. High-quality display for a colour monitor. Monopolies and Mergers Commission — Video Games: A report on the supply of video games in the UK (LONDON: HMSO Cm2781).

SWIFT

An acronym of Society for World Wide Inter-Bank Financial Telecommunications, which Society was conceived in 1973 to provide a secure method of payment instructions between major banks in different countries using a standard format for messages. *Databank Systems Ltd. v. Commnr. of Inland Revenue*, [1987] N.Z.L.R. 312 (H.C. Wellington).

Switch

"Switch" appears in MacQuari's [*sic*] Dictionary, 1981, as a colloquial abbreviation for "switchboard," in turn defined as "an arrangement of switches, plugs, and jacks mounted on a board or frame enabling an operator to make temporary connections between telephone users." "Switch," of course, also has the meaning of "a mechanical device that completes or breaks the path of the current or sends it over a different path." *Re Application by Mitel Corp.* (1985), 5 I.P.R. 260 (Aus. Pat. Office).

Switching

Switching is the process of routing traffic from one subscriber to another on the same or different networks. As noted earlier, a switched network permits traffic to move in a bidirectional fashion. Competition and Culture on Canada's Information Highway: Managing the Realities of Transition, CRTC (the "Convergence Report"), May 19, 1995.

Symmetric Cryptography

Symmetric cryptography is cryptography which uses the same key to generate and verify a digital signature. Security and Electronic Authorization and Authentication Guideline, Communications Security Establishment, Government of Canada September 1995, CID/01/15.

Symmetric Encryption

Means that the same key that is used to encrypt a message is also used to decrypt a message. For almost the entire history of cryptography, encryption has used symmetric keys. *A Survey of Legal Issues Relating to the Security of Electronic Information*, Department of Justice, Canada.

Synchronous Transmission

In the synchronous digital mode, individual characters are grouped together in multicharacter strings and sent at one invariant rate. Synchronous transmission is particularly suited for efficient computer interaction. Additionally, when compared to asynchronous transmission, synchronous techniques permit higher transmission rates to be achieved for a given channel bandwidth. *Dataspeed 40/4*, 52 F.C.C.2d. 21 (F.C.C. 1977).

Syntax

When we speak of syntax, we speak of the rules for using that command in a particular program. For example, a particular command might only be effective if followed by the name of a file. *Powerflex Services Pty Ltd. v. Data Access Corp.* (1997), 37 I.P.R. 436 (Aust. C.A.).

Programming languages are constructed to conform to a particular syntax. VX-BASIC, in common with many other languages, permits statements (essentially lines of code) to consist of identifiers specified by the programmer, reserved words (which are specified for particular purposes by the language) and operators. The identifiers can be divided principally into variables and functions or routine names. Variables are the operands of the instructions. The function or routine names are names which are provided for subroutines to enable them to be called conveniently. A variable name will refer to the cells in the memory which hold the value of the variable. The subroutine name will refer to the cell in memory which holds the first instruction of the subroutine. *Cantor Fitzgerald International v. Tradition (U.K.) Ltd.*, [1999] I.N.L.R. No. 23 (Ch.D.).

System

Means a telecommunication system and data processing system and includes all the works owned, held or used for the purposes thereof or in connection therewith or with the operation thereof. *The Manitoba Telephone Act*, R.S.M. 1970, c. T-40, as amended.

Means a telecommunication system and includes all land, plants, supplies, buildings, works, rights, franchises, easements, assets and property of every kind owned, held, required or used for the purpose of, or in connection with, or for the operation of the telecommunication system. *Alberta Gov't Telephones v. Canada (CRTC)*, [1985] 2 F.C. 472 (Fed. T.D.), reversed [1986] 2 F.C. 179 (Fed. C.A.), reversed [1989] 2 S.C.R. 225.

A program or collection of programs used to manage systems program hardware and software resources on a computer for the user. Computer Software Protection: Australia, Copyright Law Review Committee 1995.

System Information

This is a generic term that is used to refer to any information about the computer system itself. It might include such things as the type of computer, the speed of the processor, the size of available main memory, the size and availability of auxiliary disk storage devices or the maximum allowable number of users or programs active within the computer system. This term could also be applied to the information that can be retrieved from the system to determine what the current operational characteristics of the computer system are. These characteristics might include such things as the current number of users of the system, who those users are, what programs they are running and the rate at which various hardware devices are being accessed. *Delrina Corp. v. Triolet Systems, Inc.* (1992), 47 C.P.R. (3d) 1 (Ont. H.C.)

System Software

The special software (e.g., operating system, compilers or utility programs) designed for a specific computer system or family of computer systems to facilitate the operation and maintenance of the computer system, programs, and data. "Security Requirements for Cryptographic Modules", FIPS Pub. 140-1, Federal Information Processing Standards Publication, January 11, 1994, available at http://csrc.nist.gov/fips/fips1401.htm.

System Tables

Any operating system utilizes tables in order to manage the usage and operation of the computer system. It defines and builds tables to keep track of such things as the current users of the system, the various programs currently running, the amounts of various resources consumed by various users and programs, as well as the states of the various physical devices that make up the computer system. For the MPE/V and MPE/XL operating systems, these tables are documented in manuals that provide descriptive information about each of the tables as well as the layout of the data within the tables and any special notes about the usage of the tables. *Delrina Corp. v. Triolet Systems, Inc.* (1992), 47 C.P.R. (3d) 1 (Ont. H.C.)

System Tables Definition

The act of configuring or defining the size of various tables used within the operating system. This could also mean retrieving data from the tables themselves that reflect the state or contents of one or more of the tables. *Delrina Corp. v. Triolet Systems, Inc.* (1992), 47 C.P.R. (3d) 1 (Ont. H.C.)

System/360

A series of mainframe computers and related products sharing a common architecture. First announced and marketed in 1964, the IBM System/360 revolutionized the data processing industry by providing users with the ability to install upward and downward compatible computer systems. For example, a user's application program designed to run on a particular central processing unit (such as an IBM Model 30) could, for the first time, run equally well on a more powerful processor (such as an IBM Model 40). The IBM System/360 and System/370, including mainframe computers and related products such as software operating systems, achieved widespread acceptance in the world marketplace. An enormous base of mainframe computer users have made extensive investments in applications programs developed to run in conjunction with IBM Operating System Software. *IBM v. Fujitsu Ltd.*, Copyright L.R. (CCH) 20,517 (Am. Arbtn. Assoc. Comm. Arbtn. Trib. 1988).

Systems Software or Systems Program

See also Operating System Program.

Describe the material pre-programmed by the manufacturer's representatives to suit the general use to be made of the computer by the operator and which help the computer to run more efficiently by taking care of 'housekeeping' chores such as queuing jobs for the printer, or locating a particular piece of stored information. *Clarke Irwin & Co. v. Singer Co. of Can.*, Ont. Div. Ct., Keith J., December 3, 1979, summarized at [1979] 3 A.C.W.S. 807.

System software is a computer program that controls the computer hardware and schedules the execution of its functions. *Apple Computer Inc. v. Microsoft Corp.*, 759 F.Supp. 1444 (N.D. Cal. 1991).

A systems program is generally provided by the computer manufacturer and is intended to make the computer function. "It is the collection of system programs (called the 'Operating System') which converts the computer hardware . . . into a . . . functioning computer." *People v. Versaggi*, 629 N.E. 2d 1034.

A "systems program" is a computer program designed solely to help someone else program or use a computer. *Computer Sciences Corp. v. Commissioner of Internal Revenue*, 63 T.C. 327 (U.S. Tax. Crt. 1974).

Table Driven Program

In a table driven program . . . information or data used repeatedly by different parts of the program is segregated into tables rather than represented in ordinary lines of code. The use of tables simplifies maintenance and modifications, and makes the program easier to understand. *Allen-Myland Inc. v. IBM*, 746 F.Supp. 520 (E.D.Pa. 1990).

Taking down

The removal of material or information on a computer or server connected to the Web or the disconnection of a computer containing material or information for access using the Internet or an intranet so that material or information is no longer accessible in that manner. *Digital Technology and the Copyright Act 1994: A Discussion Paper, Competition and Enterprise Branch, July 2001 (New Zealand)*.

Tape-labelling

Tape-labelling serves the following functions: identification of the tape, security of the information thereon, the integrity of the information, and the interchangeability of the tapes. *United Software Corp. v. Sperry Rand Corp.*, 5 C.L.S.R. 1492 (E.D. Pa. 1974).

TCP/IP

Transport Control Protocol/Internet Protocol

Technical Data

Means recorded information, regardless of the form or method of the recording of a scientific or technical nature (including computer software documentation). The term does not include computer software or data incidental to contract administration, such as financial and/or management information. U.S. D.O.D. Directive and D.O.D. F.A.R. Supplement, Federal Register, Vol. 53, No. 209 43698.

Means data which are part of a scientific or technical nature. Technical data does not include computer software, but does include manuals and instructional materials and technical data formatted as a computer data base. Federal Acquisition Regulation (FAR): Rights in Technical Data (Proposed Rules), Federal Register, Vol. 55, No. 199.

Technical Regulation

Means a document which lays down goods characteristics or their related processes and production methods, or services characteristics or their related operating methods, including the applicable administrative provisions, with which compliance is mandatory. It may also include or deal exclusively with terminology, symbols, packaging, marking or labelling requirements as they apply to a good, process, or production or operating method. North American Free Trade Agreement between Canada, Mexico and the United States, Article 915.

Technical Specification

Means a specification which lays down goods characteristics or their related processes and production methods, or services characteristics or their related operating methods, including the applicable administrative provisions. It may also include or deal exclusively with terminology, symbols, packaging, marking or labelling requirements as they apply to a good, process, or production or operating method. North American Free Trade Agreement between Canada, Mexico and the United States, Article 1025.

Technological protection measures (Technological measure)

Devices, mechanisms or systems designed to guard against or restrict the unauthorised use of recordings or information and other material stored in digital formats. These include encryption technologies, and other software and hardware measures. Types of technological protection measures include copy-protection, access-protection codes and measures designed to restrict the use that can be made of material or information in other ways. *Digital Technology and the Copyright Act 1994: A Discussion Paper, Competition and Enterprise Branch, July 2001 (New Zealand).*

Any technology, device or component that, in the normal course of its operation, is designed to prevent or restrict acts, in respect of works or other subject-matter, which are not authorized by the rightholder of any copyright or any right related to copyright as provided for by law or the sui generis right provided for in Chapter III of Directive 96/9/EC. Technological measures shall be deemed "effective" where the use of a protected work or other subject-matter is controlled by the rightholders through application of an access control or protection process, such as encryption, scrambling or other transformation of the work or other subject-matter or a copy control mechanism, which achieves the protection objective. *Directive 2001/29/EC of the European Parliament and of the Council of 22 May 2001* on the harmonization of certain aspects of copyright and related rights in the information society.

Means a device or product, or a component incorporated into a process, that is designed, in the ordinary course of its operation, to prevent or inhibit the infringement of copyright in a work or other subject-matter by either or both of the following means: (a) by ensuring that access to the work or other subject matter is available solely by use of an access code or process (including decryption, unscrambling or other transformation of the work or other subject-matter) with the authority of the owner or licensee of the copyright; (b) through a copy control mechanism. *Copyright Amendment (Digital Agenda) Act 2000 Australia.*

Technologically Reliable

Having the qualities of: (a) being reasonably secure from intrusion and misuse; (b) providing a reasonable level of availability, reliability, and correct operation. General Usage for International Digitally Insured Commerce (Guidec), International Chamber of Commerce, 1997, available at http://www.icc.wbo.org/guidec2.htm.

Telecommunication(s)

The term "telecommunications" means the transmission, between or among points specified by the user, of information of the user's choosing, without change in the form or content of the information as sent and received. United States Telecommunications Act of 1996.

Means any transmission, emission or reception of signs, signals, writing, images, sounds or intelligence of any nature by radio, visual, electronic or other electromagnetic system. *Criminal Code* (Canada), R.S.C. 1985, c. C-46, s. 326(2).

The science of communication over distance. Such communications may involve transmission of electrical signals over wires or transmission of electrical signals by means of electromagnetic radiation through the atmosphere and/or through space. Any type of information may be carried by such signals, including sound, visible images and various types of printed and/or symbolic information. *C.P. Ltd. v. Intra Can. Telecommunications Ltd.*, Fed. T.D., Doc. Nos. T-650-86, T-651-86, Cullen J., January 25, 1988 (unreported).

The definition of telecommunication contained in *Websters Third New International Dictionary* defines "telecommunication" as follows: communication at a distance (as by cable, radio, telegraph, or television). *Intra Can. Telecommunications Ltd. v. C.P. Ltd.* (1986), 8 C.P.R. (3d) 390 (T.M. Opp. Bd.), reversed Fed. T.D., Doc. Nos. T-650-86, T-651-86, Cullen J., January 25, 1988 (unreported).

Means any transmissions of signs, signals, writing, images or sounds or intelligence of any nature by wire, radio, visual, optical or other electromagnetic system. *Copyright Act*, R.S.C. 1985, c. C-42, s. 2 [am. S.C. 1988, c. 65, s. 61].

Means the emission, reception, transmission, switching, storage and presentation of messages, communications, sounds, signs, signals, images, impressions and information by electric, electro-magnetic, electro-optical, sonic, supersonic, mechanical or chemical means or by a combination of any such means, and the processing and transformation of such messages, communications, sounds, signs, signals, images, impressions and information into useful forms, media or functions and, without restricting the generality of the foregoing, includes all means by which telephone, telegraph, wireless, data, facsimile, radio, television and other communication services are provided. *The Saskatchewan Telecommunications Act*, R.S.S. 1978, c. S-34, as amended.

Means any transmission, emission or reception of signs, signals, writing, images, sounds or intelligence of any nature by wire, radio, visual or other electromagnetic system. *Canadian Radio-television and Telecommunications Commission Act*, R.S.C. 1985, c. C-22, *Telesat Canada Act*, R.S.C. 1985, c. T-16, *Interpretation Act*, R.S.C. 1985, c. I-21.

Means a transmission, emission or reception of signs, signals, writings, images, sounds or intelligence of any nature by wire, radio, visual or other electromagnetic system. *Alta. Gov't Telephones v. Canada (CRTC)*, [1985] 2 F.C. 472 (Fed. T.D.), reversed [1986] 2 F.C. 179 (Fed. C.A.), reversed [1989] 2 S.C.R. 225.

Means any transmission, emission or reception of signs, signals, writing, images, sounds or intelligence of any nature by wire, radio or other electromagnetic system or by any optical or technical system. *Telecommunications Act* (Bill C-16, 1978), *Teleglobe Canada Reorganization and Divestiture Act*, S.C. 1987, c. 12, as amended.

From its inception, telecommunications has involved end-to-end transfer of information over communication channels (originally wires). Electrical signals transmitted over the communication channels were converted into a form intelligible to humans by devices at each end of the channel called "transducers". In telegraphy, the transducers originally were telegraph keys and sounders; these devices were largely supplanted by teletypewriters. In telephony, the transducers originally were telephone handsets. Telephones remain the most common transducers supplied by telephone carriers. Second Computer Inquiry (Tentative Decision), 72 F.C.C.2d 358 (F.C.C. 1979).

Means the emission, transmission or reception of intelligence by any wire, cable, radio, optical or other electromagnetic system, or by any similar technical system. *Telecommunications Act*, S.C. 1993, c. 38.

Means the transmission and reception of signals by any electromagnetic means. North American Free Trade Agreement between Canada, Mexico and the United States, Article 1310.

Telecommunication Facilities

Means any apparatus or combination of distinct apparatus capable of being used in the provision of a telecommunication service by the operator of a telecommunication undertaking. *Telecommunications Act* (Bill C-16, 1978).

Means any facility, apparatus or other thing that is used or is capable of being used for telecommunications or for any operation directly connected with telecommunications, and includes a transmission facility. *Telecommunications Act*, S.C. 1993, c. 38.

Telecommunications Associated Data

Means any data, including data pertaining to the telecommunications function of dialing, routing, addressing or signaling, that identifies, or purports to identify, the origin, the direction, the time, the duration of size as appropriate, the destination or termination of a telecommunication transmission generated or received by means of the telecommunications facility owned or operated by a service provider. *Lawful Access – Consultation Document, Depart. of Justice, Industry Canada, August 25, 2002.*

Telecommunications Common Carrier

Means a person who owns or operates a transmission facility used by that person or another person to provide telecommunications services to the public for compensation. *Telecommunications Act*, S.C. 1993, c. 38.

Telecommunications Equipment

The term "telecommunications equipment" means equipment, other than customer premises equipment, used by a carrier to provide telecommunications services, and includes software integral to such equipment (including upgrades). United States Telecommunications Act of 1996.

Telecommunications Service

Means a service provided by means of telecommunications facilities and includes the provision in whole or in part of telecommunications facilities and any related equipment, whether by sale, lease or otherwise. *Telecommunications Act*, S.C. 1993, c. 38.

Means a service provided by means of the transmission and reception of signals by any electromagnetic means, but does not mean the cable, broadcast or other electromagnetic distribution of radio or television programming to the public generally. North American Free Trade Agreement between Canada, Mexico and the United States, Article 915.

The term "telecommunications service" means the offering of telecommunications for a fee directly to the public, or to such classes of users as to be effectively available directly to the public, regardless of the facilities used. United States Telecommunications Act of 1996.

A service known as a computer on-line service, an electric bulletin board service (BBS), a network server or service provider or similar operation that provides for or authorizes the digital encoding, random access and/or storage of sound recordings or portions of sound recordings in a digitally encoded form for the transmission of those sound recordings in digital form via a telecommunications network or that provides access to such a telecommunications network to a subscriber's computer or other device that allows the transmission of material to be accessed by each subscriber independently of any other person having access to the service. "Telecommunications service" shall not include a "background music supplier" covered under Tariff No. 16 or a "supplier" covered under Tariff No. 17. Neighbouring Rights Internet Tariff, 1999-2002.

Includes a service known as a computer on-line service, an electronic bulletin board service (BBS), a network server or a service provider or similar operation that provides for or authorizes the digital encoding, random access and/or storage of musical works or portions of musical works in a digitally encoded form for the transmission of those musical works in digital encoded form for the transmission of those musical works in digital form via a telecommunications network or that provides access to such a telecommunications network to a subscriber's computer or other device that allows the transmission of material to be accessed by each subscriber independently of any other person having access to the service. "Telecommunications service" shall not include a "music supplier" covered under Tariff 16 or a "transmitter" covered under Tariff 17. Tariff 22 Transmission of Musical Works to Subscribers Via a Telecommunications Service Not Covered Under Tariff Nos. 16 or 17.

Telecommunications Systems

Are devices and techniques employed for the transmission of signs, signals, writings, images, sounds or data of any nature by wire, radio or other electromagnetic equipment. *Maltais v. R.* (1977), 33 C.C.C. (2d) 465 (S.C.C.).

"Telecommunications system" means "a system for conveying visual images, sounds, or other information via electronic means." Copyright, Designs, and Patents Act 1988, 1988, c. 48.

Telecommunications Undertaking

Means an undertaking in the field of telecommunication that is carried on in whole or in part within Canada or on a ship or aircraft registered in Canada. Canadian

Radio-television and Telecommunications Commission Act, R.S.C. 1985, c. C-22.

Telegram

Written matter intended to be transmitted by telegraphy for delivery to the addressee. This term also includes radiotelegrams unless otherwise specified. International Telecommunication Union, Radio Regulations (1982 Edition, Revised).

Any message or other communication transmitted or intended for transmission by a telegraph. *A-G v. The Edison Telephone Co. of London* (1880), 6 Q.B.D. 244 (Ex.D.).

Telegraph

(1) The term "telegraph" means a wire or wires used for the purpose of telegraphic communication, with any casing, coating, tube or pipe enclosing the same, and any apparatus connected therewith for the purpose of telegraphic communication; (2) Any apparatus for transmitting messages by electric signals is a telegraph, whether a wire is used or not, and that any apparatus, of which a wire used for telegraphic communication is an essential part, is a telegraphy, whether the communication is made by electricity or not; (3) An instrument or apparatus for communicating words or language to a distance by the use of electricity. *A-G v. The Edison Telephone Co. of London* (1880), 6 Q.B.D. 244 (Ex.D.).

No doubt in everyday speech telegraph is almost exclusively used to denote the electrical instrument which by means of a wire connecting that instrument with another instrument makes it possible to communicate signals or words of any kind. But the original meaning of the "telegraph" as given in the Oxford Dictionary, is: "An Apparatus for transmitting messages to a distance, usually by signs of some kind." In *Re Regulation and Control of Radio Communication in Canada (Radio Reference)*, [1932] A.C. 304 (P.C.).

An apparatus for transmitting messages to a distance, usually by signs of some kind. CNCP Telecommunications: Interconnection with Bell Canada, CRTC Decision 79-11 (May 1979); *Alta. Gov't Telephones v. Canada (CRTC)*, [1985] 2 F.C. 472 (Fed. Ct.), reversed [1986] 2 F.C. 179 (Fed. C.A.), reversed [1989] 2 S.C.R. 225.

Telegraphy

A system of telecommunication which is concerned in any process providing transmission and reproduction at a distance of documentary matter, such as written or printed matter or fixed images, or the reproduction at a distance of any kind of information in such a form; a system of telecommunication for the transmission of written matter by the use of a signal code. CNCP Telecommunications: Interconnection with Bell Canada, CRTC Decision 79-11 (May 1979); International Telecommunication Union, Radio Regulations (1982 Edition, Revised).

Telephone

Means any instrument or device into which messages may be spoken or introduced for transmission over the . . . system by wire, without wires, or by radio transmission or by which such messages may be recorded, heard or seen. The Manitoba Telephone Act, R.S.M. 1970, c. T-40, as amended.

An instrument, apparatus or device for conveying sound to a distance, especially that of the voice. CNCP Telecommunications: Interconnection with Bell Canada, CRTC Decision 79-11 (May 1979).

Telephony

A system of telecommunication set up for the transmission of speech or, in some cases other sounds. CNCP Telecommunications: Interconnection with Bell Canada, CRTC Decision 79-11 (May 1979); International Telecommunication Union, Radio Regulations (1982 Edition, Revised).

Teletext

Teletext was adopted in and has been used since 1976 by the CCITT as the provisional name for a new public text communication service proposed to be used internationally and which, in addition to the existing telex services, would offer more sophisticated features combining certain office typewriter facilities (including editing functions) and transmission functions to communicate with remote stations via the public switched networks. The name "Teletext" has been consistently and widely used in the telecommunications field to refer to the particular system of text communication. *Re Application by Siemens Aktiengesellschaft* (1983), 1 I.P.R. 1 (Aus. Pat. Office).

Teletype Exchange Service (TWX)

Teletypewriter exchange service (TWX) provides for communication by teletypewriter on a message basis between customers subscribing to the service and for transmission of a message from TWX service located at a point in Canada to a TELEX subscriber of Western Union located in the United States (including Alaska) or to a TWX service located in the United States and reached through the Western Union store and forward computer. *Alta. Gov't Telephones v. Canada (CRTC)*, [1985] 2 F.C. 472 (Fed. T.D.), reversed [1986] 2 F.C. 179 (Fed. C.A.), reversed [1989] 2 S.C.R. 225.

Teletype Service

Such communications consist of transmission of electric impulses which are reproduced in the form of printed characters. *Alta. Gov't Telephones v. Canada (CRTC)*, [1985] 2 F.C. 472 (Fed. T.D.), reversed [1986] 2 F.C. 179 (Fed. C.A.), reversed [1989] 2 S.C.R. 225.

Teletypewriter

Teletypewriters . . . originally were used purely for record communications either by, or in connection with, services offered by telegraph and record carriers. With the development of remotely-accessible computers, they became the predominant form of computer input/output terminal, although their design remained unchanged as their character of use changed. The teletypewriter art today, using technological innovations of the computer industry and in recognition of their common usage with remote computers, has progressed to the point where teletypewriting terminals no longer only reproduce input information which appears at their keyboard or paper tape reader inputs. Today's "smart" teletypewriters, or data terminals, are themselves miniature computers with information-processing capabilities used to generate information and to operate on and alter information received at their inputs. Second Computer Inquiry (Tentative Decision), 72 F.C.C.2d 358 (F.C.C. 1979).

Teletypewriters . . . generate discrete patterns of on-off electrical impulses, each of which is designed to represent a particular character of the alphabet or a particular number or symbol. The selection of a particular pattern to be transmitted is made by depression of the corresponding teletypewriter key, or by special sensing circuits which "read" patterns of holes punched in a paper tape. Thus, by simply typing a message on the teletypewriter keyboard, or inserting a prepunched paper tape, the sending part is able to transmit over the communications network a sequence of "digital" signals representing a particular textual message. At the receiving location, a similar teletypewriter employs the sequence of electrical signals received to activate the typewriter keyboard (or a paper punch) and thus reconstruct in either typewriter or punched paper from the original message text. As with voice terminals the messages are transmitted and received essentially instantaneously and as entered by the sender. Teletypewriters operate in the asynchronous mode, a method whereby individual characters can be initiated at any arbitrary time (as by the stroke of a finger at the keyboard) and at any character rate, provided that the maximum capability of the device communications channel is not exceeded. In modern teletypewriters this maximum is about 10 characters per second, or 100 words per minute. These speeds are compatible with human reaction times in operating these instruments. Dataspeed 40/4, 52 F.C.C.2d 21 (F.C.C. 1977).

A device which produces an electrical signal on the communications line in response to the depression of a typewriter-type key, or the scanning of a punched paper tape. Similarly, it imprints a character on paper, or punches it on paper tape, in response to incoming electrical signals. The teletypewriter was designed for, and is basically used for, terminal-to-terminal transmission of record (hard copy) messages. With the development of computers, however, the teletypewriter has been used increasingly for the input and output of computer data — both on-site and from remote locations via communications lines. Dataspeed 40/4, 5 C.L.S.R. 1323 (F.C.C. 1976).

Telex

Is a public switched service operating between teleprinters equipped with a dial to call the desired party. CNCP Telecommunications: Interconnection with Bell Canada, CRTC Decision 79-11 (May 1979).

Tempest-Qualified

Tempest-Qualified denotes a technological development by which computer hardware is internally immunized from external electronic surveillance, e.g., wiretaps or bugs. *Delta Data Systems Corporation v. Webster*, Comp. Ind. Lit. Reptr. 1,291 (D.C. 1984).

Terminal

Microprocessor technology has clearly made it possible for terminals to automatically perform many processing operations, which they previously performed poorly or not at all by employing techniques formerly limited to central computers. Many of the input/output processing functions necessary to establish: (a) network control and (b) interaction of a computer with specific terminals, are now done by distributed terminals. Microprocessor technology also permits terminals to perform many sophisticated arithmetic and word processing functions at the remote location while reducing the processing load at the central location. Thus technology may have rendered meaningless any real distinction between "terminals" and computers. Second Computer Inquiry (Tentative Decision), 72 F.C.C.2d 358 (F.C.C. 1979).

Terminals are simply video screens with keyboards that serve as input-output devices for the main computer. *Step-Saver Data Systems, Inc. v. Wyse Technology*, 2 CCH Computer Cases 46,503 (3rd Cir. 1991).

Terminal Attachment

Means any equipment, device or contrivance capable of transmitting, routing or receiving messages or signals through the telephone services offered by the commission through the system, but does not include a passive telephone answering device. The Manitoba Telephone Act, R.S.M. 1970, c. T-40, as amended.

Terminal Equipment

Means any digital or analog device capable of processing, receiving, switching, signalling or transmitting signals by electromagnetic means and that is connected by radio or wire to a public telecommunications transport network at a termination point. North American Free Trade Agreement between Canada, Mexico and the United States, Article 1310.

Equipment located at the customer's premises, used for voice or data communications (e.g. telephone set). *Report to the Governor in Council: Status of Com-*

petition in Canadian Telecommunications Markets, Deployment/Accessibility of Advanced Telecommunications Infrastructure and Services, September, 2001.

Tested Telex

Tested telexes are telexes which contain codes or tests which are secret between the sender and the recipient, by which the recipient can recognize that the telex has been sent by and with the authority of the bank which purported to send it . . . It is the electronic signature of the bank sending the message. By itself it demonstrates to the recipient that the message received is the message of the sending bank which can be safety and securely acted upon by the recipient without question or any further investigation. *Standard Bank London Ltd. v. The Bank of Tokyo Ltd.* [1995] 2 Lloyd's Rep. 169 (Q.B.D.).

Third-Party Maintainers (TPMs)

Third-Party Maintainers provide a maintenance service for computers designed and manufactured by others. *DPCE (U.K.) Ltd. v. International Computers Ltd.*, Q.B.D., Saville J., July 31, 1985 (unreported).

Threat and Risk Assessment

Threat and risk assessment is the process of assessing threats, vulnerabilities and assets to determine the level of security risk associated with the operation of a system. Security and Electronic Authorization and Authentication Guideline, Communications Security Establishment, Government of Canada September 1995, CID/01/15.

3DO

A technical format for the new generation of *multimedia* machines, licensed to several manufacturers. Monopolies and Mergers Commission — Video Games: A report on the supply of video games in the UK (LONDON: HMSO Cm2781).

3.5 Inch Microdisks and Media

As an unrecorded flexible magnetic disk recording media, with or without protective covering, for ultimate use in recording and storing data with a 3.5 inch floppy disk drive, a 3.5 inch microdisk is a tested or untested magnetically coated polyester disk with a steel hub encased in a hard plastic jacket. 3.5 inch microdisks are used to record and store encoded digital computer information for access by a 3.5 inch floppy disk drive. They include single-sided, double-sided or high density formats. Coated media is the flexible recording material used in the finished microdisk. Media consists of a polyester base film to which a coating of magnetically charged particles is bonded and it is intended for use specifically in a 3.5 inch floppy disk drive. A 3.5 inch microdisk is used to record and store encoded, digital computer information for random access by the head of a 3.5 inch floppy disk drive. The 3.5 inch format is smaller than the previously introduced 8 inch and 5.25 inch formats, enabling manufacturers to downsize disk drives so that computers with 3.5 inch disk drives are more compact than with previous formats. The production process for 3.5 inch microdisks involves: (1) the precise coating of a clear mylar or polyester base film with a suspension of magnetically charged particles, bonded to the film by sophisticated binders, resulting in "webs" of "coated media"; (2) the punching out of doughnut-shaped "cookies" from the webs of coated media; (3) "burnishing" of cookies to remove imperfections in the coated disk surface; (4) precise attachment of a stainless steel "hub" to the burnished cookie; and (5) assembly of the hubbed, burnished cookied inside a plastic protective "clamshell" between soft synthetic lines (which wipe the surface as the disk turns) held in place by a spring. The clamshell has a shutter mechanism that seals the disk when it is not in use but opens when the disk is in use to allow the disk-drive head access to the media. Microdisks are tested (certified) at various stages in the production process. The precise point of certification differs among manufacturers. Some manufacturers perform only statistical controls during the media coating stages, and delay certification until after assembly. Others certify after the cookies have been burnished, discard "bad" cookies, and certify again after assembly. The 3.5 inch microdisk is available in various formats, each of which represents progressive advances in memory capacity. Currently, there are single-sided double-density 3.5 inch microdisks (SSDD), double-sided double-density 3.5 inch microdisks (DSDD), and high density 3.5 inch microdisks (HD). All 3.5 inch microdisks share a common end use (as memory storage devices for computers) and perform their function in the same way (by storing encoded computer data in the magnetic particles on the media). However, different densities are not fully interchangeable, since disk drives are specifically engineered to accept a particular density of media. Use of a higher density 3.5 inch microdisk in a drive designed for lower density 3.5 inch microdisks is possible, although the higher cost makes such use unlikely, and there is increased risk of data loss. *International Trade Commission Determination re 3.5-Inch Microdisks*, 1 CCH Comp. Cases 60,024 (ITC Inv. No. 731-Ta-389).

Tie Trunk (TT)

Is a facility connecting private branch exchanges (PBX) and/or Centrex systems in two locations. While the prime purpose is to exchange traffic between two PBXs, the customer normally has universal access to local and long distance telephone service. CNCP Telecommunications: Interconnection with Bell Canada, CRTC Decision 79-11 (May 1979).

Tiering

The practice of marketing cable television in service packages comprising one or more channels each. The tiers are often differentiated by whether or not subscribers are charged for access to individual channels in the tiers. Basic tiers usually include a number of conventional off-air broadcast signals while discretionary tiers offer specialty and pay services at an increased price. Submission of the

Director of Investigation and Research to the CRTC Re Public Notice CRTC 1994-130.

Tiled Windowing System

In the tiled windowing system . . . all open main application windows are visible to the user and are arranged side by side, like tiles on a floor. The screen is always entirely filled by whichever windows happen to be opened at any given time. When one window is opened, closed, moved, or resized, all other windows must be redrawn to accommodate the change. *Apple Computer Inc. v. Microsoft Corp.*, Vol. 9, No. 6, Comp. Law. Rep. 1043.

Time-Bomb

A computer program that triggers an unauthorized act at a particular time. A Time-Bomb is one kind of Logic Bomb. Many viruses include time-bombs so that damage is caused to stored data on a given date. *A Survey of Legal Issues Relating to the Security of Electronic Information*, Department of Justice, Canada.

Time Stamping

An electronic equivalent of mail. UNCITRAL Report of the Working Group on Electronic Commerce, September 18-29, 2000, A/CN. 94/483.

Time-Sharing Computer

A time-sharing computer network consists of a central computer, which stores programs and performs all calculations, and user terminals. Individual users access the central computer through telephone connections and terminals located in their own offices. Typically, users face a monthly fee for access privileges plus an hourly rate for time actually spent using the central computer. *Flip Mortgage Corp. v. McElhone*, 841 F.2d 531 (4th Cir. 1988).

Timesharing refers to the simultaneous use of a computer by many users, each of whom can interact with that computer, i.e. ask yes-no questions and receive immediate responses. *Association of Data Processing Service Organizations, Inc. v. Board of Governors of the Federal Reserve System*, Comp. Ind. Lit. Reptr. 1,1643 (Crt. App. D.C. 1984).

Time-Stamp

Means either: (a) to append or attach to a message, digital signature, or certificate a digitally signed notation indicating at least the date and time the notation was appended or attached, and the identity of the person appending or attaching the notation; or (b) the notation thus appended or attached. *Utah Digital Signature Act* 46-3, available at http://www.le.state.ut.us/code/TITLE46/htm/46_03004.htm.

Tokens

Anything that can be used to identify the user. *A Survey of Legal Issues Relating to the Security of Electronic Information*, Department of Justice, Canada.

Are portable physical devices, such as smart cards, that have computer chips for storing information, (e.g. identifying characteristics about the token holder). Advancing Global Electronic Commerce: Technology Solutions to Public Policy Challenges, The Computer Systems Policy Project, July 1999, available at http://www.cspp.org/projects/july99_cto_report.pdf.

Toll

Toll is the word used to describe long-distance as opposed to local facilities and service. *Alta. Gov't Telephones v. Canada (CRTC)*, [1985] 2 F.C. 472 (Fed. T.D.), reversed [1986] 2 F.C. 179 (Fed. C.A.), reversed [1989] 2 S.C.R. 225.

Top Down Programming

This involves a structured plan of the total software product and permits changes and additions to be incorporated as the whole product development proceeds. *Missing Link Software v. Magee*, Ch. D., Barker J., October 18, 1988 (unreported).

Top-Level Domain

A Top-Level Domain refers to the final section of an Internet address - com, gov, net, org, and so forth. The Emerging Digital Economy, United States Department of Commerce, http://www.ecommerce.gov.

That portion of the domain name that appears furthest to the right. For example, the .ca in *www.yourbusiness.ca. Domain Name System Reform and Related Internet Governance Issues: A Consultation Paper*, Industry Canada available at *www.strategis.gc.ca*

Topography

See also Mask Works.

The design, however expressed, of any of the following: (a) the pattern fixed, or intended to be fixed in or upon a layer of a semiconductor product; (b) the pattern fixed, or intended to be fixed, in or upon a layer of material in the course of, and for the purpose of, the manufacture of a semiconductor product; (c) the arrangement of the layers of a semiconductor product in relation to one another, The Semiconductor Products (Protection of Topography) Regulations 1987 (U.K., SI 1987/1497).

A series of related images, however fixed or encoded: (i) representing the three-dimensional pattern of the layers of which a semiconductor product is composed; and (ii) in which series, each image has the pattern or part of the pattern of a surface of the semiconductor product at any stage of its manufacture. European Economic Community Council Directive, 87/54/EEC (OJ No. L.24, 27.1.87).

Means a series of related images, however fixed or encoded, which represents the three-dimensional pattern of the layers constituting a semiconductor integrated circuit; and in which series, each image has the pattern or part of the pattern of the surface of the semiconductor integrated circuit in its final or any intermediate form. Semiconductor Chip Protection in Canada, Proposals for Legislation, Consumer and Corporate Affairs Canada.

"Layout-design" (topography) means "the three-dimensional disposition, however expressed, of the elements, at least one of which is an active element, and of some or all of the interconnections of an integrated circuit, or such a three-dimensional disposition prepared for an integrated circuit intended for manufacture." World Intellectual Property Organization Treaty on Intellectual Property in Respect of Integrated Circuits.

Means the design, however expressed, of the disposition of (a) the interconnections, if any, and the elements for the making of an integrated circuit product, or (b) the elements, if any, and the interconnections for the making of a customization layer or layers to be added to an integrated circuit product in an intermediate form. Integrated Circuit Topography Act, S.C. 1990, c. 37.

Touchscreen

A touchscreen is a user-friendly input device commonly used in interactive programs. *Softel Inc. v. Dragon Medical and Scientific Communications, Inc.*, 1992 U.S. Dist. LEXIS 9502 (S.D.N.Y. 1992).

TPMs

Technological Protection Measures

Tracker ball

Hand-operated device used to move objects on the screen. Monopolies and Mergers Commission — Video Games: A report on the supply of video games in the UK (LONDON: HMSO Cm2781).

Trade Secret

A trade secret may consist of any formula, pattern, device, or compilation of information which is used in a business, and which gives an opportunity to obtain an advantage over competitors who do not know how to use it. It may be a formula for a chemical compound, a process of manufacturing, treating or preserving materials, a pattern for a machine or other device, or a list of customers. 4 *Restatement of Torts* (Philadelphia: American Law Institute, 1939).

Traffic Data

Means any computer data relating to a communication by means of a computer system, generated by a computer system that formed a part in the chain of communication, indicating the communication's origin, destination, route, time, date, size, duration, or type of underlying service. *Committee of Experts on Crime in Cyb-Space, Draft Convention on Cyber Crime (PC-CY).*

Transaction Processing Systems

Transaction-processing systems collect and keep track of information relating to a transaction. Examples range from direct marketing systems, mail order catalogue purchasing systems, telephone records systems, and so forth. Privacy-Enhancing Technologies: The Path to Anonymity, Information and Privacy Commissioner/Ontario, August 1995, available at http://www.ipc.on.ca.

Trans-Border Flows of Personal Data

Means movements of personal data across national borders. OECD Guidelines on the Protection of Privacy and Transborder Flows of Personal Data, dated September 23, 1980, available at http://www.oecd.org/dsti/sti/it/secur/prod/privacyguide.htm.

Trans-Canada Telephone System (TCTS) (now Telecom Canada)

The Trans-Canada Telephone System is a loose consortium of independent fully integrated telecommunications undertakings which work together to establish methods of planning, building plant for, and operating long distance telecommunication services within Canada in Canadian facilities. The TCTS network provides a full range of coast-to-coast telecommunications services and a wide variety of transmission facilities, including, among others, coast-to-coast microwave radio relay systems and satellite channels. TCTS was originally formed in 1931 in response to the desire to have an all-Canadian long-distance integrated telephone network on a coast-to-coast basis. TCTS serves three main purposes. First, it provides a mechanism through which each member offers national telecommunications services to its customers. Second, it establishes a process of planning, standard setting, and cooperation which permits the constructions and operation by the ten members, working together, of a national telecommunications network. Third, it provides a mechanism where members can cooperate in areas where savings and efficiencies can be achieved through joint action, e.g. certain technical or market research projects. *Alta. Gov't Telephones v. Canada (CRTC)*, [1985] 2 F.C. 472 (Fed. T.D.), reversed [1986] 2 F.C. 179 (Fed. C.A.), reversed [1989] 2 S.C.R. 225.

Transducer

A transducer is a two-port device (an input and an output port) which converts input energy of one form to output energy of another. For example, the input port might convert human inputs into electrical signals capable of transmission, while the output port would convert electrical transmission signals into a form intelligible to humans. The transducers . . . include telephones, teletypewriters, facsimile terminals, signature reproduction terminals (a primitive form of a facsimile terminal) and electronic display device such as cathode-ray tube (CRT) and luminescent displays. Second Computer Inquiry (Tentative Decision), 72 F.C.C.2d 358 (F.C.C. 1979).

Basic media conversion devices. Second Computer Inquiry (Tentative Decision), 72 F.C.C.2d 358 (F.C.C. 1979).

Transform

The processing of a data from its source to its derived form. Typical transforms include XML Canonicalization, XPath, and XSLT. *XML-Signature Syntax and Processing, W3C Recommendation 12 February 2002.*

Transient copying

The creation of temporary or incidental copies in the process of transmission of files across a computer network or the Internet, often in a cache, but the term also includes storage of information in a volatile medium such as computer memory. Transient copying is often the result of an automatic process, and users will usually not be aware of the creation or existence of temporary files. Files could reside in a cache for a period ranging from seconds to weeks (or indefinitely) depending on the nature of the cache but such storage is incidental to the purpose of transmission. *Digital Technology and the Copyright Act 1994: A Discussion Paper, Competition and Enterprise Branch, July 2001 (New Zealand).*

Transistor

A transistor is a semiconductor device with three electrodes called emitter, collector, and base region. It performs most of the functions of a vacuum tube with the added advantages of longer life, ruggedness, and small size. Its typical uses are as an amplifier and as an electrical switch. *Sperry Rand Corp. v. Rothlein*, 241 F.Supp. 549 (D. Conn. 1964).

Transiting

Is the provision of telephone company facilities to interconnect the terminals of two different specialized common carriers. *MCI Communications Corp. v. AT&T*, 4 C.L.S.R. 1119 (E.D.Pa. 1973).

Transitional Storage

Storage repositories used to hold image and related data records, other than in secure storage. National Standard of Canada, Microfilm and Electronic Images as documentary evidence, Can/CGSB-72.11-93.

Transmission

Process of transferring information over a telecommunications link or broadcast medium. *Digital Technology and the Copyright Act 1994: A Discussion Paper, Competition and Enterprise Branch, July 2001 (New Zealand).*

Transmission Apparatus

Means any apparatus that is used for: (a) the switching of information transmitted by telecommunication; (b) the input, capture, storage, organization, modification, retrieval, output or other processing of information transmitted by telecommunication; or (c) control of the speed, code, protocol, content, format, routing or similar aspects of the transmission of information by telecommunication. *Lawful Access – Consultation Document, Depart. of Justice, Industry Canada, August 25, 2002.*

Transmission Control Protocol (TCP)

The Transmission Control Protocol (TCP) is implemented in software running in the end nodes. It opens and closes the connections necessary to allow the exchange of information; its function is to ensure that any message is sent, not to interpret the message. TCP software does this by numbering the packets being sent, keeping track of them as they arrive at the destination, demanding retransmission until all packets get through, and giving them to the user in the proper order upon receipt. TCP software at the source computer will continue to send any packet until the destination computer sends an acknowledgement of receipt. TCP software will also adapt to the speed with which data is being transmitted according to the amount of congestion on the network. *Public Performance of Musical Works 1996-1998 (Tariff 22) (1999), 1 C.P.R. (4th) 417 (Copyright Board).*

Transmission Facility

Is the communications "pipeline" where channels of communication are provided for the transmission of voice and non-voice services. *Second Computer Inquiry (Tentative Decision), 72 F.C.C.2d 358 (F.C.C. 1979).*

Means any wire, cable, radio, optical or other electromagnetic system, or any similar technical system, for the transmission or intelligence between network termination points, but does not incude any exempt transmission apparatus. *Telecommunications Act, S.C. 1993, c. 38.*

Means any wire, cable, radio, optical or other electromagnetic system, or any other (similar) technical system, used for the transmission of information between network termination points. *Lawful Access – Consultation Document, Depart. of Justice, Industry Canada, August 25, 2002.*

Transmission Technology

Typical examples include signal processing, error control, and multiplexing. *Second Computer Inquiry (Notice of Inquiry), 5 C.L.S.R. 1381 (F.C.C. 1976).*

Transparent Multi-Vendor Networking Solution

Any-to-any connections such that the user remains unaware of what system it is physically connected to or what system its applications are running on. *IBM v.*

Fujitsu Ltd., Copyright L.R. (CCH) 20,517 (Am. Arbtn. Assoc. Comm. Arbtn. Trib. 1988).

Transponder

The part of a satellite that receives a signal, amplifies it, changes its frequency and transmits it back to earth. Submission of the Director of Investigation and Research to the CRTC Re Public Notice CRTC 1994-130.

A transponder is a combination of radio receiver and transmitter which receives a radio signal from a station on the ground and transmits it to other receiving stations on the ground. *The Western Union Telegraph Company v. TSI Ltd.*, 545 F.Supp. 329 (D. N. Jer. 1982).

Trap and Trace Device

Means a device which captures the incoming electronic or other impulses which identify the originating number of an instrument or device from which a wire or electronic communication was transmitted. *Electronic Communications Privacy Act* of 1986, Pub. L. 89-508 (1986).

TRIPS Agreement WTO (Agreement on Trade Related Aspects of Intellectual Property)

Agreement on Trade-Related Aspects of Intellectual Property Rights 1994; Annex 1C to the Agreement Establishing the World Trade Organisation (*WTO*). TRIPS is one of a number of trade-related agreements administered by the *WTO*. *Digital Technology and the Copyright Act 1994: A Discussion Paper, Competition and Enterprise Branch, July 2001 (New Zealand).*

Trade Related Aspects of Intellectual Property.

Trojan Horse

A computer program with an apparently or actually useful function that contains additional, hidden functions that operate once inside the computer system. Generally, Trojan Horses refer to hidden operations that cause damage to computer systems or that compromise the security of the system. *A Survey of Legal Issues Relating to the Security of Electronic Information*, Department of Justice, Canada.

A computer program whose execution would result in undesired side effects, generally unanticipated by the user. A Trojan horse program may otherwise give the appearance of providing normal functionality. *Cryptography's Role in Securing the Information Society*, United States National Research Council, 1996.

Trust

The concept that a system will provide its intended functionality with a stated level of confidence. The term is also used for other entities, e.g., trusted software, trusted network, trusted individual. Sometimes the confidence—also called the assurance—can be measured, but sometimes it is inferred on the basis of testing and of other information. *Cryptography's Role in Securing the Information Society*, United States National Research Council, 1996.

(Trusted) Third Party (TTPs)

A "(trusted) third party" is a security authority or its agent that is trusted with respect to some security-related activities (in the context of a security policy) — ISO/IEC 10181-1. Security and Electronic Authorization and Authentication Guideline, Communications Security Establishment, Government of Canada September 1995, CID/01/15.

Security authorities or agents that are trusted with respect to some security-related activities; often the term is used to refer to a certification authority operated by someone other than the data owner. A Cryptology Policy Framework for Electronic Commerce, Task Force on Electronic Commerce, Industry Canada, February 1998.

A trusted third party is the term used for an independent third party who is trusted by both the user and service provider alike (comparable to a "digital attorney"). This party can be entrusted with keeping such things as the master key linking digital pseudonyms with the true identities of their users. The trusted party knows that the relationship between an user's true identities and pseudo-identities must be kept completely secret. However, if certain conditions require it, the trusted party will be permitted to reveal the user's identity (under previously agreed upon terms) to a service provider. The conditions under which an individual's identity would be revealed must be known to both the user and service provider prior to entering into an agreement with the trusted party. Privacy-Enhancing Technologies: The Path to Anonymity, Information and Privacy Commissioner/Ontario, August 1995, available at http://www.ipc.on.ca.

An entity trusted by other entities with respect to security related services and activities, such as a certification authority. UNCITRAL Report of the Working Group on Electronic Commerce, September 18-29, 2000, A/CN. 94/483.

Trustworthy

Conducting business in a manner that warrants the trust of a reasonable person active in commerce, and having capabilities, competence, and other resources which are sufficient to enable performance of one's legal duties, and assure unbiased action. General Usage for International Digitally Insured Commerce (Guidec), International Chamber of Commerce, 1997, available at http://www.icc.wbo.org/guidec2.htm.

Trustworthy Manner

Means through the use of computer hardware, software, and procedures that, in the context in which they are used: (a) can be shown to be reasonably resistant to penetration, compromise, and misuse; (b) provide a reasonable level of reliability and correct operation; (c) are reasonably suited to performing their intended functions or serving their intended purposes, (d) comply with applicable agreements between the parties, if any; and (e) adhere to generally accepted security procedures. *Illinois Electronic Commerce Security Act* 1998 5 Ill. Comp. Stat. 175.

Trustworthy System

Means computer hardware and software which: (a) are reasonably secure from intrusion and misuse;(b) provide a reasonable level of availability, reliability, and correct operation; and (c) are reasonably suited to performing their intended functions. *Utah Digital Signature Act* 46-3, available at http://www.le.state.ut.us/code/TITLE46/htm/46_03004.htm.

Tumbling

Changing either the ESN or the MIN (or both) programmed into a particular cellular telephone instrument, often using numbers chosen at random. *United States v. Brady*, 820 F.Supp. 1346 (C.D. Utah 1993).

Turnkey Computer System

A system sold as a package which is ready to function immediately. The hardware and software elements are combined into a single unit—the computer system—prior to sale. *Neilson Business Equipment v. Monteleone*, 524 A.2d 1172 (Del. Sup. Ct. 1987).

The term "turnkey" is intended to describe a self-sufficient system to which the purchaser need only "turn the key" in order to commence operation. *Diversified Graphics Ltd. v. Ernst & Whinney*, 868 F.2d 293 (8th Cir. 1989).

Twisted Copper Pair

The transmission medium used by telephone companies for voice and data communication consisting of two insulated wires twisted together. Twisted copper pair has a much lower carrying capacity than coaxial cable, the transmission medium used by cable companies to trasmit video signals. Submission of the Director of Investigation and Research to the CRTC Re Public Notice CRTC 1994-130.

Two-Way Cable System

A cable television system with the capacity to transmit signals to the headend as well as away from it. Two-way or bidirectional systems carry data and full audio and video television signals in either direction. Submission of the Director of Investigation and Research to the CRTC Re Public Notice CRTC 1994-130.

Typeface

A typeface can be defined as a set of letters, numbers, or other symbolic characters, whose forms are related by repeating design elements consistently applied in a notational system and are intended to be embodied in articles whose intrinsic utilitarian function is for use in composing text or other cognizable combinations of characters. U.S. Library of Congress, Copyright Office, 53 F.R. 38110; *Eltra Corporation v. Ringer*, 579 F.2d 294 (5th Cir. 1978).

Typosquatting

Registering domain names that are intentional misspellings of distinctive or famous names. *Shields v. Zuccarini* case no. 00-2236 (3rd. Cir. June 15, 2001).

UCITA

Uniform Computer Information Transaction Act (U.S.)

UECA

Uniform Electronic Commerce Act (Uniform Law Conference of Canada)

UETA

Uniform Electronic Transactions Act (U.S.)

Unbundled

Services, programs, software and training sold separately from the hardware. *The Challenge of the Information Highway: Final Report of the Information Highway Advisory Council* (September 1995).

Unbundling

Unbundling involves the offering of individual components or services of the local telephone network on a desegregated (or piece-by-piece) basis in order to facilitate sustainable competition. Competition and Culture on Canada's Information Highway: Managing the Realities of Transition, CRTC (the "Convergence Report"), May 19, 1995.

Unicast

Generally speaking, information transmitted over the Internet is delivered in a unicast pull mode: pull, because the user requests or "pulls" the information when desired, and unicast, because packets go to only one recipient. Alternative delivery modes associated with audio files involve multicasting and the use of streaming software. *Public Performance of Musical Works* 1996-1998 (Tariff 22) (1999), 1 C.P.R. (4th) 417 (Copyright Board).

Universal Resource Location (URL)

Universal Resource Locator refers to the address of information or a resource on the Internet. A URL is in two parts: an indication of the transmission mechanism or protocol to be used and the location in the form of an Internet address (usually in the form of a domain name). An example is *http://www.med.govt.nz*, where the address is *www.med.govt.nz* and the protocol is HyperText Transmission Protocol (HTTP). *Digital Technology and the Copyright Act 1994: A Discussion Paper, Competition and Enterprise Branch, July 2001 (New Zealand).*

The first element of the URL is a transfer protocol (most commonly, "http" - standing for hypertext transfer protocol). The remaining elements of this URL . . . are an alias for the fully qualified domain name of the host. *Intermatic Inc. v. Toeppen,* 40 U.S.P.Q. (2d) 1412 (N.D. Ill. 1996).

The address or location of a document accessible on the World Wide Web. Ministry of Revenue Advisory Committee, Report of the Committee On Electronic Commerce, April 30, 1998, Industry Canada.

This is an acronym for Uniform Resource Locator. A URL is the address for a resource or site (usually a directory or file) on the World Wide Web, and the convention that browsers use for locating files and other remote services. URLs work something like telephone numbers, broadcast frequencies, and call numbers of books in a library. It is a unique identifier for a site or file. A URL includes a domain name (which is actually a unique Net server address) and a hierarchical description of a file"s location on the server. For example, the URL of the IPC Web site is "http://www.ipc.on.ca. The first part of a URL, before the colon, tells you the type of resource or method of access at that address. The part of the URL after the colon is typically the address of the computer where the data or service is located. Additional parts may specify the names of files, the port to connect to, or the text to search for in a database. The Internet: A Guide For Ontario Government Organizations, Information and Privacy Commissioner/Ontario, May 1998, available at http://www.ipc.on.ca.

The address that lets you locate a particular site. For example, http://www.ftc.gov is the URL for the Federal Trade Commission. All government URLs end in .gov. Non-profit organizations and trade associations end in .org. For example, http:// www.naag.org is the URL for the National Association of Attorneys General. Commercial companies now end in .com, although additional suffixes or domains may be used as the number of businesses on the Internet grows. Other countries use different endings. Cyberspeak — Learning the Language, the Federal Trade Commission and the National Association of Attorneys General, available at http:/ /www.ftc.gov/bcp/conline/pubs/online/sitesee/index.html.

Unit of Information

Although there is some blurring and a particular name is not always used to designate the same unit of information, the evidence is that a common description of units of information, in ascending order of magnitude is a character, such as a letter or digit; a field or area, which is one item of useful information such as yes or no to a question; a record, which is a few items of information, such as Mr. Smith 5 October Sheraton Hong Kong; a file, which is a collection of records which would be looked at together, such as a file of the Qantas flights for September; and a volume, which is a collection of files. *Madeley Pty Ltd. v. Touche Ross,* McGarvie, J., Aust. Fed. Ct., Dec. 21, 1989 (unreported).

Universal Access

The ability to get on-line to a network from anywhere or any place. *The Challenge of the Information Highway: Final Report of the Information Highway Advisory Council* (September 1995).

Universal Service

A policy that local rates should be kept low enough to ensure that the maximum number of persons are able to afford basic telephone service. *The Challenge of the Information Highway: Final Report of the Information Highway Advisory Council* (September 1995).

Unix

Unix is a computer operating system; *i.e.*, it is a software program that oversees a computer's internal and external activities, including processing, resource allocation, communications, and applications used. Unix is one of the most highly-regarded operating systems in the world. Numerous treatises, courses, graduate student theses and research projects have investigated, expounded, and improved upon Unix. *Unix System Laboratories, Inc. v. Berkeley Software Design, Inc.*, 27 U.S.P.Q. 2d 1721 (D. New Jer. 1993).

Unmatched Call

A telephone call placed through a cellular telephone using an ESN/MIN combination not assigned to a bona fide customer or subscriber. *United States v. Brady*, 820 F.Supp. 1346 (C.D. Utah 1993).

Up and Running

In full operation. *Chatlos Systems Inc. v. NCR Corp.*, 479 F.Supp. 738 (D.N.J. 1979), affirmed 635 F.2d 1081 (3rd Cir. 1980).

Upgrade

An upgrade is a process by which additional features or equipment are added to an existing processor so as to enable it to perform greater or different functions. *Pacificorp Capital, Inc. v. New York*, CCH Comp. L.R. 46,338 (S.D.N.Y. 1990).

Uploading

Uploading is the reverse process (from downloading), transferring computer-stored data from one's own computer to a remote computer. *United States v. Riggs*, 2 CCH Comp. Cas. 43,316 (N.D. Ill. 1990).

Third parties known as "users", of electronic bulletin boards can transfer information over the telephone lines from their own computers to the storage media on the bulletin board by a process known as "uploading". Uploaded information is thereby recorded on the storage media. *Sega Enterprises Ltd. v. Maphia*, 30 U.S.P.Q. (2d) 1921 (N.D. Cal. 1994).

URL

Uniform Resource Locator

.us

The country code Top Level Domain (ccTLD) for the United States.

Useful Article

An article having an intrinsic utilitarian function that is not merely to portray the appearance of the article or to convey information. An article that is normally a party of a useful article is considered a "useful article", 17 U.S.C. 101 (1988).

USENET

A worldwide community of electronic BBSs that is closely associated with the Internet and with the Internet community. The messages in use that are organized into thousands of topical groups or "newsgroups". As a usenet user, you read and contribute "post" to your local usenet site. Each usenet site distributes its users' posting to other usenet sites based on various implicit and explicit configuration settings, and in turn receives postings from other sites. Usenet traffic typically consists of as much as 30 to 50 mb of messages per day. Usenet is read and contributed to on a daily basis by a total population of millions of people. There is no specific network that is the usenet. Usenet traffic flows over a wide range of networks, including the Internet and dial-up phone links. *Religious Technology Center v. Netcom On-Line*, 37 U.S.P.Q. 2d 1545 (N.D. Cal. 1995).

A valuable source of information where some people exchange technical data and others engage in scientific, religious or political debate. USENET is a heady mix of news, gossip, humour and passionate opinions. *Illegal and Offensive Content on the Information Highway, A Background Paper, Industry Canada* (June 19, 1995).

USENET is a co-operative e-mail network which permits millions of people to communicate with each other on thousands of topics (each topic called a "news-group"). *Illegal and Offensive Content on the Information Highway, A Background Paper, Industry Canada* (June 19, 1995).

Consists of newsgroups or open forums on various topics. Newsgroups are either moderated (in which case a system administrator reviews any messages before they are posted) or unmoderated (in which case the messages are posted without being reviewed by any person). *Public Performance of Musical Works 1996-1998 (Tariff 22)* (1999), 1 C.P.R. (4th) 417 (Copyright Board).

USENET is one to many publication from author to readers round the world. An article (known as a posting) is submitted by its author to the Usenet news-server based at his own local ISP (the originating ISP) who disseminates via the Internet the posting. Ultimately it is distributed and stored on the news-servers of every (or nearly every) ISP in the world that offers Usenet facilities to its customers. Internet users world wide can read and download the posting by connecting to their local ISP's news-servers. *Godfrey v. Demon Internet Ltd.*, [1999] E.W.J. No. 1226 (Q.B.D.).

Is the name given to the system by which postings are sent by Internet users to forums known as "Newsgroups". A posting is readable anywhere in the world by an Internet user whose own ISP offers access to the Newsgroup in question. Newsgroups are organised into broad subject areas known as "Hierarchies". One such hierarchy is the "SOC" hierarchy which contains Newsgroups in which social issues are discussed for example the Newsgroups "soc.culture.thai" and "soc.culture.british". *Godfrey v. Demon Internet Ltd.*, [1999] E.W.J. No. 1226 (Q.B.D.).

Are a popular set of discussion groups arranged according to subject matter and automatically disseminated "using ad hoc, peer to peer connections between approximately 200,000 computers around the world". Users may read or send messages to most newsgroups without a prior "subscription", and there is no way for a speaker who posts an article to most newsgroups to know who is reading her message. *Cyberspace Communications, Inc. et al. v. Engler*, 55 F. Supp. 2d 737 (E.D. F. Ch. 1999).

User Interface

The user interface, also called the "look and feel" of the program, is generally the design of the video screen and the manner in which information is presented to the user. *Johnson Controls Inc. v. Phoenix Control Systems Inc.*, 886 F.2d 1173 (9th Cir. 1989).

The combination of a computer monitor's visual displays and the user command functions on the keyboard or other input devices is called the computer's user interface. On the Macintosh, the screen displays include icons or symbols to represent programs or information, pull down menus or lists of commands or information, use of windows to display information and the ability to move, re-size, open or close those windows to retrieve, put away or modify information, and a display of text by a proportionally spaced font in all menu items, title bars, icon names and text directories for a consistent and distinctive appearance. *Apple Computer Inc. v. Microsoft Corp.*, 1992 U.S. Dist. LEXIS 12219 (N.D. Cal. 1992).

Valid Certificate

Means a certificate that a certification authority has issued, and which that the subscriber listed in the certificate has accepted. *Illinois Electronic Commerce Security Act* 1998 5 Ill. Comp. Stat. 175.

A certificate which its certifier has issued or disclosed to another person in circumstances where that person's reliance on the certificate is foreseeable, unless the certifier gives timely notice that the certificate is unreliable, or unless the certificate is a public key certificate which has been revoked or is, at the time in question, suspended. General Usage for International Digitally Insured Commerce (Guidec), International Chamber of Commerce, 1997, available at http://www.icc.wbo.org/guidec2.htm.

Validate a Disk

In computer terminology, "validate" normally refers to steps taken to ensure the integrity or correctness of data. For instance, a user might be asked for his or her password and the response "validated" against a list of allowable values. In the case of disks, this would be a very hardware oriented operation performed to ensure the integrity of the data stored on the magnetic disk media. Data stored on magnetic media is usually recorded with a "check sum" accompanying it. This check sum is the result of some calculations performed on the data itself. When the data is read back, the original check sum is also read back and then a new check sum is calculated using the retrieved data. If the two check sums do not match, then an error has occurred either in the storing or retrieving of the data. If and when such an error is detected, various additional methods exist for attempting to recover the original data. In the case of disk devices, this process of validation and attempted recovery is usually performed automatically by the disk device itself whenever it is accessing data. Since tape media is generally much more prone to contamination, data stored to tapes is often manually "validated" immediately afterwards by the computer user to ensure that it was recorded reliably. The software supplied by computer system vendors for use in backing up (storing) and retrieving (restoring) data between disk and tape usually implements check sum style validation and detection techniques, attempts to recover data if it detects errors and performs error reporting to chronicle these occurrences. *Delrina Corp. v. Triolet Systems, Inc.* (1992), 47 C.P.R. (3d) 1 (Ont. H.C.)

Validation, Reference

The hash value of the identified and transformed content, specified by Reference, matches its specified DigestValue. *XML-Signature Syntax and Processing, W3C Recommendation 12 February 2002.*

Validation, Trust/Application

The application determines that the semantics associated with a signature are valid. For example, an application may validate the time stamps or the integrity of the signer key—though this behaviour is external to this core specification. *XML-Signature Syntax and Processing, W3C Recommendation 12 February 2002.*

Value Added Networks (VANs)

A third party communications network which arbitrates the flow of messages (usually commercial) between parties. The service provided typically include receiving, storing and forwarding messages on behalf of a party. *A Survey of Legal Issues Relating to the Security of Electronic Information*, Department of Justice, Canada.

VAR (Value Added Reseller)

It would seem that VAR is a term of art, but nowhere is this term defined. *Xec Products Inc. v. Telxon Canada Corp.*, [1989] O.J. No. 1390 (Sup. Ct.).

Variable

Each kind of data (e.g. here a part no.) must be defined by some kind of word (not necessarily English) and its nature (decimal, or alphanumeric or a mixture) and potential length given. The names of the kinds of data are called "variables". It is best to define the variables within the data division before writing the procedure division. The evidence is that programmers sometimes create variables which in the end they find they never use in the procedure division — redundant variables. Defining variables is part of the creative process. *IBCOS Computers Ltd. v. Barclay's Mercantile Highland Finance Ltd.*, [1994] F.S.R. 275 (Ch.D.).

Variable Names

In an attempt to make computer source programs more readable, symbolic descriptive names are usually assigned to areas of memory. These unique variable names are usually selected so that they describe the data that they represent. For instance, if a program is working with payroll information, the source code instructions would probably "define" or "declare" areas of memory for "HOURS", "RATE" and "GROSS2DPAY". These declarations would follow the syntax of the computer language being used and would allocate the memory area as well as assign a name to it. These variable names could then be used when referring to the memory areas and the program source code would be easier to understand. *Delrina Corp. v. Triolet Systems, Inc.* (1992), 47 C.P.R. (3d) 1 (Ont. H.C.)

VDP

Visual Display Processor. Monopolies and Mergers Commission — Video Games: A report on the supply of video games in the UK (LONDON: HMSO Cm2781).

Vector graphics

A form of graphics with an infinite number of orientations, usually looking 'square' and 'blocky' on the screen. Monopolies and Mergers Commission — Video Games: A report on the supply of video games in the UK (LONDON: HMSO Cm2781).

Verify

To determine accurately that: (a) the digital signature was created by the private key corresponding to the public key; and (b) the message has not been altered since its digital signature was created. UNCITRAL Report of the Working Group on Electronic Commerce, September 18-29, 2000, A/CN. 94/483.

Verify a Digital Signature

Means to use the public key listed in a valid certificate, along with the appropriate message digest function and asymmetric cryptosystem, to evaluate a digitally signed electronic record, such that the result of the process concludes that the digital signature was created using the private key corresponding to the public key listed in the certificate and the electronic record has not been altered since its digital signature was created. *Illinois Electronic Commerce Security Act* 1998 5 Ill. Comp. Stat. 175.

Means, in relation to a given digital signature, message, and public key, to determine accurately that: (a) the digital signature was created by the private key corresponding to the public key; and (b) the message has not been altered since its digital signature was created. *Utah Digital Signature Act* 46-3, available at http://www.le.state.ut.us/code/TITLE46/htm/46_03004.htm.

In relation to ensuring a given message (digital signature, message, and public key,) to determine accurately that: (a) the digital signature was created by the private key corresponding to the public key; and (b) the message has not been altered since its digital signature was created. General Usage for International Digitally Insured Commerce (Guidec), International Chamber of Commerce, 1997, available at http://www.icc.wbo.org/guidec2.htm.

Veronica Server

A "veronica server" is capable of searching menus on all gopher servers. *Shea v. Reno*, 1996 U.S. Dist. LEXIS 10720 (S.D.N.Y. 1996).

Version

A translation, a particular form or variant of anything. *Data Access Corporation v. Powerflex Services Pty. Ltd.* (1999), 45 I.P.R. 353 (Aust. H.C.).

VGA

Video graphics array. *Princton Graphics Operating, L.P. v. Nec Home Electronics (U.S.A.), Inc.*, Comp. Ind. Lit. Reptr. 11,126 (S.D.N.Y. 1990).

Video Compression

The process of compacting data, so that more can be stored and transmitted. *The Challenge of the Information Highway: Final Report of the Information Highway Advisory Council* (September 1995).

Video Computer Systems (VCS)

These are electronic units comprising a multi-circuit unit and auxiliary equipment. *Atari Inc. and Futuretronics Australia Pty Ltd. v. Fairstar Electronics Pty Ltd.* (1982), 1 I.P.R. 291 (Aus. Fed. Ct.).

Video-Dial-Tone (VDT)

The concept of provision of video services over the public switched telephone network. Actual implementation of such a service would require the combining of large amounts of system carrying capacity providing enough bandwidth to carry video, with the switched network employed by the telephone system. The purpose of the service would be to provide dial-up access to individual subscribers to video services. Such services would likely be offered in competition to the cable industry. Submission of the Director of Investigation and Research to the CRTC Re Public Notice CRTC 1994-130.

The two-way or "switched" broadband carriage of information. VDT technology will provide the platform for video-on-demand services. A switched communications system is one that allows two-way, point-to-point exchange of information. *The Challenge of the Information Highway: Final Report of the Information Highway Advisory Council* (September 1995).

VDT refers to the technological capability through which broadband services may be offered, not to the services themselves. VDT is therefore not a broadcasting activity. Rather, it is the use of the technology that will determine the nature of the activity. Telecom Decision CRTC 94-19, September 16, 1994.

Video dial tone refers to the two-way (or switched) (as distinct from the one-way or "dedicated") broadband carriage of information; VDT will provide the technology platform for video-on-demand services. A switched communication system is one that allows the two-way, point-to-point exchange of information. Competition and Culture on Canada's Information Highway: Managing the Realities of Transition, CRTC (the "Convergence Report"), May 19, 1995.

Video Display Terminal (VDT)

A Video Display Terminal is a device for transmitting data and instructions to the central processing unit of a computer and for receiving and displaying the computer's output. The terminal consists of a keyboard, by which the user enters the information, and video monitor which displays both the user input and the computer output. Ordinarily, a reference manual for instruction and consultation on the use of the terminal is provided with such a unit. *Digital Equipment Corp. v. C. Itoh & Co. (Can.) Ltd.* (1985), 6 C.P.R. (3d) 511 (Fed. T.D.).

Video Game

Video games can roughly be described as computers programmed to create on a television screen cartoons in which some of the action is controlled by the player. *Red Baron-Franklin Par Inc. v. Taito Corp.*, 11 C.L.R. 156 (4th Cir. 1989).

A report on the supply of video games in the U.K., Mergers and Monopolies Commission, London: HMSO, Cm 2781.

Personal video games come in two basic varieties: console games and PC games. Console games are played by loading a game disk into a console which is connected to the user's television. PC games are played by loading a game disk into the CD drive of a personal computer. *Sony Computer Entertain America v. Bleem Ltd.*, 54 U.S.P.Q. 2d 1753 (9th Cir. 2000).

Video Game Machine

A video game machine consists of a cabinet containing, *inter alia*, a cathode ray tube (CRT), a sound system, hand controls for the player, and electronic circuit boards. The electronic circuitry includes a microprocessor and memory devices, called ROMs (Read-Only Memory), which are tiny computer chips containing thousands of data locations which store the instructions and data of a computer program. The microprocessor executes the computer program to cause the game to operate. *Williams Electronics Inc. v. Artic International Inc.*, 685 F.2d 870 (3rd Cir. 1982).

A video game unit consists of an electronic printed circuit board, a television monitor, a cabinet and coin mechanism. When the component parts are connected and an electric current, activated by the insertion of the proper coin, run through the machinery, the game's audio/visual images appear on the television screen. *Red Baron-Franklin Par Inc. v. Taito Corp.*, 11 C.L.R. 156 (4th Cir. 1989).

Video-on-Demand (VOD)

An entertainment service to the home which is still in the creation stage. Such a service would allow viewers to dial up or place an electronic order for a particular movie or event directly from home through a cable or telephone network. A central repository would then transmit or download the movie or event immediately. The closest approximation to video on demand which is currently available would be pay-per-view services. However, pay-per-view programs are usually limited to one or two start times per day, whereas the goal of video-on-demand would be to provide the subscriber with access to the program at any given time. Submission of the Director of Investigation and Research to the CRTC Re Public Notice CRTC 1994-130.

A service that allows the user to dial a video-dial-tone system, choose a video and play it. *The Challenge of the Information Highway: Final Report of the Information Highway Advisory Council* (September 1995).

A service that provides programs, as defined by the [Broadcasting] Act, transmitted by means of telecommunications, where individual consumers select specific programs to be received by means of broadcasting receiving apparatus at any time of their choosing. CRTC Public Notice 1994 - 118, September 16, 1994.

Videotext

A simple means of making information visually available by means of public or provided telephone lines. The information is displayed on a television or terminal screens. *Re Application by International Computers Ltd.* (1985), 5 I.P.R. 263 (Aus. Pat. Office).

View Port

A predefined part of the display space. *Dictionary of Computers*, Data Processing, and Telecommunication, John Wiley and Sons (1984) quoted in *Re Microsoft Corporation*, Comp. Ind. Lit. Reptr. 16,485 (U.S. P.T.O. 1993).

Virtual Data Network

The use of a shared network to provide partitioned capabilities for a group of users, providing users with the appearance of a private network. *Report to the Governor in Council: Status of Competition in Canadian Telecommunications Markets, Deployment/Accessibility of Advanced Telecommunications Infrastructure and Services, September, 2001.*

Virtual Reality

Virtual reality provides the experience of entering three-dimensional audio visual environments. Study on New Media and Copyright, *Final Report* (Nordicity Group Ltd., June 30, 1994) prepared for Industry Canada, New Media, Information Technologies Industry Branch.

An interactive, simultaneous electronic representation of a real or imaginary world where, through sight, sound and even touch, the user is given the impression of becoming part of what is represented. *The Challenge of the Information Highway: Final Report of the Information Highway Advisory Council* (September 1995).

An interactive environment in which the player has the illusion of participating in the world portrayed in the game. Controlled by use of headsets, gloves or goggles and utilizing *vector graphics*. Monopolies and Mergers Commission — Video Games: A report on the supply of video games in the UK (LONDON: HMSO Cm2781).

Virus

A Trojan horse that attaches itself to legitimate programs in a computer system and reproduces itself. Viruses have a mission component, a trigger component and a self-propagating component. They can damage a system simply by filling the memory due to having too many reproduced copies or requiring the system to do too many reproduction commands. *A Survey of Legal Issues Relating to the Security of Electronic Information*, Department of Justice, Canada.

Visual Display

A visual display necessarily is what the user sees on the screen . . . It consists of or includes those features to which one would look to assess similarity for purposes of determining whether the copyright has been infringed. *Apple Computer Inc. v. Microsoft Corp.*, Vol. 9, No. 6, Comp. Law. Rep. 1043.

Visual Display Unit (VDU)

A screen upon which the operator can call up stored information to be displayed. *Mackenzie Patten & Co. v. British Olivetti Ltd.* (1984), M.L.R. 344 (Q.B.D.).

Visual Display Unit. *Eurodynamic Systems Plc v. General Automation Ltd.*, Q.B.D., Steyn J., September 6, 1988 (unreported).

Voice Mail

Voice mail is an electronic telephone messaging service that allows for non-simultaneous voice communication between two or more individuals. Like answering machines, the service takes messages for an individual who is unable to answer a call. However, because it is computerized, the powers and capabilities of voice mail are considerably greater. Privacy Protection Principles For Voice Mail Systems, Information and Privacy Commissioner/Ontario, October 1995, available at http://www.ipc.on.ca.

Voice Service

A voice service is the electronic transmission of the human voice such that one human being can orally converse with another human being. Second Computer Inquiry (Tentative Decision), 72 F.C.C.2d 358 (F.C.C. 1979).

Means a two-way telecommunications service involving direct real-time voice communication between two or more natural persons, but does not include a service the purpose of which is limited to the coordination or setting up of a data service. CNCP Telecommunications: Interconnection with Bell Canada, CRTC Decision 79-11 (May 1979).

Means a two-way telecommunications service involving direct real-time voice communication between two or more natural persons, but does not include a service the voice aspect of which is limited to the coordination or setting up of a data service. Tariff Revisions Related to Resale and Sharing, Telecom Decision CRTC 87-2 (Feb. 12, 1987).

Voice Terminals

(Telephone Instruments) Convert sound into electrical "analogs" for instantaneous transmission over the telephone network, and then reconvert these analog signals to sound waves at the receiving site. Dataspeed 40/4, 5 C.L.S.R. 1323 (F.C.C. 1976).

Volatility

If a DVD disc is inserted into a DVD player or personal computer, playback occurs by passing the computer instructions to the RAM in the DVD player or computer, on a temporary basis. When the consumer's session is completed, and the program terminated, all instructions associated with that program are no longer protected against overwrite within the RAM. When the DVD player or computer is turned off, all the contents of the RAM are lost. That characteristic is usually referred to as "volatility". Australian Video Retailers Assn. Ltd. v. Warner Home Video Pty Ltd. (2001) 53 I.P.R. 242 (Aust. F.C.)

VPN

Virtual Private Network

Vulnerability

A weakness in a system that can be exploited to violate the system's intended behaviour. There may be vulnerabilities in security, integrity, availability, and other aspects. The act of exploiting a vulnerability represents a threat, which has an associated risk of being exploited. *Cryptography's Role in Securing the Information Society*, United States National Research Council, 1996.

VRCs

Visible Records Computers. *Mackenzie Patten & Co. v. British Olivetti Ltd.* (1984), M.L.R. 344 (Q.B.D.).

WAN

Wide Area Network

WATS

Wide Area Telecommunication Service. *MCI Communications Corp. v. AT&T*, 4 C.L.S.R. 1119 (E.D.Pa. 1973).

WCT

The *WIPO* Copyright Treaty 1996. *Digital Technology and the Copyright Act 1994: A Discussion Paper, Competition and Enterprise Branch, July 2001 (New Zealand).*

Web Browser

In order to access the Internet, most users rely on programs called "web browsers". Commercially available web browsers include such well-known programs as Netscape and Mosaic. *Intermatic Inc. v. Toeppen*, 40 U.S.P.Q. (2d) 1412 (N.D. Ill. 1996).

Web Page

One way to establish a presence on the Internet is by placing a web page, which is, ultimately, a computer data file on a host operating a web server within a given domain name. *Intermatic Inc. v. Toeppen*, 40 U.S.P.Q. (2d) 1412 (N.D. Ill. 1996).

Webcasting

Webcasting gives Internet users the ability to watch their favourite television programs on their computers. The Emerging Digital Economy, United States Department of Commerce, http://www.ecommerce.gov.

Broadly, Webcasting is the transmission of audio or video over the Internet. The Economic and Social Impact of Electronic Commerce: Preliminary Findings and Research Agenda, OECD August 7, 1998.

Using the Internet as a transmission medium for sound (radio) or video. A webcast is like a broadcast in that it is to a wide potential audience that can include anyone with access to the Internet. A webcast can also be simulcast, which involves the simultaneous transmission of a broadcast or cable programme service via the Internet. It is also possible to webcast to a selected group of recipients, which is also known as "narrowcasting" or "multicasting". *Digital Technology and the Copyright Act 1994: A Discussion Paper, Competition and Enterprise Branch, July 2001 (New Zealand).*

Web Site (See also Site)

A web site is an Internet address which permits users to exchange digital information with a particular host. *Edias Software International, Inc. v. Basis International Ltd.*, 947 F.Supp. 413 (D. Ariz. 1996).

A document ("page") or collection of documents in HTML format, stored on a server, that is accessible to users of the World Wide Web. The Web site of an individual, business, government, or organization is usually accessed first through the home page, which typically provides an overview of the contents of the Web site. Commercial Web sites often include software applications that allow consumers to order and pay for products advertised on the site. Report of the Committee On Electronic Commerce, April 30, 1998, Industry Canada.

Means an Internet destination where you can look at and retrieve data. All the web sites in the world, linked together, make up the World Wide Web or the "Web". Cyberspeak — Learning the Language, the Federal Trade Commission and the National Association of Attorneys General, available at http://www.ftc.gov/bcp/conline/pubs/online/sitesee/index.html

The Web site is a collection of network services, primarily HTML documents, usually called Web pages, that are linked together and exist on the Web at a particular server. As an example, the IPC's Web site is located at http://www.ipc.on.ca/. All of the information contained on the different screens are collectively considered to be the IPC's Web site. Exploring a Web site usually begins with the home page, which may lead you to more information about that site. The Internet: A Guide For Ontario Government Organizations, Information and Privacy Commissioner/Ontario, May 1998, available at http://www.ipc.on.ca.

A web site is "a collection of Web pages [published on the Web by an individual or organization]. . .Most Web pages are in the form of 'hypertext'; that is, they contain annotated references, or 'hyperlinks,' to other Web pages. Hyperlinks can be used as cross-references within a single document, between documents on the same site, or between documents on different sites." *Universal City Studios, Inc. v. Reimerdes,* 55 U.S.P.Q. 2d 1873 (S. D.N.Y. 2000).

A location on the Web usually containing a collection of hyperlinked documents and files. A website has a unique URL, which normally, but not necessarily, points to the entry point (or home page) for the site. *Digital Technology and the*

Copyright Act 1994: A Discussion Paper, Competition and Enterprise Branch, July 2001 (New Zealand).

Website addresses are identified by a uniform resource locator ("URL"). Most URL's begin with the letters "www", which represents the World Wide Web. Those three letters are usually added to the SLD and the TLD to form the main portion of a URL. Following the example of the Jones & Company's Domain Name, Jones & Company's URL is *"www.jones.ca"*. *British Columbia Automobile Assn. v. OPEIU. Local 378* (2001), 10 C.P.R. (4th) 423 (B.C.S.C.).

Website is a collection of pages available at the same general URL. *Society of Composers, Authors & Publishers of Canada v. Canadian Assn. of Internet Providers* (2002), 19 C.P.R. (4th) 289 (Fed.C.A.)

Webcrawler

An Internet software application that is used to access file servers and collect Web site information, such as each Web page's title and URL. Report of the Committee On Electronic Commerce, April 30, 1998, Industry Canada.

Webzine

Web magazine. In the case *Primedia Intertec Corporate v.. Technology Marketing Corp.*, 50 U.S.P.Q. (2d) 1079 (D.Kan. 1998).

Wideband

A service enabling the two-way transmission of voice or data communications with speed in either direction of greater than 64Kbps up to and including 1.544 Mbps. *Report to the Governor in Council: Status of Competition in Canadian Telecommunications Markets, Deployment/Accessibility of Advanced Telecommunications Infrastructure and Services, September, 2001.*

Wide Area Network (WAN)

A communications network made up of a number of Local Area Networks (LANs) and/or Metropolitan Area Networks (MANs), allowing access to data physically located at widely disparate distances. *The Challenge of the Information Highway: Final Report of the Information Highway Advisory Council* (September 1995).

The microcomputers on a local area network may be connected by telecommunication lines to another computer or another local area network to form a wide area network. When that occurs, one of the microcomputers communicates over the telecommunication line and is known as a "communication server". The communication server gives each of the other microcomputers in the local area network access to communication over the telecommunication line. The communication server has a device called a "modem" which links it to the telecommunication line and converts the electrical impulses from the computer system to impulses which will be transmitted over the telecommunication line. At the other end of the line, another modem converts those impulses to impulses which can be understood by a computer. Within a local area network the microcomputer, which is the communications server, may or may not be the one which is the file server. *Madeley Pty Ltd. v. Touche Ross*, McGarvie, J., Aust. Fed. Ct., Dec. 21, 1989 (unreported).

Window

A window can also be a logical view of a file. By moving the window, you can view different portions of the file. Philip E. Margolis, *The Random House Personal Computer Dictionary, (1991)*, quoted in *Re Microsoft Corporation*, Comp. Ind. Lit. Reptr. 16,485 (U.S. P.T.O. 1993).

[A window] is an enclosed, rectangular area on a display screen. Many operating systems have graphical user interfaces that let you divide your display into several windows. Within each window, you can run a different program or display a different file. Philip E. Margolis, *The Random House Personal Computer Dictionary, (1991)*, quoted in *Re Microsoft Corporation*, Comp. Ind. Lit. Reptr. 16,485 (U.S. P.T.O. 1993).

Windows are particularly valuable in multi-tasking environments, which allow you to execute several programs at once. By dividing your display into windows, you can see the output from all the programs at the same time. To enter input into a program, you simply click on the desired window to make it the foreground process. Windows are also useful with word processors because they allow you to edit two or more files at once. Philip E. Margolis, *The Random House Personal Computer Dictionary, (1991)*, quoted in *Re Microsoft Corporation*, Comp. Ind. Lit. Reptr. 16,485 (U.S. P.T.O. 1993).

A window is a separate viewing area on a display screen as provided by the software. Operating systems can provide multiple windows on screen, allowing the user to keep several application programs active and visible at the same time. Individual application programs can provide multiple windows, as well, providing a viewing capability into more than one document, spreadsheet or data file. *The Computer Glossary*, 4th ed. American Management Association, (1989), quoted in *Re Microsoft Corporation*, Comp. Ind. Lit. Reptr. 16,485 (U.S. P.T.O. 1993).

A window is a reserved area of main memory. Same as buffer. *The Computer Glossary*, 4th ed., American Management Association, (1989), quoted in *Re Microsoft Corporation*, Comp. Ind. Lit. Reptr. 16,485 (U.S. P.T.O. 1993).

A portion of the screen to which activity is currently limited. *Computer Professional's Dictionary* (Osbourne McGraw-Hill, 1990), quoted in *Re Microsoft Corporation*, Comp. Ind. Lit. Reptr. 16,485 (U.S. P.T.O. 1993).

In computer graphics, a window is a predefined part of the virtual space. *Dictionary of Computers, Data Processing, and Telecommunication* (John Wiley and Sons, 1984), quoted in *Re Microsoft Corporation*, Comp. Ind. Lit. Reptr. 16,485 (U.S. P.T.O. 1993).

Is a formally-specified text editing program which exploits the graphics capabilities of CRT terminals. Terminal screens are divided into several "windows." Each window displays text from any of a number of simultaneously open files. Through the notion of linked "ponters," operations upon one file may invoke corresponding operations upon other files. Douglas Gerhardt, *et al.*, *Window: A Formally Specified Graphics: Based Text Editor* (June, 1973), quoted in *Re Microsoft Corporation*, Comp. Ind. Lit. Reptr. 16,485 (U.S. P.T.O. 1993).

In applications and graphical user interfaces, a window is a portion of the screen that can contain its own document or message. In window-based programs, the screen can be divided into several windows, each of which has its own boundaries and can contain a different document (or another view into the same document). Each window might also contain its own menu or other controls, and the user might be able to enlarge and shrink individual windows at will. In some programs, windows are opened side by side on the screen; in others, open windows can overlap one another. *Microsoft Press Computer Dictionary* (Microsoft Press, 1991), quoted in *Re Microsoft Corporation*, Comp. Ind. Lit. Reptr. 16,485 (U.S. P.T.O. 1993).

In computer graphics, a window is a software tool for scaling (sizing) an image to fit within certain boundaries on the display screen. In this sense, a window not only provides a working area for a program and a view into a particular portion of a document or graphical image but can also be used as a reference area for translating an image based on three-dimensional coordinates (points on x-, y- and z-axes) into an appropriately scaled pattern of pixels (dots) on the screen. *Microsoft Press Computer Dictionary* (Microsoft Press, 1991), quoted in *Re Microsoft Corporation*, Comp. Ind. Lit. Reptr. 16,485 (U.S. P.T.O. 1993).

A window is a software device, used in multiprocessing environments, that allows a terminal to be used to run several processes at once. The terminal screen is divided up into several windows, each of which is dedicated to a particular processor's set of processes, just as though it were an entire terminal screen. Windows are particularly popular in integrated software applications. *Computer Dictionary*, 4th ed. (Howard W. Sams & Co., 1985), quoted in *Re Microsoft Corporation*, Comp. Ind. Lit. Reptr. 16,485 (U.S. P.T.O. 1993).

In computer graphics, a defined area in the world coordinated system. Michael F. Nordeski, *The Illustrated Dictionary of Microcomputers*, (3d ed.) (Tab Books, 1990), quoted in *Re Microsoft Corporation*, Comp. Ind. Lit. Reptr. 16,485 (U.S. P.T.O. 1990).

A rectangular, on-screen frame through which you can view a document, worksheet, database, or other application. In most programs, only one window is displayed. This window functions as a frame through which you can see your document, database or worksheet. Some programs can display two or more parts of the same file, or even two or more different files, each in its own window. *Que's Computer User's Dictionary* (Que Corporation, 1990), quoted in *Re Microsoft Corporation*, Comp. Ind. Lit. Reptr. 16,485 (U.S. P.T.O. 1993).

Window Features

One typical system offers ten user-designated macro keys to combine up to 20 keystrokes in one: on-line help in its own window; full screen windows, overlapping, or side by side for quick reference between programs; directory that lists all programs and files available, indicating the last program used in the current window; personalized windows to change color, size, shape, and location; simple menus, prompts, and one-keystroke commands; and vertical or horizontal scrolling within one window, without affecting other windows. *Computer Dictionary*, 4th ed. (Howard W. Sams & Co., 1985), quoted in *Re Microsoft Corporation*, Comp. Ind. Lit. Reptr. 16,485 (U.S. P.T.O. 1993).

Window Systems

Make use of on-screen windows to display a range of application options. *Re Microsoft Corporation*, Comp. Ind. Lit. Reptr. 16,485 (U.S. P.T.O. 1993).

Windowing

The ability to display simultaneously a collage of material, *i.e.*, graphics or different parts of text from the same document, on a computer screen. *Dictionary of Computers, Data Processing, and Telecommunication* (John Wiley and Sons, 1984), quoted in *Re Microsoft Corporation*, Comp. Ind. Lit. Reptr. 16,485 (U.S. P.T.O. 1993).

The division of a single display screen into several different viewports, each belonging to different programs running concurrently on the same computer. The viewpoints may overlap each other in the same sense that papers on a desk may overlap, partially concealing the papers underneath. Windowing allows the user to manipulate the viewports to place one on top of the other and to control their placement on the screen. Michael F. Nordeski, *The Illustrated Dictionary of Microcomputers*, (3d ed.) (Tab Books, 1990), quoted in *Re Microsoft Corporation*, Comp. Ind. Lit. Reptr. 16,485 (U.S. P.T.O. 1993).

Windowing Environment

A windowing environment carries multiple windowing even further by enabling you to run two or more applications concurrently, each in its own window. *Que's Computer User's Dictionary* (Que Corporation, 1990), quoted in *Re Microsoft Corporation*, Comp. Ind. Lit. Reptr. 16,485 (U.S. P.T.O. 1993).

An applications program interface (API) that provides the features commonly associated with a graphical user interface (such as windows, pull-down menus, on-screen fonts, and scroll bars or scroll boxes) and makes these features available to programmers of application packages. *Que's Computer User's Dictionary* (Que Corporation, 1990), quoted in *Re Microsoft Corporation*, Comp. Ind. Lit. Reptr. 16,485 (U.S. P.T.O. 1993).

An operating system or shell that presents the user with specifically delineated areas of the screen called windows. Each window can act independently, as if it were a virtual display device. Windowing environments typically allow windows to be resized and moved around on the display. The Apple Macintosh Finder, Microsoft Windows, and the OS/2 Presentation Manager are all examples of windowing environments. *Microsoft Press Computer Dictionary*, Microsoft Press (1991), quoted in *Re Microsoft Corporation*, Comp. Ind. Lit. Reptr. 16,485 (U.S. P.T.O. 1993).

Windowing Software

Programs, such as Microsoft Windows, that enable users to work with multiple onscreen windows. Windowing software acts as an intermediary between an operating system, such as MS-DOS, and application programs designed to work within a windowing environment. *Microsoft Press Computer Dictionary* (Microsoft Press, 1991), quoted in *Re Microsoft Corporation*, Comp. Ind. Lit. Reptr. 16,485 (U.S. P.T.O. 1993).

Uses windowing techniques. *Re Microsoft Corporation*, Comp. Ind. Lit. Reptr. 16,485 (U.S. P.T.O. 1993).

Software that uses windowing techniques to display information or get input. *Computer Professional's Dictionary* (Osbourne McGraw-Hill, 1990), quoted in *Re Microsoft Corporation*, Comp. Ind. Lit. Reptr. 16,485 (U.S. P.T.O. 1993).

Taking the integrated approach, one typical system offers windowing that permits users to access up to 10 windows, each containing several modules at a time. They can work with each program in a separate full-screen window, or have several programs in window side by side for easy reference. *Computer Dictionary*, 4th ed. (Howard W. Sams & Co., 1985), quoted *Re Microsoft Corporation*, Comp. Ind. Lit. Reptr. 16,485 (U.S. P.T.O. 1993).

Allows users to access numerous windows through the use of icons. *Re Microsoft Corporation*, Comp. Ind. Lit. Reptr. 16,485 (U.S. P.T.O. 1993).

Windows

When spelled with a capital W, Windows is short for Microsoft Windows. Philip E. Margolis, *The Random House Personal Computer Dictionary, (1991)*, quoted in *Re Microsoft Corporation*, Comp. Ind. Lit. Reptr. 16,485 (U.S. P.T.O. 1993).

Windows is a windows program from Microsoft Corporation that runs in IBM compatible PCs under Microsoft's DOS operating system. With Windows, two or more applications can be open at the same time and users can switch back and forth between them. If the applications are written to run under Windows, data and graphics can be copied and moved from one application program to the other. Data and graphics from normal DOS applications can be copied and moved into Windows applications. Windows also provides print spooling, which allows printing to take place in the background. *The Computer Glossary*, 4th ed., American Management Association (1989), quoted in *Re Microsoft Corporation*, Comp. Ind. Lit. Reptr. 16,485 (U.S. P.T.O. 1993).

Windows provides a desktop environment similar, although not identical, to the Macintosh. Multiple application programs, or multiple copies of the same application program, can be opened into windows that can be sized and located anywhere on screen. The applications can be also converted into icons and placed on the desktop when not used. Windows makes it easier to work with subdirectories than normal DOS, but it does not create folders into which documents are placed as does the Macintosh. *The Computer Glossary*, 4th ed., American Management Association (1989), quoted in *Re Microsoft Corporation*, Comp. Ind. Lit. Reptr. 16,485 (U.S. P.T.O. 1993).

Because many people frequently work on more than one task at once, Windows lets you divide the screen into separate areas called windows, each of which can display a separate task. If you start a new task, Windows will automatically resize the existing windows for you, to make room for a new window to display the new task. You can easily switch from task to task and transfer information between tasks and their windows. Nancy Andrews, *Windows, the Official Guide to Microsoft's Operating Environment* (Microsoft Press), quoted in *Re Microsoft Corporation*, Comp. Ind. Lit. Reptr. 16,485 (U.S. P.T.O. 1993).

Common or "street" name for Microsoft Windows, a multi-tasking graphical user interface environment that runs on MS-DOS-based computers. Windows provides a standard interface based on dropdown menus, screen windows, and a pointing device such as a mouse. Programs must be specifically designed to take advantage of these features. *Microsoft Press Computer Dictionary* (Microsoft Press, 1991), quoted in *Re Microsoft Corporation*, Comp. Ind. Lit. Reptr. 16,485 (U.S. P.T.O. 1993).

Windows are sections of computer screens in which various activities may occur simultaneously. "Windows" are features of all graphical user interfaces. In *Re Microsoft Corporation*, Comp. Ind. Lit. Reptr. 16,485 (U.S. P.T.O. 1993).

The evidence is clear that the trade, consumers, and the public, consider the term "windows" to name a type of software, and a function of software or a particular software feature. In *Re Microsoft Corporation*, Comp. Ind. Lit. Reptr. 16,485 (U.S. P.T.O. 1993).

Windows/386

Windows/386 is a special version of Windows from Microsoft Corporation that runs under Microsoft's DOS operating system only on IBM compatible Pcs using the 80386's CPU. Windows/386 takes advantage of the 80386's virtual mode and allows multiple DOS applications to run in a multi-tasking environment with memory protection. Memory protection prevents the entire computer from stopping if a single application program crashes. Windows also simulates the EMS 4.0 memory standard in normal extended memory without requiring special EMS boards. *The Computer Glossary*, 4th ed., American Management Association (1989), quoted in *Re Microsoft Corporation*, Comp. Ind. Lit. Reptr. 16,485 (U.S. P.T.O. 1993).

Windows Environment

A windows environment is a computer that is running under an operating system that provides multiple windows on screen. DESQview, Microsoft Windows, Presentation Manager, Finder, MultiFinder and X Window are examples of windows environments. *The Computer Glossary*, 4th ed., American Management Association (1989), quoted in *Re Microsoft Corporation*, Comp. Ind. Lit. Reptr. 16,485 (U.S. P.T.O. 1993).

A computing environment characterized by an operating system that allows multiple windows on the display screen. Examples of such environments include DESQview, Microsoft Windows, Presentation Manager, and X Window for the IBM, and Finder or MultiFinder for the Macintosh. *Computer Professional's Dictionary* (Osbourne McGraw-Hill, 1990), quoted in *Re Microsoft Corporation*, Comp. Ind. Lit. Reptr. 16,485 (U.S. P.T.O. 1993).

Are operating systems allowing for multiple windows on display screens. In *Re Microsoft Corporation*, Comp. Ind. Lit. Reptr. 16,485 (U.S. P.T.O. 1993).

Windows Program

A program written to run under Microsoft Windows. *Computer Professional's Dictionary* (Osbourne McGraw-Hill, 1990), quoted in *Re Microsoft Corporation*, Comp. Ind. Lit. Reptr. 16,485 (U.S. P.T.O. 1993).

Is software that adds a windows capability to an existing operating system. In *Re Microsoft Corporation*, Comp. Ind. Lit. Reptr. 16,485 (U.S. P.T.O. 1993).

WIPO

World Intellectual Property Organization

Wire Communication

Means any aural transfer made in whole or in part through the use of facilities for the transmission of communications by the aid of wire, cable, or other like connection between the point of origin and the point of reception (including the use of such connection in a switching station) furnished or operated by any person engaged in providing or operating such facilities for the transmission of interstate or foreign communications for communications affecting interstate or foreign commerce and such term includes any electronic storage or such communication, but such term does not include the radio portion of a cordless telephone communication that is transmitted between the cordless telephone handset and the base unit. *Electronic Communications Privacy Act* of 1986, Pub. L. 89-508 (1986).

Wireless Technologies

Such as cellular and PCS transmit data and voice signals from a user's device to a network where it can be switched to other wireless devices, wireline networks and the Internet. Advancing Global Electronic Commerce: Technology Solutions

343

to Public Policy Challenges, The Computer Systems Policy Project, July 1999, available at http://www.cspp.org/projects/july99_cto_report.pdf.

Wireline Service

Telecommunications services offered over wires. *Report to the Governor in Council: Status of Competition in Canadian Telecommunications Markets, Deployment/Accessibility of Advanced Telecommunications Infrastructure and Services, September, 2001.*

Wireless Services

Telecommunications services via the airwaves - radio, cellular, satellite, microwave, etc., and includes fixed wireless. *Report to the Governor in Council: Status of Competition in Canadian Telecommunications Markets, Deployment/Accessibility of Advanced Telecommunications Infrastructure and Services, September, 2001.*

WLAN

Wireless Local Area Network

Word Processing

Applications include: interactive information retrieval systems, management information systems, text editing, translation, typesetting, etc. Second Computer Inquiry (Supplemental Notice), 42 Fed. Reg. 13029 (F.C.C. 1977).

WIPO (World Intellectual Property Organization)

A specialised agency of the United Nations (UN) with a mandate to administer intellectual property matters recognised by the UN member States. WIPO carries out a number of tasks related to the protection of intellectual property rights, such as: administering international treaties; assisting governments, organisations and the private sector; monitoring developments in the intellectual property rights field; and assisting in the harmonising and simplifying of relevant rules and practices. WIPO has 175 member states. Its headquarters are in Geneva, Switzerland. *Digital Technology and the Copyright Act 1994: A Discussion Paper, Competition and Enterprise Branch, July 2001 (New Zealand).*

WIPO "Internet Treaties"

The *WCT* and *WPPT*. *Digital Technology and the Copyright Act 1994: A Discussion Paper, Competition and Enterprise Branch, July 2001 (New Zealand).*

WPPT (WIPO Performances and Phonograms Treaty)

The *WIPO* Performances and Phonograms Treaty 1996. *Digital Technology and the Copyright Act 1994: A Discussion Paper, Competition and Enterprise Branch, July 2001 (New Zealand).*

WTO - (the World Trade Organisation)

An international organisation dealing with the rules of trade between countries. The WTO was established in 1995 as the result of the 1986-94 Uruguay Round of the General Agreement on Tariffs and Trade (GATT). Most of the trading nations of the world are WTO members. The WTO administers a number of international agreements relating to international trade, including TRIPS. *Digital Technology and the Copyright Act 1994: A Discussion Paper, Competition and Enterprise Branch, July 2001 (New Zealand).*

World Wide Web (WWW)

The worldwide web was created to serve as the platform for a global, on-line storage of knowledge, containing information from a diversity of sources and accessible to internet users around the world. *American Civil Liberties Union v. Reno*, 929 F.Supp. 824 (E.D. Pa. 1996).

The graphical, hypertext portion of the Internet. Report of the Committee On Electronic Commerce, April 30, 1998, Industry Canada.

Is an information (data, sound, graphic, etc) search and retrieval service which allows a user to select key-words or phrases and then provides all matching information locations on the Internet. *A Survey of Legal Issues Relating to the Security of Electronic Information*, Department of Justice, Canada.

The exact definition for the World Wide Web (popularly known as the Web or WWW) varies, depending on whom you ask. In practice, the Web is a vast collection of interconnected documents, spanning the world. Three common descriptions are: A collection of resources (Gopher, FTP, HTTP, telnet, Usenet, WAIS and others) which can be accessed via a Web browser; A collection of hypertext files available on Web servers; A set of specifications (protocols) that allows the transmission of Web pages over the Net. The Internet: A Guide For Ontario Government Organizations, Information and Privacy Commissioner/Ontario, May 1998, available at http://www.ipc.on.ca.

The "web" is a vast decentralized collection of documents containing text, visual images, and even audio clips. The "web" is designed to be inherently accessible from every Internet site in the world. *Blumenthal v. Drudge*, 1992 F. Supp. 44 (D.D.C. 1998).

The most commonly used name for the World Wide Web. *Image Online Design, Inc. v. Core Association*, 2000 U.S. Dist. LEXIS 10259 (C.D.Cal. 2000).

An Internet application which provides a means of storing and accessing multimedia documents and files which can be located, accessed and retrieved using the HyperText Transmission Protocol (HTTP). *Digital Technology and the Copyright Act 1994: A Discussion Paper, Competition and Enterprise Branch, July 2001 (New Zealand).*

The Web, a collection of information resources contained in documents located on individual computers around the world, is the most widely used and fastest-growing part of the Internet except perhaps for electronic mail ("e-mail"). With the Web becoming an important mechanism for commerce, companies are racing to stake out their places in cyberspace. Prevalent on the Web are multimedia "web pages" computer data files written in Hypertext Markup Language ("HTML") which contain information such as text, pictures, sounds, audio and video recordings, and links to other web pages. *GoTo,com v. Walt Disney* Co., 53 U.S.P.Q. 2d 1652 (9th Cir. 2000).

The World Wide Web ("the Web" or "WWW") is often mistakenly referred to as the Internet. However, the two are quite different. The Internet is the physical infrastructure of the online world: the servers, computers, fiber-optic cables and routers through which data is shared online. The Web is data: a vast collection of documents containing text, visual images, audio clips and other information media that is accessed through the Internet. *DoubleClick Inc. Privacy Litigation,* Civ.0641 (N.R.V.) (S.D.N.Y. Mar. 28, 2001)

The World Wide Web is comprised of electronic documents called "webpages". Webpages are stored on computers known as "servers". A "website" is a collection of related webpages stored on a single server. A "homepage" is the "front door" of the website. *British Columbia Automobile Assn. v. OPEIU. Local 378* (2001), 10 C.P.R. (4th) 423 (B.C.S.C.).

The World Wide Web (Web) allows an end user to obtain access to information stored on a server. The files or Web pages are assigned character names known as Universal Resource Locators (URLs) which may be translated into the IP address of the server on which the files are stored. *Public Performance of Musical Works* 1996-1998 (Tariff 22) (1999), 1 C.P.R. (4th) 417 (Copyright Board)

The World Wide Web provides a facility for one to many publication. "Web Pages" are held at a particular site (usually operated by an ISP) in such a way that they can be accessed by Internet users world wide. The creator of Web pages sends them to his local ISP who stores them. An Internet user can access and download copies of the pages by connecting to his own local ISP and requesting transmission of those pages via the Internet. *Godfrey v. Demon Internet Ltd.,* [1999] E.W.J. No. 1226 (Q.B.D.).

The Web is a vast network of cites which are collections of Webpages stored on a single computer. Webpages are graphical, audio and textural presentations of information that can be revised and updated. *Technical Committees' Internet Task Force Report*, International Organization of Securities Commissioners, September 13, 1998.

The Web allows users to publish documents, also called "Web pages", that can then be accessed by any other user in the world. The Web comprises millions of separate "Web sites" that display content provided by particular persons or organizations. Any Internet user anywhere in the world with the proper software can create her own Web page, view Web pages posted by others, and then read text, look at images and video, and listen to sounds posted at these sites. There are Web sites now by large corporations, banks, brokerage houses, newspapers and magazines, and government agencies and courts. *Cyberspace Communications, Inc. et al. v. Engler*, 55 F. Supp. 2d 737 (E.D. F. Ch. 1999).

The World Wide Web is one part of the Internet which allows for the display of graphic materials, photos, text and audio. Individuals around the world can easily access and interact with the World Wide Web. Information is "published" on the Internet by any individual working with proper software in their home or business. *Hasbro, Inc. v. Clue Computing, Inc.*, 45 U.S.P.Q. 2d 1170 (D. Mass. 1997).

The Web, a collection of information resources contained in documents located on individual computers around the world, is the most widely used and fastest-growing part of the Internet except perhaps for electronic mail ("e-mail"). *Brookfield Communications, Inc. v. West Coast Entertainment Corp.*, 174 F. 3d 1036 (9th Cir. 1999).

The World Wide Web is a group of documents electronically stored in different computers all over the Internet. *American Network, Inc. v. Access America/ Connect Atlanta, Inc.*, 975 F.Supp. 4940 (S.D.N.Y. 1997).

A massive collection of digital information resources stored on servers throughout the Internet. These resources are typically provided in the form of hypertext documents, commonly referred to as "Web pages", that may incorporate any combination of text, graphics, audio and video content, software programs, and other data. A user of a computer connected to the Internet can publish a page on the Web simply by copying it into a specially designated, publicly accessible directory on a Web server. Some Web resources are in the form of applications that provide functionality through a user's PC system but actually execute on a server. *United States of America v. Microsoft Corporation*, 87 F.Supp. 2d 30 (D.D.C. 2000).

The World Wide Web (the "Web") is "a massive collection of digital information resources stored on servers throughout the Internet. These resources are typically provided in the form of hypertext documents, commonly referred to as 'Web pages', that may incorporate any combination of text, graphics, audio and video content, software programs, and other data. A user of a computer connected to the Internet can publish a page on the Web simply by copying it into a specially designated, publicly accessible directory on a Web server. Some Web resources are in the form of applications that provide functionality through a user's PC system but actually execute on a server." *Universal City Studios, Inc. v. Reimerdes*, 55 U.S.P.Q. 2d 1873 (S. D.N.Y. 2000).

Worm

In the colourful argot of computers, a "worm" is a program that travels from one computer to another but does not attach itself to the operating system of the computer it "infects". It differs from a "virus", which is also a migrating program, but one that attaches itself to the operating system of any computer it enters and can infect any other computer that uses files from the infected computer. *United States of America v. Morris*, 2 CCH Comp. Cas. 46,419 (2nd Cir. 1991).

A program that creates a complete copy of itself. Unlike a virus, a worm does not need to attach to a host program. Like a virus, a worm may access, alter, destroy, or consume system resources using the rights and privileges of its host program or user. *A Survey of Legal Issues Relating to the Security of Electronic Information*, Department of Justice, Canada.

Writing

"Writing" is the instruction to the computer to transmit data to a record in a data file. The programme assembles the data that goes into each field, determines the order, type and encoding specified by the file layout and then transfers the data for each field to the records on the computer disk, inserting field separators between each field. The position of the record in the data file is identified by the key, also derived from the file layout. If a programme can write to a data file, the programme incorporates some, but not necessarily all, of the file layout information into the data file. *Geac J & E Systems Ltd. v. Craig Erickson Systems Inc.* (1993), 46 C.P.R. (3d) 25 (Ont. Gen. Div.).

WTO

World Trade Organization

xDSL

Stands for Digital Subscriber Line, a technology which compresses signals allowing them to be transmitted over twisted pair copper infrastructure at much higher transmission rates than normal. Advancing Global Electronic Commerce: Technology Solutions to Public Policy Challenges, The Computer Systems Policy Project, July 1999, available at http://www.cspp.org/projects/july99_cto_report.pdf.

X Window

X Window is a windowing environment for graphics workstations that was developed at the Massachusetts Institute of Technology (MIT) with participation from Digital Equipment Corporation and IBM. X Window differs from traditional windowing programs that work on a single computer system. It is designed to allow graphics generated in one computer system to be displayed on another workstation in the network. X Window, designed to run under any operating system, is supported by all major graphics workstation vendors. *The Computer Glossary*, 4th ed., American Management Association (1989), quoted in *Re Microsoft Corporation*, Comp. Ind. Lit. Reptr. 16,485 (U.S. P.T.O. 1993).

A standardized set of display-handling routines, developed at MIT for UNIX workstations, that allow the creation of hardware-independent graphical user interface. *Microsoft Press Computer Dictionary* (Microsoft Press, 1991), quoted in *Re Microsoft Corporation*, Comp. Ind. Lit. Reptr. 16,485 (U.S. P.T.O. 1993).

Zeroization

A method of erasing electronically stored data by altering the contents of the data storage so as to prevent the recovery of the data. "Security Requirements for

Cryptographic Modules", FIPS Pub. 140-1, Federal Information Processing Standards Publication, January 11, 1994, available at http://csrc.nist.gov/fips/fips1401.htm.

80286

The 80286 was and is the most valuable Intel microprocessor. It is another generation of the iAPX family with started with the 8086. *Advanced Micro Devices, Inc. and Intel Corp.*, CCH Comp. Cases 60,218 (Arb. Award. 1990).